MARGARET STORM JAMESON was born in Whitby, Yorkshire, on 8 January 1891. Her forebears had lived in Whitby, then a small fishing and shipbuilding port, for uncounted generations: her grandfather was a shipowner, her father a sea-captain. She was educated at a private school, followed by one year at the Municipal School in Scarborough. Awarded one of the only three County Scholarships available in the North Riding of Yorkshire at that time, she took an honours degree in English Language and Literature at Leeds University in 1912 and was given a one-year research scholarship, to be held at University College, London: she found University College dull, and transferred herself to King's College. Her thesis, on Modern Drama in Europe, finally approved by Leeds University, was rewarded by the Degree of Master of Arts; it was published in 1920, by the firm of William Collins. In the meantime she had married and had a son.

In 1919 she returned to London, becoming for a year a copy-writer in a large advertising agency. She published her first novel, and began a two-year editorship of an obscure weekly magazine, *New Commonwealth*. From 1923 to 1925 she acted as the English representative of the American publisher Alfred A. Knopf, and later, for two and a half years, was co-manager, with her second husband, Guy Patterson Chapman, of the short-lived publishing house of Alfred A. Knopf in London. She married Guy Chapman in 1925, a deeply happy marriage, broken in 1972 by his death, after a distinguished career beginning with the publication in 1933 of *A Passionate Prodigality*, his classic account of trench warfare in France, and ending in a study of the politics and history of the Third Republic of France.

Between the years of 1919 and 1979 Storm Jameson published a total of forty-five novels. She has also written short stories, literary essays, criticism, and a two-volume autobiography. In 1939 she became the first woman president of the British section of International PEN, where she was an outspoken liberal and anti-Nazi, and a friend and helper of refugee writers. In 1952 she was a delegate to the UNESCO Congress of the Arts, held in Venice. She was awarded a D.Litt. from Leeds University in 1943, and is a member of the American Academy and Institute of Arts and Letters. With her husband, she has been an inveterate traveller, mostly in Europe. She now lives in Cambridge.

If you would like to know more about Virago books, write to us at 41 William IV Street, London WC2N 4DB for a full catalogue.

Please send a stamped addressed envelope

VIRAGO
Advisory Group

Andrea Adam   Zoë Fairbairns
Carol Adams   Carolyn Faulder
Sally Alexander   Germaine Greer
Rosalyn Baxandall (USA)   Jane Gregory
Anita Bennett   Suzanne Lowry
Liz Calder   Jean McCrindle
Beatrix Campbell   Cathy Porter
Angela Carter   Alison Rimmer
Mary Chamberlain   Elaine Showalter (USA)
Anna Coote   Spare Rib Collective
Jane Cousins   Mary Stott
Jill Craigie   Rosalie Swedlin
Anna Davin   Margaret Walters
Rosalind Delmar   Elizabeth Wilson
Christine Downer (Australia)   Barbara Wynn

Book Tokens

Give them the pleasure of choosing
Book Tokens can be bought and exchanged at most bookshops.

Autobiography of
Storm Jameson

JOURNEY
FROM THE NORTH

Volume II

Virago

Published by Virago Press Limited 1984
41 William IV Street, London WC2N 4DB

Journey From the North Volume II first published 1970
This edition of Journey From the North Volume II offset
from the Collins & Harvill Press
edition of 1970

· Copyright © Storm Jameson 1970

All rights reserved

Printed in Great Britain by
The Anchor Press at Tiptree, Essex

British Library Cataloguing in Publication data

Jameson, Storm
    Journey from the north.
    Vol. 2
    1. Jameson, Storm   2. Authors,
    English – 20th century – Biography
    I. Title
    823'.912   PR6019.A67Z/
    ISBN 0-86068-506-3

The cover shows a detail from 'Bomb Damage in the City ' by Eve Kirk, reproduced
by kind permission of the Imperial War Museum.

For Guy

Contents

Part I: Turn as You May

Turn as you may, lap after lap, in front of the black
Eumenides who are bored and cannot forgive.

GEORGE SEFERIS

Chapter 1

The deviate approach of a war many can see coming is a hand clapped over the eyes. Ridiculous to look back, over the waste months, to a time already irrelevant when some current of action might have set in and swept us past the teeth of the rock. And though this can still happen, we don't look forward, we have lost the sense that the future is our business.

In the early spring of that year I moved us to the house we were to share with my young sister, her husband and her two very young children. It was a big house, solid, and dignified in a pleasantly shabby way, like a plainly-bred Victorian dowager. It had lawns and a great many old trees and an orchard, and this, with the large kitchen garden, was what we counted on to see us through the war. My room on the first floor was vast, with windows looking down towards the high south wall of the garden; there were nectarines on this wall. Guy's room downstairs was equally large, but darkened by the elms and a strong old yew-tree. The village itself was small and unspoiled, in the middle of open heath.

I have never been happier.

The autumn before we moved, in the middle of the Czech crisis, I began writing a novel that had been knocking on my skull to get out. It was about Europe—portraits of Europe seen in this and that light, from this and that angle, as a painter might go on trying to get at the truth of a man or woman, looking for it both in himself and his model. I wrote it with consummate pleasure, without a moment's boredom. For once I was too sure of the probity of what I was writing to feel either bored or impatient.

I know well that to be perfectly happy all I need is an unearned eight hundred a year, or its equivalent in our depreciated money, and the courage to live abroad and write a book every seven or ten years.

There were to be four portraits, long *nouvelles* or *récits*. I wrote the last first—'The Children Must Fear'—about Budapest, and finished it in November. But already, in October, I had begun writing another novel, completely different in kind, and just as determined to get itself written. This one, which I meant to call *The Captain's Wife,* was the story, after her wilful marriage, of Sylvia Russell, one of Mary Hervey's daughters—Mary Hervey being the central figure in three novels about shipbuilding I wrote in my green twenties. It sprang from a deep nostalgia for a life I knew only through my mother, and through my childhood in a society of captains' wives of the old sort, as much at home in small cargo boats as in their own houses. Sylvia Russell is not my mother. But I drew from that powerful ghost and from all I had absorbed, consciously and unconsciously, from her memories, the portrait of *a* captain's wife who resembled her in looks and gestures. (When, in the underworld, Odysseus tried to take his dead mother in his arms, she slipped through his grasp.)

At the same time another of the stories of *Europe to Let* was nagging me. This was 'The Hour of Prague'. I began it, and after writing ten and eleven hours a day for a fortnight dropped it to get on with *The Captain's Wife*, which I finished in February—to my grief I had to find another title for it in England—and went back at once to 'The Hour of Prague'.

In April and May I spent five weeks in Paris, alone. My mind has saved only one image of what must have been at least a near approach to complete happiness, that of the evening when Benjamin Crémieux took me to the *répétition générale* of Giraudoux's *Ondine*. At that time I still adored Giraudoux, and would have listened to Jouvet's incomparably moving voice with equal pleasure had he been reciting a time-table. I was madly happy—in spite of the ironical surprise I felt that, at this moment, when, Vienna lost, Prague lost, Paris was really in danger, we should be applauding fervently this piece of enchanting nonsense about a German knight. The work of a rather tired enchanter.

'Would you like to speak to Giraudoux?' Crémieux asked.

If I had had the courage I should have refused: I knew that I should be too timid to utter two consecutive words. We climbed a mean dusty staircase to an even meaner room, and I listened dumbly for ten minutes while Crémieux talked amiably and volubly to

Giraudoux, who was grey-faced and smiling, and looked for all the world like a Foreign Office clerk.

Over supper in Weber's, Crémieux described the scene there after Munich, men and women in evening dress, sweating violently with relief, excitement, and too much wine, waving their arms and parts of garments, and shouting, '*Merci, Daladier! Vive Daladier!*'

'Too many Frenchmen are less afraid of the Nazis than of socialism,' he said harshly, with a harsh grief.

Simply out of politeness, I answered, 'They have their counterparts in England, eminent respectable men and politicians who believe that Hitler is no threat to their interests and so need not be opposed.'

This was true, but I had not said what I thought, which was that in any event we were sounder than the French, and more likely, at the last minute to stand. Or were we only less intelligent?

(After that night I did not see Crémieux again. When, some time in 1944 I was told he had died in Buchenwald I felt only a conventional regret, and for twenty years never gave him a thought. Then, on the 29th of March 1964, I was reading the fifteenth volume of Paul Léautaud's *Journal Littéraire,* and came on the entry of Wednesday the 19th of May 1943.

'*Paulhan m'a reparlé de Benjamin Crémieux. Averti par des amis qu'on allait l'arrêter et se dépêchant de filer et de se cacher. Il a été arrêté, chez le petit bistro de . . . (je n'ai pas retenu) où il vivait caché, par deux agents de la Gestapo, revolver au poing. A ce moment, Paulhan a eu ce mot, avec une sorte d'expression douloureuse sur le visage: "Ils vont le torturer." Il m'explique que Benjamin Crémieux, lieutenant dans l'armée française, s'est occupé de la formation d'une sorte de groupe militaire armé.*' Léautaud has no use for such senseless gestures, and says so. Paulhan answers that Crémieux is '*de ces gens qui n'acceptent pas, qui ne se résignent pas.*' Strangely, this touches Léautaud, who had always liked Crémieux, although he did not like Jews. '*Qu'est le mieux,*' he reflects, '*le plus estimable, le plus noble même, si on peut dire—et, en écrivant ce mot*: noble, *le mot* bête, *je l'avoue, me vient en même temps—de ne pas se résigner, de ne pas accepter, de protester, de continuer à agir* contre *selon les moyens qu'on a, courant le risque qui peut en résulter, ce qui tout de même donne à cela un certain caractère, ou d'être comme moi à se ficher à peu près de tout ce qui est et qui se passe, se refusant à être dupe de toutes les rhétoriques de circonstance? . . .*'

Suddenly I was seized by a piercing grief for Crémieux, seeing

him very distinctly, a ridiculous figure with his black Assyrian
beard and short clumsy body, playing tennis, in shapeless white
trousers on the point of falling down—he invariably hitched them
up at the last second, in time to save himself from disgrace—and in
P.E.N. committee meetings watching the English with a savage
determination not to be tricked by us, and applauding one of
Giraudoux's more sterile plays because Giraudoux was part of the
literary establishment to which he himself, urbane conscientious
critic that he was, belonged. This middle-aged Jew, the last person
in the world to be, in Léautaud's phrase, duped by the rhetoric of
events, to turn into a hero of the Resistance—I had tears in my eyes.
Why had I laughed at him so often?

When I returned to England in May, Ria Braatoy, who had just
come back from visiting her father in Germany, told me that the
highly-placed Nazis who were his business friends and associates
had amused themselves by telling her that a Russian-German treaty
was as good as signed, the British Isles would very soon become
untenable as one European country after another fell to Hitler, the
King and members of the government and the aristocracy would
bolt to Canada, the remaining English would be serfs in a German
Gau.

'What did you tell them?' I asked.

'All I said was: Don't be too sure,' she said, with her fine smile.

'But you, Ria, what do you think?'

She shrugged her shoulders. 'Your ambassador in Berlin is an
incredible fool, and your people haven't the faintest idea how arrogant, how brutal, the Nazis are. When you realize it you'll fight
back. One can only hope it won't be too late.'

'They say God watches over fools,' I said. 'No doubt He'll look
after us.'

After six weeks, I was too restless to sit writing all day waiting for
war to break out, and went back to France with Guy. The mortal
certainty that we were seeing France for the last time heightened
every colour, every image, every sensation. In Saumur, a little
drunk from reading too much Péguy—the eve of a second war had
seemed the moment for him—I saw the Loire, 'notre blonde Loire',
as he might have seen it, in a ravishingly gentle light, a benediction
of light; every shadow of leaf or stone, every bank of sand, every
crumbling strong old house, recovered in it the innocence of man

before he learned—or had learned only a little—how to be cruel.
Bordeaux was unbearably hot, the sky a sheet of blistering white
metal. Without looking it up I don't know whether the Gironde is
masculine, but certainly it is a male river where the Loire, even in a
sullen mood, is as unmistakably feminine. Despite the heat, I walked
from end to end of the quays and in crowded streets, gathering up a
café table, a crane, an old woman with a head from some *jolly* Dance
of Death, if you can imagine that, every wrinkle a toothless smile, a
scent of limes, a small child lifting its single garment over a gutter,
and putting them away against a dry future. Except in Bordeaux,
the days were only gently warm, and the light a caress.

I am never unhappy in France. This time it was happiness, gaiety,
a lively contentment, above a thin cold current. How much of this
would exist after the war?

Still lower, colder, as cold as ice, the narrow stream into which,
again and again, without meaning to do it, I dipped a finger. The
shop windows in Bordeaux were full of things, gloves, handbags,
scarves, any one of which would have pleased my mother. Even
here there were times, even in France, when the whole world, its
June sunlight, its lime-trees, was only the form taken by my grief,
nothing, an absence of her.

Chapter 2

Six months before I had made one of my more insane blunders,
tricked into it by the comedian in my skin who again and again in
these confused middle years led me farther and farther out of my way.
I ought, when its International Secretary, Hermon Ould, invited me
to become president of the English Centre of P.E.N. to have rejected instantly an office that would involve me in the anguish of

making speeches and meeting people. For six years, from 1938 to 1944, my life was bedevilled by this folly. But for one circumstance I should have invented a reason for resigning at the end of a year.

As an establishment, P.E.N. has one indubious virtue: no one is forced to join it and it has no power to bind or loose, even though its centres—except the amiable well-meaning English—are wormholed with literary politics. European writers, from Erasmus to Sartre, are political animals. The politics run a different fever in each capital. In Czechoslovakia, say, or Indonesia, they are likely to be ferociously nationalist. What do you expect of countries which have had to plot and struggle for their right to become or remain a nation? In these countries a writer is held to be as accountable for his actions as a financier or a baker.

In Paris an active member has his eyes fixed on the next stage in his career—a literary prize or the Academy—and cannot lift an eyebrow without asking himself whether it will do him good or harm.

'Now that I am *académisable*,' a French writer I like and respect said to me, 'I must be a little careful what I do.'

I felt no impulse to laugh. To be *académisable* . . . frightful, but is it worse than the disorganized struggles, vanities, discretions, of English writers?

I began my presidency by writing a long letter to the *Manchester Guardian* on the duty of writers to abhor racial intolerance. A most worthy letter. Any good Victorian liberal could have written it. None of my hard-tempered sceptical ancestors would have dreamed of doing so. I daresay that is why I wrote it.

The circumstance that kept me from resigning was not political. In 1938 the gas-ovens for disposing of human beings had not been invented, but Hitler's bloody harrow had been at work for five years, and in the thin stream of refugees able to reach England were a number of writers, German and Austrian Jews and non-Jewish liberals and socialists. Now, after Munich, many more began trying to escape it. Letters—from Vienna, Prague, Brno—poured into our shabby office, and since we had only one half-trained typist, Hermon and I were in the situation of a man with a piece of frayed rope trying to save hundreds sinking in a quicksand.

There were too many of them.

We answered every letter, we tried to get the visas needed, an effort involving us in hundreds of letters to the Home Office and visits to overworked refugee organizations. For one person we got out, ten, fifty, five hundred sank.

On the day when the German troops entered Prague, I came into the office and found a Czech writer, a big man, standing there: when he fled he had had to leave his wife to follow: her visa did not come and she was trapped. Until he put his hand over his face he did not know he was crying. Surprised, he stammered, 'What is happening? Excuse, please, I don't sleep. She is alone. What can I do?'

If he had been flayed, he would have been less exposed.

An exile understands the words *solitude*, and *death*, in a sense to which an Englishman is deaf. I realized this again twenty years later, in November 1959, when I was sitting, the only English writer who had taken the trouble to come, in a room full of exiles. As one after the other, Albanian, Czech, Estonian, Hungarian, Latvian, Lithuanian, Polish, Roumanian, Ukrainian, recited the names of the writers in his country who had been imprisoned, deported, murdered, an icy cold came from him. I felt a useless familiar despair and anger.

'There is only one way to help people,' A. R. Orage once said to me, 'and that is to give them money.'

At the time I was surprised to find him cynical: I realized now that he was absolutely right.

'We *must* get hold of some money,' I said.

Hermon looked at me wearily. 'Where on earth do you imagine it can come from?'

'We can try.'

I drafted two letters, paying attention to every word. One we sent to the Centres in every non-European country, asking the secretary to send it out to newspapers; the other went to English publishers.

It did not surprise me that the richest firms sent the smallest amounts. The rich are often mean, it is one reason why they remain rich.

From one source and another we raised almost three thousand pounds, not a great sum. Had we been appealing for some superb cause . . . but our exiles were not famous writers—these could make shift to live anywhere—and they had been victimized by their own people, a suspicious circumstance. My grandfather used to say, 'A man who says he has been ill-used by his family doubtless deserved it.'

After a time I knew that I would rather go out scrubbing floors than write any more begging letters.

Chapter 3

The Swedish Centre had arranged to hold a Congress in Stockholm, in the first week of September. All through July and the first week of August we went on preparing for it in London, as though there were no Polish crisis. In a civilization which is fundamentally insane, always liable to fits of homicidal mania, it is the only way to live. I knew, when I sat down to draft a motion to submit to the Congress, that it would never be submitted, that the English delegate, E. M. Forster, would never present it, never make the speech he was preparing. I took no less pains over it.

It was a fine motion, plumped out with *les rhétoriques de circonstance* like a stuffed partridge, every word of it sincere and useless.

'We, the members of the English P.E.N., hold it advisable now to call the attention of all Centres to the need to remind their members of their pledge, which forbids them to disseminate hatred in any cause; that they owe a duty to truth and reason and that if they allow truth to be destroyed and hatred to triumph they will be betraying their own country, other countries, civilization itself.'

'It will be a great pleasure,' E. M. Forster wrote, 'to speak to a resolution which is so sympathetic to me, and so sympathetically phrased . . . I had thought of a reference to the Antigone and an (unfavourable) one to Plato just to show that the problem isn't a new one, but coeval with civilization . . . '

The same day I ran into the writer and Liberal journalist J. L.

Hodson and asked him whether he thought there were any chance of our going to Stockholm.

He smiled his good gentle ironical smile. 'I never prophesy. But I visited Holloway prison this week, and found the women busy making thousands of red ties for the wounded.'

This very minor symptom of our insanity shocked me, and I stammered something about the frightful wickedness of people so obsessed by their idea of Hitler as a barrier against socialism that they forgave him the concentration camps, the invasion of Prague, everything.

'That isn't the whole of it,' he said. 'It's difficult for an essentially dull decent man like Chamberlain to believe that anyone is so paranoically ambitious as to want to dominate Europe. It's very difficult for anyone to believe in the reality of evil men. If Hitler were patient and subtle he would wait to swallow the Poles very slowly, and we should probably turn away our eyes. For good reasons—horror of war is a good reason—as well as bad. Luckily or unluckily he's neither patient nor subtle.'

'Do you believe that war is the worst thing that can happen?'

If he had said yes, I should, I think, have closed my mind to every other conviction. He was a good man, very brave, a natural Christian.

'No, I don't,' he said, smiling. 'We have to die sooner or later. To surrender and let the country fall into the hands of men capable of inventing artificial hells, Dachau, Buchenwald, would be far worse than anything I remember about war.'

'For men,' I said, 'even young men. But children?'

'The price of fighting for what you believe gets higher all the time, I don't blame anyone for deciding that it's too high. But you were asking me if I believe that death is the worst thing that can happen. I don't.'

My most grotesque memory of those days is of arguing with H. G. Wells. I am astonished that I was able to argue with him in his arbitrary and bad-tempered moods. The credit was his. I did not suddenly become morally brave, I was still anxious to say what would please, but from the time I came to know him fairly well I was never tempted to placate him.

My feeling for him swung between two extremes. At times I believed that he was a crystallized mass of vanity and self-will. Again and again our arguments deteriorated into an unseemly wrangle before witnesses. On my way to a committee in August, I saw the first Air Raid Warning notice pasted on the colonnade of the Ritz, and decided that nothing was more ridiculous than to talk of going to Stockholm on the 30th. I had just told the committee so when the door opened and in walked H.G., very jaunty, always, with him, a sign of intransigence.

'Of course we are going,' he said brusquely. 'We're going there to prove that we're not afraid of the Germans and to defend the dignity of English letters. It's no good your consulting the French, they're all bureaucrats, afraid to call their souls their own. *We* must go, and speak for freedom in a voice that will be heard all over the world.'

Vexed by this gasconading, I said recklessly, 'The world isn't interested in hearing from us at this moment, and we shan't impress anyone with our courage in being out of England when a war starts.'

The others waited dumbly for the teeth to close on my head, but he remained good-humoured and smiling.

'Very well,' he said, 'if you're afraid, I shall go alone, and while the rest of you are cowering in England—'

'The war is not going to be fought in Sweden,' I said.

'—I shall be in Stockholm, telling the Swedish writers that you are all cowards.'

'They may cancel the Congress.'

'Short of their turning out to be as weak-kneed as you are, I shall be at Tilbury on Thursday to sail in the *Suecia.*'

I corrected him. 'Wednesday.'

Delighted to be able to quip, he began turning the pages of his pocket diary. 'It would be strange,' he said, chuckling, 'if I were saved by a subterfuge while you all sailed to a Swedish concentration camp.'

This was one of the moments when I loved him.

'We'll meet here again the day after tomorrow,' he said to me genially, 'and you'll have the pleasure of agreeing that I'm right.'

In his old half-inaudible voice, shaking with passion, Henry Nevinson said, 'I must tell you all and Storm that I have written to the Italian Centre to protest against a poem in their journal. It's a very bad poem but that's not the point. It runs like this: We thank our Duce for the joy of machine-gunning the Abyssinians from the air like black ants . . . Abominable. I couldn't wait to consult Storm before protesting.'

'What was the phrase?' H.G. asked.

'Like black ants.'

'Black—? Oh, yes, ants. Well, Italians . . . '

He was in a less amiable mood at our next meeting, and told me sharply that it was not only his duty but mine to go to Stockholm 'to speak for freedom.'

Feeling like Alice trying to reason with one of the incomprehensible and specious monsters of her dream I said, 'Your metaphors might be misleading; a speech made about freedom in Stockholm won't be worth a snap of the fingers.'

'Your feebleness shocks me,' he retorted. 'I've worked very hard to put a little self-respect into the French, they spend their time on their knees to the Quai d'Orsay, and now I see that you're just as much under the thumb of our rascally Cabinet.'

The next morning I heard from the Swedish embassy that their government would much rather we did not hold a meeting there now. When I told H.G. he said drily that he would go alone, as a private person, not as a member of a society of cowards.

He sees himself, I thought, standing up on the eve of war, demonstrating, with the world listening. He is an ape.

In the same breath I thought that he was one of the most generous of men, with no vanity in him. Or he would not allow me, a nobody, to quarrel with him.

I thought: I should write and tell him so.

He answered my letter at once, in his small firm hand. 'Don't you worry. About values there is no argument. We go our several ways and no doubt we shall find ourselves in alliance again later.'

As we did. In 1941 I let myself get involved in a prolonged time-wasting argument with Jules Romains, who had gone off to New York and there, exasperating to blind fury the European writers sitting it out in London, formed what he named 'The European P.E.N. in America'. Certainly he did not expect the London exiles to take offence. As for the English—he held suavely the common French view of England as a hypoborean island of dubious origins.

Talking to H.G. at a luncheon we were giving the Greeks, in Frascati's, I asked, 'Have I your support if I am driven in the end to try to rid us of this turbulent Frenchman?'

'Certainly.'

'Will you take his place as International President? If you won't, what will be the use of my fighting him?'

'Sooner than leave him in charge, I would even agree to that.'

After the lunch, when Hermon and I came down the staircase into the wide foyer, we saw him sitting there with Moura Budberg. He looked small and tired.

'You really will take Romains's place?' I said to him.

'I'll do all I can,' he answered, 'though I am an old worn-out man, and may die at any moment. What would you do if I dropped dead now?'

Without reflecting, I said,

'I should cry for my lost youth.'

'Ah.'

I could not read his expression, but I had the sense that he was not vexed . . .

Six months after this we quarrelled violently. It was at a meeting of the International Executive. He attacked me at once, savagely. What he said was too grotesque to be disproved.

'It has become obvious to me that you are an agent of the Foreign Office. You're plotting with the rascals to bring P.E.N. under government control.' His voice rose to a high-pitched scream. 'You want to make it an instrument of Foreign Office propaganda. I won't have it!'

I glanced round the long table, at the dozen or so foreigners, half of them presidents of the several Centres-in-exile in London. Only five faces have stayed in my memory: William Kielhau, the Norwegian, whose ordinary speaking voice was the screech of a gull; the smooth diplomatic face of the Swedish delegate; the Catalan's small black eyes set in old yellowed ivory; Antoni Slonimski's delicate Polish features, and Salvador de Madariaga, his delicate lips stretched in a finely mocking smile.

Which of us is he mocking? I wondered: me, or H.G. in the part of an unscrupulous bully? None of them would come to my help. Except for Madariaga, their respect for H.G. kept them silent—that, and their sense that it was an Anglo-Saxon quarrel—whatever sympathy they might feel for me. My own poor forces were all I had.

I (or my grandfather) thought: I'm damned if I'll give way in front of a lot of foreigners.

'What you're saying is absurd,' I said. 'There's not a word of truth in it.'

'I don't believe you,' he retorted.

'You'll do as you please,' I said calmly, 'but the truth is that we have never been asked to do propaganda, for any Ministry. If we were asked, I should refuse.'

I have forgotten the rest—and lost the notes I made afterwards. The more violent a scene, the harder it is to recall it clearly.

A fortnight later he repeated his accusation.

'I've been lunching with the Minister of Information,' he said, eyeing me. 'He left me in no doubt that he considers you one of his errand-boys.'

'I have never met him.'

'He believes he can do as he likes with you—you. You're not experienced enough to deal with these people. I daresay you mean well, but I don't like the way you're going.'

Before I could check myself I said, 'You talk like my mother.'

He looked at me with such malevolence that I felt momentarily excited. 'I shall leave the society,' he said. 'I've done my best to keep you straight and you have abandoned me.'

'It's you who are abandoning us,' I protested.

'No, no, this is a parting.'

He stood up. I got up at once, none of the others moved, and stood while slowly he put on his overcoat and adjusted the straps of his gas-mask. Smiling round at the silent committee, he said, 'I notice that some of you are not carrying your masks, it's foolish and very anti-social, you should be setting an example, as I am.'

I opened the door for him, we shook hands, and he went. No one seemed sorry. I was so sad I could have wept. He had been behaving badly, but my respect for him was too great to be destroyed by a fit of hectoring, and I regretted our quarrel bitterly. Why, I asked myself, did you choose him, of all the people in the world, to prove that you are not timid?

When I was adolescent he had a prodigious influence on me and on all my friends. He formed a whole generation, throwing himself at us in a rage of energy, overwhelming us with his ideas, some absurd, all explosively liberating. Unlike Bernard Shaw, who did no more than instruct and amuse us, he changed our lives. A pity that so many of us were killed before we had time to do him credit or discredit, and without knowing what the world he had been trying to shape would be like. It died between 1914 and 1918, with several millions of half-formed young creatures.

To share the bitterness of my regret now you would have to be twenty or less in 1913, living in cheap lodgings in London, poor and continuously happy.

Short of apostasy, I could not mend things. I could do nothing.

Suddenly I felt certain he would not leave. He won't, I thought, cut himself off from the body he still dominates. Next week, he'll turn up as though nothing had happened.

He did. Smiling and in the best of tempers.

Chapter 4

It must have given George Fox enormous satisfaction to run through the streets of Lichfield crying, 'Woe, woe, to this bloody town.' More satisfying than waiting, in an atmosphere which is that of a painting by Bosch, full of unrelated objects, each as sharp as a nail and casually distorted: a web of letters secreting useless hopes, fears, defensive evasions; voices repeating the mobilization order, notices about food hoarding and the evacuation of children from the most threatened areas; an eloquent speech by Daladier—oh, the eloquence of these comedians who used none of the powers they had to avert war—about honour (the honour of an adroit politician), liberty, the judgement of history, *la chère patrie,* and the rest of it and the rest of it, raising in advance a memorial to young men who are still alive.

I went on working at 'The Hour of Prague', which was turning out to be the longest and most difficult of the *récits* making up *Europe to Let*. After a few minutes, I was sunk in it, and—to be honest—perfectly happy. The air coming through the widely open window was warm and soft, and there was a scent of leaves and scythed grass. As soon as I dropped my pen, the voice started again in the darkness at the back of my skull: You may not see your son again . . . It was seven weeks and two days since he had written.

These icy thoughts went on below the pleasure of sitting writing in this large tranquil room, *and did not alter or destroy it.* So long as I knew he was alive, I could not only go on sinking myself over my eyes in a half-written book, but feel this intense happiness.

A writer, even a minor writer, is something of a monster.

The war began on a day of unusual beauty, clear hot sun, dazzlingly white clouds below a blue zenith, a high soft wind. An old man's dry croaking voice, full of bitterness—more, it seemed, because he had been duped than for any other reason—reached us in the garden.

'Consequently we are at war with Germany . . . '

We were filling sacks with earth to protect the windows of the cellars. Nothing could be more naked than my sister's glance at her two children. For less than a moment. Then her face closed: she would not give herself away. I helped her to carry down the stone stairs, into the largest of the four cellars, a table, chairs, rugs, a box of toys. In another cellar a huge frog squatted in the middle of the floor. Startled, she clutched me, laughing wildly, herself a child.

I went up to my room and began to draft an article for *The Times Literary Supplement.* It was not due until October, but I wanted it out of the way. In effect it was a genuflexion before the ghost of Erasmus, one of the idols of my adolescence, and his Europe. I set down the title: *Writing in the Margin, 1939,* and then another ghost, living, this one, tapped me on the shoulder and I went to look for my copy of the letter 'A soldier' wrote to the *Spectator* in 1916.

' . . . You seem ashamed, as if they were a kind of weakness, of the ideas which sent us to France, and for which thousands of sons and lovers have died . . . You make us feel that the country to which we've returned is not the country for which we went out to fight . . . We are strengthened by reflections which you have abandoned. Our minds differ from yours, both because they are more exposed to change, and because they are less changeable. While you seem— forgive me if I am rude—to have been surrendering your creeds with the nervous facility of a Tudor official, our foreground may be different, but our background is the same. It is that of August 1914. We are your ghosts.'

A few persons, even in 1916, must have recognized the voice, made hard by contempt, of Sergeant R. H. Tawney.

He at least, I thought, will not tell me that when half the world is in agony it is indecent to sit writing about the need to save a few ideas, the idea of brotherly respect, the common man's instinctive mistrust of authority, the need to doubt. If only I can avoid rhetoric . . .

I see now that it is only possible to avoid it when the first person for whom one writes, to whom one writes, is oneself. The double effort, to recall the past without inventing forgotten details, and to see clearly one's own failures, lies, hypocrisy, illusions, cuts the throat of rhetoric. Wherever I detect its traces in this manuscript, I know that they hide a failure of attention or honesty, or of both.

Writing to a crowd of people, even to a narrow or friendly crowd, rhetoric is probably almost a form of politeness. The long eloquent Statement I wrote in the middle of September, to go out to the Centres in all allied and neutral countries—I have forgotten why we sent it as well to bishops and archbishops—is full of a modest rhetoric.

I believe that rhetoric in war time has another use—as an incantation. As a savage makes his most ceremonious gestures before a menace he cannot face nakedly . . .

In September 1939 it seemed highly unlikely, as well as slightly indecent, to think of earning a living as a novelist. I wrote to Humbert Wolfe, my one friend in the upper reaches of the civil service, and asked him to help me find other work.

I had known him for years, well enough to see as real and solid a man very many people saw as unreal, an assiduous player of parts he invented for himself. He had been born in Yorkshire, of an Italian mother and a German father, into one of those continental families which gave nineteenth century Bradford its distinctive colour among the dark cluster of textile cities in the West Riding—not my Yorkshire. His mother when I knew her was a formidable old lady, as slender and straight as a rod—as she was to her dying day—a foreigner, uncompromising in her refusal to take on the protective colouring of a native. She was a very Calvin of morals, without any intention to be cruel. She set a mark on Humbert he never effaced.

He spends his life, I thought, effacing the mark of Bradford.

For all its intake of continentals, Bradford is West Riding to a monstrous degree, a trough of smoke-blackened stone, majestic Victorian Gothic, factory chimneys, mills, steep grimy streets. The child a good half Italian set down in this dark place might, by a miracle of adaptation, of mimicry, have been happy. Humbert chose —at what age?—to mimic instead everything that Bradford was not.

His body seemed to have learned its gestures by heart, and his voice to have studied its inflections under a master unwilling to leave anything to chance. The first creative effort of his mind, carried out with unbelievable thoroughness, was one of self-creation. The creation of a self whom no one, not even Humbert Wolfe, could accuse of a Bradford virtue or vice. Hence the ceaseless spinning round an invisible centre, the play of impudence and irony, the underlying melancholy, the amused invention of personae, which made him so gay and often disconcerting a companion.

There are many people, especially bureaucrats, whom no one, not the most miserable, dreams of asking for help, because it is manifestly useless and ridiculous. At the opposite pole are those it would be ridiculous not to beg from, since they as manifestly lack the self-importance to defend themselves. Humbert was incapable of learning the simple creed of the bureaucrat, for whom human beings are the raw material of an experiment which can only be a complete success if the human beings are dead or witless. Objectively, he was an immensely competent civil servant; morally, he had never been a member of the sect, he had been too early saddled with a sense of responsibility for other people, their unhappiness, disappointments, mistakes, cruelties.

Perhaps it was on this side that my mind was able to touch his and discover that he was real.

He used himself mercilessly, living his two lives, as official and writer, as though each had a right to the whole of his nervous energy.

Absurd to talk of his two selves. He had a score of selves, each quick-witted, adroit, and well able to defend itself. It would have been stupid to think that there was nobody at the centre except the puppet-master, too busy inventing the play to have time to reconcile himself to himself.

His kindness was the first paradox of this most paradoxical of men. He handled misfortune and unhappiness with the greatest delicacy, and took an intense pleasure in annoying and mocking self-important and respected persons, with whom his tongue did him as much harm as did what they called his affectations.

They would have forgiven these more easily if he had not been affecting an intelligence, a wit, a shrewdness, which were genuine.

A few days after I wrote to him, an editor invited me to lunch in the Ivy. Ridiculously, I expected that three weeks of being at war would have transformed a restaurant which was a habit with the better-known or better-off actors, writers, journalists, politicians. Looking round when I came in, I was surprised that nothing had changed; there was not a uniform in the place, not one of the young men I half expected—foolishly, since they were dead or no longer young. My eye caught one after another of the faces seen on other visits: two middle-aged writers lunching with their publishers; Princess Bibesco; Aneurin Bevan with the political editor of one of our less polite newspapers; a celebrated actor with a very young man whose hand he kept touching; and Humbert with Pamela Frankau. Even in repose, or in the act of attention, Humbert's face had the look of a mask. An impressive mask, haggard, strongly drawn, bony, the eyes remarkable, the eyes of a comedian, perhaps a great clown, made more remarkable by the circle drawn round the pupil with a fine pen dipped in Indian ink.

After a minute I realized that my first impression of the place had been an illusion. With a light shock, as if a skin were being peeled from it, or from my eyes, I saw that it had in fact changed, in a very odd way. It was not the famous scene at the end of Proust, there had not been time for any of these people to become deformed or old; but they had suddenly, even Humbert, even Pamela, young, elegant, witty, become old-fashioned. A hand passed across them had effaced colours and displaced the figures themselves into a colder distant background.

A few of them, I thought, will be able to catch up again with their time, the others will one day notice suddenly that they have ceased to exist.

It did not cross my mind that I should be among these.

Towards the end of the meal Humbert came across the room to speak to me.

'How soon do you need a job?'

'I'd like to finish the book I'm writing.'

'Of course. How long will it take you?'

'Until the end of the year.'

'Very well,' he said lightly, 'I'll ring you up then. Don't worry, I can certainly do something.'

Watching him as he made his way, moving with practised negligence, between the tables, pausing to speak to Elizabeth Bibesco, my host said, 'Extraordinary fellow he is. I can never believe he's real.'

'He's really kind,' I said.

This was not the place, nor had I the quickness to say that his immense skill in impersonation sprang from the fact that, for as long as it amused him, he was, wholly—almost wholly, leaving aside the part of him reserved, as we say, to God—whoever he happened at any moment to be impersonating, the witty diner-out, the tactful handler of a social crisis or its deliberately unscrupulous provoker, the malicious story-teller, the poet ... .

Chapter 5

I was writing 'The Young Men Dance' for *Europe to Let*. Set in Cologne in 1923, it twisted three cords, the short-lived separatist movement in the Rhineland, that strange bitter episode, the friendship of two young men, and a foreshadow of the German damnation in the form of a young Goebbels. It is probably the best, because the only purely imagined, of the four nouvelles, and I enjoyed writing it.

I wrote through every sort of interruption, letters and telephone calls from and about our exiles, anxious letters from English writers about Alain and Jean Giono, who had been jailed as subversive characters—the first indeed was, as subversive and unmanageable as Socrates.

A minor symptom of wars is the cancerous growth of committees. I have deliberately wiped out my memories of all those I was trapped in, including one, secret and high-powered, formed to save a few young writers from the slaughter to be expected—which I admired coldly. Did anything come of it? I have completely forgotten. It remains in my mind as a noble torso, shoulders and a pelvis, but no limbs ...

A hard-working writer can count as one of the benefits of his obsessed life his trick of living simultaneously, with equal intensity, in two scenes. Driving through Hyde Park, a few minutes after nine o'clock on the morning of the 8th of November, I saw vividly the dirty grey-green balloons resting their hindquarters on the ground between the air-raid shelters for their crews, the lounging groups of soldiers, sea-gulls, cavalry in steel helmets exercising their restless horses: the day before there had been a violent thunder-storm, long tearing claps, flashes of lightning across a livid sky, and torrential rain; now, in the mild sun, the grass was a luminous green, fleecy clouds grazed the pale freshly washed blue of the sky, and a few yellow leaves, very precisely drawn, clung to the branches between drops of water or mist. In the same instant of time I watched the Czech actors on the evening of the 27th of June 1938 playing *Romeo and Juliet* in a seventeenth century palace. The illusion was complete, the white pillars of the garden-room, the darkening sky, the swallows, the superb freshness and vigour of the young men and their word-play, were as solidly present as the actual scene, not im-posed on it or seen behind it, but reflected with it on the sides of the bubble formed by sky and grass.

I did not know then that the man, Dr Franke, Minister of Edu-cation in Beneš's government, who had had the lyrical idea of playing *Romeo and Juliet* in a room built when Shakespeare was alive, was in the hands of the Gestapo in Prague; he died a month later, of the tortures they were using on him.

(I have been sitting for an hour, staring at that sentence. To go on writing seems impossible, if not indecent.)

Some time that month I finished the fourth nouvelle for *Europe to Let,* the last—'Between March and April'—set in Vienna, immedi-ately before and after it fell into the same hands. There is a portrait of the young Lilo in it, too ingenuous but fairly accurate: the story itself and the other characters I invented, *after* the truth, as one says of a painting that it is after Rubens. All I had heard, seen, felt in Vienna in July 1938, went into it, in some form.

As soon as I had sent the manuscript to the publisher I began mak-ing notes for a novel which had been at the back of my mind, half patiently waiting its turn, ever since the day when, reading Wheeler-Bennett's *Hindenburg, the Wooden Titan,* I felt, with the indescribable excitement a woman is said to feel when her unborn child moves for the first time, theme and plot move in my brain. I conceived my Hindenburg as the head of a family of Alsatian wine-growers—

somewhere I found an old book on the history and methods of wine-growing and read it with passionate interest and enjoyment—and characters and scenes germinated in my mind with delicious ease. Nothing in this novel came from my own life, yet to speak of it as an improvisation would be absurd, since no other novel I have written was, as this was, lived intensely in the writing.

I had written less than a chapter when, opening *The Times* on the 8th of January, I read that Humbert had died the day or was it two days before, in his sleep.

In the first moment it was difficult not to think that this was another of his half-malicious, half-mischievous jokes, another mask invented and slipped on to mystify, amuse, and disconcert friends as well as enemies: behind it he was surely smiling, delighted by the success of his latest deception, delighted to have created an effect, even of dismay.

It is the first time he ever gave up, I thought.

I remembered a fellow Yorkshireman, J. B. Priestley, speaking of him as 'a damned show-off', and thought: Imbecile! Couldn't he see that this supple worldly mercurial figure was terribly vulnerable, this teller of malicious stories considerate to a fault, this damned show-off a man with no image of himself as admirable, no vanity, and no egoism, if egoism consists in thinking of oneself as more important than the obscure, the young, the weak?

How dull the world is beginning to be, I thought . . .

After a time I reflected that my chances of a war-time job had vanished. I felt completely indifferent to this, even relieved, and went back to *Cousin Honoré*.

On the 28th of January, as if to ape the immobility of the armies, the earth itself turned to ice. The day before, after several weeks of intense cold, with thick frost, there was a thaw, and torrential rain. The temperature must have dropped again suddenly. Towards midnight, opening a window in my bedroom, I noticed the curious sound a very light wind was making in the trees. In the morning every blade of grass, thin branch, weed, telegraph wire, had its thick sheath of ice. Each single leaf of the privet hedge was encased in ice, and the separate sprays of the evergreens; the grass stood erect in fine lancets of ice, each veined by a thin greenish-brown blade; every reed, dry thistle, bare twig and branch of the trees in the orchard was enclosed in a cyst of ice; the ground was covered with ice to the depth of more than an inch, and wherever a wall had been still wet it was masked by a dark clear film, curiously striated. The sound I had listened to at midnight was made by the slight movement of all these ice-imprisoned leaves and twigs, a chinking or creaking note, strangely dull.

> . . . rat's feet over broken glass
> In our dry cellar.

During the day the wind strengthened a little, and the creaking sound became louder.

Snow fell during the night, so that leaves and branches now had a thick double sheath, snow on ice, and the ground was inches deep in snow. The electricity failed; we dressed and ate breakfast by the light of candles, and then tried to ring up the town, but the wires were down. Outside, the cold forced the breath back into the lungs. No sun, no thaw.

The next day a heavier fall of snow began to crack the branches. The big rhododendrons turned into a strange form of cactus, each leaf swollen by the ice to monstrous thickness, looking like limbs of grey green-tinged dead flesh. Ornamental shrubs round the lawn, frozen to the brittleness of glass, broke at a touch.

It crossed my mind that Europe might be dying under this ice, and the war would be stopped by famine.

I had accepted, I forget why, an invitation to a party, given by a publisher, in the Café Royal. On my way across the hall, I caught sight of J. L. Hodson disappearing into the brasserie, and ran after him. He was not going to the party, and I sat down with him on one of the plush benches. He had been in France as a war correspondent. He said he was trying to make up his mind whether, since he could write so little about what he saw, he could in honesty go back.

'What *is* happening?' I asked.

'Very little—except to the Finns. It makes me uneasy and I don't feel any easier here. No one has any sense that we're fighting for anything except to patch up the kind of world where the same few are comfortable and privileged and the rest remain half-educated and half-fed. The country will go bad if it isn't given a hope for the future: the old men who got us into this—out of their natural sympathy with the Nazis and anxiety for themselves—are fighting it without a rag of energy or vision. There's no moral basis, our leaders have none, they can't see outside their class—one or two of them would make terms with Goering now if he promised them a gentlemanly capitalist Germany and a war on Russia. The Labour bosses have accepted the ends and means of a mechanical civilization and don't offer anything more. Hence the feeling that nothing is worth a fight. And yet how decent our people are! We went into this war with no lift, but our young men are magnificent—believe me. Give us hope and a faith, and you'll see . . . '

He smiled. 'Don't think I'm a pessimist. I'm not . . . Are you writing?'

'I began a novel. But isn't it wrong to sit writing now?'

'Good God, no. Write as long as you can. This interlude isn't going to last, the Germans aren't in it for a joke, or for what—when it was a question of a few muddy yards a month—we used to call a limited objective.'

I left him, with reluctance, and went upstairs to the party. The immense room was so brilliantly lit, and there were so many people, hundreds, not counting the scores of waiters running about with a surfeit of food and champagne, that I almost turned back from the door, cowed by the numbers and the tearing rattling noise of voices. It was exactly the sound, enormously magnified, made by the branches with their membrane of ice.

A man I knew slightly, an eminently successful novelist, spoke to me and I asked him, 'Are all these people writers?'

'My dear girl, of course not, they're reviewers and journalists and broadcasters and civil servants, and an ambassador or two—and a few writers like you and me who are still, as they say, in full production.'

I thanked him for comparing me with himself. We talked for a few minutes about 'the novel', with a certain delicacy, as if it were a disreputable relative of his or mine. He moved away and I left at once, knowing that if I stayed I should say the most idiotic things to people who had no more wish to talk to me than I to them. I am not an imbecile, but slowness of mind, and boredom, often make me talk like one. I had been a fool to come. If you must talk and drink, I said to myself, let it be with one or at most two others, friends.

The fourth day of the ice began in thick mist, a grey wall behind the lines of spectral trees. A large old acacia, the tallest tree in the garden, had every one of its main branches split down the middle. Smaller trees and bushes had snapped off at the roots. The lawn was an extraordinary sight; in places, spikes of ice, each the sheath of a blade of grass, thrust above the snow, looking for all the world like miniature tank-traps. The children amused themselves by running against shrubs and trees in a clatter of glass rods and cracked branches.

In London I had picked up from Hachette's dwindling stocks a copy of Valéry's *Variétés 2*. Cutting the leaves this evening, I had a few minutes of piercing happiness; it contained essays on Stendhal, Baudelaire, Mallarmé, and for a moment this seemed worth the trouble of living.

A slow thaw began, and went on during the night. On a branch of yew under my window stems and ice-sheath had parted company, the leaves fell to the ground, but the sprays of ice clung to the tree, still marked by the fine veins of the leaves they had killed.

Paul Morand was in London that week, and P.E.N. gave a luncheon for him at the Café Royal. We asked E. M. Forster to take the chair, and I found that I should have to sit between him and the First Secretary of the French Embassy. Never had I felt less sure of being able to entertain either of these distinguished men, and I asked Denis Saurat to stand with me in the doorway and help me through the first moments with the Frenchman. He was called away, and said, 'You won't have any trouble recognizing him. He has spent years trying to look like Proust, but I think he has given it up as a bad job.'

A minute later I saw, coming up the staircase, a man who did not look more than thirty, but in every other way fitted Saurat's malicious description: he was slight, elegant, with heavy eyelids, and moved languidly.

'Monsieur de Charbonnières,' I said.

When we were seated, he asked, 'How did you know me? Do I look so like a diplomat?'

I said recklessly, 'Professor Saurat told me that when I saw someone coming in who looked as though Proust might have written about him, it would be Monsieur de Charbonnières.'

'That is a compliment,' he said, without a smile.

But he was not displeased, and roused himself to speak, in a faintly animated way, about the news. With *Cousin Honoré* in mind I had been reading the lately published French Yellow Book, and I made a polite remark about the difference between Neville Henderson's reports, clumsy and full of self-justification, and those of the French Ambassador. 'Perhaps under Federal Union, we might educate our diplomats in Paris to write with that splendid clarity.'

'But everyone knows that your late Ambassador to Berlin is a fool,' he said, without a trace of irony. 'They are not all like him.'

Somehow I found myself talking about the failure of intellectuals. 'My only criticism of your English intellectuals, he said, 'is that they are not serious. I see H. G. Wells here. He has drawn up a Declaration of the Rights of Man, and is debating it in the *Daily Herald*. Why doesn't he write about what is happening to these famous Rights in Poland now?' He went on with the same limpid nonchalance, 'The information we have is so frightful that much of it can't be printed. The Germans are systematically shooting professional and educated men and women, with the idea of reducing Poland to a nation of peasants and workers, uneducated men without leaders. They hand the women of these classes to their soldiers. They have emptied whole towns and villages of their inhabitants, turning them out to die in forty degrees of frost. They bring in a Baltic German, show him round the house, ask him if he likes it, then tell the Polish owner he has two hours to clear out. "This is not your house any longer, it belongs to this man."—"Where am I to go?"—"That is not our business."—"What can I take?"—"What you can carry in your hand." There is no other house for him to go to. He and his family join the thousands dying on the icy roads.'

'What are we to do with the Germans?' I exclaimed. 'What can one do with a European nation which has no respect for the individual?'

He lifted a small finely shaped hand. 'I don't know. We can't hold them down forcibly for ever, we can do it for a time, but then people get tired.'

'The English get tired first,' I said.

He smiled for the first time. I reflected that I was doing a little better than I could have hoped. His neighbour on the other side spoke to him, and I turned to E. M. Forster. I admired him so much that what confidence I had froze again into timidity, and I could not think of anything fit to say. He helped me by asking about Monsieur de Charbonnières.

'Mr Morand tells me he never speaks, I am afraid you must be working very hard.'

'He has been talking a great deal about Poland,' I said. I repeated what I had been told.

The great writer moved his hands in a light gesture, very charming. 'But is there any evidence?'

I was taken aback. It had not crossed my mind that I was showing myself eager to believe in atrocities. I assured him hurriedly and untruthfully that I knew there was evidence. He did not dispute it and talked about something else. I had been quietly reproved. Shocked out of its confusion and diffidence, my mind fell into its trick of attending to what was not said, and I thought: He is good, honest, cares a great deal about justice, and is very slightly cruel, in a feminine way . . .

After the luncheon, with an hour to wait for my train, I sat in Paddington station and listened to a shabbily-dressed woman talking to her friend. She repeated the same phrases over and over, as though to make them harmless.

From thinking about Poland and wondering whether I had been misled, I tumbled into a black pit of despair about the war itself. Oh, God, I prayed, let it end, now, quickly, and set us free from this nightmare, this fear. Anyone who justifies it is forgetting or pushing out of sight the misery of poor women unable to pay their rent, the children running loose in London with gas-masks knocking against their skinny shoulder-blades, the anger of young men, the useless deaths.

I told myself, and I believed, that to accept, as genuine pacifists do, anything rather than war, total disrespect for freedom, the systematic crushing or deformation of the spirit, is to accept a death as final as the death of the body. Even in hell, one could not give up fighting for freedom of mind.

But this was merely reason. My black despair came from another source, and did not lift until I was giving the children their bath that evening. Then it lifted—for no reason.

During these months I came to know President Beneš a little. I felt for him an affection—I dislike politicians on principle —I never felt for any other public figure. He had the failings and weakness of a man of reason who believes that reason *ought* to prevail. In a crisis he asked himself involuntarily: How would Thomas Masaryk act? His desperate struggle to bend together two extremes, two utterly incompatible ways of thinking and living, Masaryk's solid nineteenth century idealism and good sense, and the hideous violence of his own time, drove him into expedients and into devising ambiguous formulas which gave the impression, sometimes, of slyness and cunning. But the dislike, no, hatred felt for him by a number of powerful men in London and Paris was not based on this. It was based entirely on their sense of being confronted by a decent sober-minded reasonable man who was hindering them from coming quickly to terms with his would-be murderer. They actually spoke of him as ill-bred and unreliable, transferring to him the epithets that applied with complete accuracy to Hitler. It would have been interesting as a semantic irony if it had not been a disaster.

One day near the end of February there was a memorial service in London for Karel Čapek. Henry Nevinson made a speech, and Jan Masaryk, and Czech actors put on scenes from his plays. The whole performance was anything but polished, even shabby. When one of the young women lifted her arms on the stage, you saw that none of them shaved their arm-pits, and the Czech folk-song sung during the recital of Čapek's superb prayer for his betrayed country almost drowned it. Yet I had to keep back tears.

I was sitting between Beneš and Madame Beneš, and he talked about his long friendship with Čapek. 'After a difficult day, I would go and sit with him for an hour, two hours, three, we did not speak much, but it was a great help to me.'

'The time you will miss him most is when you go back,' I said.

'Yes. How did you know?' he said.

In fact I had only wanted to bring on the idea that he would go back. He sat for a minute, sunk in himself, then said abruptly, 'I can give Germany three narrow strips of country and still keep a defensible frontier, but that way I shall get rid of two out of our three million Germans. Half the remaining million will have been killed off by our people before I get back. Those left can be given their choice of going to Germany or becoming Czechs. There will be no more German schools, no German language used, no parliamentary representation—this time we shall be drastic.'

His calmness when he spoke of the killings gave me a strange muffled shock. Not that I had the impudence to approve or disapprove. And I understood sharply enough that his countrymen would want to efface in blood the memory of humiliation and worse. But what was this future that threw its shadow backwards over streets lively with the springing feet and clear candid faces of the Sokol children and over the free village women heaping a table with food and wine for their foreign guests, and over Jiřina's tranquil confidence? And who said that justice can be more bitter in the belly than it was honeyed in the mouth?

Chapter 6

There was something peculiarly horrible about the invasion of Norway. Why? I think because it was like seeing that a cancer which is killing the older members of the family has begun to work in the children. Listening to the first news on the wireless I was shaken and afraid as at no other time in the war, not even during the air-raids.

When we went to Norway, in 1935, the ship put us off at a tiny port in the Oslo fjord at four o'clock in the morning, a June morning as clear as fine glass, sun, a light wind off the water, silence. Not a cat was awake. Walking along a narrow street, past the door with my name, Storm, over it, I caught the sharp hemp smell of new rope and felt not only a keen pleasure but relief, as though a weight had suddenly been lifted from me—as indeed it had, a weight of years, of regret and errors, letting me go back into one of countless mornings in Whitby when I was walking with my mother in a narrow street in the oldest part of the town, the air cool, the salt wind from the harbour light and friendly: if, on our errand, we went as far as a large ramshackle storehouse and loft she always said, 'Your grandfather's sail loft was here, I used to like the smell of tar and rope,' and I would answer, 'There is still a smell of rope,' which was not true, but it pleased her and made her smile. I was not conscious then of being safe and happy, but now, in the empty Norwegian street, glancing into a flagged passage which might be any one of the dark narrow alleys in Whitby called ghauts, an exquisite sense of freshness and lightness of mind and body seized me. It was not mine, it belonged by right to the child who was still living in a Whitby I had long left, but it was I who felt it.

This defenceless little port, Horten, the Germans had bombed. It seemed an appalling irrelevance, even in war time, and the shock of grief I felt was sharpened by an instant when I saw the bombs wipe out my grandfather's sail loft and the old, very old street with one foot in the upper harbour and another in the roots of the cliff. Not knowing how much or little damage had been done to Horten, I tried, walking up and down my room, to hold it in my mind exactly as it had been when I saw it for a moment with the senses, new, intact, of a child . . .

After the endless winter, spring was late. The first warm day came at the end of April, with a gentle wind and rain as fine as blown hair.

I spent the last week of the month in a country hotel near the Liddell Harts. During those days I understood, for the first time, the intense fascination of the study of strategy, a logical or mathematical exercise of which the terms are living bodies and minds and geographical features (as in *Alice Through the Looking-glass*), with the subconscious bite of danger. There was something criminal in the pleasure with which I listened to his lucid account of what was happening in Norway, an account completely different from those we were being offered in the newspapers. On the fourth evening I was there, the B.B.C. announced, as though it were an unimportant item, that our troops were withdrawing from a position covering a town of which I have forgotten the name—Dombaas?—but it was one Basil Liddell Hart had pointed to on the map, four days earlier, and explained why it was essential to hold this insignificant place and why, unless our people moved very quickly and were lucky, they would not be able to hold it.

Delighted to show myself off in the role of attentive pupil, I said, 'I suppose it means we shall leave Norway.'

'Yes,' he said, 'I give us three days, perhaps only two.' In his quiet only half audible voice he went on, with no emphasis of any kind, to explain why the situation was serious, far more serious than we were being allowed to know. 'The truth is we were never in so dangerous a position in the last war as we are in this, and we have never been so threatened. Compared with the Germans we are ill-equipped, and'—he hesitated and went on with a half-smiling grief —'the French are not altogether dependable allies. From all I can gather they're in a worse muddle than we are.'

It was on the tip of my tongue to ask: You mean we may lose the war?

I said nothing. For two reasons. I was as reluctant to talk about the possibility of defeat as if England were a member of my family who had disgraced himself. And equally diffident about saying that I did not believe we could possibly be defeated, it wasn't one of our habits.

I felt that it would be impudent to ask him what he felt. Possibly —the most English as well as the most rational of men—he was able to contemplate the idea of defeat with the whole of his mind where mine lost the power to think or understand as soon as it was a question of our losing the war (not, after all, an impossibility: other countries had been defeated, Poland, France in 1870, Germany in 1918).

On the 2nd of May I went, rashly, to see the Braatoys. Bjarne was not there, but two other Norwegians were in the small living-room with Ria, a man now at the Legation who had crossed into Sweden and left his wife in Stockholm: the second, whose name was Rytter, had been a broadcaster in Oslo. Ria, who loved heat and spent any sunny day on the dusty ledge miscalled a balcony overhanging Albany Street, was looking particularly handsome, her bare arms and shoulders a smooth dark brown like oiled teak.

'We're waiting for Bjarne to ring up from the *Herald*,' she said, 'there may be news.'

Rytter was unable to keep still or be silent. Walking, with difficulty, about the room in the few feet between Ria's bed and the table, he answered her polite question by a torrent.

'We began getting queer news on the night of the 7th of April, about ten, that German warships were moving up the fjord, we didn't understand it, then air-raid warnings, we gave these out, over and over, and then, about midnight, the order to mobilize, and we gave that out. We didn't know at all what was happening. Some time after four we heard that a German warship had been sunk in the fjord, and we said: Ah, the English have come, thank God. Suddenly, about seven, the Nazi planes were overhead. Then about half-past nine we were ordered to leave Oslo at once, we packed a lorry with stuff and went off, passing the aerodrome where we saw German planes landing, we got to Hamar, Haakon was there, and after a time the Nazi planes began to hunt for him, and we went with him into the wood—it was the only wood they bombed. Who, I ask you, had given away his whereabouts? There were only five traitors among well-placed Norwegians. Five.' He stopped abruptly in front of me. Staring into my face he said, 'How many would it need to betray England? Do you know?'

The other Norwegian smiled. 'I haven't reached that point of despair yet.'

Picking up a newspaper, Rytter demanded, 'Who is this R. H. Tawney who wants your Air Force to bomb the Ruhr?'

'My God, it wouldn't be so bad,' Ria said, smiling, 'why should only Norwegian towns be bombed?'

At this moment the telephone rang. We watched her as she listened. Her face, under its tan, paled, and I knew that Basil had been right even to the day. She put the receiver down and stood frowning for a moment.

'Are we retreating?' I asked.

'Yes. Chamberlain has just told the house that we—your troops—are evacuating all southern Norway.'

Neither of the others looked at me, and Rytter said hurriedly, 'I was not anxious about my father—he is a strong socialist—and the others, because, although they lived near the Oslo aerodrome they had a hut in Hallendal and they got away there. This means that the country will be overrun by the Nazis, and they will be caught.'

'I don't understand very clearly,' Ria said. 'What does it mean?'

'It means,' the Legation man said calmly, 'that Scandinavia is gone, Sweden will have to make terms, Italy will come in on the German side, the Balkans will capitulate . . . '

Rytter looked at me. 'Let me say this, please. We knew quite well, if we resisted, it meant that Norway would be a battlefield. All right —we put it at your disposal as a battlefield. Fight the Germans here, we said, and you'll never be invaded. Now they can sit down behind the Siegfried Line and build a magnificent fleet, and attack you directly. Your Prime Minister talked about Germany losing our iron ore. Not at all, *you* have lost it, it will pour out through Lulea, the Swedes won't resist.' He laughed. 'Does your poor Chamberlain think that the ice lasts all year up there?'

'That's enough,' the other man murmured.

I had nothing to say. Rytter went on, with the same dry anger, 'If you had only landed enough men and supplies *in time*, and gone straight for Trondheim, risking your ships, we should have pushed the Germans out.'

'You won't be a battlefield,' I said.

'Listen. If every town in Norway had been destroyed and the Germans thrown out, we should still be happy. But if you are leaving us we are finished, we can't fight alone.'

'Enough, enough,' his friend said.

When Bjarne came in he went straight to the wireless set and switched it on. 'Chamberlain will be on the news,' he said, smiling sharply. 'It would be a pity to miss it.'

I have rarely heard a more adroit or vainer speech, or of worse quality. He implied that Norway was a trap, and almost gave the impression that we had been extremely clever to go there in order to be able to withdraw so skilfully. It was painful hearing. I felt sure he would not lie in his private life: as a politician he lied without noticing it, and that was surely much worse than the lies everyone tells privately.

'Will he get the country on this?' Rytter asked.

'Almost certainly,' Bjarne said, with his mad laugh.

'The Swedes will be able to exercise their splendid talent for neutrality.'

After a few minutes, Bjarne took both men away to dine in town, and as soon as we were alone, Ria asked, 'Have you made any plans? I mean, if we lose the war.'

If she had not said *we* I should not have remembered at this moment that she was German.

'We can only keep very cool, and our eyes open,' I said. 'If we are occupied, the Germans will kill some of us. If we make terms'— I had been going to say: If we capitulate . . . I could not get it out— 'I shall try to get the children and ourselves to America. But I won't be an exiled writer, it's a ghastly life, I'll char, or get a job as housemaid.'

Ria smiled, showing the edge of magnificent white teeth.

'I shall kill myself before they can touch me,' she said calmly, almost gaily.

I reflected that there was no doubt she would. At this moment she looked as though she had been very narrowly bred, a look of race, like a fine animal. Beside her, I was slow and inelegant. I doubted whether I should kill myself.

I left her and walked up the hot shabby street towards the underground station. Grief and a feeling of shame raged in me. And yet . . . There is a sharp old northern saying: No man dies of another's wounds . . . *We* are not defeated, I thought.

Is it absurd to say that I have never felt the life of England stronger in me and in the people I passed in the street and sat opposite in the underground than on that evening of the 2nd of May 1940?

Chapter 7

People lived sharply that May, with the double sense of being driven by time as by a strong following wind, and of each minute of this scudding time being dilated to infinity.

On the ninth I was in London. We were giving one of our refugee parties that evening: they cost us a little money, but they (we hoped) gave the exiled writers a brief sense of being still part of a community. The greater number of our guests were German or Austrian, and most of these were Jewish. Walking about the long room in the New Burlington Galleries, I picked out the dark-skinned skeletal face of one of our Catalans, and the two or three Czechs—what had become of the young writer who sent us desperate letters from Brno, whom we had failed to get out? The thought of the speech I should be forced to make was nearly intolerable. I detest making speeches, and to have to make one to people for whom the present was an insoluble riddle and the past a kaleidoscope of fears, anguish, and the deaths of friends, shamed me. Moreover, not many of them would be able to hear my light voice. Perhaps more heard than I could have expected, they were so quiet when I got up on a chair and began speaking that I felt their attention like a hand clutching my arm. I said what I could about the difficulties of their lives, I said I knew we could not give them back their lost certainties, their lost streets, cafés, friends, I said that our friendship for them was a plank thrown across an abyss, I tried to warn them not to show anger and impatience when they met, as, if the war took a bad turn they would meet, suspicion and injustice . . . It does not matter a toss what I said. If I had had the tongues of men and of angels I could not have lightened their obsessions for longer than a breath.

I was staying the night with Noel Streatfeild in Bolton Street, within a step or two of Green Park. When I knew her first in the twenties, this daughter of the vicarage was a lovely and charming

young rake of an actress (I daresay an indifferent one): she dropped
acting to write gay well-mannered novels and lively sensible quick-
witted children's books, and without losing a feather of her gaiety
arranged for herself a hard-working and eminently well-run life. It
ought not to have surprised me that she turned out to have an active
social conscience; she was not a descendant of Elizabeth Fry for
nothing.

In the morning, Nellie, her shrewd friendly housekeeper, a
Londoner to her ill-fitting teeth, brought my coffee to me in bed. I
was taking it from her when Noel came in, smiling, merry as a grig.

'Well, girls, we're on. The Germans invaded Holland and Belgium
this morning. I've just heard it on the French wireless.'

'I suppose they would know,' I said.

'They certainly do.'

'I've a sharp kitchen knife out there for any parachutists who land
in the Park,' Nellie said pleasantly.

'You won't,' Noel told her, 'need it this morning. Later, perhaps.'

I listened with pleasure to her strong self-possessed voice as she
talked on the telephone to some knowledgeable friend. Like the
well-born women of a much earlier generation she spoke with
traces of a tart accent, learned in the nursery.

'Yes, yes, but what *sort* of help are we giving them? The sort we
gave the Poles? . . . My cue? Yes, of course. Anything is better than
waiting . . . '

She had been training as an air-raid warden since the first week of
the war. Laying down the telephone, she sent a quick smiling glance
round the room. 'I wonder how long all this will be here.'

(It disappeared one night during the Blitz, with parts of Piccadilly
and Jermyn Street. Noel was on duty outside—or was it one of the
nights when she toured Deptford during raids with a mobile can-
teen? She worked in Deptford to the end of the war: what she saw
and heard there—with her acuity about people, even the barely
articulate—made her contradict me sharply when I said, of the
crowds cheering their throats raw for Churchill one day in June
1945, 'They'll keep him in power.'

'Don't you believe it, my sweet. They're saying goodbye to him.')

It was a deliciously warm clear day. Unwilling to go back to
Reading, I dawdled about London. A news poster had it that Antwerp had been bombed, and I walked attentively about the streets
round the Cathedral rearing above the old houses squatted at its

feet, and looked with love at shabby buildings on the near-by wharf which could not be expected, without my help, to stand up to bombs. Antwerp gave me my first foreign memories, my first taste for departures. Did my restlessness, my impotent hatred of being settled, start there? No, earlier—long before I was born . . .

During the next fortnight the speed of the German advance across Belgium and northern France numbed a part of the mind while keeping another listening intently, whatever else it was busy with, and even in sleep, to sounds too distant to be audible: voices that were and were not the voices of young men, my friends, killed in 1914 and heard now for the last time below the voices of young men I didn't know and thought about with an anxiety I was incapable of feeling in 1914; sounds of wheels grinding to a stop on hot dusty roads crowded with refugees; cries of terrified children.

'Is it true,' I asked one of our airmen, 'that the Germans make a habit of flying low enough to machine-gun the refugees?'

'Perfectly true.' He added reflectively, 'I don't know that habit is the right word, it seems more like a game they play.'

What sort of boys were they who played this game? Perhaps Hitler's only unforgivable sin is to have turned a generation into robots, or conscienceless *routiers*, who killed, as the guards in the extermination camps did later, not mindlessly, but with minds bent to a pattern and anaesthetised to feelings that might disturb it.

The one of us to whom listening became anguish was Guy. As the names of the first war succeeded each other in the bulletins, Vimy Ridge, St Quentin, Amiens, Arras, Abbeville—dear time-worn Abbeville—a buried landscape, an area of grotesque corruption, its clusters of splintered houses, corridors, tunnels, stench, obese rats, treacherous parapets, rose again in his mind, and he sickened with a fever which was only a poisoned abscess of memory.

I realized what I had always known. For its survivors that war did not end on a day in 1918: they are the survivors of themselves.

Chapter 8

From the moment the Germans broke into France, May had been superb, skies without a cloud, clear dawns widening to a day-long bright warmth, springs, fountains, rivers of hawthorn, chestnut, lilac, apple blossom, cherry: the acacias were more splendid than I ever saw them, large old trees heavy with ivory-white flowers, scenting the air for a distance of twenty yards.

On one of these cloudless days I went to a reception in the Chinese Embassy. To step from the hot street into the coolness of the hall was like walking into the sea, a sea without waves, and the staircase was noticeably quiet and cool. It was only when I reached the top that the voices came out, like so many crossed tentacles. The large rooms were crowded. I recognized some of the faces; at a first glance it seemed that all Dr Quo's English guests were Left-minded intellectuals, writers, journalists, publishers, politicians—likely enough. A few Chinese women, young exquisite creatures, stood about in the eddies of nervous excitement, unmoved by them, holding plates of sandwiches, minute, very delicate, and bowls of strawberries.

After some minutes I thought that everyone in the room was saying the same thing, circling round it like a hen round a knife lying on the ground.

'It's a question of time, the French are completely demoralized, completely unable to stop the German advance units, and they—the Germans, of course—are magnificently equipped. Their parachute troops are firing villages behind the French lines——'

'If there are any lines now.'

'—smoking ruins, and no one knows what the civilian casualties are, but they must run to a hundred thousand. The first German troops will reach the coast facing us in less than a week.'

'A nice prospect.'

'My dear fellow—' a short laugh—'you haven't been attacked in the *Völkischer Beobachter* as often as I have. I don't mind telling you that I've made my doctor supply me with poison, I couldn't stand being tortured. I know too much about it.'

'Why don't you go to America?'

'I can't do that, I should be discredited: all I've worked for would be discredited.'

'Have you heard the latest? The Ninth Army has been captured.'

'Whose Ninth?'

'The French, of course. Giraud's army. So far they haven't admitted it, but it's certainly true.'

'Surely you know *why* Churchill went to Paris? It was to back Reynaud in dismissing Gamelin and giving Weygand the job.'

'Too late. The capitulation party is too strong. Influential people there are already in touch with the German Foreign Office.'

'You see how ridiculous it was to depend on France, and how sensible *The Times* was in the days when it was advising us to make friends with the Germans. What we ought to have done—I said so at the time, to several people, including Attlee—in 1933, was to hold out a friendly hand to Herr Hitler, and join him in reorganizing Europe. We shouldn't, if I'd been listened to, be in this mess now.'

Herr Hitler? Why this respect?

'. . . a Gauleiter taking the place of the Lord Lieutenant of the county, and German administrators—but no doubt the civil servants will stay in their jobs. After all, the country must be run.'

I stood knee-deep in the currents converging from all sides. I felt stupid. I was not taking in what I heard. Because of this protective stupidity—a habit—I believe in a disaster only *after* it has happened. Did all these people believe we were defeated? They seemed to . . . I had not spoken to my host; I had never seen him in my life, and I asked Kingsley Martin to point him out to me.

'You don't know him? Come and talk to him, he's a splendid fellow, you'll like him.'

Certainly he had a splendid, sculptured, serenely intelligent face: one could look at it for a long time, as at a wide landscape, without coming to an end of it. Fortunately I had no need to talk, Kingsley talked. He, like the others, assumed that France was lost and that the Germans would assault England in a matter of weeks. Politely drawing me in, Dr Quo said: 'What do you think?'

'Surely,' I said, stammering, 'the Fleet—so long as the Fleet is intact we can't be invaded?'

'Absurd,' Kingsley said kindly. 'We could be devastated from the air before they risk landing troop-carrying planes and parachutists.'

'But are you sure the French are going to give in? Defeat—it isn't my idea of France.'

'We all know how infatuated you are with France,' Kingsley said, laughing.

'I think they're done for,' Dr Quo said. 'This isn't the sort of war they're equipped to fight, their generals are too old, it's not a war for old men.'

Coming from him, this shook me as nothing and no one else had. But it did not penetrate far into the fog of stupidity. Nor did even Kingsley's account of the situation, now, of our soldiers: in the next two or three days, he explained, they would be caught in a triangle of the coast with a choice between surrendering or being massacred when they tried to get away.

'Couldn't they fight their way through?' I asked.

'My dear girl, three hundred thousand of them—at the most— and the Germans have eight million men under arms!'

With the least noticeable of smiles, Dr Quo said, 'It reminds me of an incident in northern China in the fifth century. One of our poets . . .'

I have forgotten, I believe I did not catch, the name and most of the details. The episode seemed to belong to the fifth century B.C., and I had the impression that he was trying, out of kindness, to reassure a barbarian that a break in the short and brutish history of her country would not be the end of civilization.

I watched him carry his smiling calm from one to another of the groups of excited, too well-informed men and women. I was certain that, if the worst happened, they, or all but one of them, would behave as well as the dullest and simplest, but I wished sharply that they would keep quiet in front of the politely undisturbed Chinese.

If the worst happened—like a dog shaking itself after a plunge into the sea, my mind shook off any image attached to the words. I was staying the night with the Kingsley Martins. My son had given me a Hendon telephone number, no use, he warned me, before half-past eight or nine at night. To please Susan Lawrence I had agreed to speak at—of all absurd things—a Fabian dinner, and I gave Kingsley the number and begged him to go on ringing up until he got an answer. I went off, distracted between the fear of missing Bill and fury at having, once again, been too weak to say No. The dinner was being held in the ballroom of a Bloomsbury hotel, a place of purgatorial decency and gloom. A number of silent, noticeably square-bodied men were sitting about the comfortless hall. I was told that they had crossed from Holland in fishing-boats. My spirits rose. At least one of our allies was worth having. In two rooms I crossed to reach the ballroom, furniture and wall-mirrors were shrouded in dust-sheets, as for a funeral. Surely a little premature? Susan Lawrence was in the chair; I sat between her and Margaret Cole, and saw with despair and rage that it was already eight o'clock. You fool, I thought, you ineffable fool, what a way to spend one of your last evenings! I was not the chief speaker, but as the dinner, which was atrocious, dragged on, I lost patience and my manners, and said that I must be allowed to speak first. As soon as I had made my speech, I fled.

Opening the door of the flat to me, Kingsley said quickly, 'It's all right, my dear, I got the boy. He's on his way in.'

He arrived almost at once. Kingsley went away to make a telephone call, and I had a few minutes with him alone. For all my inability to direct or discipline him, or tell him any of the dull truths about the way sensible worldly people live, I had never told him lies. I saw no excuse for starting now, and I told him brusquely that many people believed we were going to lose the war.

'Do you believe it?' he asked.

'No. Yes. I don't know.'

'Not very clear of you.'

'Thank God you and I haven't the same name.'

'Do you think the Germans are as dumb as that?' he said, smiling.

Kingsley had come back. 'Quo says he very much wants to meet Dr Jameson again, and though he's very tired, he'll come round.'

I did not believe this, but I was enchanted that it had been said in Bill's hearing. Some sorts of vanity are innocent. Almost innocent. That, for instance, of appearing in a good light before one's children.

Dorothy Woodman came in from a committee meeting, something to do with help for China, bringing with her an attractive young man who was Stafford Cripps's secretary. Behind her warm placid looks and soft voice, she is the perpetual revolutionary: impossible to imagine a society in which she could not find an under-dog to defend. When Dr Quo came he began questioning the young man about an affair not yet in the papers: Cripps was being sent to Moscow, with plenary powers.

'Why Cripps?' I asked.

'Because,' said Kingsley, 'he is *persona grata* there, hates the Labour Party, and can't possibly be considered an Imperialist.'

'I spoke about it to Maisky two days ago,' Dr Quo said, 'and asked him what chance there is of the approach succeeding. Maisky said: I don't know, it's late, it's late.'

My only reaction to this startling piece of news was, again, pleasure that my son was listening to it. He must, surely, find the conversation entertaining, worth the trouble of coming into town to hear. I felt modestly pleased with myself.

It will seem fantastic, I thought, if we *are* defeated, that we sat here, in this quiet pleasantly untidy room, with the Chinese Ambassador, and discussed the reasons why France is collapsing, the strength of the French Fifth Column, the abject failure of social democracy in Europe, the length of time, days or weeks, we can hold out, the meagre chance that America might help us. I tried and failed to imagine a German-occupied England in which such gatherings had become unthinkable. Instead, a ludicrous image flickered at the back of my mind—myself haring across the fields at the back of our house, a little ahead of the Germans, dragging with me a large canvas bag stuffed with unfinished manuscripts and notebooks.

When Bill was leaving, to go back to Hendon, Kingsley said, 'Can't you get Storm away in an aeroplane? As a known anti-Nazi she'll be in real danger.'

I said swiftly, 'He has a wife.'

'You must get them both away,' Kingsley said with energy.

It was two o'clock before I went to my room. I lay awake a long time, thinking of Bill, of my young sister and her children, and of the novel I was writing. The thought that, if we were invaded, I should not have time to finish it vexed me.

Chapter 9

In the morning I sent a telegram to Amabel Williams-Ellis, asking her whether, if it became necessary, she could find lodgings for Do and her children in her North Welsh village. I expected and got the answer: Yes, of course.

The internment of B class aliens was under way, and some of our exiled writers had been taken, among them the Austrian writer, Robert Neumann: he had been in England since 1934 and I knew him and his second wife very well. That is, I knew the amiable side of a complex character; I suspected that in private he used his witty tongue, sharpened in the literary café society of Vienna, on his English friends, whom he found provincial, but I believed him to be kind, and I was truly vexed that we had thought it necessary to intern this quick-tongued soft-bodied friendly intellectual. I felt more anxious about his young wife, Rolly, left alone in their cottage in a small Buckinghamshire village.

I was to see her this afternoon. Waiting for her in the United University Club, I was greeted by a man I knew very slightly, a youngish diplomat; he had been at the Hague and was not yet tired of talking about the ease with which troops, guns, and even small tanks are landed from planes or by parachute on aerodromes and arterial roads. I reflected that our house in Berkshire was ringed by aerodromes. Ought I to hurry Do and the children off to North Wales now, at once?

'Are we going to be invaded?' I asked.

He laughed. 'Who knows? Churchill has gone to Paris again to try to stiffen the dear French. How do you stiffen a puppet that has lost all its sawdust? France is finished.'

I had the civility, or the servility, to smile.

When Rolly came into the room, I thought she had shrunk. She is small and slender, a Rhinelander, gay and very stubborn: that afternoon she looked smaller than ever, her gaiety pinched out like a candle. Since Robert left with the friendly policeman who came for him, she had heard nothing, not a word. She had been to see every English friend they had who might help to get him released. Some of these had made excuses not to see her. H. G. Wells, although he allowed her to come to the house, had said drily that he didn't know enough about Robert to speak for him.

'I said, "But you have known him for four years! You know he is an anti-Nazi," and he said, "Yes, but how do I know whether he is reliable or not? He could be blackmailed by them." Margaret, what can I do now? I am defeated. And what are they doing to him that he doesn't write to me?'

She spoke evenly, without raising her voice, using as few words as possible. I did not say what I thought: that Robert's worst or only suffering would be metaphysical.

'It's extremely likely that his letters are lying on some official's desk, with a great many more, waiting for someone to decide whether they are to be posted or censored first.'

'They ought to know how frightful it is to hear nothing.'

I caught sight for a moment of the anguish of the stateless, accepted on sufferance for a time, and rejected abruptly as *not one of the family*.

'The worst of all,' she went on, 'the thing that really frightens me is—if the Germans land—the Government may hand the refugees over to them.'

'Oh, no, that's impossible,' I said, shocked.

'You say that because you wouldn't do it yourself. But that doesn't mean a defeated Government wouldn't do it. One can't trust any politician.'

I did not argue the point, which struck me as absurd—we did not then know about the German political exiles in France who were handed over, in many instances deliberately, in others out of a brutal indifference, to the Nazis. Instead I wrote down all the details she could give me about herself and Robert, to use in writing to the Home Office.

'Promise me one thing,' she said. 'If I am arrested, will you go on trying to get him out? It doesn't matter about me, I can stand it, but please don't forget him.'

'I promise. On condition that you tell me when you are short of money.'

Her small face closed as though she had suddenly gone blind. 'I don't need any money, the garden is full of vegetables I planted, and I put down twelve dozen eggs in water-glass when they were cheap; I can live on them for a long time.'

I hardly knew which made me feel clumsier, her look of brittleness or her stubborn pride.

She was swept into internment long before she came to the end of her preserved eggs.

I was hoping against hope to see my son again this evening, and at eight I began to ring his number: I rang at intervals of ten minutes until at last a man's voice said, 'They were late leaving.'

'What did you say?'

'They were late leaving.'

This time I understood what I was being told. There was no point in staying a second night in town, we caught the last train and I sat staring at a sky so abnormally still and clear that it was menacing, as though the darkness were a mask. This unreal darkness thickened when a huge violently yellow moon rose on the left; the water of the Thames near Reading was absolutely still, as if turned to ice, the reflections of the trees imprisoned in it like the naked branches during the four-day ice at the sterile beginning of this year.

Do must have been awake, listening. As we came in she appeared at the head of the staircase, her hair falling about her shoulders; she may have hoped it was her husband, who was working a twenty-hour day at his biscuit factory to replace the supplies lost in France.

I had forgotten, I thought absurdly, that she is beautiful: excitement had laid a patina of soft brilliance over her face and darkened her eyes. For a moment the thought that she would grow old, and tired, and lose her air of fineness and perpetual youth, was shocking.

'Is there any news, Dear Dog?'

I told her what there was, and said, 'Perhaps you had better take the children to Llanfrothen for a few days, until we know what's going to happen.'

She shook her head. 'I can't go now, with the fruit ready to pick and bottle. We shall need it.'

'Well—we'll see.'

'The French are going to give in,' she said contemptuously.

Suddenly convinced that it was impossible, I cried, '*No*! Not France.'

Two or three days after this, on the 14th of May, *Europe to Let* was published. I did not notice it at the time, nor, so far as I recall, did anyone else. Except, perhaps, the Czech exile who later gave up his allotted period on the B.B.C. to telling his listeners in Czechoslovakia about 'The Hour of Prague'. And except, oddly, a Soviet writer called Rokotov who translated 'Between March and April' for some Russian journal and cabled to the Ministry of Information in October 1941 to tell me that a sum in roubles was owing to me. I answered telling him to give them to the Russian Red Cross. Possibly he did.

Through the Ministry at this time I used to exchange passionate telegrams and letters with the secretary of the official body (VOX) of Russian writers, he exhorting me to stand shoulder to shoulder with them against the bloodthirsty (debased, treacherous, abject) tyrant (traitor, fascist hyena), and I replying, a little more austerely, in the same spirit—I had small hope that any adjective I used was better than abjectly counter-revolutionary.

On the 24th of May, between errands to the village shop, picking our gooseberries, and bandaging Nicholas's cut knee, I drafted a long and eloquent appeal 'To the Conscience of the World'. We had it signed by a score of our most important writers, and sent it to all the neutrals.

Who received it in silence. It drew a single reply, a finely sincere letter from the woman librarian of the Dallas (Texas) public library.

Anyone, especially any young man, reading it today, twenty-four years after the hot bright day when it was written, would jeer not only at the naïveté of the sentiments, but, if his ear is fine enough (unlikely), at their profound unreality. These well-cut sentences are not the real sentiments of a human being who may or may not be in danger, they are phrases which float to the surface from the level where simple feeling comes up against the debris from a lifetime of reading, and is deflected into speech.

The young man would be deluding himself if he believed that the sacred cows of rhetoric are less sacred than they were. Their bones may be sticking through the hide, but they can't be killed.

It is now (1964) nearly a quarter of a century since our soldiers, trapped in a corner of the French coast, were brought back. Nothing during this quarter-century has come anywhere near the intense excitement of those few days, starting in anguish and rising on this side of the Channel to a pitch of exultation no one could expect to feel more than once in a lifetime.

I shall begin to tell lies if I try to describe this feeling to anyone who was not there.

Chapter 10

To be thought well of, I should imply that the fears and anxieties of these weeks made it impossible to write a novel. The truth is, I have never, as a writer, been so voluptuously contented as I was during this time.

There was nothing I could do to stop the barbarians invading us. I might just as well go on with my ordinary life. Better in any event than bolting, or wringing my hands.

Except on days when I had to go to London, I wrote from early in the morning until six at night, whatever the news I had swallowed with my breakfast coffee—heaven be praised that coffee was never rationed during the war. Mantes had been bombed, Paris was in mortal danger: I recalled briefly the evening in Mantes less than a year ago when we sat drinking, glasses of cheap yellow wine, at a trestle table outside one of the two small cafés in the dusty square; it was the evening of the 14th of July, and young men swung their girls across the cobblestones, round the dry cracked fountain, to the music of a concertina and two drums: the Seine was a short walk away. ('You have your coasts to protect you,' a Frenchman said to me, 'we rely on our rivers.' This year not even the Marne kept its word.) Think about all that this evening, I told myself obscurely, when you are bathing the children, or in the half-dark garden watching low-flying swallows, but now write.

This was not only the invincible egoism of the writer—when it comes off, his trick of pressing the marrow of feelings, sights, sounds, into language gives him such astonishing pleasure that only an immediate shock, a disaster taking place under his eye, can distract him from it. But, as well, I was driven by a subconscious wish to pretend to safety, and a stubborn need to finish what I had begun.

I was working at *Cousin Honoré*. Not only because, at this moment, nothing was worth doing except the best I could do, but because it had been living on a deep level of my mind too long, the process of *crystallization* had gone much too far: to abandon it now was impossible.

This one of my too many novels is the one in which it is easy to watch the maturing of an honest book—one, that is, which exists as an organism, not as a construction, a neat scheme. The actual source or sources of such a book may differ widely; the process of growth is the same. As soon as I had transposed the Germany of Wheeler-Bennett's life of Hindenburg into an estate in Alsace, the characters began transposing themselves. Honoré Burckheim revealed the strengths and weaknesses Hindenburg might have shown if he had been the head of an Alsatian family of ironmasters and wine-growers, with a modest Renaissance house in Strasbourg and a château and vineyard in the village, Burckheim, which had belonged to his family for six centuries. In turn this Alsatian Hindenburg merged with my idea of Stanley Baldwin, and the two together fused into the complex figure of Cousin Honoré. I was not for a moment concerned with the real Baldwin, of whom I knew no more than I knew about the real Hindenburg (less, since Wheeler-Bennett is an admirable analyst, and what little I knew of the Conservative statesman came from the gossip of his colleagues and opponents), but with an imagined human being able to absorb all I felt about the men who had led us to disaster, politicians for the most part, obsessed with the need to safeguard not only the spiritual values of their class (as much an instinct in the rather stupid Hindenburg as in the astute Englishman) but its possessions, self-satisfied, disingenuous to the point of lying, eminently respectable, with respectable emotions and an actor's ability to use them to create an impression, solid men, pragmatists, not ill-willed or in the worldly sense inexperienced.

The process bears no resemblance to the act—the folly, rather—of copying a living model. What takes place is a crystallization of feelings, insights, memories, ideas, round the bare outline, the germ, of a character: a living model, a man or woman known to the writer, can only hinder the process: his imagination is embarrassed by irrelevant facts instead of working freely and easily on the unknown, the half-seen, the half-begotten, the barely conceived.

Other characters in the book were born by the same double process of crystallization and the fusion of two or many persons. Wheeler-Bennett's Brüning attracted to himself the little I knew of Beneš and became Edward Berthelin; Schleicher offered the germ of Sigenau, and Sigenau and his English wife took on the physical, only the physical, likenesses of two people I knew and admired, so that he became a more likeable character than the slippery opportunist, General Kurt von Schleicher; Henry Eschelmer, Burckheim's illegitimate son by a peasant mistress, who murdered both Sigenaus, drew life from the idea of a young Goebbels; and Jules Reuss from the equivocal figure of Otto Meissner who served both Hindenburg and Hitler. A few of the characters were invented—but what is invention?—the peasant farmer, Dietrich; the two young people, for whom I felt indulgence and liking; Burckheim's second wife, an American; Anne-Marie Eschelmer . . .

The change of milieu produces its own complexities and depths of meaning, one change involving another, and another, until the original chain of events is completely overlaid. The personages move farther and farther from their point of origin and become truly autonomous, and are enriched, complicated, changed in depth, by the working on them of circumstance.

And, of course, the fusion of all these many elements is fed and animated by personal memories and emotions entering it spontaneously at every level.

This digression will be of interest only to a writer, and one who cares more about his writing than about the impression he is making.

I wrote *Cousin Honoré* with unfailing happiness, no feeling, not a trace, that I had set myself a task, only the exquisite pleasure of following the action as it unfolded and the self-revelation of the characters. A pleasure without anxiety, an angelic pleasure. No insoluble problems. Everything I knew or could learn about French politics and society between the wars offered itself willingly to be used or discarded, and my passion for walking about foreign cities (and anger at being deprived of it) sharpened the image of an Alsace I had not, at that time, seen. I worked surrounded by photographs and engravings of Alsatian towns and villages quickened into life by the breath of a remembered France. Remembered with love, with grief.

Years of hard work had suppled my writing brain, and I was—I realize it now—at the peak of such intellectual and emotional energy as I possess. *Cousin Honoré* was one of the last novels I wrote with pleasure. It was written, too, in what, for me, are the only satisfactory conditions, a quiet room, looking over a wide view or a garden, and—the one really essential thing—no responsibility for running a household, the one task in life I loathe and resent. My young sister ran the house for both families, hers and mine. I had duties, as might a child in its home—I made beds, washed clothes and dishes, picked fruit for jam—but no responsibility. My mind was free.

Looking back at those months, across the errors, restlessness, drifting, of succeeding years, I see that I was being offered a sample of my real life as a writer. At the time I did not see this clearly.

No one, unless he is of the family of Goethe or Tolstoy, stays on his peak long. The moment of greatest energy reached, a descent begins. All I can say is that if I had had the sense or the luck to go on living as I lived then, I should have put off my moral and spiritual old age ten or even twenty years.

I wrote the last lines on the 15th of June. The Germans had been marching into Paris since the day before, and the book ended in a Strasbourg emptied of all but a handful of its citizens.

'It seemed to Berthelin that he was walking through any moment, it might be as distant in the past as the first Roman fort set here, in which the city was in danger, and through his own life, and the life at this time of every man in Europe. Streets, houses, the Cathedral itself, with its spire and pinnacles of endurance, were the thoughts and fears, the solitude, the endless curiosity, the sins, the crowded estate of pain and helplessness, the unconquered mind, all he is, all he has lost the habit of, all that is only habit, proper to a Frenchman. He remembered that Péguy said, "Christendom will come back in the hour of distress." Would it, when it came back to France, find all this untouched, this body made lightly of stone? Or would these be broken, the past smouldering, and the future a weight lying across the living bones of a hand? Of whose hands?

'Let there be French hands and feet and a brain, Berthelin prayed. Risen behind the spire, the sun promised at least that.'

Who would have guessed that the answer to this lyricism was General de Gaulle? . . .

A minute or two after I had laid my pen down and stretched, I was called downstairs to the telephone. With a slightly crazy gaiety Bjarne Braatoy told me they were leaving in four days, for New York.

'And listen. An American journalist tells me he saw your name on a Nazi black-list in Berlin. You're in as much danger as anyone, and it would be only sensible to leave now.'

'Let me speak to her.' Ria's voice had kept its undercurrent of laughter. 'The sensible reason why we are going is that a German woman married to a Norwegian socialist would be a fool to stay here, the real reason is that I couldn't bear to drown in that Nazi filth, my father might be able to save me, but I should have to live with it.'

'Of course you must get away,' I exclaimed.

'Come with us.'

The revulsion I felt had nothing to do with my will. I did not answer at once, and after a moment she said gently, 'Forgive us for going.'

'But it would be idiotic to stay,' I said. 'You must go.'

'Yes.'

'I'll come up to see you before you leave.'

My sister was waiting to talk to me. Something in her clear look, a certain hardness and fixity, struck me.

'What's the matter?' I asked.

'Nothing. Nothing really. I've been thinking, I've talked about it to Robert, and we think, I think, if you know someone who would be the right person to keep them I'd take Nick and Judy to America, now.'

She had spoken simply, coldly. Without hesitation, without asking myself whether to send them away was the right or the wise thing to do, I said—as I would have said to my mother about something she wanted, 'Yes, of course. I am sure I can find someone—if you're sure you want them to go.'

Her face did not change. Still looking at me fixedly she said, with the same coldness, 'If we're going to be invaded . . . they're so small . . . and even if we're not invaded this autumn there won't be any food.'

The fear that it was already too late to arrange anything seized me, but I said calmly, 'I'll get advice.'

'All right.'

She turned quickly and went away. Afraid, perhaps, that I was going to say something that would trick her into giving away feelings she would think it shameful, indecent, to show to anyone, except her husband.

That same evening or the next I had a visitor, a middle-aged German woman I had met in Berlin, a cultivated warm-natured woman, half-Jewish, talkative and very gay, earning a tolerable living as a translator from English. She came to London in 1935, bringing with her a little money, enough to rent the ugly house in north-west London she had turned into a boarding-house.

It was another of the warm velvety evenings of that inconceivably generous summer. We sat in the garden and she told me why she had come. To my astonishment, it was only to beg me to go to America while there was time. I interrupted the flood of words to say, 'But, my dear Sophy, you're in worse danger than I am. Why don't you go?'

She began to cry. 'I'm tired of running away, I ran to San Remo in 1933, and then to London, I can't run any farther. But you can go, you must. I beg you to go. Go now. You don't know what they're like, the Nazis, they can do worse than kill you, other English writers have gone, Auden, Isherwood, if they weren't ashamed to leave why should you be? And they were right! Think of the German writers—Erich Kästner—who didn't leave when Brecht and Thomas Mann did, even if they're still alive what good are they doing? Oh, I'm right, you know I'm right.'

'Probably you are,' I said, 'but——'

'But what, in God's name?'

'But there is a difference in kind between running away from your own countrymen who are trying to murder you, and running away from an invader, when millions of your innocent fellow-countrymen can't. And don't think I haven't considered doing it.'

She shook a wildly dishevelled head. 'The Gestapo can't kill everyone, but they'll kill you.'

I tried to clear my mind. There is no logical reason, I thought, why I should feel this mild contempt for young men who remove themselves from the danger of a violent death—and not only themselves, their unwritten books. No one need be ashamed of fearing air-raids, and no writer can help feeling a mad exasperation at the prospect of dying before he has finished his work. In the last war I felt a cold respect for conscientious objectors who bore witness to their hatred of war in prison, and contempt only for the obscene women safe in England who handed white feathers to young men in civilian clothes. It is harder to feel respect for a witness living two thousand miles out of danger. Moreover, a clever young minor novelist is scarcely worth saving, though a good poet may be—if he feels that the most important thing is to survive. Nor is there any good reason to save a middle-aged woman novelist.

My flesh shrivelled at the thought of falling into the hands of the Gestapo, but . . . between the wars I had been a pacifist, and I had not had the moral firmness to stand by my pacifism in this war. To run away would make this worse.

I looked at poor Sophy, sitting, snuffling, her imploring eyes fixed on me like a gentle untidy intelligent dog, and felt for her suddenly all the respect, all the love, all the sympathy I could not feel for our prudent intellectuals.

I patted her arm. 'Dear Sophy, we're not going to be invaded.'

'You are mad,' she said, sighing.

But for the time it took me to say it, I believed it. And, without better reason, how could I leave the country which held my son, my young sister, my husband?

Chapter 11

In the morning, I went up to London to give lunch to the Oldens.

What set Rudolf Olden apart among our exiled writers was not that he was a scholar and a humanist where the rest were novelists, journalists, critics, but the almost impersonal nature of his hatred of tyranny; he hated it with every fibre of a fastidious intellect rather than for its disruption of his own life. Living since his arrival in England in a cottage near Oxford, on Boar's Hill, belonging to his friend Gilbert Murray, he could have been almost content, but for the war, to use himself up in writing—himself and his passion of hatred. He took two things for granted, the English care for freedom and the unfailing quiet devotion of his young wife. They had a two-year-old daughter, born in England, and her birth had opened in him a spring of pure happiness, something he had never, I think, known; he was too complex and self-lacerating an egoist.

It took the first internments to shake his belief in English justice. At the beginning of the war his sole anxiety was to find ways of using exiled writers, of every nation. He had almost forgotten that, officially, he was an enemy.

'I regretted deeply,' he wrote to me, 'the postponement of the Stockholm Congress. There would have been the very occasion to show to the world that the writers of the world are not divided into different camps, that they are not "enemies". This is the great difference between 1914 and 1939. Then they said: My country right or wrong. Not so this time. Poor Hitler who does not know the value and weight of spiritual things saved us from so terrible a mistake . . .'

This was the first moment when I caught sight of a naïve innocence behind the delicate, ironical, and ambiguous smile with which he watched the workings of vanity and ambition in his fellow-writers.

When the internments started he began writing to me about his idea that the American government could be persuaded to invite the German writers in France and England to carry on 'the great struggle' in the States. They might even, he thought, found a publishing house there to save the tradition of Goethe and Heine.

This was worse than naïve.

'No one would wish to give the appearance as if he run away from potential dangers.' (No one, dear Rudi?) 'I should say almost all of these men living in France or here would have had the possibility to go to the States in past years and they remained deliberately in Europe although they foresaw the coming war with certainty. Some of them just wanted to remain nearer the great decision, some of them did it for love of Europe, some felt sure they would be used and wanted to fight the Nazi. This was perhaps foolish but it was so . . . The trouble of being interned is not so much to live for some time without the usual comfort and liberty used to—but it is this: to be entirely idle whilst one hoped for utter activity . . .'

Before leaving to go to London, I turned on the seven o'clock news. Reynaud had resigned. So, I thought instantly—and instantly strangled the thought—the French do mean to give in.

In the drawing-room of the United University I listened to the lively conversation of two men—one I knew to be a War Office official—about 'the latest plan'—whose?—'to fight a retreat across France, evacuate the French army to English and French North Africa, make this country impregnable, blockade Europe, and wait for the Yankees.'

The Oldens cut short my eavesdropping—not to overhear I should have had to move away or put my hands over my ears.

Rudolf's friendly twisted half-smile was a thin mask: behind it, the tense knot of anger, refusal, and under everything else, hope. His face was thinner than ever, and more deeply lined, as though the bones were working inside it, like the wood of a tree, to age him rapidly. As always, Ika showed none of her anxiety. Was there a nerve in her body which was not vowed to him?

He talked for some time about his schemes, and I tried to imagine the quickest way of helping him to approach what he called the two *hommes de lettres* in the government. (Who were these two mythical animals? I have forgotten.) Then, abruptly, he told me they had decided to send their child, the little lively Kutzi, to a friend in Canada.

'It is better—I may not have much time.'

'Our English subject,' Ika said, smiling. She had a low even voice, comforting the ear. 'I must tell you that the clerk in your passport office treated me with such kindness as if *I* were the child. My troubles only started now, this morning, in the American consulate; I went to ask if they would give her a visa so that, if necessary, I could send her in an American ship, and the man I saw when I went in was brutal. I told him I wanted to make an enquiry. "What's the passport?" he said. I told him, "British nationality."—"Parents' nationality?"—"Stateless." He looked at me like a stone and said, "She'll go on the quota of her parents' nation."—"That seems hard," I said, and he said, very rudely, "We don't give visas on compassionate grounds." I said, "But I'm not asking you for compassion, I came to make enquiries."—"Come at 9.30 tomorrow, I'll give you another chance," he said, and pushed me to the door.'

'Let me go for you tomorrow,' I said.

'Oh, no,' she said calmly, 'I'm not afraid. You forget, I'm half English.' She smiled. 'I told them that, when they said I couldn't be an Air Raid Warden any longer, and they said sweetly, "We trust both your halves, but . . ." '

'Nothing would matter if they would allow us to work,' Rudolf said, with polite anguish.

'I am sorry,' I said. 'But that's no comfort. Try to forgive us.'

'Don't think it is not comfort,' he said swiftly. 'And don't speak about forgiving. You are one of the great assets of the world, found on the way through many countries. *Eine Frau mit einem grossen Herzen*—excuse my talking in my own language—what great, rare, reassuring comforting occurrence.'

I have rarely felt more ashamed. How had I deceived him to this extent about myself? Hurriedly, to distract his notice, I repeated the gossip about 'the latest plan'.

'But you have no troops in France, nothing you can fight with,' Rudolf exclaimed. 'And the French—my God!'

Now what peered through the mask was the Prussian gentleman's wholly involuntary contempt for a Latin race: I had seen it before, when he was watching Jules Romains give his arrogance and vanity a run in committee.

'Surely,' I said, 'if they meant to surrender they wouldn't have called on Pétain?'

This had only just occurred to me. Rudolf looked at me with

aloof amusement, and said softly, 'For a really dirty trick they would be sure to call in a general.'

When I went to the back of the room to pay the bill, the head waiter whispered, 'The French have ratted, it was on the one o'clock news.'

I let the Oldens go away without telling them. A minute or two later, the hall porter brought me up an evening paper with the news headlined; Ika had bought it in the street outside the club and told him to take it to me.

In the village that evening, I went with Do to order wood at the store. There were other women waiting, from the cottages, and they talked calmly among themselves about our going on alone. One said, 'All I hope is they'll get the children away.' Later, an old man fetched the logs to the house. I helped him to carry them from his handcart and stack them in a shed. He smiled at me toothlessly.

'Now we got rid of them foreigners we s'll be as right as rain,' he said.

He had not the slightest idea what he was talking about, it was the sort of thing my father, with his unthinking distrust of every other nation except the Scandinavians, would have said. But he was a consoling contrast with the agitated intellectuals in the Chinese Embassy. So was Churchill's grim short speech. He made no appeal to the Americans. Thank God—that would have been unbearable . . . His style as a writer sets my teeth on edge, I detest inflated eloquence, but again and again during these years, as at this moment, he thrust his strong harsh voice to the roots of our hearts.

The light striking on my thin eyelids woke me at five a.m., and—I must have been thinking it in my sleep—I thought: They're going to let us down . . . This must have been how the Czechs felt after Munich, and I wondered whether the French would turn against us as they turned against the Czechs as soon as they had given them away.

I had a few moments of soaring exhilaration, worth a lifetime of sober existence.

During the next four or five days I worked frenziedly to finish typing *Cousin Honoré* from the manuscript, to get it to New York before we were cut off.

Never, I shall never forget the opulent summer of 1940; no single thread of cold in the air, a sky without a flaw; the branches of the trees in the orchard were dragged to the earth by their weight of pears and green plums; on the long south wall nectarines offered themselves by scores, by hundreds. The sun roared overhead like a young lion, the grass of the lawn became as brittle as ash, and wide cracks opened in the dry iron-hard earth.

I interrupted my typing once, to go up to London and stand for almost three hours in a queue in the passport office to get an application form for my sister's passport. I finished it two days later, in time to hear the wireless news at nine p.m. Listening to the armistice terms the French had brought themselves to accept, I did not look at her—I felt sure we had left it too late.

Day followed rainless day, with a light dry hot wind. We were now so certain that the Germans would invade—and the French had not even sent us their Fleet—that we expected the first landing every mortal day of that time. Troops arrived in the village to dig emplacements for machine-guns and deep trenches at the side of the roads. The barricades of barbed wire and wood looked crazily homemade, like the chains of crochet-work which were all I ever learned to make as a child.

I spent the last day of June reading the typescript which he had just sent me, of *The Behaviour of Nations*, by that tortured old Quixote, Morley Roberts. I read it in the garden. In spite of its strength, the sun had not bleached the sky; intensely blue, with towering white clouds too large, too swollen, to be moved by a gusty south wind. No book could have been more apt to a day expecting violence than this bleak hard work, written (as I knew) in conditions of mental and physical stress which did not so much as crack the clear surface. It was an examination of the social conduct of nations, of their behaviour among themselves, made in the light of his conception of the world as 'the great nutritional field of hostile hungry nations', leaving aside questions of morality and dignity, and looking at the naturally morbid state of Europe as a surgeon would look at his patient.

'Man in the mass,' I read, 'is not man, but a low organism of gross instincts and irresistible tropisms, an animal incapable of reason . . . Such an organism recognizes no effective claim but the power to hold . . . Ideas of right and even righteousness, morality and moral laws, the sacredness of treaties, honour, kindness, mercy and nobility found only in a very few units among the animal mass have no meaning for the threatened or aggressive organism.'

There was something astonishingly exhilarating in the company, at this time, in this moment, of a modern Hobbes.

He was the embodiment—a lean hard embodiment, graceful even in extreme old age—of nineteenth century materialism and humanism. The book was written with coolness, lucidity, a natural elegance and a courteous avoidance of all ambiguity. Who could believe that it had been written by a man over eighty, in bad health, enduring, without a thread of comfort or consoling hope, an agony of grief for his dying step-daughter?

Planes, fighters, began to pass in formation across the blue gulfs overhead. Surely, I thought after a time, many more than usual. Had it begun?

It struck me that if the country were occupied I should have to leave this house for the sake of the others. Moreover, I mustn't leave anything behind, any letter or paper, that could compromise them or any friend or any of our exiles. I had heard too many stories about the meticulous work of the Gestapo to think it absurd that they might come here.

I keep very few letters or documents. I don't understand my own passion for destroying these things since, unless they are cracked or broken (I detest all scarred and defective things and only want to get them out of my sight), I cherish any number of useless objects. On the day when, in a final desperate effort to free myself, I sell all my possessions, long heavy bookcases, antique tallboys, old china and tables, I shall for sure keep my mother's small exquisitely useless Chinese cabinet, the case of war medals, scores of photographs, the parchment from the République Française conferring his Médaille Militaire on my brother, and a round dozen more things no more good to me than the confusion in the rag and bone shop of my mind, its darkness broken into by shafts of light picking out a lace table-cloth in my mother's room, rank salt-bitten grass on the cliffs at Whitby, cobbled streets nearer my eye than the very lines on my palm, a smile, fugitive idly-dropped words. But I destroy what most writers keep—reviews, articles written about me, or documents to do with me. Why am I so anxious to sink without trace? Because the traces I make on the earth are not so clear as I hoped they would be?

I do keep a few papers. Among these was a bundle of letters about *No Time Like The Present*—kept, I daresay, because this book was closer to me than any novel. I had not the heart to re-read them, but as I tore them up I recognized some of the hands, Gerald Bullett,

Michael Sadleir, Morley Roberts, S. K. Ratcliffe, R. H. Tawney, Sir
Michael Sadler, A. R. Orage, Edward Thompson: many of them
were from strangers, several had come from abroad. I dropped the
fragments into a carton, and threw on top of them every letter from
an exile, only keeping back—to be destroyed when the invasion
started—papers about them.

In the same tallboy, in one of its two awkwardly-placed secret
drawers, I came on Duckworth's reader's report on my absurd first
novel, *The Pot Boils*. How the devil had I got hold of it? I must, in
my innocence, have asked for it at the time (1917).

'This is a distinctly clever tract, gibing at the young intellectuals
who take up social reform. It is not so much satire as irony and it is a
difficult book to place. Amid much cleverness and insight, there are
streaks of self-conscious smartness and labouring of the point. Still,
I think it is worth some attention.

'It is loosely constructed; starts nowhere; ends nowhere; tries
apparently to follow the French model [*already?*] of throwing in jabs
of light on a given character from many angles. Each chapter intro-
duces new characters, who re-appear at odd moments; and the
characters are so many and so ill-defined that the reader becomes
confused in sorting them out. They do not live [*not even my dear
Poskett?*]; they are vehicles for the author's theories and the ex-
pounding of his theme.

'There is no plot. The book rambles round the thoughts, ideals
and struggles of a group of young people from a northern university,
their dissatisfaction with life as it is, their forlorn miseries over
things that don't matter.

'I think it should be considered, though hardly for immediate
publication. Later, the Labour question will become acute, and
reconstruction will be in the air, and it might then have a chance . . .
If it is a first book, it shows considerable promise, and the author
would in any case I think be worth encouraging for his next book.
There would hardly be much in this, but the man can write and is
worth watching.'

Alone in my room, I laughed. Not at the awkward shabby young
woman—even in her blind self-confidence and energy crazily more
simple-minded than today's newest writer, the dupe of ideas,
knowing too little about too much—but with her: she was irrepres-
sible, alive with infinite hopes and childish arrogance.

In a worn-out despatch case forgotten on the top of the tallboy and thick in dust, I found the six tiny calico bags I made in 1915 when I went into my first loathed house, and labelled in marking ink: Rent and Rates; Clothes: Payments on sofa 10/-; Savings: Food: Coal Light and Gas, sharing between them each month something under ten pounds. I threw them quickly into the carton, afraid to see rising, in the wide sunlit room, a commonplace small house and the ghost of a girl lifting her heavy baby into his cot . . .

Instead, before I could turn away, I saw my young brother on his last leave. He was looking down at the sleeping child. 'He'll never have to fight,' he said in his young indistinct voice, *'we're* seeing to that.' He turned to me for a second the face of a boy, smooth, unformed—I saw it with shocking clarity—and asked, 'How old is he now?'

'Twenty-five.'

'I'm nineteen,' he said . . .

Shivering with cold, I felt an intolerable regret for my confused wasteful life.

We had a bonfire going in the kitchen garden. I emptied the carton on to it, then went back into the house and dragged from their shelves every book on economics, sociology, world politics, all Gollancz's Left Book Club works, every political pamphlet, carried them out, and flung them on the bonfire, mad with rage at the thought of the hours, days, months of my life I had wasted on them when I might have been pleasing myself, or learning to read Homer in Greek.

Watching them begin to smoulder—twice they put the fire out—I swore to myself that if I escaped the barbarians I would withdraw from the world and try to write a book, one book which recorded only the essence of my life, the one or two ideas that were mine, not picked up from other people or books, the one or two feelings, impulses, acts, in which my whole self had been engaged.

It would be so difficult not to invent that I should have to write a thousand lines for ten I kept. And what a devil of a lot of paper I should waste . . .

27th of August 1964

This chimera of a book has haunted me all my life, as relentlessly and uselessly as the impulse to withdraw from the world. Naturally I have not written it (although each page even of these memoirs has been rewritten at least four or five times and the waste of paper prodigious). I have continued my improvident life and the fatal inattention to outer events which has bedevilled and bedevils it. I march with great energy—still—glancing neither to right nor left, now and then pausing barely long enough to notice that my garments are covered with burs, hopelessly lost. But without the lucidity, hardness, will, to turn back . . .

Why write? Why write either about myself or about the ghosts who stray into my mind—from where? Imagine that you are looking from the deck of a ship at night at the dark limitless expanse of sea; look down at it, fix your eye on a speck of foam sliding past, gone, lost in the black depths. Surely the impulse to write is as absurd as if this speck wanted to explain itself, cry out, praise or blame the sea and its works?

Chapter 12

The contrast between Jules Romains standing up and Jules Romains seated always surprised me, however often I saw him transformed from a Roman emperor to a short stocky peasant. I respected the titanic energy of his ambitions as a writer: it was less easy to like the political impulses of a French writer who was gratified when the Nazi government turned out a guard of honour for him in Berlin at a time when liberal German writers—these included Karl von Ossietsky, who died in Oranienburg—were already in concentration camps.

What impersonal esteem I felt for an immensely intelligent writer died a sudden death the day I read copies of his letter to MM Bonnet and Daladier, thanking them—*vives félicitations et profonds remerciements*—for their noble conduct at Munich. '*Je me suis souvent félicité,*' he told Bonnet, '*au cours de ces mois tragiques, de la chance que c'était pour nous de vous avoir à ce poste.*'

There was no need for him to write to them. He could just as well have said his prayers to them in private. I hoped passionately that the Czech writers who had been heartened by his eloquent protestations in Prague in June 1938 would never know how warmly he had congratulated two of their murderers. They did, alas, and in December their president, Madame Tilschova, a very courageous old woman, wrote me a sorrowfully dignified letter of protest.

As soon as war broke out, he sensibly moved the Présidence Internationale to his country house at Saint-Avertin near Tours. From here he involved me in a ridiculous time-wasting tussle of wills over a 'Projet de Message' of unimpeachable patriotism, with a twist in the tail telling all writers to give unreserved support to their governments. I was in violent revolt against giving unreserved support to any politician. My idea of the writer's function in the state is that of uncynical sceptic, Socratic questioner: even if he is a soldier, and so under orders, he ought to keep his mind's eye open.

There was some malice in my feelings. For a moment the irresponsible young Eikonoklast of 1913 returned to life, delighted to mock the imposing great man under the eyes of my young dead friends. 'Let him advance himself how and when he pleases,' I said, 'but not involve us in his devotions,' and I wrote a polite letter explaining our doubts on this part of his Message, adding that democratic practice required it to be submitted to the Executive before it was sent out.

'No one,' Hermon said as he signed it, 'is so respectful of democracy as you are when it suits you—except H. G. Wells.'

The argument dragged on. In June we heard from him that he was leaving France for '*les risques, les sacrifices et les tristesses de l'exil*' in America.

'If he wants risks and sacrifices, why doesn't he come here?' Hermon grumbled.

'God forbid,' I said.

Another letter announcing his departure for Lisbon said he was moving the Présidence Internationale to New York, and taking with him all the papers to do with refugee writers in France. At this stage, unnecessary. The Czechs, Poles, Hungarians, were already making their way to England, and the Germans and Austrians were still in the internment camps where, unless they were exceptionally lucky, their Nazi compatriots caught up with them.

The relief I felt that we were not going to be ruled in London by this jesuitical figure was not unlike the childish pleasure of the old countryman confident that all would be well with us now that we had 'got rid of them foreigners'. At the same time I felt that he ought to have come to England.

On the 23rd of July we had a cable from him, from New York. It ran: 'Well. Arrived. Hurrah for England fighting for liberty. Jules Romains.'

Reading it, I burst into the jeering laughter of an ill-mannered Yorkshire schoolboy.

'What an ape!'

After a moment's rather shocked surprise, Hermon began laughing, less unkindly.

We were not left without the support of France. Denis Saurat, the director of the French Institute in London, moved quietly into the vacant place.

Saurat was one of that handful of Frenchmen who have loved England. Loved it not blindly, as many Englishmen love France, but with a clear-sighted understanding of our faults and virtues. His passionate friendship with England did him lasting harm with his countrymen.

I did not at that time suspect how many persons inhabited his skin: the ambitious administrator, the scholar, the mystical poet, the dreamer with a nostalgia for the primitive, the philosopher fascinated and a little repelled by the unconscious myth-making energies of the mind. He was not only bilingual, writing English as he wrote French, with ease, lucidity, wit, not only a scholarly critic of our literature, not only a poet in the tradition of English mystical poetry; he had an English heart living in what seemed complete amity with his mercurial French mind.

When Romains left for New York, Hermon and I invited him to lunch with us in the grill room of the Café Royal. We waited for him with a little anxiety. Since France collapsed we had not seen or heard from him, and he might—why not?—resent us.

We saw him standing in the doorway, his small frail body half hidden by the hurrying waiters. (This delicate body had a peasant toughness. During the air-raids a bomb brought his house down on him, dislocating his joints; he endured weeks of pain by coolly and subtly examining the nature of pain in a remarkable book, *Death and the Dreamer*.) He saw us and came forward, with his light dancing step, and a fine smile which, already, offered us his heart.

As he seated himself, he said, 'Well, my children, this is a writer's war, it is being fought for us.'

'So long as you don't insist on my taking an oath of loyalty to Bonnet,' I said.

He laughed gently. 'This war isn't a tragedy, it's melodrama or farce. I say that although my son is missing, perhaps dead. Individual tragedies, yes—but we are making the whole into a tragedy by thinking of it as one.'

'Has anything been heard of Giraudoux?' I asked. At that time, the two living foreign writers I cherished were Giraudoux in France and Ludwig Renn in Germany.

'No. His son is here: he got himself to Lisbon and sent telegrams to England signed, naturally, Giraudoux, asking to be picked up. They sent a plane and out stepped this young man. He can't be any use, and his father might have been.'

'Tell me something,' I said, 'there is a journalist here—Elie Bois——'

'I know him, he edited the *Petit Parisien*. I am sure he didn't sell himself, but it was a rotten paper.'

'What did he mean by a phrase he used in the *Sunday Times*—about the hold Baudouin had over Reynaud?'

'A woman,' Saurat said curtly. He added after a moment, 'More than one woman has been playing a shabby part in our politics. No, I am not going to tell you the story. Find it out for yourself. Better still, make it up.'

'I have been reading Euripides,' I said. 'He says in the *Orestes*, or he makes Apollo say, that the gods used Helen to set the Greeks and the Trojans at each other, to rid the earth of its too many inhabitants.'

'Oddly enough her name is Helen. But you must track the story down for yourself. It's not important. Novelist's nonsense . . . You know, there wasn't any need for France to give up, the government lost its nerve, tanks were no use except in the northern plain, it would have taken them months to get through the Central Massif. Reynaud should have said: Marseilles is now the capital of France . . . The truth is the rottenness spread right through the upper layer and seeped down. The Republic is finished, its only friends were decent poor men with no energy.'

'Then what's the next thing?'

'Far too early to think about that.' The ripple of gaiety spread from his eyes to his voice. 'The military imbeciles wasted our tanks by chucking them like pebbles against the German tanks instead of driving them into Germany behind the backs of the German army and creating exactly the same confusion and panic there that the German tanks were creating in France. Then we could have said: All right, you're in Rouen or Paris, what does it matter, here we are in Munich, we'll exchange capitals.'

His gaiety shrivelled abruptly. 'Let me tell you something, my friends. The English should sing small about Mers-el-Kébir. It wasn't a victory. The *Dunquerque* was the finest warship afloat, if she had fired there would have been heavy losses in your fleet. The French sailors can't have fired at all.'

Then, to comfort himself and us, he began to talk with fierce quiet devotion about de Gaulle. 'Keep your eyes on him, he isn't only one man, he is France, my France. I'll do anything on earth for him. It rather looks as though no writer has had the sense to follow him to London.'

'What do you think Gide will do?'

'Get himself shot, some *acte gratuit*! No, no—behind that ambiguous mask, he is too fond of himself. Alain is probably agreeing with Pétain, he hates war. Paul Morand will go on climbing discreetly, Mauriac—well, he is a good Catholic and a good Frenchman, he'll have to choose—Pétain, that eighty-year-old virgin, or France. As for Storm's beloved Giraudoux, he'll retire to the Limousin and write a play. Let's hope it's better than his pitiable propaganda! Romains—where is he, by the way?'

'Didn't you know?' I said. 'He's half way to New York.'

His fine smile knocked twenty years off his age. 'So it's true! I didn't think he'd go. Well, we must do without our great man.'

'Are you sorry?' I asked.

'Now, why did he go? I suppose—yes—if he had come here he'd have had to do what de Gaulle told him. He wouldn't like that, he'd rather play at *la haute politique* with the nobodies in America. Or—' his eyes sparkled—'perhaps, for once in his careful life he is backing the wrong horse.'

Chapter 13

Had I been working on a novel I could have gone on with it, but with invasion only a few days or weeks off, I could not begin a book which might never be finished. Hearing that the Ministry of Labour wanted volunteers, unpaid, to clear up its Special Register, I offered myself, and began work there on the 3rd of July, on a confused mass of files into which letters from writers, scholars, and other well-known or well-educated men had been thrown in no sort of order.

I made and illegally kept a copy of one of the letters I found.

'. . . as, however, it seems that no one over 65 (Prime Ministers excepted) is considered of any use by this Government I would be willing to push babies' perambulators for 2 hours daily for mothers employed in war work.'

It was signed by General Sir Hubert Gough, K.C.B. etc. etc.

I was involved, continually, with our refugees. The third wave of exiles had broken over us when France collapsed and the intellectuals who had fled there from Czechoslovakia and Poland had to move on if they did not want to be caught and handed over to the Gestapo. A few, very few, Germans escaped at the same time, escaping first of all from the defeated French.

Government officials, who knew something about the damage done in France by the Fifth Column, had a good excuse for exercising their habit of expecting the worst of human nature. It is true that they had less excuse than they supposed—there were no aliens in the French Fifth Column, it was a purely native industry, and included well-to-do respectable bourgeois up to the wealthiest, corrupt politicians, and a few corrupt fascist-minded soldiers. But men and women who had spent their adult lives opposing fascism in all its forms, and had already, many of them, endured the annihilating misery of concentration camps, were not tempted to betray the country they had entered in the belief that it was free and tolerant.

Very often I could only think that the jailing of these helpless refugees opened a crack into an abyss of dull meanness like the final disgusting irrelevance of Dostoevsky's cockroach.

For a bone-dry official to say that all aliens must be interned on the off chance that one of them is a spy is logical and arguable. This is not true of private individuals who suddenly discovered that their foreign, perhaps Jewish, friends were an embarrassment.

One of our interned writers had highly-placed English friends, who had known him for many years. I went to see them—after failing to get them on the telephone—to ask them to write to the Home Office about him. They were polite, friendly, evasive.

'After all,' X. said, 'think of the temptation it must be to a German, at this moment, to try to put himself right with his own government? I don't dream of blaming him. We're all capable of weakness.'

'But why suspect a man you have known for so many years of turning coward overnight?'

'My dear lady, do let us keep a sense of proportion. He may be perfectly innocent and reliable, I hope he is, it would grieve us both so much if he weren't—my wife, you know, adores him. And suppose he is, in fact, innocent, what a splendid chance for him to show his gratitude to this country by refusing to complain about a few months of comfortable internment! Why, I have often thought how restful a term of imprisonment would be!'

'Would you really enjoy being kept behind barbed wire for months or years? And I don't know that the camps are comfortable.'

'But no hardship for a strong healthy man!'

I tried to appeal to his wife. 'He asked me to tell you that the only book he was allowed to take with him is one you gave him.'

'Oh, the dear man,' she said tenderly. A shadow crossed her face. 'Is my name in it, I wonder?'

'I rather think so,' I said maliciously.

'You should be more careful,' X. reproved her. Turning to me, he said, 'I'm sure our friend appreciates that as a Jew he is safer where he is. I needn't tell you that I have no feelings against Jews, but there is, don't you know, a certain feeling among unthinking people that they are not, what shall I say? altogether singleminded. Both of us, I

do assure you, my foolish warmhearted wife especially, are only
thinking of his comfort, physical and moral.'

There was nothing to be done with two people so convinced of the
nobility of their motives for not lifting a finger to help their friend. I
left, turning over in my mind phrases to soften the blow it would
be to him.

Others, the obscure nobodies, were much worse off: the women
who were not told that a son or a husband had been shipped off to
Canada until the shipload had been sunk; the unimportant elderly
professor remembering his two years in Dachau, who killed himself
when the police came for him.

Rudolf Olden had been moved from his first camp to another, a
disused cotton mill, bare and verminous. When I gave Ika lunch she
was as composed, above a fathom of despair, as always, and her
voice—delighting me by its undertone, which was the start of a
single vibrating note, perhaps a low C—as warm and quiet. Kutzi
was on her way to Toronto, and she was alone in the cottage, where
the most innocent objects took a spiteful pleasure in reminding her
of the one thing she and Rudi had refused to admit, that they were
living in exile. The silence in her room was so hostile that she could
not sleep.

She would not let me say that it had humiliated me to learn how
callously England could behave.

'Oh, no,' she said, 'that's ridiculous. England is you and the
Murrays and many others. After all—except Kutzi—we are Germans; you can't expect bureaucrats to realize that the lines dividing
people now are not national, but intellectual and spiritual . . . What
is breaking Rudi is that Gillies says he will be released if the Americans take him. He wanted desperately to share your dangers here—
he was so confident, too confident, that he was useful.'

She had decided to leave the cottage—'We should have known,'
she said, smiling, 'that a permanent address was one of the things we
had given up . . .'—and move their few possessions to London,
where it would be easier to work for Rudi and the others. There was
only one thing I could do for her—persuade the Home Office to dis-
gorge their documents, including Rudi's military papers; she could
not take a step without papers, and every letter she had written
begging for them had been ignored.

I took the list, promising recklessly that I would get them for her
somehow.

When she was leaving she said lightly, 'We have been very happy here—and very lucky. In a way it is more comfortable to be like everyone else.'

This summer, for the first time in my life, I became aware that my body had a will and an existence of its own. Until now—I was forty-nine—we had been on the best of terms.

Here is an account of a single day, written badly in that thin canvas-backed little notebook I shall destroy (any day now), not worth calling a diary—the entries are too few, with gaps covering months or a year, and too erratic. Why, for example, did I take the trouble to record at some length the whole of this day? I have forgotten.

July 25 (or 29—the figure is half illegible)

Left the Ministry at 5 and went to 90 Piccadilly, Hugh Walpole's flat, to talk to him and J. B. Priestley about J.B.P.'s scheme—does he want to be our first Minister of Culture?—to force Ministries to employ writers. A room crammed with half-suffocated paintings and sculptures, jostling each other for breathing-space on the walls. I believe that Hugh, always asking himself anxiously: Am I loved?, is never entirely sure he exists; he goes on frenziedly adding possession to possession to give himself an illusion of solidity.

The view from the window, across the Green Park to Victoria's monument outside the palace—exquisite. If I lived there—and when I had cleared out nine-tenths of the paintings—I could write a masterpiece.

J.B.P.'s 'several pigeons'.

I made one suggestion, brushed aside. Perhaps I had laid a finger on one of those pigeons. The list of eminent writers included two women, Rebecca West and Virginia Woolf, Clemence Dane thrown out as not in their class. Obviously I am included only as president of P.E.N. and not as writer.

Nothing will come of it. If either Hugh or J.B.P. had worked on the Special Register he would know that the last thing the authorities want to do is to employ writers: any writer they give a post to will have been commended for other qualities than his status as novelist or poet. Furious with myself for wasting time on a discussion of no interest to me. Shall I ever have the courage to say No to these music-hall turns? I haven't even any talent for literary politics, I am mortified by my incompetence, and bored, bored.

Ran almost the whole way to the New Burlington Galleries. The second of our refugee parties. Our guests this evening Czechs, Poles, French, and the three or four of our Germans who have not been interned. Standing outside the door, I thought: Is the little we can do for them any sort of weak bridge across the *abyss* dividing writers who understand treachery, cruelty, insecurity, with their living nerves and flesh from us who know them only by name? Obviously not. The signs we make to them, from behind our façade of security, must be like the twittering of birds or children.

The effort needed to go in and talk, talk, shake hands, smile, pronounce the foreign names correctly, was ridiculously heavy. Germans first. Old brave gay Dr Federn, the historian, looking more than ever like a frock-coated grasshopper—the frock-coat is getting shabby—talked to me anxiously about another German he wants us to save from internment. Listened, knew I should have to ask him about his own son, who is ill, a diabetic, and has been interned. When I did, and told him I am ashamed of the internments, he laid his skinny old hand on my arm, smiling sweetly, and said in a comforting voice, 'You are not to mind, England is still the best people in the world.'

Talked to the Czech poet, Viktor Fischl; he thanked me for writing about him to Stephen Spender and Paul Selver, but his young healthy serious face remained severe and guarded; I noticed he stood about alone the whole evening. Shy? Cautious?

Talked to dozens of people before noticing a young woman with a magnificent head, very blonde, a smiling Valkyrie. Anna Mahler, daughter of Gustav Mahler. Why, I asked one of the Germans, doesn't she join her mother in California? Would *you* want to live with Alma Mahler? he said: she is terrified of her.

The president of the Polish Centre, who has been living in Paris, is here. Maria Kuncewiczowa, a ravishing creature, clear delicate face, arched nose, small ears chiselled by a silversmith, slender hands and wrists. An elegance of the bone. Speaks halting English in the most enchanting voice. Later I heard that she was a concert singer before she became a writer, she trained in the Warsaw Conservatoire and in Paris, and has sung in Italy and Germany. Well-known in Poland: in 1937 she won the Warsaw Literary Prize given to the finest work of the year: has translated from the Russian and—this one could expect, they are birds of a feather—Giraudoux. Everything about her, voice, gestures, is charming, a controlled gaiety,

Lopokhova in the Boutique Fantasque. Her parents, she told me, were exiled to Russia after the Polish insurrection of 1863, and she was born there, in Kuybishev.

'You see, I learned the habits of an exile very early, all I need is a little practice.'

Hands rising like two very young birds.

I can't imagine what it is like to be exiled not only from your country but from your language. A writer writes a little from his memory, but much more from the memories of his ancestors. These come to him stored in the words they and he have always used for the commonest things, cup, bread, sleep, grass, loyalty, treachery, kindness, death. In his turn he passes on what he has received, adding anything of value he has. I can't guess what goes on in his mind when he is suddenly and brutally cut off from both past and future, when the nerve joining him to his tongue is cut. Not more than one or two of our exiles will ever learn English well enough to write in it (the poets never)—I try and fail to imagine the force of will, the desperate courage, needed to make the effort, and the even greater courage to persist against the whole weight of the past and the protesting murmur of dead voices—all the others will be faced by every sort of barrier, the hazards of translation, reluctant publishers, lack of interest in their alien experience. How can Maria Kuncewiczowa survive when her hand, her writing hand, has been severed at the wrist?

Thanked Kingsley Martin, sincerely, for coming here, and making himself amiable to dozens of unknown foreigners. He may be an egoist, an aggressive unbeliever in the uses of tradition, but he is genuinely kind. Took the chance to ask him what he thought now about the war. He is convinced that fascism will come here, and soon—the boredom of a prolonged war, bombing, the military disasters we have to expect, will give the men who were behind Chamberlain their chance to emerge, push Churchill out, and make peace.

He said a great deal more, and I repeated part of it to dear Moura Budberg. She listened with a faintly ironic smile, and said in her marvellous voice, 'What do you make of the way the Left sees fascists under every bed? Why do they? Their own suppressed dictatorial impulses? I must tell you that H. G. believes fascism is coming here . . . I suppose he would go to the States.'

'Could you live in America?' I asked her.

She made a queerly evasive gesture. 'You know, I have lost all my family—my sister, my closest friend. Since they were driven from their small Baltic estate and sent to German Poland I have heard nothing, complete silence. I should hate to leave Europe without knowing whether they are dead or alive.'

Her voice moved me. I thought: In a sense you are Europe itself, in one carelessly warm body.

'Step by step you've been pushed to the edge of Europe here,' I said.

'Yes.'

She and I might be happier in French Canada than in the States, its politics wouldn't touch us closely, we could imagine we were living in the eighteenth century.

Elie Bois. Slack broad shoulders and an intelligent face, yellow, heavily lined, the face of a village mayor—good living and astute thinking together shape a face that could only be French. Questioned him about Reynaud's woman; he told me readily the whole story, and talked, with many details, about Baudouin, Mandel, Laval. I came away with a novel about France, and a play or *récit* about both wars, ours in 1914, and this, leaping together in my brain, scenes, characters, fragments of talk.

Both must be forced back, out of sight. There is no time, invasion or air-raids are too close: everything now is provisional, even or especially the things that used to demand the greatest attention.

3 a.m. Switched off the light for a minute, to look out. Low clouds have come up over what was a superbly starry sky, very clear. A fan of searchlights opened and shut, opened and shut, between two layers of cloud. A moment's quiet, long enough to give me the energy to go on typing. I have been at it since I came home—first these notes, then letters, letters, letters: to the Home Office about old Federn's friend; about Ika's documents; to Ika; to Rolly to ask her whether she has had the chocolate I sent and to reassure her about Robert; to the Home office about both of them; to Bill, who hasn't written; to Jim Putnam in New York to ask him to meet Do and the children; to Miss Hockaday about them; to poor Frau Dr H. about her crippled husband who is in Pentonville, to the Home Office about him. The words *I have, Sir, the honour to be Your obedient servant* will be found on my heart.

When I shut my eyes for a second they run against thorns and spring open.

I am ashamed of the momentary exasperation I feel, turning over Robert Neumann's already thick file. Can't he pretend to be a monk and possess his soul in patience? (These are obviously the reflections of someone who has never been shut up in prison, and is ashamed of showing emotion, even a reasonable emotion.)

Must sleep. Must turn all these poor anxious shades out of my room, I feel my last ounce of energy draining away into their fathomless anguish, I am exhausted.

Postscript

A strange feeling of absence. The light was coming when I drew the blackout curtains, and I saw myself in the glass near my bed. But I saw a woman who had nothing to do with me, I looked at her impersonally, and made notes. In repose it is a smooth face, a little morose; a line draws down each end of the long mouth, others cross a high prominently rounded forehead above thin eyebrows; the eyes are large, long-sighted, an opaque grey-blue—colour of the North Sea on a day in late summer . . . A bird woke in the garden, two runs of a triple note. The face in the glass changed at once, and became young and gay, the face of a girl who had been little encouraged to exist in her own right, at her rightful time, and seized every chance to snatch another look at the world before being shown out of it for good.

Chapter 14

All through July I chased the formalities needed to get my young sister and her children to the States. In these days when jealousy of America's wealth and power makes us seize every chance to damn Americans as materialists, violent, shallow, crude, we lack the grace to remember that in 1940 they behaved to us with a generosity it would be impudent to praise. No doubt they are crude, violent and the rest of it, with a leaven of civilization no larger than ours. And they give way to a generous impulse as foolishly and simply as if they did not know the value of money. Women who knew nothing about me, friends of friends, who heard I needed a sponsor for my sister, wrote and cabled that they would be financially responsible for her and hers. The offer we accepted came from Texas, from a Miss Hockaday, founder and head of a girls' school in Dallas. Not that my sister had the slightest intention of staying over there; all she wanted was to find suitable foster-parents for Nick and Judy and hurry back. An official in the American consulate warned her, 'You may find you can't get back.'

Her eyes started at him. 'What nonsense! I'd like to see anyone forbid me to come home.'

They left the house on the evening of the 1st of August, to catch the night train to Liverpool, the two-year-old girl in a rage at being wakened after a short sleep, Nicholas, as always, lively and sweet-tempered.

This was the first and only time I caught a glimpse of the agonized struggle that had been going on in my sister, in her slender body as cruelly as in her mind, for weeks. Except her husband, the two children were her dearest possessions, and she was as fiercely possessive as all the women of our family. She had to make the decision. She would not have allowed anyone to make it for her. No doubt, alone with her husband, she thought aloud, and cried, but with me she was always laconic and off-hand.

Only at the very last, before she turned to get into the car, she clung to me, her face that of a child trying not to cry. (Exactly like the very early morning when I came away, leaving her in her Swiss school: she had seemed not to care, but at the last minute, lying in bed, she locked her arms round my neck like an iron hoop.)

'Daisy, don't try to keep me in America,' she said hurriedly. 'They don't need me as much as *he* does.'

A letter from Ika that Rudi had been released. He wanted to see me. He was in a wretched state and could not leave the flat.

Taking with me an enormous parcel of German books and an old typewriter promised to one of our Germans, I went up to London. The door of the flat in a narrow Mayfair street was open. Ika, at the telephone in the hall, tears running down her face—our composed quiet Ika!—was turning the pages of the directory with one hand. 'Rudi is really ill, and I can't find the doctor's number.' I found it for her. She went back into the bedroom, and after a minute called me to come. My savage dislike of illness seized me, I went dragging my feet. He was lying on his side, his face grey under its thick film of sweat; he tried to take my hand, and stammered an apology for asking me to come, then suddenly broke down, convulsed. I fled.

When Ika came into the sitting-room, perfectly calm now, I asked, 'What did they do to him in that camp?'

'He isn't strong. It was one of the bad camps. But—no, that's nothing. It is really his disappointment that we can't stay in England. After six years. Gillies is still trying to persuade the Home Office, but . . . You know that Columbia University has offered him a professorship? It's very kind, and of course we shall go unless the Home Office relents. The difficulty at the moment is that we have to leave this flat tomorrow, sooner than I expected, and I can't leave him alone to go and look at two places I've been told about.'

I went off to look at them for her. It was very warm, no direct sun, a colourless leaden sky pouring down a blistering heat. Waiting in Park Lane for a taxi to come by, I felt giddy: the railings and the fronts of the houses rippled in my sight like a snake, bulging in one place and flattening out in another.

Neither of the furnished rooms I saw was tolerable for an invalid. I dropped my burdens at the agreed place, and telephoned Ika that I would go on looking, but, praise be, she was able now to go herself, and I galloped off through the furnace to meet Hermon.

We went slowly through the piles of letters and documents about the internments. The weight of so many nagging insoluble problems pressed on me until I became a fly crawling over the floor. Hermon had lost his voice.

'My God, you look frightful,' I said.

'Have you seen yourself lately?' he croaked, smiling.

We had arranged to dine at Chez Fillier, early, before going to a meeting of the Polish P.E.N., at 55 Prince's Gate. Too exhausted to eat, I drank lime juice and ate a zabaglione.

The young Pole who gave a long almost ironical account of the state of German-occupied Poland spoke with the greatest calm about the new Dark Age: the deliberate policy of the Germans to wipe out all intellectual life, by destroying the cultured and professional classes; scholars and the staffs of universities are killed off in the concentration camps and their libraries destroyed; nothing except time-tables, cookery-books, and writing paper may be printed; museums and galleries are being stripped: the German scientist who had been a guest of Cracow University, and knew where the gramme of radium was kept, wasted no time in collecting it. 'If any of us supposed that the German was *bon enfant*, he has been cured by this trick of stealing from your host. Obviously, too, there is a metaphysical side to their cruelty, it is an idea, a *volupté*, as well as a policy.' He made one or two good jokes, of the Peter Fleming type, but, alas, I forgot to write them down.

I talked to the Foreign Minister, Zaleski; he seemed tired, old, and without confidence. His young compatriot, who had fought in France, was infinitely gay and calm, but that is a Polish trick.

Almost until the last minute, Rudolf Olden hoped for a reprieve—until the moment when he looked at the Travelling Paper he had been given, in which the clause allowing him to return had been crossed through again and again, in red ink. This emphasis offended him, as though he were being not shown out but kicked out.

'Please, do not forget our little family,' Ika wrote, an hour or two before they sailed. He, too. 'Do not forget me. I hope for a better revoir. I regret to leave this country in this moment. But no choice was left to me. Please do not forget our unhappy comrades in the camps—when there will be more calm than it is now. For instance, a man as Burschell should not remain in internment . . .'

How many days before I stood still in a London street to read, cold with horror, that the *City of Benares*, full of children on their way to America, had been torpedoed and sunk? The vision of a terrified child in the instant of drowning in those black depths stopped my heart. The sea is every man's enemy, and to sink an unarmed ship is naked treachery. And children . . . My eye caught Ika's name. She hadn't, it was forbidden, told me the name of their ship. They were both lost. An English officer tried to force Ika into a boat, but she would not go without Rudi, too ill to move. I am sure she refused calmly, disengaging herself with young dignity.

My dear Ika, my poor stubborn quiet Ika.

A few lines I wrote about her in the *Manchester Guardian* drew a letter from one of our interned writers, the account of 'a Commemorating Gathering in this Internment Camp to honour the memory of Rudolf Olden, his wife, and the poor children who died with them. Our great old actor Emil Rameau recited from Goethe's *Faust*, the famous pianist Robert Friedmann plaid Beethoven's Death March, Ernst Urbach sang from Schumann . . .'

There were moments this autumn when it seemed that the whole of our civilization was living only in the internment camps where they played Beethoven and in the minds of a few hundred exhausted young airmen, boys of twenty-three who looked forty. These last not only saved England from the fate of Poland, Norway, Denmark, France, but (though they did not know it) repeated in their own way the very words of Homer's Achilles—

'Yet even I have also my death and my strong destiny
  and there shall be a dawn or an afternoon or a noontime
  when some man in the fighting will take the life from me
  also . . .'

A narrow seamless strip of time joins both fighters, both generations of young men, in the same elegance of spirit, the same hard gaiety, the same unspoken belief in human superiority to the forces crushing it. And finds room in the margin for a shabby handful of exiles listening to Beethoven in an internment camp.

Chapter 15

In September the weather broke, suddenly an icy vein, the chill of autumn, and a yellow leaf, for no reason, not a breath of wind, letting itself flutter to the ground.

We were still waiting to be invaded, but with growing disbelief: only every now and then a nerve, somewhere in the ear, touched lightly, gave off a faint sound.

This month the P.E.N. was appointed by the Home Office to advise it on the standing, past life, and claims of every refugee writer who had been or might be interned, and on all appeals from 'men of letters' for release. The Royal Academy and the R.I.B.A. were advising on artists and architects, and there were committees for musicians and lawyers. No doubt these bodies had staffs to do the donkey work. Hermon and I laboured alone, to exhaustion, knowing that to make only one mistake would compromise every refugee.

This, and the house, and a report for the Ministry of Supply on women in arms factories, which involved me in a great many long train journeys, left me no time for writing. The faceless ghost of the play about both wars clung to the back of my mind, and I made a few notes for it at night. But suddenly I thought that I must re-read the whole of Chaucer, from the beginning. It was the one thing I wanted to do now. No reason, except the impulse to go back to one of those April mornings of first youth, the air cool and clear, the sharp colouring of the first spring flowers, the first stirring of sap in the trees, the first thrush, the early morning smell of the wet grass.

At this time I was ignoring a recurrent pain in my body.

Blackout curtains turned my room into a comfortable cell. It was simple to go on reading through the noise made by a German bomber, lost or delayed on its way home . . .

> My lord, ye woot that, in my fadres place,
> Ye dede me strepe out of my povre wede,
> And richeley me cladden, of your grace.
> To yow broghte I noghte elles, out of drede,
> But feyth and nakednesse and maydenhede . . .

But I can't bear to sleep in a cell, and no sooner was I in bed, windows open, the darkness outside and inside the room split open at regular intervals by the finger of the searchlight nearest my bed, than the sound changed its accent. The first bomb sent an electric current to the very tips of my fingers, but only the first. In place of the excitement and suppressed panic of nights spent in London during raids, there was this acuity of separate sensations, very odd indeed, less disturbing, but infinitely more poignant: one had time to pay attention to it.

There was an extraordinary irrelevance about these bombs dropped casually in open country, due, I think, to the certainty that corn will go on ripening, gulls open their cruelly strong wings over the ploughed fields, whatever the destruction. When my father wrote that Whitby had been bombed, it seemed as foolish an irrelevance: but the bombs dropping in the field below the ruins of the Abbey and close to the place where my mother was lying uncomforted sent a shudder to the root of my life and disturbed the child sleeping in the dark quiet of a small old sea-port.

In this new war, the indecent gap between civilian and soldier closed. We were back in the time of Froissart: there is no difference between a city bloodily sacked by fourteenth century mercenaries and a modern city after an air-raid: the dead children look as dead and small.

No one, I thought, will ever again be deceived about the nature of war, as civilians were deceived when the slaughtering was done out of their sight.

This was an illusion.

Talking, in 1963, to an intelligent young man of twenty, I discovered that both wars have become as insubstantial as Troy. I wanted to pass on to him my recurrent image of one bombed house among many, nothing left except the wall at one side and, clinging to it, part of a landing and half of what had been a handsome Queen Anne staircase: when I saw it, the bottom of the flight went down into a pool of water covered thickly by a film of white grit and blackened fragments of paper: I stood close to it in the May sunlight and watched two people move across the polished floor of a room not there, out into the vanished hall, to the staircase. Nothing, I thought, is lost, nothing ends, every trivial mortal thing lasts exactly as long as the cradling mind.

I sympathized with his boredom. It was exactly mine before the excavations at Glanum. A searing Provençal sun beat down on the crumbling fragments, the white broken columns of Greek temple and market-place, the ground plan, empty sunken walls, of two streets of Gallo-Roman houses with traces of mosaic in the dry earth, the whole place very small and, to me, meaningless.

I stared at it and thought: Is this all it was?

It never crossed my young sister's mind that she could stay in America. Between the anguish of leaving her children and the indecency of abandoning her husband and country, just when it was going to be invaded and perhaps defeated, there was no choice. Told, in Dallas, that there were no passages from New York or anywhere in the States, she went to Canada and took ship there.

Early in November we had a cable that she was on her way to Montreal. Delivered by post, it had been five days coming and there were reports in *The Times* that day that a German pocket battleship had attacked a convoy 'half way between Ireland and Newfoundland', and next day a report that 'losses in the convoy are likely to be heavy'. The Canadian Pacific office in London could only tell us that, so far as they knew, their ships did not sail in convoy.

Not able to wait at home another day, her husband went off to Liverpool to wait there. He was anxious, but young enough to feel certain she was alive.

At that time I got up at six, so that Guy could take an early train to London, to his publishing office. In November it was still pitch at that hour; I dressed in the dark to avoid shutting windows and adjusting black-out: also I was half-asleep and the electric light jarred. That morning I heard wild geese, and saw them, a line of long winged arrows, flying very fast, black against a dark sky mottled by darker grey clouds. In the east a thin pencil of very clear pale yellow made it any one of pre-dawn skies I had seen at home, but there it is drawn above moors. The familiar longing to go back seized me—why am I forty-nine, not four or fourteen? Then I remembered that the wild geese hunt dead souls, and I had a fearful vision of Do's thin body sinking in icy Atlantic waters.

The next day, the 11th, I read in *The Times* that a boat, the *Empress of India*, had been bombed and disabled four hundred miles west of Ireland; a Japanese ship had picked up the S.O.S.

I rang up Guy in London at once to tell him to talk to the Canadian Pacific people, and while I waited I ran about the house, cleaning, dusting, so that she would be pleased when she came. I remembered the Two Minutes Silence in time to stand for two minutes, thinking about my brother. But it seemed infinitely distant, as if it were part of my childhood, as if he had been killed then. He, my mother, that life, the I who lived it, were all dead.

All, suddenly, was well. The shipping office said that the *Empress of India* was no longer in their service, and that Dorothy, if she had left Montreal on the third, would be on a smaller boat which was now docking in Liverpool. Thank God, thank God . . .

The house, as soon as she was back, seemed to come to life after fifteen weeks of suspended animation. None of us realized then that the heart had gone out of it with the children.

Invasion or no invasion, I had to do something with my new freedom and I began planning the war play. Perhaps because it was written entirely in dialogue, and only later turned into a short novel, all the characters in *The Fort*, French, English, German, are over-articulate. The time, June 1940, the setting, the cellars of a farm near the village of Beaucourt-sur-Ancre in northern France in the path of the advancing Germans, made violence natural and inevitable, but my real interest was in the thoughts, obsessions, memories, of all these men, most of all in the older half-crippled English officer, in whose mind the images of both wars cross each other, until, at the very last moment, he is seized by a single dominant image.

The pain I had been trying to ignore, hoping it would cure itself, became acute, and very reluctantly I took myself to a doctor. It turned out to be nothing worse than a duodenal ulcer, and I was told to live on milk for six weeks.

I finished the play version of *The Fort* on the 13th of January. The moon woke me that morning, shining full on my face, at five o'clock. 'This is a little exaggerated,' I said. I turned over and lay for an hour, looking at the garden. There was nothing gentle about the light, it was ambiguous, very bright, threatening, and the trees were remote and in some way bestial. Their unkind insistence puzzled me. There was something behind it, but what?

I put *The Fort* away to revise later, when it had settled.

During the past months I had been questioning Frenchmen and reading everything I could lay hands on that might help me to live in the France that had capitulated. There were few days, even at my most preoccupied, when I did not live in it part of the time, and I was becoming a great deal too familiar with the old and young men and women, how many old, how many young, soldiers, politicians, officials, priests, peasants, workers, schoolmasters, journalists, police, who pressed on me from all sides, begging me for the life I owed them. I made careful notes of things heard or overheard, snatches of dialogue, stories of courage, treachery, intrigue, political illusions, and of scenes, the blond Loire under a cloudless May sky, the light, like no other in France, of that wide valley, the bridge at Saumur, a village—Montreuil-Bellay?—a woman dying at the side of a road choked with refugees . . .

The first deep crack had opened in our lives. Since July or August of last year Guy had been desperately trying to get back into the army, ostensibly because of 'the usual bloody Boches' and because he was exasperated by the idea that they were planting their hard bottoms on café chairs in France and looking round with the half-indulgent, half-brutal gaze of conquerors. In fact, because, for all its vile cruelty and filth, he remembered the years of the first war as a time when he had been acutely alive and happy. In November 1918 a life which used up the energy of every nerve in his mind and body and gave him in return friendship, and an inescapable purpose, ended.

Without knowing it, he was longing to return to that. And to his youth.

Not for a single moment did it cross his mind that he was acting with the greatest imprudence and want of foresight. What any sensible man of his age would do now was so clear that only an in-corrigible un-worldling could miss it: he should stay with the publishing firm where he had been working for four years as editor, and where he was needed, and become, in due course, a director. Instead, as his exasperated employer pointed out, he 'deserted to the army', throwing away his chance of a solid future.

Neither did it cross my mind that he was behaving idiotically.

Neither of us thought or think in these terms. From a worldly point of view, we have less than half a wit between us. Sad, sad.

On reflection, I cannot explain my own lack of sense. Guy's is easily explicable; he was never, as child or young man, given any notion that his future depended on his own cunning and persistence. But I knew better: I had had to claw my way out of a narrow insecure world, I had been ambitious, possessive, shrewd.

After failing again and again to get himself taken back any other way, he was invited into the Army Education Corps, and went off, gaily, in the middle of January.

Just then, new rumours of invasion made me think I had better revise *The Fort* at once. I did this quickly, turning it into a very short novel. A pity. In spite of two or three excellent scenes, it is a respectable skeleton.

For several weeks after I had finished it, I worked on the French book, driving the characters back, keeping them firmly at arm's length. This was a sound instinct. A novel should be years in the cask. No other method gives the writer time to eat away all that is obscure or trivial in his ideas and impressions, and uncover as many as possible of the relations between feelings, events, people.

This (or any) year's crop of novels is the proof. The new X, the new Y, the new Storm Jameson, appearing duly every spring or autumn, ought to have been kept back at least six years, to mature, if capable of maturing, and its author subsidized or given honest employment . . .

One day in mid-April the idea for a short novel rose to the surface of my mind with the agility of a young trout. I had been wakened, very early, by the sirens, and was lying in the half-darkness listening drowsily to a succession of sounds, first that half-perceptible shudder in the air, then the planes, the first cock-crow, taken up by every cock for miles round, distant bombs, silence, an owl, another five or six bombs, the sound, dying away, of the retreating aeroplanes; last of all, a magpie calling out sharply in the garden.

I closed my eyes against a broad streak of moonlight, and in that instant the theme of the novel moved behind them. Suppose a German scientist had discovered a means, some quite simple interference with the brain, of turning the men and women of an occupied country into obedient docile animals, with healthy bodies, and neither individuality, in the human sense, nor will. Would anything, any memory, survive or revive in the nation so treated?

I began *Then We Shall Hear Singing* at once, and put it aside twice, to write an essay and a long very difficult pamphlet.

Milk is no diet for a writer, and I was often maddeningly exhausted. I could not always control my mind. Occasionally, when I was drawing the blackout, I caught it thinking: I may be killed before morning and not see this again. Then I looked long and intently at the crimson gash below a dark dove-grey cloud mass, traces of a rosy fleece in the pale zenith, bare trees, the bird in the long grass.

All this time, too, I was struggling to justify to myself my desertion, as in the first war, of my pacifist friends. I tried to dodge the knot by writing (for *The Times Literary Supplement*) an eloquent essay on the not very original theme that the crisis in our civilization is first and last a crisis of the spirit, semantic in so far as words no longer have even approximately the same meaning for two men of equal intelligence in different nations, of different political faiths, moral in that the enormous intellectual effort of the last fifty years has landed us in a situation the intellect cannot control. Rhetoric? Of course—but also the unravelling of something I believe deeply: that human nerves and sense need more time to adapt themselves than they are being given (no one has told us at what speed of change the mind ceases to think sanely; it may be quite low, the speed, say, of a man on horseback); that science has been in some way disgraced by the cruelty of its applications (this feeling is much derided); that, this time, we may well have been too clever and created a world in which our instincts cannot live. If what we think of as our civilization collapses, another may, in time, a long time, take its place, but it will not be the heir to our Christian-Graeco-Roman world. It may be Mongolian . . . I ended, for the gallery and for my own amusement, by comparing lengthily the virtues of France, Germany, England. Very poetic.

After this I decided, with fearful reluctance, that I ought to give a truthful account of my change of mind about this war, since, after all, I might have misled other people. To go on dodging it was a little too cowardly.

The End of This War did not run to more than twelve thousand words, but it cost me three months' hard work. Easy enough to stress that during the last quarter-century Europe has become a continent in which atrocious cruelties are practised on more and more people. That if man is a spirit he cannot be less in danger as a spirit than as a creature enjoying the sun, wine, books, dog-racing. That the cruelties the Nazis practise on Poles, Czechs, Jews, in the name of racial purity and on their own countrymen in the name of order may inflict a mortal injury on the human mind and spirit. Humanity, if this creed triumphed, might be reduced to the level of the mindless Nazi slave, or the still lower level of the Nazi master. There are things, precariously won human qualities, which must be saved.

But at any cost? The boy pressing his hands over a stomach ploughed by a shell, the child dying in an air-raid? They it was who had to be answered. No one else.

Of course they could not be answered. There is no answer. Answers are ruled out. Peace of mind is ruled out. For pacifist and non-pacifist alike, there is a choice between two guilts, two prices. The price of surrendering to the Nazi barbarian is Auschwitz, the camp guards pushing the living bodies of children into the gas chambers, the killing of prisoners for pleasure, the corruption, in the long run deadly, of language. The price of war is a million, ten million, broken tortured bodies, broken minds, and the destruction of long-living cities and villages.

No answer, no answer.

I turned aside to write about the absolute necessity, after so much suffering, to recast society in a form which did not, as did the one we had inherited, outrage every instinct for justice and decency in minds not deaf from birth or blind from self-abuse.

Of some hundreds of letters the pamphlet let me in for answering, I kept one, from the Archbishop of York (William Temple), for the sake of a single passage. 'We have at all costs to avoid two things: the tendency through sheer fatigue to shirk the responsibility which military success will involve, and the eagerness of the bosses to re-constitute an order which gives them power and wealth . . .'

During these early months of 1941 I lost control of my mind again and again, dragging it back with growing difficulty from a pit. I knew, my least nerve, the last cell of my brain, knew that war bred as much evil as it destroyed, perhaps more. Yet I could not, with the pacifists, cry: Submit, submit. The price was too high; the smell from the concentration camps, from cells where men tortured men, from trains crammed to suffocation with human cattle, choked the words back into my throat.

My despair was such that I could only let myself cry over the last war.

Now and then I had the sanity to reflect that this despair was at

least partly a narrow personal grief. Again and again, trying to
find my way in the darkness, I met the lighthearted girl with her
child, her face turned away from home. Useless to tell her that she
was making a mistake.

I was about to write that not a soul knew I was half-mad. It has
just struck me, but only now, that probably one person knew—an
elderly Jewish refugee. A conversation I had with him seems to
belong to this time. We were standing looking at a hillside of oaks
and young birches, the ground below the trees covered by a fine
half-transparent cloud of bluebells, subtler than the blue of the sky,
clearer than the blue of deep water, a miracle of living colour.

'You are thinking,' he said in his uncertain accent, 'that in so
lovely a world the horrors are bearable.'

'No,' I said. 'I was thinking about the last man. The human race
has been wiped out by a disaster which has left natural things
intact——'

'Human beings are not natural?'

'They are naturally cruel. I have wiped out the animals, too. He
is alone and old, this man, absolutely alone, looking for some place
he remembers from the past, and can't find. He comes on this wood,
and it gives him a moment of such happiness, ecstasy, that he is perfectly willing to die. Better, perhaps, an old woman. What do I know
about the emotions of an old man?'

'Yes, perhaps an old woman,' he said. 'But you do know about
the emotions of a man, you are of the line of old blind Tiresias.' He
patted my hand with his dry fingers. 'Smile, little Tiresias, smile.'

The first days of spring came at the end of April, with a warm wet wind and freakish bursts of sunlight. My irrational despair began to move off. At the same time I gave up living on milk. It is mortifying to reflect that this may have had everything to do with the rise in my spirits.

Very early in May, time doubled back on itself to give me a moment of the past. A letter from Loftus Hare, living now in poverty, thanking me for my small part in the present his friends gave him on his seventy-third birthday, went on:

'I have a confession to make to you. Twenty years ago Visiak brought me a typescript on William Blake, written by a young undergraduate of Leeds University. It was too long for me to use, but I retained it, I must suppose, by some accident, and when Visiak called for it I could not be certain what had become of it. I was convinced that I had returned it to him. Now in going about I have lately found the typescript and been ashamed at my lapse. Even though twenty years late, you shall have it.'

I supposed that I had written and tried to get published an article on Blake. But what turned up at the end of the week was the bulky manuscript of the thesis for my Honours degree, written in Leeds in the stiflingly hot July and August of 1911. I had never been able to remember what had become of it.

Will anyone believe that a writer could be so indifferent to a manuscript which had involved months of hard work as not to ask for it back, and then to forget it completely?

Turning the pages gingerly—it must be unreadable—I was run through by the most acute longing for the pale smoky sunlight of the north, falling on those vast troughs of grimy streets, mills, warehouses, chapels, sluggish canals, tall factory chimneys vomiting a stream of smoke across hillsides scarred by rows of bestially ugly houses. Grey even in the light, black under icy wind-driven rain, none of them is farther than a few miles from moor roads the Roman legions took into Yorkshire a trifle of two thousand years ago.

You were a fool, I told myself, ever to leave that country of bitter winters and late heart-ravishing springs . . . I have always, as if by instinct, not simply disliked but hated certain things about Yorkshire people, that derisive glint at the back of the eye, their shrewd irony, their wish to jeer and deflate. But these are—surely?—outweighed by a habit of self-mockery, patience, deeply secretive kindness, and a hard incoercible temper which may yet save us from the bureaucrats.

I saw myself in the sitting-room of the house in Whitby, copying out this damnable great thesis, night after spacious September night, kept awake until daylight by the green tea I persuaded my mother to buy for me. I was as strong as a young horse. And so confident, so ignorant, so radiantly discontented, so happy, that a minute of those few years is worth at least a decade of the present.

I put the typescript away carefully. It might have a use . . .

The B.B.C. arranged for me to broadcast to the New York P.E.N. on the night of the 3rd of July. This meant that I should have to speak at 2.30 in the morning of the fourth. I slept a little on the floor of a friend's two-roomed flat. Wakened at a quarter to two by a call from the B.B.C., I walked to Broadcasting House through completely empty streets: it was a night of soft fine rain, the sky high and cloudy, the wind warm: the all but obliterated traffic lights down the length of Oxford Street drew it out to an infinite distance. After I had made my broadcast I walked slowly back. The rain had stopped and the wind from the south-west was stronger. The curious feeling I had of solitude and nakedness did not spring from the empty streets and the height of the faintly dappled sky, but from the sense that I had been, however lightly and briefly, in touch with a vast crowded mainland from which I had cast off suddenly. I felt the island under me lifting to the movement of the sea.

This sense of isolation persisted until I fell asleep again on the floor.

As soon as I was at home, I took the thesis on Blake from its cupboard, and destroyed it. Why keep a single useless fragment of my past?

Looking back today (18th of September 1964), I see that my life during the next eighteen months was quite ludicrously unnatural.

'He leads an unnatural life' is said of a person who guards himself, by rudeness if he must, from throwing away energy on social life when he has something better to do. In sober truth I had something better. For me, an unnatural life is one of dining out often, using up in amiabilities the hours, days, of silence and apparent idleness essential if one is to write anything worth the effort. To spend four or five hours talking to comparative strangers exhausts me: the amiabilities should be compressed into a few weeks a year entirely devoted to them, not allowed to gnaw the margins of every day.

I did not grudge the time spent on the exiles. Here not only conscience, that virus, but liking and fellow-feeling were involved. Time spent on merely social affairs was thrown away. Even when it fed the curiosity about human beings that my mind secretes endlessly, an unloving curiosity—I know less about the few men and women I love than about scores to whom I am totally indifferent—it was ill-spent.

One day, during a luncheon the Poles gave for a Scottish writer—there is a link between the Scots and the Poles very like the link between Scotland and France, founded, that is, on romantic misunderstanding, with a hostile side-glance at England—I caught a glimpse of the truth. The guest of honour made a long speech, larded with sharp jokes against the English. I had the Polish Ambassador on my right. 'I notice that you all laughed,' he said. 'Don't you object to his making fun of you?'

'Not in the least. The Scots do it when they get a chance, it amuses them and doesn't hurt us.'

'That is rather arrogant.'

'No, forgive me,' I said, 'you're wrong, we're very simple, and until they slap us in the face we believe that other people must like us.'

He laughed. 'That may be true. It isn't true of any other nation I know. But you have so few close neighbours. For example—you don't have to consider how to get the Russians out of your country after a war which has exhausted everyone else and left them untouched. The Germans will be defeated and, unless we are all out of our minds, not destroyed, not penalized, but kept strictly neutralized. But a strong greedy Russia—*there* is the serious problem.'

'Surely—in the end—it will depend on America?'

'Of course. But to be only a little safe we must be in East Prussia, and do they, the Americans, even know where East Prussia is? I hope fervently that you English will remain in Europe after the war, I hope to see many Gibraltars in Europe, some of them on the Polish frontiers.'

I had the malice to ask him about Czechoslovakia. He said gravely,

'I like the Czechs—in spite of their bourgeois ways. In fact, because of them. Beneš is a really great figure. He made mistakes, he relied too much on liberal doctrine—perhaps he learned that at Geneva. You know, I was for several years at Geneva: I went there believing that I should be able to speak frankly. I was disappointed, and felt that I was all the time being duped, because all the nations, especially the smaller nations, spent by far the greater part of their energy thwarting each other. Then I began to take a hand in it, and after a time I enjoyed the game immensely, and became quite clever at it!'

Either because his neighbour on the other side was mute, or out of professional good manners, he went on talking throughout the meal, about Poland, the war, politics, the politicians. I listened, I asked questions it amused him to answer, but the better half of my mind was occupied with the atrocious thought: *You* are beginning to enjoy this fatuous game of meeting people you don't care tuppence for, nor they for you. What good is it? Why are you destroying yourself?

I felt a ridiculous dismay.

I had only to withdraw from everything except the effort to help the interned writers. Why didn't I? Out of fear. The fear of finding myself *nothing but a writer*.

I let myself be sucked deeper into the vortex. I wasted days, weeks, on the absurd quarrel with Jules Romains. If I had dared to be frank I would have told the angry exiles that—in the middle of a war—the public gestures even of a great writer are no great matter. My impulse was to leave him in peace, to do as it pleased him. The Polish, Czech, Norwegian, Catalan, German and Austrian writers living in London were less light-minded. They were so angry that I did not dare let them see how indifferent I felt.

'He's in a devil of a hurry to bury us,' I said indiscreetly.

'This,' the Norwegian reproved me in his grating voice, 'is not a moment for English sense of humour.'

Do you want my opinion of intellectuals? It is that if the next (nuclear) war leaves fifty assorted writers alive, they will have formed themselves into Academies and committees before you can say Aristotle.

I spent hours drafting eloquent letters of remonstrance to the *archifumiste* himself. Damnably long letters. When I try I can be just as boring as Cicero and as high-principled. A day when I had to write one of these rhetorical exercises was ruined for any other sort of writing.

What astounded me in him was his disregard for our vanities. Why in God's name, couldn't he use a little tact with us?

Months before this grotesque episode, we had decided to hold a Congress in London during the autumn. It was not my idea—I had lost my earlier belief that writers ought to make splendid public gestures—but I took it up with decent enthusiasm. Now, without my suggesting it, but with my approval—it would rid us of a sacred monster, and I should be spared writing him any more letters—it was decided to seize this chance to vote Romains out of office and H. G. Wells in.

All I insisted was that it ought not to be done in his absence. I wrote to him in June, begging him to come to the Congress. He refused politely—*Veuillez croire, chère Storm Jameson, à mes sentiments bien amicaux*—he was sure already that his engagements would keep him in New York right through the autumn. I tried a second time— he could come easily, since an aeroplane had been laid on to bring writers from America. I failed again. Had he come, his eloquence, eminence, energy, would almost certainly have overwhelmed his critics.

During the Congress, H. G. —as I had suspected he would—went back on his promise to take Romains's place and, without consulting anybody, invited Robert Sherwood into it. When he told me, I said, 'I hope sincerely that he will refuse.'

'And why, pray? He's a good writer and a fine man.'

'Of course. He's also too busy with official work to be anything more than a nominal president. We don't want a figurehead.'

H.G. gave me a half-malicious, half-friendly glance. 'My impression of you is that that is just what you would like.'

Luckily, Sherwood refused. We elected a presidential committee of four: Thornton Wilder, Dr Hu Shih, the Chinese Ambassador to Washington, our dear Saurat, and H. G. Wells himself.

'In my capacity as thorn in your flesh,' he said to me.

Chapter 17

The supreme benefit to us of holding a Congress in London in 1941 —other than the pleasure of bragging that London had taken the place of Paris as a cultural hive (alas, without cafés)—was that we were not embarrassed by the indifference to writers which is the mark of all English governments, from right to left. We had not to apologize to the foreigners for not entertaining them as they had been entertained in Buenos Aires, Prague, Warsaw, and elsewhere. Let them suppose that in any other year they would have been offered opera at Covent Garden, supper at the Mansion House, sherry with the Prime Minister. We offered them instead the chance of being bombed, and three days of uncensored discussion of writers' problems and duties in the post-war world, the whole world except Russia. The only Russian we were able to entice, and only to lunch, and only after he had taken a fortnight to scrutinize the list of guests, was the Ambassador, Maisky.

Two tiny incidents delighted me.

All our interned Germans had been released, and one of them, Frederick Burschell, chosen as delegate by his Centre, came to ask me, 'What must I wear, please? I have not very good clothes—' he had on a badly-worn grey flannel suit—'I have this, and also I have a black suit.'

'You should wear the grey during sessions, and the black for parties,' I said, very seriously. 'That is, if you wish to be correct.'

'I wish only to show my respect for the great, the unforgettable joy to be invited to the occasions.'

The second incident concerned the Polish woman I talked to for several minutes during the Lancaster House party. Impossible to guess her age, she had a thin sallow lined face, worn hands, and the angular body of a girl. On the lapel of a jacket shabbier than Burschell's she had pinned three or four medals. They were her war decorations, earned as a soldier in the Polish underground army during the months before she and her scholar husband escaped.

I felt the greatest respect, and told her so. Her eyes in their discoloured sockets came smilingly to life. 'But I came here to tell you that today for the first time I am not a stranger, and to thank you, you yourself, for making me know I exist.'

'Would you say that the others—I mean the other exiles—are happy?'

'They are reassured.'

If we have done nothing more, I said to myself, than reassure two exiles, a Pole and a German, that they exist, the effort was well worth it.

We had so little money, about two hundred pounds, that I decided, as any Yorkshire housewife would have done, to spend the greater part of it on a splendid luncheon, not fritter it away in small sums. Very early in our preparations, I had a sharp argument with Hermon about the need for a show of great names.

'You mean the names of great writers, E. M. Forster——'

'Nothing of the sort,' I interrupted him. 'What we need is a list of patrons so eminently respectable that the Government will be ashamed to do nothing for us—Beneš, Haakon of Norway, Jan Masaryk of course, Sikorski, a few persons like Kenneth Clark, the various ambassadors——'

'My God, why do you want ambassadors? Shall we have to stand the beasts lunch?'

'Can you think of a cheaper way of putting up a show of grandeur with nothing behind it? A line of ambassadors will take the place of Beneš's garden party and the huge official receptions and the rest.'

'It's a revolting snobbish idea.'

'Listen to me,' I said. 'We are governed by snobs, surrounded by snobs of all kinds, political, social, artistic, literary—yes, literary. They write the music. Either we play it, or we get no official help, not the very meanest, and we shall be seen—by the dear French and the others—for what we are, rogues, vagabonds, poor relations.'

He agreed, with the greatest reluctance, and our patrons numbered four heads of governments in exile, thirteen ambassadors and ministers—we did not invite the Spanish Ambassador—six High Commissioners, a round dozen eminent Englishmen, and Saurat, who was lending us the French Institute.

We were not in a position to refuse alms. The Free French, who ought to have been our guests, invited the Congress, the whole of it, to a reception in Dorchester House. For the rest, we wrung from the Government a small cocktail party in Lancaster House, for the fifty or sixty delegates only, and the use of an aeroplane to bring over two American writers.

The president of the New York Centre, Robert Nathan, excused himself in the most friendly way from sending delegates. As a neutral country, he explained, America had to move 'with Indian quiet'. I went happily behind his back to invite Thornton Wilder and John Dos Passos. Later, tongue in cheek, I apologized when he complained of my 'high-handed behaviour'.

Our two Americans were arriving at Paddington late in the evening. When Hermon and I went there to meet them, the station was in darkness and completely empty; we walked about it, losing hope, until suddenly the shadows at the far end of a platform thickened into human shape, two gay and excited shapes, our Americans. What we felt for them at that moment was love.

We had put them up at the Savoy, thinking that nothing less luxurious would be good enough. We took them there, and I said, 'My goodness, what can we do to amuse you? There's nothing.'

'S-show us the b-blackout,' Dos Passos said, stammering and smiling. 'It's the one thing we want to see.'

We walked about the unlit moonless streets, laughing, stumbling over piles of sandbags, for two hours. Then Hermon and I went back to a borrowed room to work, as we had been working for the past two weeks, until four in the morning. Afterwards, walking across Kensington Gardens, in the early light, I realized that I was not even sleepy. I was in a state of grace. When not a single cell of my mind and body is bored, I have energy for anything. Or at that time I had.

I had spent a fortnight preparing three orations, the first one to be delivered at the inaugural luncheon, before two or three hundred people (including the ambassadors). The thought of it wiped out every other fear, even the biting fear that I should not be able to find a word to say to the guest of honour, the American Ambassador, John Winant. 'He never speaks,' a member of his staff had warned me. That makes two of us, I thought gloomily, two people as mute as carps. A friendly demon put it into my head to ask him where in America he came from. He replied by two words.

'Describe it to me,' I said.

Speaking very slowly, for quite several minutes, he talked about a stretch of country, his voice suggesting by its peculiar resonance that there was an immense stretch on one side of him, and a hill on the other. When he stopped, I told him about Whitby. I cheated a little—I saw no reason to tell him how much of the simplicity and dignity it had in my childhood had been defaced by imbeciles. The place where I was born is as much part of me, and therefore still alive, as my skin and my dread of loud angry voices.

It reminded him, he said seriously, of Maine.

He talked about his own childhood. I listened attentively, and made up phrases about him: middle-aged, sensitive to a degree, nervous, humane, perpetually careful not to give himself away, detests rhetoric, a highly complex nature behind a simplicity which is only at the surface, shrewd, prosaic but with a quality not of this world, strictly speaking, unworldly.

Abruptly, because I was listening with intense concentration, I had a familiar sense of *overhearing*. I heard or rather felt for a moment a desperate effort he was making to hold together in himself the two ends of—of what?—a state of mind, a process, a thought?

To my relief, his neighbour on the other side spoke to him, and I turned to listen to Jan Masaryk.

He was in the highest good-humour. Grinning, he repeated part of a conversation he had had in the ante-room with a French journalist.

'A terrible fellow, proper——, wanted me to explain why the Czechs lost their nerve in 1938. What will Storm say to me if I kick one of her guests into the street? I said to myself, and let him off. As you know, I'm a tolerant fellow, by God I'm tolerant, but . . .'

'Perhaps he has a bad memory,' I said, 'or a bad conscience.'

'If you can lay hands on a French journalist with a conscience, not a dupe, not an impostor, tell me. I'll come a long way to look at him.'

His impressive public mask might have been all I saw of a great man. But the same week John Winant invited me to dinner—his other guests were R. H. Tawney and his wife. I could not dine, I had some Congress duty or other, but I went in after dinner to drink coffee with them. I found a Winant so different he might have been his own younger brother, smiling, peaceful, at ease with Tawney, who—dear Tawney—as shabby as usual, had thrust a lighted pipe into the pocket of his tweed jacket, where it had burned a large hole. Much he cared!

What surprised me was to discover that the two men were alike. Each had a dignity, a nobility, so unselfconscious that, like Tawney's shabbiness, it was part of him. I had read lately a passage from André Gide's Journal in which he orders himself '*ne pas se soucier de* paraître. Étre, *seul est important*.' The distance seemed to me infinite between this theatrical attitude, a man practising an expression of sincerity in front of a glass, and the innate inviolable self-possession—using the word in its literal sense—of these two men. I suppose that Harry Tawney was more casually arbitrary than the American—he had not had to school himself to patience with fools and knaves.

The fact that Winant acted a part in public—the part of the taciturn dependable envoy—is irrelevant. Almost everyone acts a part. Even a truly great man—think of Goethe—may see *the others* as spectators against whom he has to guard himself. Often he is himself one of the spectators.

Tawney never threw these spectators a glance, I doubt if he noticed they were there. He was completely, carelessly himself, in any company, and no doubt he paid a price for his indifference. With him, Winant felt safe enough to be careless, talk readily and gaily, say what jumped into his head, laugh. He had the gestures, the smiling energy, of a man at least twenty-five years younger than the man I had seen a day or two before this evening . . .

I have forgotten almost all the events of that week. I remember, very sharply, a few faces, Hsiao Ch'ien's fine smiling mask, Arthur Koestler's, heavy, imposing, clumsy, and—at the time this surprised me—good, Salvador de Madariaga's look of contemptuous distaste when he was quarrelling with H. G. Wells about a passage in the *Outline of History* on the behaviour of the Spaniards in South America.

They were a buffalo confronting a fiercely controlled lynx. Later in the day, the buffalo charged briefly: talking about something else, H.G. interrupted himself to say in his highest most piercing voice, 'I am not going to say very much about my nimble-minded friend, Madariaga. I have known him for a great many years and I always have a dazzled admiration and appreciation for his extraordinary nimbleness. So I, being a heavy-footed, slow-going journalist, will not attempt to do anything more than say that I hope he will continue nimble to the end of the story, and that any answer I could make today would be like trying to pick up a very nimble drop of quicksilver which had got to the bottom of a bath of hot water.'

When, shaking a little, I stood up to make my Presidential address on the responsibilities of the writer, poor driven wretch, I caught sight in the audience of the editor of *Horizon*. For some reason which had nothing to do with him, I did not know him except as a lively editor, a gust of jeering Yorkshire irony rose in me—What the devil does *he* know about life as it is?—and stiffened me to recite my long eloquent speech without much awkwardness. Afterwards, a friend who had been seated immediately behind him told me, 'Conolly said you had a pleasant voice and did it very well.'

'Damn his impudence,' I said.

I was none the less pleased.

This week was the farthest point I reached as a public figure. I was never, at any moment, tempted to go on climbing. Vanity, which has lifted so many writers of my day on to so many platforms, acts to keep me off them: I have no virtue as a speaker, and no quickness. All I can do is write, even enjoy writing, a piece of rhetoric, and deliver it as well as a not very talented actor, and that with fearful effort.

Anything more would have been teaching a bear to dance.

I have a clear memory of the furiously angry Frenchman who came up to me, when I had been making a speech about France, and accused me of sentimentality.

He may have been right. It is difficult, and in 1964 a little ironical, to recall that in 1941 not only middle-aged English writers believed passionately that they were fighting to save France.

'Sacrée Dordogne,' the Frenchman, a little man with the face of an elderly Robespierre, said violently. 'It's a river, not a reason for going into a swoon. And generous humanity! Don't you understand that we shall never forgive you because we made fools of ourselves, because we began the war with less than a dozen modern bombers, all as carefully hand-made as if they had been tooled by engravers, and because our politicians were all either fools or rascals. That's the country you've been talking about like the sentimental Englishwoman you are!'

'But not the country that will come to life after the war,' I said.

'Of course not. But don't delude yourself that the new one will be any fonder of you. On the contrary!'

'At least it will be forced to notice that we are well-meaning.'

'Error, error! It will take the first chance your politicians give it—they won't fail to find one—to notice that you are provincial and disloyal.'

The real error might only be to forget that, in one of its aspects, love is a purely selfish activity, indulged in for the pleasure of being in love. Why should the French thank us for being infatuated with the Loire, the Dordogne, the Lot? . . .

When I went home after the Congress week, I found that our two sixteen-year-old servants had left, to go into munitions factories. Useless to dream of finding others in the tiny village, we should have to keep the large old house in order without help. When I was ironing the sheets I had washed—I iron atrociously, I always did, from the first time I had to do it, in my very first detested house in Liverpool at the beginning of the first war—I laughed at the contrast between last week's Madame la Présidente and this week's washer-woman with the aching back. Not that I minded in the least having to take my share of cooking, scrubbing, washing linen. What I detest is being responsible for running a house.

My only other memory is of trying to take the edge off Salvador de Madariaga's just wrath. After the Congress he exchanged letters with H. G. Wells, and sent me copies. His first letter was long and courteous. The second, also very long, began, 'I must keep things on the plane of reason, much as you try to drag them down to lower levels . . .'

The last was short: 'My dear Wells, I can waste no more patience nor courtesy. No. You are not the man you pretend to be. The plane of reason is not accessible to you. Farewell. Salvador de Madariaga.'

I had always deferred to him. In the first place because at that time he still expected the resurrection of a Spain which would summon him to its side, and I felt sure he was going to be disappointed; even if a few persons in Spain remembered him they were already living in an age and a country he knew nothing about, which would reject him. Secondly because, in an unguarded moment, he had told me drily that certain people had dropped him now that he was no longer in a position of power . . .

He was, is, that noble and now mythical animal, the uncompromising European liberal. His ideas and ideals are clear, hard, precise, and would make sense to Voltaire, Herzen, even to Unamuno: in Europe now they are dry leaves rattled by the east wind.

He left the P.E.N., and the last time I saw him, in November

1959, after the meeting of exiled writers where I was the only Englishman, he reproached me for its laodicean politics.

'It is no longer my business,' I said. 'Why did you leave? You should come back and put it right.'

He gave me a hard, not unfriendly glance, and said evenly, 'I have no time for whims, irrationality, disloyal compromises, ignorance.'

Chapter 18

We had to decide at once whether or not to renew the lease of the house in Mortimer in the coming March. My sister hesitated. Her own much loved house in Reading would be free then, and this house, without the children, was a vast empty husk. Had I said: Let's stay, and bring the children back after the war, she might have agreed. I didn't say it. Instead, I talked of taking a flat in London.

Ever since Guy went into the army, I had had the sense of being a third beside a closely devoted pair: I missed him acutely, his lively intellect, his violent changes of mood, his spontaneity, so unlike my tortuous doubting mind. In a marriage which is an intimate friendship, what Blake called Minute Particulars count infinitely. I was bored without him. His letters from all over England, gay, lively, observant, exasperated my feeling of loss. Just at this time he was posted to the War Office. He travelled up daily by train, but the trains now were crowded, often delayed, and in winter icy.

Under cover of the truth, I am lying. A restless devil possessed me, the same restlessness and indiscipline, like the energy of an untrained retriever, that account for all my *departures*, from the first.

Then, too, like the Master sunning himself on the Janiculum in Rome on the morning of the 16th of October 1832, I had discovered—*Est-il bien possible!*—that I was fifty. The idea of writing my life did not then smile at me. If it had, I might have stayed where I was.

At the end of October, I took a small flat on the top floor of a house in Portland Place. No one wanted to live a few yards from Broadcasting House, thought a German target, and I got it on a war lease, at a fantastically low rent.

In those years London, air raids apart, was infinitely pleasanter than it has ever been since, shabby, quiet, friendly, and magnificently alive. It smelled better, too. For the first time in its long history, perhaps for the last, it was a European capital. At moments I had the sense of being in another country, all the pleasures of escape, a body suddenly younger and lighter, a mind leaving its berthing, bound away.

But, for my sins, I knew too many people.

'As I was passing, I came in . . .' Spoken in every variety of foreigners' English, German, Polish, Czech. Several of our exiles were working now for the B.B.C.: the coming and going was terrible.

I can write anywhere, in any discomfort, kneeling on the floor, resting my paper on the edge of a shelf, cold, tired, ill, hungry, but only if I can count on a day without a single interruption. I was deeply attached to some of the people I saw, but I should have liked to see them only in the evening, at a meal I had not had to cook . . .

L— A— might have been used by a Czech sculptor modelling the likeness of his country—quick sturdy body, thick fair hair, blue eyes with a gleam of peasant malice. She was not a peasant, but an intelligent highly cultivated young woman, the translator of T. S. Eliot into Czech and herself a poet. Her close friendship with Jan Masaryk was that of cat and dog, or foil and horse-whip. He wanted her on the State Council, and she stubbornly refused, unable to endure the intrigues and jealousies infecting every exiled government (except possibly the Norwegian—one of the unexpected benefits of a monarchy, with its immovable centre). Losing his temper, or pretending to, he shouted at her as if she were a refractory recruit: his obscenities and scurrilous irony amused her . . .

During the Congress I had been shocked by Arthur Koestler's description of Rose Macaulay as a charming old lady. Rose, old! In my eyes she had not altered a hair since the evening twenty years before when, timid and dazzled, I saw her for the first time. Now, listening to her rapid talk, watching the movements of her small head and abrupt flickering smile, I thought that in some persons age makes a sudden leap; overnight the flesh shrinks from the bones and hidden lines rise to the surface. But age did not account for a trace of sadness, or lassitude, given away by her voice, for all its liveliness.

Five months earlier, in May, she had lost everything she possessed when her flat was destroyed. She had written to me at the time. Her first letter was purely despairing.

'Yes, dearest Margaret, Luxborough House is no more. I wish I had been in it, I might have saved something, but I was away for the weekend and all is lost. It got first an H.E., then fire started, and wasn't put out, and everything was consumed. I can scarcely bear it —all my dear books, and everything else gone. I can't start again, I feel. I keep thinking of one thing I loved after another, with a fresh stab. I wish I could go abroad and stay there, then I shouldn't miss my things so much, but it can't be. I loved my books so much, and can never replace them. I feel I am finished, and would like to have been bombed too. Still, I suppose one gets over it in the end. I haven't a cup or plate to my name, so am stopping in a furnished room near . . . It is better to be alone, and to sulk by oneself . . .'

Written only two days later, the second was very slightly less like the movements of a numbed limb. '. . . my own books leave a gaping wound in my heart and mind, that is the worst part of it all—all my lovely seventeenth century books, my Aubrey, my Pliny, my Topsell, Sylvester, Drayton, all the poets—lots of lovely queer unknown writers, too—and Sir T. Browne and my Oxford Dictionary. Gradually I hope to replace some of them, but it will take years. My Animal book, that Daniel George was helping me with, sending references he found, is gone for ever; *all* my and his notes for it, and all the books I was getting the stuff out of for it. I hate that. And my partly-written new novel gone, too, but I don't mind that so much, nearly. The Animal Book was my heart's blood—it was to have been *such* a nice book! And all my seventeenth century travellers— Purchas and the rest—oh, I can't think of them, it simply doesn't do. Even Vera B. wouldn't say I was "totally unmoved" now, for my "pale sardonic eyes" keep wanting to cry, just like her pansy ones. I have been climbing about my ruins (staircase gone, but I climb precariously up charred and frail laths, up to where No. 7 was). And lo, among burnt wreckage I found my kitchen dresser, unconsumed because sheltered by the roof that had fallen across it, and out of it I extracted (at 7.30 a.m., before anyone came to stop me) several glasses and china things and actually a jar of marmalade and a little tea, and my old silver mug! What a find! It's all there is—the charred fragments of my books mock me everywhere. There may somewhere be some silver buried, but the demolition men won't go up and dig for it, they say it's not safe. But when it all comes down, may I be there to watch, for no silver gets past the demolition men, they say; it all goes into those much too big pockets of their dungarees—"You're telling me," said a policeman bitterly when I said I didn't think silver was safe with them. He says they all take what they can. He seemed really shocked at human nature—and indeed it does seem cruel of them . . .'

Despite these letters, I did not believe that the change in her had much to do with the loss of her books and manuscript. Something sharper was biting her.

I thought: I shall never know.

One day, when she was leaving, she stood for several minutes, still talking, on the stairs leading down to the lift. I looked at her, profiled on the wall, narrow shoulders, delicate arched nose.

'You're very tired,' I said.

She moved down a step, paused, and looked back at me. 'Margaret, you don't know what it's like to watch the person you love dying.'

She spoke calmly, and I felt her anguish pricking the ends of my fingers. I supposed, for no reason, that the person was a man, perhaps already dead. I forget my reply, but it was not a question: when a thing of this kind is said to me I don't ask questions, I am afraid to touch the wound, and afraid that the speaker may regret, as I should, the impulse to demand help or pity. Nor, for fear of putting other persons on the track of a secret, did I question any friend of hers.

Now (October 1961), I see the story told in a Sunday newspaper, for strangers to read, with the letters she wrote a priest . . .

The difference between the French exiles and the others was deep. When a German came into the room, and especially if he were a Jew, he brought with him part of the blackness of Europe, the sense that he had his back not to a country he had for the time being lost but to a gulf he would never recross: the Poles had their habit of exile, which almost took the place of a country they could not lose: the cautious watchful tough-fibred Czechs knew or thought they knew exactly how they would tidy the place up when they went back. All, in their different ways, had made themselves at home in England, much as a woman rearranges a hired room to give it an air of being lived in.

The French noticed that they were in another country only when it exasperated them or roused their derision. The rest of the time they went about their business with the self-absorption of travellers changing trains, glancing indifferently at the foreign signs and newspapers.

There were exceptions—dear Ignace Legrand, novelist, who had flung himself, at the last minute, with his wife and young daughter, on to an English cruiser leaving St Jean-de-Luz, expecting confidently to be made use of by his countrymen in London. Perhaps he was unusable. Certainly they did not want him, and he was in the depths of misery and poverty when D. L. Murray rescued him. He adored the English, forgiving them faults and weaknesses he was too intelligent not to see, for the sake of their, as he saw it, natural decency and goodwill. He was doomed: he could not become English; climate, language, food, all defeated him, and he went back to France after the war—with his utterly devoted wife, an angelic being camouflaged as a small pale gay well-bred woman—to be neglected as an alien eccentric.

At the other end of the spectrum, a man high in General de Gaulle's political service—a member now of the Conseil d'État—asked me blandly, smiling across the glass of sherry I had just handed him, 'Tell me, ought I to try to learn English? Is there anything to read?'

He was completely unconscious of the fatuity of his question, and innocent of offence.

Moving serenely between the two extremes, Denis Saurat almost brought off his attempt to be a native of both countries. How much more narrowly French he was than English I realized during an evening when he dined with us with Harold Butler (late of the I.L.O. and Warden of Nuffield), and they talked about Germany. The Englishman, loathing Hitler and his creed—it was not a creed, it was opportunism as an art—could still seem a spectator, like Dante in hell: Denis was involved as a spirit in torment.

'What,' Harold Butler asked, 'are we going to do after the war with the pure-bred Nazis, the real young thugs?'

'I don't know,' I said.

'Kill them,' Denis said quietly. He added, in a meditative voice,

'There won't be a German problem. What there will be, when the Germans are retreating, is another Night of the Long Knives. They believe they have picked up France and the other countries without paying. Every second adds to the debt.'

A vision I had of one of our Czechs, a middle-aged man with a broad good face, large hands, and small penetrating eyes, drawing his knife across the throat of one of these young thugs, wormed at heart but young, almost a boy, turned me briefly cold. I said diffidently, 'If we try to strangle Germany, the carcase will poison Europe. Think of last time.'

'One German will survive,' Harold Butler said, 'the banker Schacht. A real Prussian, brutal, sure of himself, a *large* brute. I remember an immense dinner in the Berlin Bourse, two thousand people, a river of champagne flowing from eight p.m. to five a.m. The Bourse had been closed for two days while it was prepared. Schacht was in the chair and made an arrogant speech . . . "In those days there were bankers in Vienna—" there were five Austrian bankers at the table—"We had to close the Bourse for this occasion, but other Bourses are closed for worse reasons, I notice that the French Bourse was closed today—" it was one of the French crises: the French Ambassador, sitting next but one to him, shouted in German, "That is an insult." Schacht didn't care. Yes, an imposing brute. I was with him and two other bankers at Basle, a meeting of the International Clearing Bank, when Hitler sent his troops into the Rhineland, the three of them were cats on hot bricks. I was sure then, as I am now, that if the French had marched, the Germans would have withdrawn and the army would have got rid of Hitler.'

'We should have had to march alone,' Denis said very drily.

Later, when Harold Butler had been saying that after the war Russian influence and prestige would be so high that the whole of Eastern and Central Europe, except just possibly Czechoslovakia, would go communist, Denis said, smiling, 'I was told last week about a Norwegian who refused to come to England from Narvik. He said he knew the Germans would go some time, but if the Russians ever got into the country there would be no getting them out again, and he must stay to see that they didn't, the English might try to help, but they always came too late and left too soon.'

'Will France go communist?' Guy asked.

'Only if we, I mean the English, make a mess of it. Throats will be cut, and there'll be a degree of civil war. The essential is for us to go in in force, every man, plane and tank we have. I want to see a company of English soldiers in every village! Unless the French *see* us defeating the Boches there'll be no union of the two countries, which is the only thing that can save civilization in Europe.'

'Union would solve one of your problems,' I said. 'In the last few minutes you have been a Frenchman talking about England, and an Englishman talking about France. Which are you?'

He laughed. 'I dream in French. In a dialect at that.'

'Well,' I said, 'don't, when you're awake, speak English the whole time. It won't do you any good with X.,' and I repeated X.'s question about the need to learn English.

'He is a rotten branch,' Denis said lightly, 'a left-over from the République des Camarades, sweating vanity and lies. He won't— believe me—last two minutes in the new France.'

My poor Denis! Was it possible to make more mistakes about the new France and your place in it than you did?

Chapter 19

Some little time after the United States came into the war, the head of a department in the Ministry of Information asked me if I could think of anything English writers could do to cement Anglo-American relations. Flattered as I was to be asked the question, I saw the trap open at my feet.

'Do they need cementing?' I asked.

He answered very seriously. 'You know as well as I do that there is always some degree of suspicion of us in American minds. Less at this moment than usual, but it's all the same a habit. And since no one thing is more important to us than good relations with them . . .'

My heart sank as I suggested that it might, perhaps, be an idea to get a score of well-known writers to make up a volume of stories, essays, poems, and sell it in America, only in America, for the benefit of the U.S.O., the body which looked after their servicemen.

He was delighted. 'Have you ever edited such a book?'

'Yes,' I said, 'once. It was hell.'

I came away from the Ministry raging against my folly and my inability to say No. But this time it was not, not only, a weak longing to be approved. I had the strongest possible sense that we were in debt to the Americans for a generosity which outweighed infinitely any suspicions they may have had that we were trying to drag them into war. The value, enormous in money, of their gifts after 1939 could not be reckoned in money.

That was one reason, the strongest, for my walking, eyes open, into the trap. The others were a wish to keep a good conceit of myself, and the absolute impossibility it is to me, in any circumstances, to say: My own writing is too important to interrupt . . .

As I had known it would be, the work was atrociously time-wasting. I made a list of writers, thirty-two, of every sort, from the serious to the entertaining. I wrote to G. M. Trevelyan and the Poet Laureate, wondering whether the second of these, seeing my name at the end of a letter, would remember that in her book on Modern Drama in Europe, an insolent young student had savaged joyously one of his plays. The great historian's essay was the first manuscript in my hands, John Masefield's poem not the last. I asked for and got poems from Walter de la Mare, T. S. Eliot, Edmund Blunden, Helen Waddell, Edith Sitwell, C. Day Lewis. To my friends and contemporaries who were not poets I wrote *sans façons*, prepared to bully those I could reach. It was not necessary. With one exception, the thirty-two agreed at once.

The exception was George Bernard Shaw. This singular man, in whom a poet and a fine poet lived uneasily, sharing a bed with the Fabian politician, the professional heretic, the buffoon, carried his reluctance to be duped by a generous impulse to a degree of warmth rarely seen. (I should like to be born again at the moment when Shaw the polemist and clown, so anxious to shock by his antics that he was ready to flirt with dictators, has been totally forgotten, and the author of certain scenes in *St Joan*, *Heartbreak House*, *John Bull's Other Island*, is seen for what he was, a passionate man who, for some reason known to his Maker, denied his heart oftener than he let it speak.)

His letter refusing made me grin.

'Dear Storm Jameson,

'You are most welcome to write to me at any length, at any time, on any subject.

'But I am no use in charitable matters. The work of the Red Cross should be done by the Government and paid for out of the National revenue to which everyone has to contribute. This line in preaching is not my line. I have never bought a poppy: the whole rosebud garden of girls has rattled its tins at me; but I have run the gauntlet of them all. I have never autographed a book for sale nor allowed a play of mine to be performed without payment of author's fees. Would you have me, at 85, break this glorious record to enable our warmongers to exploit your generous heart and pay their way by private cadging? Since the winter of 1939 they have had £50,000 from me.

'I tear up all MSS that I do not publish. My Irish Protestant stock revolts against relics. Anyhow my MSS are all in shorthand. The printed ones are all in the shop window. So you must write me off as N.B.G.

'Otherwise I am yours always
G. Bernard Shaw.'

I believed I could play the ape as naturally as he did, and I spent an hour proving it, certain that I should draw a reply.

'Why, yes I would like you to go on breaking records, that is, the conventions you have made for yourself, until you are 185, and then break any convention which lays down 185 as an age to die. I can imagine no reason why you should not break any intellectual or moral record—or any physical one, either. You have taught us to look to you for it. My own hard upbringing laid it down that it is disgraceful to ask again for what has been refused once; experience, equally hard, taught me that you can avoid this disgrace and some-times have what you want by asking in a different way. You know well that this book is not being put out to earn money for the American Red Cross. If famous and well-advertised writers run forward with saleable manuscripts in their hands it is because they hope that the Americans will say, "They must like us, they're giving us the money they have left over after they've paid their taxes. We've been mistaken, they're fine fellows and friends of ours." And perhaps the effect is not great—but I was also taught to do my best and then to do it again. You'll think: Now this ape is trying to persuade me to save the British Empire. I am not. I do not want to save what is already gone the way of other empires. What I hope for —if you can call hope what is probably only Puritan pigheadedness —is a world in which the properly English virtues can work and in which Englishmen can use their thick skulls to feel their way. Such a world will not come into being if we are on bad terms with America and the Soviets. (But let someone else ask you for a page or two to please the Soviets, I can't bother with two continents at once.) So, if I have thought of a way in which writers in this country can make modest advances to America, I am stricken in my heart by your refusal to help me.

'As a student I was one of a small society of Eikonoklasts. It was a sound instinct which drove us to demolish you with our tongues ten times for every time we attacked our other idols. We must have known that the others would end like Dagon, as stumps, but you would live on to console us, a green tree among stumps and dry wells. So it was, so it is, so it will be,

'I am always your humble servant.'

This letter was preposterously disingenuous. He had never been an idol of mine or my friends. We thought of him as a construction, something that might have been conceived in the mind of an abstract painter or sculptor, an affair of spirals and fragments of steel and wire, rather than a human being.

But he replied to it. At a tangent.

'Bless your innocence, do you suppose I have not yet expressed my sympathy with Soviet Russia? What you propose would be the most ridiculous anti-climax. From 1920, when relations between England and Russia were at their worst, and Lenin was the bogey man of the west, I sent him one of my books with a dedication that left George Washington nowhere; and lithographed facsimiles of it were still current in Russia when I was there in 1931, and was treated as if I was Karl Marx in person. Since then I have lost no opportunity of preaching friendship with Russia. I have spent years of my life preaching communism from every platform in the country.

'As to America, the newsreel which I made for them last year has had an enormous success there, and ran for many weeks in the chief New York Cinema as a star attraction.

'You will see that your notion that I could make any further impression, much less announce my much hackneyed Bolschevism as a novelty, is founded on a happy ignorance of the public antecedents of an obsolete dotard. It is 60 years since, full of Marx, I delivered my first propagandist lecture on Socialism. Your grandmother might have been present if women had been admitted to the Woolwich Radical Club, which was the scene of that obscure beginning.

> 'So you see it's impossible,
>   Always yours'

The old devil has had much the best of it, I thought, and gave up trying to trick him into making an unprofitable gesture.

It strikes me as I write that perhaps he expected me to ask permission to print his letters in *London Calling*. It never crossed my mind.

With the gift of two poems, Walter de la Mare's letter pushed me, before I could step back, face to face with an awkward girl, confident and timid, already adrift. I could do nothing for her, not even warn her.

'. . . How odd memory is! It slaughters so many innocents, and retains others without the least trace of any danger they may have been in of the same fate. I recall with peculiar vividness one evening when I came to the Station with you, and we shared the top of a tram. You weren't wearing a hat. But why just that? And another glimpse of when we were talking at 14 . . .'

You thought yourself so undefeatable, so intelligent, I said coldly, and you were blinder than a bat to your blunders, your worse than blunders. I am not sorry for you.

Before I started on this absurd labour, I had finished *Then We Shall Hear Singing*, and returned at once, with relief—even, on days when I had nothing else to do but write it, with the liveliest pleasure—to *Cloudless May*.

Then We Shall Hear Singing is a curious book, curious as a proof that even a minor writer is able, now and then, to overhear the future. There are more ways of killing a cat than choking it with butter, but that serves, and it is not necessary to interfere physically with the brain to condition human beings to be apathetic or docile atomies in a dangerously overcrowded world, no nuisance to their betters . . .

I was working to exhaustion, trying to write as many hours a day as if I had not to keep the flat clean, shop—the burden of war-time shopping—and cook meals. Usually I sleep as soundly as a child, but I began to lie awake, wondering how, or why, I had got myself into this nightmare of wasted time and strength, hornets' nest of people, nameless boredom of what Quakers call creaturely activities.

About this time I finished my first reading of André Gide's *Journal* in the Pléiade edition. It had been my companion for months. I am not foolish enough to compare my mind with his, but I felt myself as I read in profound sympathy with him. (His homosexuality does not interest me, I can neither feel nor condemn it, I accept it as one of his ambiguities.) And in nothing more closely than in his recurrent laments over the way his days are broken into and his time and energy devoured by people wanting help or advice. As I have, he had a moral inability to say No. And, as I do, he longed to agree with the person he was talking to, and he listened, trying anxiously to guess what the other wanted to hear, more than he talked. And he imagined that he had made a fool of himself in company. In short, we are egoists of the same breed, if not of the same intellect.

A half-comic interlude. In March, Guy was ill, very ill, with mumps. He needed skilled nursing, and a ravishingly pretty young Swedish woman, one of Lord Horder's nurses, spent the day with us, except when she was lunching, at my charge, at the Dorchester, the only restaurant she knew. During this time I had to go down four times to Mortimer, to pack up for storing our thousands of books and other things left there. It was icy weather, I stood for hours in the overful corridors of trains, and caught a heavy cold. One morning, luckily after the Swedish girl had left us, I fainted, a rare occurrence with me, one I enjoy—the delicious sense of escape and irresponsibility as the world fades into blackness.

Reluctantly, when the doctor came to look at Guy, I let him examine me. He talked in a portentous way about an overworked heart and an anginous precondition. I did not ask him what, if anything, these dubious terms meant. I thought him a fool and suspected him of inventing them to alarm me. I knew perfectly well that my loyal ass of a body was capable of simulating any illness to get me out of the domestic trap I was in. Twenty-eight years ago, I reminded myself, in 1914, I was making ready to move into the house in Liverpool Garden Suburb, with despair, rage, tears, *knowing* that the trap had closed on me. Since then I had torn myself out of it, again and again, with bitter guilt, and again and again been driven back . . . If there were anything wrong with my heart, *which I did not believe* (and I was right), it was something my body had invented, as a last effort to free me. Bless the good kind ass, but I could not take advantage of its cunning.

Because of Guy's illness we were in quarantine, and I had to warn people who were in the habit of coming to the flat. One day, I opened the door to a ring, and there stood Ernst Meyer, in his long terribly shabby overcoat. He held out a bottle of milk and four eggs.

'For you,' he said, in his gentle musical voice, smiling.

I could not refuse to take them, but I felt like tears. Gifts, and such a gift, from a refugee, hard put to it to live . . .

My trick, if it was one, failed. I can never keep myself in a state of exhaustion. By the end of April I was in full delirium of people again. God be thanked I have forgotten every incident of this time except two or three.

The four American writers, women, sent over to take a look at us, with one of whom, Maxine Davis, a charming vivid creature, I fell into friendship at sight (another of them, a very pretty young woman, confessed that she fled precipitately to the basement of the Ritz during alerts—'Was I yellow!' she said disarmingly).

Richard Hillary's fiercely pitiable mask . . .

The oranges . . .

Noel Streatfeild and her housekeeper were each given one orange by her greengrocer, and they decided to give them to me. No one now will be able to imagine what inconceivable generosity this was. I had not had one in my hands for at least two years. As she went off, Noel said, 'They're small and probably sour, but an orange is an orange.'

She was wrong on both counts. They were not sour, and an orange is sometimes a miracle.

Chapter 20

That old captain, my father, crosses my path again and again in the underworld, glancing at me very briefly from pale long-sighted eyes, not with reproach—he did not expect from me more than the little he got—with indifference and a faint, very faint and unwilling hope of being recognized.

It seems to me that I recognize him—a little. And a little more distinctly now than when we were children and my mother set us down to write to him to Buenos Aires or Vera Cruz or Valparaiso, and we sat frowning, gnawing the ends of wooden penholders, struggling to drag a stiff sentence or two from minds empty of any other feeling than boredom, any image of the man who would stretch out a long sun-blackened hand for the letters pushed towards him by the ship's agent in those far-off places—'Letters from home for you, Captain.' Did he, when he read the few lines, know that they had been written by heartless strangers? Probably not. Long before this, he had learned to live to himself. And with himself—with all his selves except the very last.

There were so many of them in one lean hard weathered body: the friendly almost affable man known to passengers he thought well of, full of stories you could believe or not as you liked; the man his officers respected for his toughness and magnificent seamanship, even when, as happened sometimes, they disliked him for some grudging trick he had played them; the handsome first officer a quick-tempered spirited girl fell in love with and married; the man she came for good enough reasons to detest, and at the end of her life could not endure in her sight and treated with unforgiving coldness; the thirteen-year-old child setting out in the icy darkness of a January morning to begin his life as apprentice in a sailing-ship—lucky for the child that he could not look ahead, it was a brutal life; the tall shambling old man, eighty-three when his wife died, living on alone in a house built for a large family, contented, even in his own way happy—loneliness was no new experience for him, and for the first time he was master in his house.

No one knew what went on in his mind. Would he himself have known, if it were pulled out suddenly like a dog from the burrow it had run into? This burrow was tortuous; he must have lost himself continually in blind passages, inventing triumphs, past and to come, a word, a look, a deed, forcing everyone, forcing *her*, to respect him, pursuing memories as vivid as the scream of a gull, faces, voices, cities, the changes in cities. He had been about the seas for more than sixty years; there were more harbours in his mind than feathers on the gull's wing, and he saw each of them distinctly: set him ashore in the dark on some wharf he had visited once as third mate and he could have walked without stumbling the shortest way to the agent's office.

He had become an obdurate liar. But did he know when he was lying? In the long silences, he told himself tales in which truth and lies were inextricably mixed, memory aiding and abetting. Say he recalled a street in Santiago. What easier than to imagine something happening there, and he the centre of it? Life showed itself to him with astonishing vividness, but he became uncertain where this or that belonged; he took a house from its secretive courtyard in a Spanish port and set it down in Gravesend and himself in it, carrying on a fantastic conversation with the King's surgeon whose photograph he had seen in the morning's newspaper.

At times, after he came home for good to live his stealthy isolated life in the house, unwanted, refused a trace of the respect and authority he had had in his ship, I felt a brief sympathy for him, even warmth. Some buried nerve in my mind or body knew him. Knew why he lied: knew that on his day-long solitary walks over the moors he was accompanied by a well-meaning boy no one had ever seen since the 29th of January 1868: knew why he locked up in his wardrobe a jackdaw collection, probably of rubbish: knew why, faithfully, perhaps hopefully, at Christmas, New Year, Easter, he remembered to buy and bring in some sort of gift: knew why he kept his better garments put away and went about shabbier than a tramp, not expecting the occasion when he might want to cut a figure, but waiting for it.

He had a virtue I respect and envy—*he did not fear ridicule*.

In the five years he lived alone, I went up to Whitby twice, and stayed the inside of a week, laying myself out to be pleasant. That was as far as my very slight feeling for him moved me.

Nothing of my mother remained in her house, which was decaying more quickly than you would expect of so solidly-built a place. He had taken possession of the whole of it, all the rooms from which, in her lifetime, he was silently excluded. He slept in the larger of her two bedrooms, in a disorder he did not notice. When a bomb blew in several windows at the back of the house, he had them boarded up, darkening the shrouded rooms. Delicate old rugs became filthy with the soil and dirt he trod into them. Clumsily, mishandling or trying to mend them, he destroyed fine old pieces of furniture, one after another. Everywhere were cobwebs, dead leaves, a dry smell of earth and dust. The elderly housekeeper who came in every day for an hour or two could not have kept so many large rooms clean, even if he had not thwarted her irresolute efforts.

I wrote to him fairly regularly. Once or twice, after I went to live in London, he sent me a shoe-box full of half-dead flowers, and once a handful of woodruff I dried and kept.

I paid him my second visit this year, in September.

The winter before, he had been ill, the first illness of his life. Looked after, in a fashion, by his housekeeper and the district nurse, he recovered quickly, but it had marked him. For the first time, he looked his age, almost eighty-eight. The skin of his face, still the colour of saddle-leather, and grained like old timber, had fallen in: it was covered by a network of dark cracks—he seldom took a bath —and hair stood out in thick quills from his long narrow head.

I asked him some indifferent questions about his illness.

'Ha, it was nothing,' he said carelessly, 'I pay no attention to such things, the sea air keeps me healthy. I never swallow medicines; a passenger we had in the *Saxon Prince*, a very clever fellow, one of the King's doctors, told me they were no good, he only ordered them for the look of it. Plenty of long walks, that's all you need. If your mother had walked more, she'd have been healthier.'

After more than twenty years, I am still trying to explain to myself a trivial incident of that visit. Bombs fell one night, about one o'clock, very near the house. Startled awake, I lay still. After a moment, the door of my father's bedroom opened softly: he came out on the landing and stood outside my door. I opened my mouth to speak to him, and felt—felt is the wrong word, but there is no other—a hand laid on it. The impulse to speak died, and I let him turn away, to pad quietly about the house in the darkness. After a few minutes he came back to his room and closed the door with the same care not to make a sound.

Why didn't you let me speak? I asked. Why did you want to deprive an old man of a companionable word at such a moment?

There had been so many nights—in fact, every night of his life after he came home for good—when he paused at the door of her room on his way to bed and said, 'Good night.' And waited for the dry answering, 'Oh, good night,' he did usually get, but not always . . .

An evening two months later, he wrote the daily entry in his log, in a hand little less firm than it had always been, clear, open, and sloping sharply back.

'Light NW-SW winds. Weather fine clear cold during night.
8.00 am Light SEwd. Wea. fine clear cold. Stamps -/7, papers -/7
Noon ditto. Sea strong on beach and bar, pm ditto. Cold.'

Laying the pen down, he began raking the stove before settling to his scrapbooks, or one of the newspaper competitions he was never within a universe of winning, and when the stroke fell he pitched forward, burning his hand on it. Half-conscious, he lay through the long November night until the woman came next morning.

I was in North Wales, and the war-time journey across England took eleven cold hours, until eight in the evening.

There were two women in the house when I came in: the housekeeper had moved in, and the bony loud-voiced district nurse had waited to talk to me.

'Go up and see him,' she said jauntily, 'he's expecting you.'

He was awake, and looked at me without interest. His face had become indifferent and remote, hard. I had not kissed him since I was a child, and it would be futile now.

When I went down again, the nurse said, 'The captain needs proper nursing. The nuns down the road will take him, if that's what you want. Y'know, he's the most stoical gentleman ever was, and considerate and gentle and tries not to give trouble—a gentleman in the thousand. I see people as they are, y'know, and I've known few as polite and modest, yes, modest.'

You know a man none of us ever saw, I thought. Perhaps what he was meant to be, but who knows? Is one real at the moment of death? Or is the reality the long confused groping deluded years of iving from moment to moment? His heartless treatment of my young brother, or his courage and seamanship and a child's endless curiosity?

The housekeeper was sleeping in my bedroom—none of the others was habitable. I made myself up a bed on the floor of the sitting-room, and fell instantly into a dead sleep. It was the room immediately under his, and some time during the night I half roused to hear him call out. Less than half—my body was a log. No, I can't help him, I thought. He called three or four times. Then the woman went to him.

This is not my only failure to love, but I remember it whenever I catch sight of the tall shabbily-dressed old man, coming towards me with his long shambling rapid stride and passing me with scarcely a glance.

In the morning I let them carry him from his house to the nursing home run by nuns, where he died the same day, easily and simply, more quietly than a ship comes to anchor.

So they said. I was not there.

When I went to look at him, lying with closed eyes in a bed not his own, tears rushed from me. 'He had such a hard life,' I said, excusing myself. The nun standing beside me smiled with a serene indifference. No doubt she was used to such useless tears, or she supposed I was crying for myself.

Do came to help me clear the house to be sold. She and I forced open the locked drawers in the room on the top floor, and found them crammed with the detritus of voyages, old yellowed newspapers, mildewed photographs, fragments of exotic shells, dried flowers, manuscript books going back fifty or more years, into which he had copied anecdotes and poems that had caught his eye, and traced comic drawings of clowns and women in boned stays. They filled four sacks.

But, there remained the more than forty large folio log-books, in which every single day he recorded in close detail winds, currents, the state of sea and sky (Midnight on the 4th of January 1908, was unusually dark, the sea like fire and full of phosphorus intensified by the dense black sky to the NW), minute incidents of the day's run, and the look of ports, harbours, foreign streets, markets and the price of fruit, a view of the world as one sharp-eyed eccentric captain knew it. After he came home, he still noted faithfully, every day, the changes of wind, sea, sky, with a few very brief soliloquies. 'Thus ends the year with a great feeling of something was wrong, for I don't seem to care whether I sit or walk about, my heart is heavy although I try to shake it off by the thought of the happy recollection this day brings forth. W.S.J.'

Millions on millions of words, his hand moving slowly across the page, day after day, year after year.

'What,' I said, 'are we to do with these?'

'Destroy them, of course,' Do said contemptuously.

I suppose we must, I thought: I can't carry them about for the rest of my life.

It took us several hours to destroy his life's work. I deserved the remorse I felt when the director of the museum, to whom my father had spoken about his diaries, asked me to let him have them.

'I destroyed them.'

'What a pity,' he said quietly, 'they would have been of great value. He was a remarkable man.'

Not many people came to see him buried: a few cousins I did not know, hard-eyed friendly men and women, and two or three of the old retired captains he gossiped with when they met on the cliff-top or the pier; they may not have liked him or believed all he said, but they were of the same almost vanished race.

'So you h'an't laid'm wi' your mother,' one of them said.

I knew that flyting tone, half-sarcasm, half-rebuke. 'There was a place for him with his own family,' I said, staring.

It may be only the living who recall clearly anger, resentment, enmity. Might she have said, '*I knew you in the dark* . . . *Let us sleep now* . . .'? I could not have risked it, I had to arrange it as, thinking of her closed door and silences, I supposed she would want.

Seen from up here, the coast line curves finely to the north, the estuary widens into the outer harbour and flows silently to the foot of the perpendicular wall of sea, the ancient Church crouching on the edge of the east cliff looks stonily down at flights of worn steps and roofs half as old as itself. There is nothing more useless, more unjustifiable, than pity when it is too late. It would have mortified me to cry in front of my young sister's indifference—and for what? Because one old sea-captain had been stopped hurrying through the secretive old streets down there, making his meagre purchases, glancing from side to side as he crossed the bridge, at a sunken mooring-post, a flash of wings.

Guy met our train in London, at King's Cross. I said goodbye to my sister and her husband on the platform; they were going underground to Paddington Station, and we decided to take a bus to the hotel. We changed our minds and went back, and ran into them at a turning in the underground passage, they hurrying one way, we the other. Pleased to be going home, Do was laughing. Excitement had heightened the colour in her cheeks and darkened the clear blue of her eyes: in that place her beauty startled by its freshness. Smiling, raising her hand, she turned the corner out of sight.

Chapter 21

There is a moment immediately before the tide turns to go back when a child standing knee-deep in the waves feels an all but imperceptible current, not yet the ebb but the turn.

I had been living in North Wales since the end of October. Guy had been posted to Harlech as commandant of the new ABCA school for officers, and as soon as I had stored books and furniture I followed him there, half reluctant to leave a flat I had made habitable, half deeply, blindly, eager to get away from London and its devouring duties and distractions. Subconsciously, I had begun to draw back, turning without noticing it towards a mole's retreat into obscurity.

Guy lived in Coleg Harlech with his staff, and batches of young officers sent to do a short course in current affairs, a project that a great man disapproved of; the Prime Minister's nose imagined a faintly subversive smell—the only current affair a soldier need have in his head was his part in the war, everything else should be left to higher authority.

I found myself two rooms in a house looking across the estuary to the hills on the other side.

Even under an overcast sky these hills were beautiful, bare, with a down of fine grass stretched across the ancient stone skeleton. The perpetual changes of light across them were as calmly sensual as the touch of a feather, and in sunlight the bay filled with light, a fleece of light in rapid ceaseless movement. Below them on the edge of the estuary, facing Harlech, distant about two miles as the gulls and cormorants flew and a great deal farther by road and bridge, was Portmeirion, the hotel-village imagined and built by Clough Williams-Ellis, landowner, architect, physically and mentally the most elegant of men, an eighteenth century wit grafted successfully on to the twentieth. A trace of the involuntary admiration one feels for a superb natural object, a mountain or a splendid tree, entered into my liking for him. My affection for his wife, sharpened by her calm insistence on using her Strachey genius exactly as she pleased, was of long growth, born at a time when her elegance, unconscious air of authority, quick racing mind, a little intimidated a badly-dressed young woman whose gauche provincialism she either did not notice or gaily ignored.

The society that had grown up round the hotel, on the edge of the park or in houses and cottages on the nearer hills, reminded me sharply of the Spanish fishing village I stayed in in 1935. Here as there a foreign body had pushed its way into old veins, with the difference that the Welsh smiled and went out of their way to be amiable where few of the Catalans, the women never, smiled or made any effort to narrow the abyss between themselves and the invaders. And, here as there, several of these were Germans and Central Europeans, writers, painters, a scholar or two, but not poor. (After a time I noticed that the friendly talkative Welsh drew a subtle distinction—an inflection of the mind, not a demonstration—between these other foreigners and the no less foreign English who, politically speaking, were the oppressor, alien in a graver sense than Germans, Austrians, Hungarians.) For all its pungent cosmopolitanism, it was a society very unlike the one I had fled from, a curiously brittle growth. I was not bored. To live in a foreign country sharpens my brain as do books, music, the theatre, and—a little less—the society of men and women more intelligent than I am, when all I need do is listen to them, as I listened to Michael Polanyi or Arthur Koestler.

I have a vivid image of Michael Polanyi walking ahead of me through the pitch-black tunnel of a disused slate railway, towards the end of a strenuous climb across rocky hills. To lighten the way through the mud and the fatigue of falling in and out of unseen holes and jumping the wooden blocks between the rails, he repeated verse after verse of Verlaine, in an enchantingly gentle voice.

An incident no less distinct and trivial taught me about Arthur Koestler that neither his formidable intelligence nor his fits of black temper nor his natural charm lie as near the bone as his kindness. He had George Orwell staying with him in the farmhouse he rented in the hills behind the hotel: ill, exhausted by the journey, Orwell was sleeping heavily in the same room as his baby son: the child woke early, and to keep him quiet, so that Orwell could sleep on, Arthur sat beside the cot for an hour and amused him silently by pulling faces. Nothing I know about him pleases me so much.

Living in Harlech at this time was one of those astute and intelligent Welshmen who have no wish to separate themselves from an England which gives their energy infinitely wider elbow room than it will find at home—T.J. To look at—and to talk to—this elderly man, the *âme damné* of Lloyd George and Baldwin, might have been a schoolmaster or an unfrocked priest: short, sallow, his long large beak and narrow half-closed eyes gave him the air of a not unfriendly cockatoo. He was as nimble-witted as the devil, very capable of genuine idealism, blandly Welsh in his charm, shrewd, vain, and had been so delighted to find himself, by his unusual talents and persistence, intimate with the great, keeper of their secrets, in a position (he imagined) to manipulate them, that for him a Ribbentrop came to have the same weight and moral value as a Baldwin or a Lionel Curtis. I did not dare to ask him whether he still believed that as 'a man of peace' Hitler, tactfully handled, could have been coaxed into leaving western Europe alone. He was anything but a fool, but it is difficult for an idealist who is also a metaphysical politician to admit error . . .

I had here every condition I needed to write as well as I am capable of writing: no responsibilities, and a room with a wide view. Each time I glanced up from the small table where I had just room for an elbow and the manuscript of *Cloudless May*, I saw the estuary, the opposite hills, the light. Impossible to find words for the felicity of living at the same time here and in the Loire valley: it is not the same light, but in both places it is incomparably spacious, suave, alive.

In writing *Cloudless May* I found, as with *Cousin Honoré*, that the initial act of transposing an unmanageably vast national theme into a narrow local one releases immense energies. The provincial Laval, the provincial Reynaud, Pétain, Mandel, Weygand and the rest, are not miniatures of the national figures: each is a person in his own right, freely available, free to manifest every passion and twisted reasoning likely to spring from his nature and situation, and to act in whatever way a human being does or may act under great stress.

This transposition avoids the basic artificiality of novels placed supposedly on a national level, with *a* Prime Minister, *a* Minister of this and that, *a* Permanent Secretary, *an* editor of *The Times*, on whom the skin hangs loosely in great wrinkled folds round a thin kernel of flesh and blood—very much as if a slender actor were impersonating Falstaff, with the garments of the real Falstaff hanging round him, three-quarters empty. Inevitably, these invented eminent persons are overshadowed and the colour and substance drained out of them by the reality hovering behind. The motives working in the *préfet* in a provincial capital may be essentially those of a Prime Minister, but their local habitation encloses them in a space which does not reduce the human being to a life-sized puppet.

This is always true. And in *Cloudless May* I was blessed by the peculiar circumstances of France in May and June 1940, when national breakdown forced a greater degree of autonomy on the province, turning it into a small State and compelling its officials to act freely, that is, to take charge of events.

It was a very difficult novel to write, and I was intensely happy.

Early in February I reached the last two or three chapters.

On the afternoon of the 10th of February, a single German aeroplane, flying at a great height, perhaps lost, perhaps avoiding a more dangerous target, dropped its bombs on Reading, a small completely undefended town, killing only civilians, among them my young sister.

After more than twenty years, I cannot write about it calmly.

The telegram from her husband was delivered to Guy at the college. When he came into my room with it, I supposed for a moment that I knew what he was going to say.

'Is it Bill?'

'No. Dorothy.'

There was no train out of Harlech for three hours. Left alone, I actually finished the sentence I had been writing when he came in: like the body of a decapitated hen, my brain went on twitching for several minutes.

You don't mind my doing this, do you? I said to her.

I reached Reading at eleven that night, without having taken in clearly what had happened. My body knew and went on shivering, not from the cold, but my mind was still stupefied by the inhuman abruptness of it.

She had been on duty, a volunteer worker, in the kitchen of the civic restaurant when the bomb crashed into it. An older woman working beside her, who was seriously hurt but not killed, told my brother-in-law that when they heard the bomb coming she had time to say very quietly, 'That's for us.'

If we had kept the children, I thought, she would not have had the time to do war work.

Since there was nothing to identify her, she was taken with others to an undertaker's house, and Robert found her only after hours of distraught search of the hospitals and casualty stations.

Early the next day, I went there with him. Disfigured but, thank God, not maimed, her young cold face, lips lightly parted, accused me of going on living. I cried difficult tears over her in that small ugly room, staring at a crack in the wall behind her, along which a small moth was fluttering as though caught in it.

My first thought was that she must come home at once: I forget how we arranged it . . .

Unlike every other house I have cleared up after a death, what I touched and folded and sorted in hers was the future, only the future. She had begun preparing for the children's return the very day she came home. She had very little money to spend, but each week she bought some one thing and put it away for them: there were tins of food, books, material for clothes, toys, even, dear God, the birthday cards for three more years. Such frivolities, she thought, might disappear from a straitened England.

The doll's house she was furnishing for Judy, covering chairs with scraps of silk, making and hanging curtains, lacked the final touches. For less than a minute when I was staring at it, I had the sensation of a short quick finger pointing out what remained to be done.

After so many years I still at moments have to remind myself that it is true.

Her husband had been trying to get himself into the Air Force: he had a few weeks to wait, and during this time we sold the house, and I went back to Harlech, to *Cloudless May*.

Working at it all day, I finished it by the end of the month.

For a long time I lived two distinct lives, one in which I wrote, and another at night, in the small bare icily cold bedroom, and in the daytime when I went out and walked along the coast road or into the village. Even if I had wanted to, I could not have dismissed the images, they were always close to me, waiting for me to put my pen down.

Chapter 22

After a winter and spring in Harlech, I moved to a small old hotel a few miles inland. Here the estuary narrowed to a trout stream, the valley was a desert of reeds and grass, the hills separating it from other valleys were partly covered by oak and the fine hair of pines, in the clear streams the water was soft, soft, and the air gentle. Where the hills closed in, a slate village, crushed between higher naked hills, sent rivulets of money trickling from the quarry along tributary valleys.

I had travelled farther from my own coast than if I had crossed Europe. Possibly these black-haired slender-boned men and women had been pushed to this edge of the island by my savage ancestors. I have never liked any place better, nor felt more irreconcilably an alien.

The hotel was run by a slender handsome woman, gay, friendly, sharp-tempered, at once business-like and pleasure-loving. Thus, the bath water was always hot, the food well-cooked, and the atmosphere of the place easy-going and very faintly louche. By nature and up-bringing I am strait-laced, but dissolute enough in spirit to find the combination of cleanliness, order, and a not obvious licence ex-tremely pleasant. It suited me well.

Now and then commandos from the near-by Rehabilitation Centre arrived, all young, lucidly reckless, and very imperfectly rehabili-tated: bagpipes at three in the morning disturbed less sound sleepers than I am, but complaints were not even listened to . . .

After weeks of planning it, and brooding—and some duty writing, a long story for the volume the Czechs put together in memory of Lidice—I began to write the partly autobiographical book I called *The Journal of Mary Hervey Russell.*

Hervey Russell is a character from *The Mirror in Darkness*, that Balzacian monster I abandoned in 1935, and my shadow. The impulse to disguise myself—not new, after all: I give way to it every time I have to talk to people I don't know—had been encouraged by reading Kierkegaard. If so scrupulous a writer could manage it, I could at least try not to lie while masking the truth.

Something happened in writing the disguised Hervey Russell's journal which may be a little like what happens in the writing of a poem. Image after image, level after level of thoughts and sensa-tions, rose to the surface as I worked, each of them attaching itself to a great many of the others. I wrote slowly, and felt more acutely than ever the pain of writing and the intense physical pleasure of using words, and of recognizing the, so to speak, consanguinity of the images.

Somewhere, I forget where, Léautaud says that '*le vrai talent littéraire, c'est d'écrire des livres comme on écrit des lettres, absolument. Tout ce qui n'est pas cela n'est que pathos, pose, rhétorique, enflure. Se laisser aller, ne pas chercher ses phrases, se moquer des négligences de style même . . .*'

If he is right I have no literary talent. But is he? I was not as I wrote conscious of cheating, but certainly I did not let myself go, and my mind was invaded by phrases like a torrent of swifts fighting for a claw-hold in the ruins of a house. (May the ghost of old Léautaud forgive the metaphor!) . . .

Except for the hours when I touched the icy current of my young sister's death flowing through me, I was at ease with myself . . .

During the whole summer I watched with amusement and misgiving the hand-over-fist climb of an ambitious young man, not in the least a jesuitical figure, a clever office-soldier with a great deal of charm and any number of personal virtues, capable in good faith of arranging to advance himself at the expense of less adroit colleagues, by any means except violent ones. He was not vain, not unscrupulous in anything except the turning-points of his career.

Since there was nothing else I could do I memorized him for possible future use . . .

I am not certain when I finished the *Journal*, I think at the very end of the year. Published in May 1945, it drew from R. H. Tawney a letter I read in fear and trembling, trembling with joy, fearing that I could never deserve his praise again. A miracle.

If only this one book can outlive me, I thought, if only . . .

(When I was asked for a manuscript to be sold for the benefit of the American War Bond Committee, I gave this, as the best I had: it is in a Pennsylvanian public library. Not to forget, I add a list of the others I gave away: the manuscript of *That Was Yesterday* to the library of St Andrews University, the three books of *A Richer Dust* to the Central Library in Leeds. Two others—*No Time Like the Present* and *The Voyage Home*—I had bound and gave to American friends for whom I could do nothing else: they in turn handed one to Wellesley College, the other to Kenyon. Odd to reflect that, after I am dust, these hundreds of pages my hand wrote with some pleasure and more labour, in every sort of place and condition, will exist.)

Some time late in 1943, Guy was dislodged from Coleg Harlech and posted to Northern Command, in York . . .

When I was packing my book box I came on a large folder crammed full of notes for unwritten volumes of *The Mirror in Darkness*, and began tearing them up. But mischief had been done, ghosts from the three books I had completed swarmed in my brain, demanding more life—one in particular, the tortuous uneasy figure of David Renn, to whom I was joined by more than one nerve and vein. Others leaped forward, I saw them move from the darkness into the atrociously unquiet months between May 1938 and the outbreak of war, and knew that I could not get rid of them without violence.

Almost without intending it, my hand reached for a sheet of paper and began to erect the skeleton of a novel about Renn . . .

With comical displeasure I realized that I had become *une machine à faire des livres*. I am without the egotism needed to dignify the role. An egotist, yes, but unable to take seriously a talent no greater than that of a score of my fellows. Such pleasure as I get out of writing is not the delight and agony of the air-borne. But—even today—if I am not writing I feel with exasperation and despair that I am failing in a task laid on me by some crack-pot god. I envy, my God, the free and sane who can look at the patient face of an old woman without feeling obliged to memorize the wrinkles.

'What did you do,' the bored interrogator will ask when I present myself in the underworld, 'with the things you were given for your journey, the North Sea in summer, the great white cherry tree, the coast line, the dazzling fields of marguerites, the undersea note of the bell-buoy, and the cries of gulls?'

'I made phrases.'

'What an idiot!'

Chapter 23

In April that year, when I was in York, the weakness I had been ignoring on the theory that I was inventing it, got out of hand. I was very ill. Later, I went down to the south coast to be nursed back to strength by Leonora Eyles, wife of D. L. Murray. He was editor at that time of *The Times Literary Supplement*, an office of which he was deeply proud: his abrupt dismissal after the war mortified him deeply.

A remarkable woman, Leonora. How old was she then? Sixty? A few years younger? Her smooth unlined face, broad and flat across the cheekbones, narrowed to a small pointed chin and a firm small colourless mouth: she had pale sharp eyes and a finely arched nose—

it was the face of a Flemish madonna and a benevolent spiritual bully, used to taking things and people into her hands, self-assured, a little hard, paradoxically a little voluptuous; there was even a nearly unnoticeable trace of cruelty in the short mouth, but it had been turned round to kindness. (Oddly, she and I had a trivial link she knew nothing about. In the days when I was Alfred Knopf's agent in London, Charles Evans of Heinemann told me about his vain efforts to free her from a disastrous contract with a publishing shark, and that she was desperately poor; I gave him a little money I happened to have on me, I was on my way to buy a coat I could very well do without, to give her anonymously.)

It was a strange household: David, who looked like a good-humoured priest, large, soft, delicate in mind and manner, with no vanity and not a great deal of male energy, a secretary known as Bardolph (his face 'all bubukles, and whelks, and knobs, and flames o' fire'), a one-armed woman servant, taken by Leonora out of pity, a young married daughter and her penniless husband (later, after their divorce, he became the film actor, Alexander Knox), and Charles Murray, David's father. This extraordinary man dominated the family, simply by being eighty-seven, rather deaf, rich, an ex-fencer, a dandy, and as stubborn as Leonora herself. Not that he was spared her coercive tongue, but in a curious way he imposed himself.

What at that time I saw as a Shavian comedy turned out a tragedy in the blackest manner of Strindberg. I know too little about her early life to guess why Leonora was driven by the need to punish herself—that hint of sensuality? self-destruction is *also* a pleasure. She used up her youth in calamitous efforts to save human wrecks, and then, when marriage to David could have saved her, arranged to be defeated by making herself nothing more than a household slave to Charles and the others. At my last sight of her, less than ten years after this, in a large seedy Edwardian house in London, she had become an old woman, bent almost double, moving about the vast dingy rooms in draggled clothes. David, as well-dressed and quietly genial as always, had changed little: neither had Charles: at ninety-six, he was still slim, dandified, and now stone-deaf; he was sound asleep in a small upright chair, a rather sinister figure at the back of the room. The sense of decay, deathly weariness, hatred, did not come from either of the men. But, at the end, the impulse to self-destruction overtook and trapped even David, the innocent man, the one person in the family devoid of hatred, the one in whom a delicate kindness failed only at the very last.

The preparations for the landing in France were going on round us, and I was still there when Paris was freed. David loved Italy and had little feeling for France; since he knew I had a great deal, he set me down to write his editorial about it. I had had to force back tears when the Marseillaise, violent and triumphant, sprang from the wireless, but as soon as I started my thousand words, genuine feeling withdrew, and all I wanted to do was to write as much as possible like Giraudoux at his best and least metaphysical.

If I had the patience to look it up, reprinted in *The Writer's Situation*, I should know how far I succeeded in this pious exercise.

Later that month I began to hear stories about the ugly face of Liberation. Not merely comic or ironical stories of half-innocent corruption—'*Ce qui est étonnant, ma chère Margaret, c'est la célérité de la décomposition: deux mois, et l'assiette au beurre est devenue le plat de la Résistance!*'—the subtle self-corrupting of the brave maquis fighter become a powerful official overnight, with a car, a position he is not fitted for, intellectually or socially, who succumbs almost at once to all the temptations of the abject languid Marianne of the 'thirties. But there were grim coldly detailed rumours of private and political killings done under cover of Liberation justice. I was fascinated by these. I listened avidly, trying to penetrate to the roots of the cruel tortuous acts of men who were neither monsters nor naïve scoundrels. The village Orestes, the small town Robespierre, exist in our veins, and can be understood, a little, by looking at a drop of blood under the microscope.

At the same moment I did not want to believe these stories, and sometimes shut my ears.

An item I discovered in a French news-sheet about a young Frenchwoman who had married a German officer in Normandy during the Occupation gave me the germ of a play. I felt that the young woman Vercors had imagined refusing to speak one word to the decent well-meaning German with whom she was in love was little more than a respectful gesture made towards things, not as they are, but as they would be if men were consistent: what would she have become if she had behaved as a human being rather than as a symbol? . . . Still too weak to write for more than a short time, I put together the skeleton of a play, acts and scenes, and wrote fragments of dialogue.

At the end of July, I insisted on leaving Leonora. She was very angry with me, but I had had as much generous bullying as I could stand.

I began writing again at once, and finished the play in November. By now, it was certain that we were in for another winter of war; I set about turning it into a short novel, and finished that in February. In its ironically emotional way, *The Other Side* is an intelligent account of a young woman, meant by her nature for happiness, who is stretched to breaking point by the tension between her feelings and her acts. There is a plot, exciting enough—but leave that. It was not the last, but one of the last of my books to be freely praised. I think it deserved it less than later novels which have been treated with cold justice.

I went back at once to David Renn, who was hunting down his friend's murderer. But this book meant as the fourth volume of *The Mirror in Darkness* multiplied in my brain until I was forced, reluctantly, to divide it into two—no publisher wanted to set eyes on a manuscript half the length of *War and Peace*. Dividing it encouraged the two parts to grow unequally, the action of *Before the Crossing* taking place immediately before the war, and of *The Black Laurel* after it, chiefly in occupied Germany. David Renn's hunt ended where in effect it began, in his own passionately ambiguous heart and mind. After the overgrown prelude, the second book became an altogether more complex affair, with a great many characters not conceived in the original series. Regarded as one work, the two form a whole I am not ashamed of, and if any soul in the future, if there is a future, is moved to turn the pages of a forgotten novelist, may his glance fall on it.

3rd of April 1945

The photograph in today's *Daily Mail* of a sixteen-year-old German soldier walking to his prison cage, head down in a vain effort to hide his tears, a boy's clumsy fingers twisting a handkerchief, moves me to a grief as useless as his. I have no need to look at it closely to etch his features in my memory. He is the spit image of my seventeen-year-old brother in his clumsy uniform of the R.F.C. in 1914.

On the day I finished *Before the Crossing*, in July 1945, I had the first letters, two, sent by different hands, out of Czechoslovakia. Jiřina Tůmová was alive, but her husband, the quiet seriously friendly young man I saw in Prague in 1938, had died atrociously.

'. . . when you will come to Czechoslovakia next time you will not find my husband . . . He was the sense of my living, we have gone through life nineteen years together, the last seven working illegally against the Germans. Since 1944 the danger was approaching, we got several warnings, but it was necessary to go on. At last on the 23rd of February of this year we have been caught on account of a clandestine broadcasting station. They learned nothing from him, not a name passed his tongue, neither mine. Five so-called 'heavy examinations' and after these he was not any more able to speak. I saw him on the 16th of March. He was not himself any longer, he did not see me, though I stood but a few steps before him. I was held by one of the Wachtmeister and I could not speak nor move otherwise they would either have beaten me before him or him before me, it was one of their pastimes. I tried to put all my love in my eyes, but was obliged to shut them again. It was too much to stand, and we never wept before the Gestapo . . . The image of his face and body has not left me since that time. I dare not and cannot tell you the details. I have them in statements of his fellow prisoners and doctors who have seen him. Only this: there was not a single place on his body that was not tortured, bloodily beaten, his ribs and one leg broken, and he was left with pneumony and septic fever in his cell up to the 20th of March. Up to the 31st of March he was left in his prison. Then he was transferred to the prison hospital until the 9th of April. On that day he was brought—he could not walk—to the so-called small bathing room and strangled. I learned about his death only the 10th of May. Since the 5th when I had been set free with the other prisoners, from Pankrác, I looked for him everywhere. I could not believe that he should be dead, he who loved life so much. And then, both of us have been guilty and only he paid for it . . . The very sense of living is lost, the duty to live remains. Believe me, dear Margaret, you are the first person to whom I dare speak about these things. My dearest, we must not lose hope that some day people will comprehend that life was meant to be lived and not to be destroyed. It is quite unimaginable that so few understand it . . . My husband said: If everybody went away who will work here? I must follow his words. And I will not leave him here alone. Kind souls in the Prague crematorium have saved singly the

ashes of those who have been burned. So he is home again. One
Friday in February he went away, one Friday in May I brought him
home. A handful of ash and it represents my earthly happiness. My
beloved boy . . .'

She asked for a letter. I had written already, I wrote again, but
what can one write to a woman whose husband has been tortured
and shown to her by his jailers? Words.

I had a frightful dream. There was an insect I thought dead, but
when I bent over it I saw it twitch, and someone told me that what
twitched in it was the nerve of cruelty. The sky, when I looked up,
was immense and full of light, and a circle of hills descended in great
curves to a sea covered with tiny curled waves. I looked down again,
and there was still this insect, nothing else living.

On the 6th of August, the age, or rather the interregnum which had
lasted some twenty odd years, came suddenly and violently to a stop.
Hiroshima marked, too, the end of the classical and Christian eras,
of the Middle Ages, of the Renaissance, of the Enlightenment—in
short, of civilization as historically conceived. The fact that the epoch
into which we have moved may be mankind's last alters every per-
ception, underlines with a peculiar anguish or gaiety every gesture,
from that of a mother taking her new-born into her hands to that of
a painter before his canvas or a writer with a blank sheet of paper in
front of him.

Nothing is more ridiculous than a writer, an animal whose re-
sponse to disaster is a phrase. All I could imagine doing was to write
a letter to the *Manchester Guardian*, still, on the whole, a calm decent
organ of liberal opinion: 'Sir, it is difficult to imagine on what
grounds Mr Churchill and the leader-writers base their pious hopes
that the atomic bomb will "conduce to peace among nations", or
"become a perennial fountain" of anything but death. Since we have
not refrained from using it to blot out a city of 300,000 inhabitants,
why should we hope that the consciences of future users will be more
sensitive or merciful? The example has been set.'

After I had posted it I reflected that life had become much
simpler now that it was no longer a question of happiness or freedom or any other of the baits that have made the fortune of so many
ambitious men, *leaders*. Now that for the first time the human species
can, if it feels like it, put a bullet through its silly head and finish, we
can laugh at politicians and other serious-minded buffoons mouth-

ing 'the great questions of the day'. There is only one: Can we survive?

Before Hiroshima, a writer who feared that civilization (that is, his freedom to write) was in danger could think of finding a monastery, or could remove himself and his brain to another country, less immediately threatened by the barbarians. Now all he can do is to keep his head, listen to the warning voices from present and future, and report them accurately.

Anything more? Yes, a little.

Many people are competent to tell us what to do to survive. Only the artist—a class of persons which includes the man who set a pot of geraniums outside his hovel in the ruins of Warsaw—can tell us how, in what conditions, men can survive as human beings. I mean a being who is not only human, not an existential animal, but a creature possessed of a divine instinct to create pleasure for himself and others. It was because he had lost his faith in this saving instinct that H. G. Wells died in despair . . .

I had a feeling of exhilaration, even gaiety. Now that none of us is safe, we can really laugh, really mock our pedantic teachers, really live.

Part II : The Eatage of the Fog

My life is light, waiting for the death wind,
Like a feather on the back of my hand.

T. S. ELIOT

Chapter 1

Had I been asked, that summer of 1945: What do you most want to do? I should have answered: To get out of England.

A chance came at the end of August. The Polish Embassy in London, not then the embassy of a wholly communist government, wanted to send an English delegation of four or five people to Warsaw, to a 'cultural conference'. It seemed in the highest degree unlikely that such a conference could be held there at this moment, but, I reflected, there is no accounting for Poles.

The plane chartered by the embassy left Hendon very early in the morning, with four English passengers, the rest Poles who might or might not want to stay in Poland. One of these was the poet Antoni Slonimski. To distract myself as we took off, I went over the messages I had memorized from Maria Kuncewiczowa to her sister-in-law and to various writers (if they were alive), and from B., a poet, to his closest friend (if alive). Like all but one or two of the exiles I knew, B. was fanatically certain that a Poland controlled by Russia was unfit to return to. I was regretting sharply that I had refused to take money as well as messages: we had been told that it was strictly forbidden to take more than five pounds, and I had decided that to be caught trying to smuggle money would compromise more than myself. It was only when we were hurried through the controls without examination or any but the most perfunctory questions that I realized I could have taken as much as I liked, provided I did not declare it.

The day was marvellously clear, a sky without a cloud, and the sea as flat and unwrinkled as a duckpond. We flew at fifteen hundred feet, staring down at a Europe as empty as it may have been on the 9th of September 1145—emptier. Between Hanover and Magdeburg, I counted four vehicles on the roads. There were no trains, the junctions were a tangle of smashed lines, there were not even ferries to take the place of the bridges sagging into the rivers. Looking down at the bombed towns was like peering into the black rotted centre of a decayed tooth, grim enough, but for some reason a less disturbing sight than this collapse of Europe into mediæval conditions of travel. The few aeroplanes hurrying officials from point to point in chaos took the place of the angels a mediæval painter puts in the upper corners of his canvas.

As soon as we took off from Berlin, I gave Antoni my window seat, so that in the moment of crossing the frontier he could look down at Poland. To me, Brandenburg, East Prussia, and neighbouring Poland look the same, a flat country of fields, lakes, trees, but long before the navigator came in to tell us that in five minutes we should be crossing the old frontier, our Poles were tense and silent. I did not look at Antoni. I have no doubt that his calm delicate face did not change. One or two of them wept, and another, on his knees at a window, prayed.

The moment I felt like praying was when we circled Warsaw airfield, and I looked down and saw that it had been badly mauled and was as full of holes as a colander.

The young secretary from our Embassy who met us said, 'We were only told last night that you were coming. God knows where you'll sleep.'

The drive into the centre of Warsaw was disquieting, like the onset of a nightmare. The head-lights picked out shadowy figures emerging and vanishing between broken-off walls in a landscape so familiar that it was some time before I realized where I had already seen it. Like vultures, the surrealist painters had smelled it out.

The car stopped at last, in front of a whole building, the Polonia Hotel. One of only four buildings still standing in Warsaw, the Polonia housed all the legations in rooms that were bedrooms and offices in one, and every room was in use. We sat for a long time, an hour, two hours, on a first-floor landing, while W——, the gentle withdrawn Pole sent by the Foreign Office, tried weakly to find a place for us. An old man, one of the hotel staff, shuffled past at intervals, each time murmuring sorrowfully, 'Very difficult.' It was Chekhov, not Warsaw.

In the end room was made for us, and I was given an attic on the top floor, bare and very small. There was a bed, a cupboard, a chair, a wash-basin—nothing else. A naked electric bulb, black with flies. The lavatory next door was suffocatingly hot, and stank. I had not had time in London to be inoculated, and wondered whether I could escape typhoid.

By now it was going on for midnight, and we were hungry. Expecting nothing, we followed W—— to a restaurant on the ground floor and were served a superb dinner: vodka, smoked salmon, jellied eel, mounds of red and black caviar, cold meats, escalopes of veal with fried eggs, vegetables, ices—I avoided these, waiting to see whether the others were poisoned by them—real coffee, such a meal as none of us had eaten for years. A long narrow side room was crowded by dancers, girls who might be shop-girls, young men looking like clerks, all very shabby, dancing with inconceivable energy and gaiety. All round us older men and women sat eating meals as lavish as ours. But where did the food come from?

Antoni questioned the manager, and told us, 'He says that Russians eat here, and they supply the food. These other people, including the dancers, are wives and sweethearts of government officials, or are employed in Ministries; they are badly paid, but they can afford a night out now and then.' He added drily, 'No doubt they have other sources of income, this isn't London.'

Before going to bed, I walked out of the hotel and stood, a few yards from the door, breathing the coolness. At once, a man began talking in an undertone, behind my shoulder. It was too dark to see his face clearly.

'You're a visitor? English? Don't believe what they'll tell you about dead Jews. They're coming back, with their filthy tricks. Let me tell you about these——'

I walked away from him, and before I reached the doorway of the Polonia a second shadow came out from the wall and asked me whether I had pounds or dollars, he would pay four hundred to the pound: the official rate was forty-five. Afraid—he could cut my throat and vanish—I stepped back quickly into the doorway.

The bed was clean, as hard as a board, and I slept like a log.

In the morning I stared from my single pane of glass at sprawling pyramids of rubble under a hard blue sky. So far as I could see there was nothing else, only these ossuaries of fractured stone and brick. A great tangled arc of steel sprang from the collapsed skeleton of some large building to hang grotesquely in mid-air. Nothing we had seen on the way across had prepared me for a city destroyed as a human body is destroyed by a shell, a mess of torn entrails and splinters of bone.

Shaken, I went down to the first floor and found that I could get coffee in a small room set aside for chance visitors. Antoni was there, and one of the others.

There was, of course, no cultural conference. None had been planned. Smiling, lifting his thin shoulders, W—— said, 'Who knows where these ideas come from?'

Since we were here, the authorities wanted to do their best for us, and we were given zlotys, two interpreters, young women, and W—— was arranging interviews for us with Ministers. Even, unless it broke down, there would sometimes be a car we could use.

'For this morning,' he said, opening his arms widely, still smiling his patient smile, 'you are free.'

Seen at eye level, the desert of dust and bricks fell apart. In the street outside the hotel, the ruins had a solemn beauty. Hard to believe they were freshly made, they had every air—except the deep peace of age—of having decayed slowly through centuries: defaced carvings and the crumbling heads of statues clung to the façades, which might be a whole roofless front, or part of one, or only a few feet of jagged wall, or a single broken column in sunlight. The prevailing colour of the stone was a greyish rose fading to soft cindery pink or darkening to rust. Behind the disembowelled fronts, cataracts of rubble and dark dust. The wide street itself was as lively as a fair-ground. For its volume, the traffic made an incredible noise—a few lorries crammed with soldiers or workers, country carts, shabby horse cabs, a few open seatless carts plying as buses, and odd wooden contraptions pushed by a bicycle, to hold two persons.

On every side narrow lanes traced the lines of vanished streets between the scorched shells of houses, each vomiting its dust-choked torrent of rubble. With only spades and bare hands, men and a few women were working headlong to clear them. The faintly sweetish stench of the bodies rotting under the rubble still clung to it. In London all these streets would have been roped off as dangerous—as they were. But to give a thought to safety would have put the whole of Warsaw behind ropes. Small stalls backed against the collapsing ruins were selling bread, a few pounds of butter, uninviting scraps of meat, eggs, cakes, and, believe it or not, flowers. On one stall, flour in German bags, loot from the new provinces. Countrywomen with bare dusty legs squatted on the rubble behind scraps of food, and bare-footed young boys, agile dirty gutter-rats, stood about with trays of cigarettes monstrously too dear to buy—

who bought them was a mystery of the same order as the channels by which they reached Warsaw.

'Poles take to smuggling as to the black market,' Antoni said, 'by a disreputable sixth sense.'

Here and there, a woman stood offering silently a single linen sheet, folded across her arm, or a curtain, or a piece of lace. A girl with a calm beautiful face held out a box of ivory chess-men. Who in this place would buy it from her?

I was ashamed to look at them.

And yet, what sprang from these stones was not sadness, not defeat. It was an inextinguishable energy. The man or woman who had cobbled together a room without light, heat or water on the upper floor of a tottering building, reached by fragments of a staircase jutting precariously from the shaky wall, would not have set a pot of geraniums on the fire-blackened sill unless he had decided fiercely not only to live, but to live gaily. And the tenant of one of the exposed cellars roofed with strips of canvas or corrugated zinc had marked the entrance to this hole in the earth by a green leafy branch.

A narrow room at street level, cleared of rubble to be used, with mad disregard of the wall about to fall and crush it, as a shop, was selling a few saucerless cups, a single pair of worn shoes—and flowers.

One part only of the ruins was without life, an emptiness—that was the vast level plain of broken brick where the ghetto had been. Here nothing existed, no single line or form, not even a seed fallen among thorns, nothing.

Warsaw was badly knocked about during the four weeks' siege in 1939, and again during the Rising. After the Rising, as a final act, the Germans destroyed, deliberately and with method, everything that was left, an act prepared long beforehand, during the Occupation, part of the plan to remodel it as a German city. Buildings were mined, staffs and demolition squads trained. During their last days they had only to blow up and burn, quarter by quarter—the libraries, the Cathedral, the Royal Castle, the baroque palaces, archives, collections of ancient documents, old churches, streets of houses, all. Warsaw when they left it was this monstrous heap of scorched refuse, covering the bodies of the killed.

When the soldiers of a mediæval invader sacked a town they had taken, it was a cruel business—and simple. A simple pleasure in smashing, objects and bodies, an instinct any woman has seen at work in her tiny child. The destruction of Warsaw was darkened by something worse, by the perversion at source of reason itself. The Germans did not occupy Poland in the way they occupied other countries, as a military measure. In that sense it was not an occupation. It was a first stage in colonization. They were going to settle in Poland. Towards the defeated Poles they behaved with the ruthlessness of brutal colonists who have no public opinion to fear.

'Are you married?' Antoni asked one of our interpreters.

'I was,' she said quietly. 'My husband and all my family have been killed. My mother—this is really strange—was in hospital. The Germans wanted it, and to clear it quickly they killed everyone, doctors, nurses, the patients.'

The plan, insane but reasoned, to Germanize Poland involved exterminating anyone—writers, scientists, scholars—who might keep the mind of the country alive. Not allowed, even if left at large, to do their work, these died also of poverty. When the terror ended, the continuity of Polish culture had been broken. In every field, in the schools and universities, in the theatre, in music, literature, research, the older trained workers were gone, dead, part of the charred dust of Majdanek and Auschwitz, or prematurely aged, and the young not yet able to fill their place.

After a day or two in this ruined city I began to see that the pot of geraniums was saying calmly, joyously, even devoutly, 'To hell with the past.' And saying it with the energy and deep instinctive gaiety that had decided the authorities to start rebuilding a theatre; it was almost finished, a clear solid building rising from the heart of the ruins.

A pleasant young man from the Ministry of Culture took us through the National Museum. This building, modern, had not been demolished because at the end it was in use as a barracks. It was almost empty. Since 1939 it had endured all the vicissitudes of a villa in Roman Gaul during successive barbarian invasions: intelligent looting by German savants with lists made when they visited it before the war; then four or five years of care-free looting by army officers, Gestapo, and clerks of the civil administration, and the delightful habit German dignitaries formed of offering each other birthday presents, a Rembrandt, a jewelled sword, a tapestry, chosen from its collections. But it was not finished off until 1944, during the Rising, when four battalions were quartered in it. There were still some paintings and tapestries, and a great many cabinets

filled with old glass and china, coins, prints, and other things—
these included robes and uniforms of eight centuries. Bored, the
soldiers amused themselves by dressing up in the ancient costumes
before tearing them to shreds, cut up the Gobelins tapestries to use
as blankets, bayonetted the Egyptian mummies, fired with bows
and arrows and revolvers at paintings until they hung in ribbons,
used Limoges enamels of the sixteenth century as oven dishes, used
and then joyously smashed the old china and glass, pocketed the
Greek, Roman, Byzantine coins, and left everywhere, between
ceiling-high mounds of broken shards, splinters of old wood, torn
stained manuscripts, perforated canvases, those heaps of excrement
which are the characteristic German gift to houses in every country
they invade. It is said that infants think of their excreta as gifts
offered to a mother or a nurse so that they will be noticed and loved.
How inarticulate and deep must be the German wish to give and
receive affection.

'Such strange people,' Zelinsky said, smiling. 'The man, a Dr
Professor Frey, who set aside the Canalettos for export to Germany,
had tears in his eyes because of their beauty. And you see this—' he
pointed to a damaged sixteenth century cabinet, all but three of its
engraved silver plaques ripped off. 'The German expert knew at
once, when he touched them, that those three are fakes, and that the
others were worth a great deal. Such knowledge, such delicate
fingers, and a common thief . . .'

At this moment, I thought of the Elgin marbles.

'And here is something so terrible I do not like showing it.'

We stared in silence at a large greyish-pink notice, carrying a list
of names: one of the bi-weekly lists of men who had been rounded
up in cafés and houses and shot in the street, and their bodies slung
into lorries, like sides of meat. To the young Pole it meant a line of
men, young, old, some of them boys, standing against a wall, naked,
so that their clothes were not spoiled, their mouths perhaps filled
with clay or cement to prevent their crying out. A black tablet with
a cross now marked the places of execution: there were a great many
of them, we had noticed one a few steps from the Polonia, the crumbling wall pitted by bullets.

Realizing that we did not see the faces, Zelinsky said lightly, 'If
you hadn't seen a friend for a day or two, and you saw the notices
going up, then hurrying across the street to read the names, it was
like——'

He broke off, with a delicate indecipherable movement of his hands.

'Such strange people. You know, when a German officer walked past the tomb of our Unknown Soldier—it was charming, a colonnade—he always saluted it. Later, of course, they blew it up. What you call a split mind, I think?'

Perhaps . . .

During our interviews with Ministers I took notes in my own form of shorthand of what these overworked men told us, and typed them late at night, sitting in my small hot room next door to the stinking lavatory, typing, typing, until three and four.

I formed a curious double vision of a country stripped to the bone, without machinery, livestock, tractors, lorries—what the Germans left the Russians took—nothing left for the most elementary needs, authorities, from Warsaw to the smallest village, struggling to the point of deathly exhaustion with difficulties repeated in every single personal life: men and women without a change of clothes, workmen using their hands to clear the ruins, schoolmasters without books, peasants without seeds for sowing.

And a country on the edge of being swallowed by Russia: the secret police—not a new fashion on this side of Europe—were already in its efficient hands, as well as every form of propaganda. There were still four parties, only one of them communist, and non-communist politicians and Ministers—the Minister for Agriculture, a large smiling Buddha—able to joke with each other about their differences. Listening attentively at the dinner given for us by the Minister of Culture—Kowalski, a genial old boy, once a writer of peasant novels, very like R. H. Tawney to look at, which endeared him to me at sight—I could not detect any malice in the witticisms with which he peppered his colleagues.

The thousands of words I typed, and dutifully used in articles, have vanished. What remains, what I shall carry in my skull to the last, is faces and gestures. The face of the young officer who interpreted for the Vice-Foreign Minister, a smiling mask of such fatigue that if it had been possible I would have left. The strange eyes, pale and half-mad, of the young woman, Kowalski's secretary, who told me that her husband had been tortured all day, then killed, in the living-room of their house, by Germans who were looking for her.

'The neighbours listened to it going on—and told me. They were right to tell me. Our two children ran out of the house and for a week I did not find where they were . . . Are you going to tell me that vengeance is mine, saith the Lord? The vengeance I want is justice . . . even if there is no end to it . . . crime, punishment, justice, vengeance for justice. Yes, yes, next time, the next war, will be the end. It doesn't matter, I tell you, I shall smile in its face! . . . Why did you come here, by the way?'

'A Polish friend in London——'

She interrupted me. 'Don't talk to me about the London Poles.' Her voice became a thin howl, like a dog. 'Cowards!'

I found B.'s friend in one of the Ministries, and repeated the message I had learned by heart. 'If you like,' I said, 'I'll take a letter to him.'

'Is he coming back here?'

'No.'

Turning away from me, B.'s friend said calmly, 'Then I have nothing to say to him.'

'Am I to tell him that?'

'As you please.'

The interpreter for the Minister of Culture was an aristocrat, a Radziwill. He was a very bad interpreter, stuttering, looking from one to the other of us with the sad eyes of a comedian. Five years in Buchenwald had left him very lame; he walked painfully, with a stick. Later, talking to me, he said carefully that although he was not a communist he knew that the only hope for Poland was to work peacefully and loyally with the Russians. He went over the arguments for this again and again. Clearly, he was unhappy. I wanted to tell him that I did not feel that he or any other educated man or woman ought to refuse to work for the government, at a time when two generations of administrators and teachers had been wiped out by firing-squad and concentration camp. But it would, I saw, be entirely the wrong answer. He was desperately anxious to justify his position as a *rallié*—but he had to do it as though no justification were needed. I did not think it was. But then I was not a Polish landowner who had taught himself to talk with conviction about kulaks and the need to eliminate them.

'You will explain, please, in London—you are a writer, you must know many people—that in a totally ruined country one must work with the tools at hand, whatever they are.'

'Of course,' I said.

Speaking English was an effort for him: he kept on dropping into French in the middle of sentences. 'We cannot be sorry for les possédants, ils sont les survivants *inutiles*.' He passed his hand slowly over his face. 'You know, I did not expect to return from Buchenwald. Why did I? Ah, c'est que mes enfants ont beaucoup prié pour moi.'

One afternoon a young professor, and his very young wife, came from Lódź to see us. Both had been for some time in prison camps. I took the young woman to my bedroom, to give her a spare jersey I had. Sitting on the edge of the bed, she touched it with her fingers, gently, as if it were alive. She was very shabby and very pale.

'May I ask questions?' I said.

'Please.'

'Not for myself . . . How difficult is it to live here?'

She shrugged her thin shoulders. 'Few of us have more than the clothes we stand up in, everything, except bread and potatoes, is very dear—no family can live on the wages or salary of any ordinary person. If there are two or three in the family able to work, or if they have something to sell, or—' she moved her fingers, a gesture of distaste or mockery—'they speculate. Others who are in government service take bribes, there are high-ups who steal boldly—do I mean boldly?'

'And the Russians?'

'They control the police. What more do they need? People disappear. Like in the sea or a nightmare . . . As for the rest—what could you expect, with masses of soldiers moving through the country? I can't be shocked when they mishandle Germans—the sufferings of a German seem irrelevant—but they rob and rape decent Polish women. Only this morning the shop we use was looted by Russians with guns. But why are we talking of these things? Others are more serious. It is more serious that the line between old and young scholars has been interrupted. It is serious that so many of our libraries are ash. Imagine setting fire deliberately to a great library! Has there been anything like it since the great library in Alexandria was burned? And that was an accident.' She smiled. 'What is *not* serious is to have lost everything you had. It is not a bad feeling.'

'I asked about conditions because a friend in London—Maria Kuncewiczowa——'

'I had one of her books, until I was arrested.'

'She is hoping I can advise her about coming back.'

She laughed. 'It's still true that Poland is a land for heroes or swine. Those who want to fight should come back. No one else.'

'I have messages for a writer called Nalkowska. Is she alive?'

'Very much so.' She laughed again, shortly. 'She has become a communist deputy. Don't think I disapprove of writers who work for the government. A great many do, who are not communists. She is. She is very ambitious.'

'You mean—a writer who wants to be a success and safe must be a communist?'

She smiled. 'Now I will ask a question. I have been told—is it true?—that Dresden has been destroyed. I went there with my father when I was twelve. I loved it very much.'

'Almost completely destroyed. Somewhere I read that when the Russians went in they made stacks of dead bodies in the market-place and turned flame-throwers on them.'

'I am sorry about Dresden.' She hesitated. 'But only a little sorry.'

We were invited to tea—that is, coffee, cakes, and nauseatingly sweet thick marsala—by the President. Beirut. He was excessively polite. I had seen eyes like his—quick, sly, greasy, hard—in the faces of Yorkshire business men, but his were without humour. Elongating thin lips, he said, 'Note this, my friends. I want all Poles to return. But they must be Poles who look to the new Poland.'

No, I can't advise Maria to return, I thought.

Later, talking to our Ambassador in his room in the Polonia, I said that Beirut was a thug if ever I saw one.

'I can show you someone far tougher,' he said, smiling, 'the head policeman, the Minister of Public Security, Radkiewiecz. I like these people, they are brave and in a hell of a mess and working like heroes, and I'm inclined to think that the proportion of thugs in the administration is surprisingly low.'

There is a face moulded by hard work, patience, poverty, which has always been and still in some sense is *the* human face, the one I cannot look at without a pang of grief and rage. In Poland it was the haggard unutterably patient face of the keeper in what remained of a zoo outside Cracow. He was shivering a little in his worn-out jacket. During the war, he had listened to the broadcasts from London.

'You promised to send us so many things,' he said quietly, with a poor smile, 'but nothing has come.'

He refused money, pushing the hand offering it gently away.

No doubt he had expected too much of England.

The formidable difficulties involved in transporting anything, a visitor or a truck of food, would have been farcical if it had not been so nearly a tragedy. We had not fully understood this when W——— said he had arranged for two cars to take us to Cracow, and he was disappointed that we did not recognize a miracle when we saw it. They were wretched cars, but no car would have lasted on roads as dilapidated as the road between Warsaw and Cracow.

We left shortly before twelve and reached Radom at two o'clock, to find ourselves involved in a state funeral of people killed when seven hundred 'men from the woods' attacked the little town and broke open the jail to free their friends. Every shop and eating-place was closed, but a boy led us deviously through alleys to the back door of a shuttered house: it seemed to be the local night-club, a bare room with jazz instruments leaning against a wall, and four large playing-cards as decoration. We sat here a long time, and at last were brought an admirable lunch: coarse potato soup with sprigs of fennel, escalopes, vodka.

We drove on, slowly, hour after hour, jerking violently out of deep ruts and over improvised bridges, across a country of flat planes, the lines falling over one another like folds in an endless linen sheet. Here and there in the all but treeless fields, a cluster of stone chimneys marked the place where a wooden village had been burned down by the retreating Germans: when they had time to spare for it, they killed.

Before long we became stupefied. It grew dark, and the car I was in had a burst tyre. We were starting again after the repair, when the car ahead turned back in search of us, and broke an axle in one of the prodigious ruts. Too exhausted to behave well, we abandoned it, promising to send our car back from Cracow, and went on, leaving Slonimski, the two young women, and another Pole, to be murdered by brigands.

It was ten o'clock when we reached Cracow. A deputation of writers had been waiting for us in the hotel since five, most of them had left, but a young man, a poet, called Milosz, a couple of young women, and a shabby old gentleman who had been Bernard Shaw's translator, were still there. I went to my bedroom, changed, and came down to find them still talking in the hall. At last, all went except Milosz, and we invited him to dine with us. I had found out about him from one of the young women. As they had, he had escaped from Warsaw after the defeat of the Rising: during the Occupation, when to be caught with an English book cost either a concentration camp or a quicker death in one of the bi-weekly executions, he taught himself English to be able to read our poets, and translated *The Waste Land*, finishing it, with a fine sense of justice, the day the Rising started. Young, he seemed solidly self-possessed and very attractive in spite of it, with a pale rather broad face and a mouth flattened like Pushkin's, except that his was colourless and he had an engaging smile. At the table, I was too far from him to hear what he said in his slow English. Suddenly, raising his voice, he said with calm savagery, 'No. People in Cracow have not suffered enough. Warsaw . . .'

At this moment, a robust middle-aged woman walked across the room from the door, with terrific energy, and seated herself in the chair next to mine.

'I expected you all hours ago,' she said. 'I am staying here, I am Nalkowska.'

I told her my name, and she professed, with a fine smile, to have read two of my novels. Then I gave her Maria's messages: she had sent a great many, more than to any other of her friends, and a question: Did Nalkowska's sister know that her husband had been shot dead on the Spanish frontier, trying to reach England?

'She doesn't know. I knew, I was told a year ago, but why tell her? She is dying herself, let her die thinking he may return to-morrow. What does it matter? She is as good as dead. Tell me, please, is Aldous Huxley alive? And Virginia Woolf?'

I answered her questions, and began talking again about Maria. She listened in silence; I got, very strongly, the impression that she was no longer Maria's friend, and reflected, for the second time, that I could not let Maria come back. Finally, tapping my hand, she said genially, 'You are tired, my dear friend. Tomorrow I have questions to ask you—not about the Poles in London, I am not going to waste this chance of talking to an English writer by discussing fools. Let me see you often, often, but for serious talk.'

I was tired to death, but I could not go to bed without knowing that Antoni and the others were safe. It was after midnight when they turned up, exhausted, and very cool about our desertion.

After Warsaw, Cracow was curiously a little unreal. Untouched, since the Russians got there in time, it was the place where the lines of past and future crossed to form a fragile present, palpitating with energy, almost violent, below a dull provincial surface. It was full of writers, painters, musicians, many of them survivors from Warsaw, working feverishly—with every material condition against them, without books, with one dress, one suit of clothes, one pair of thin shoes, living in one room—and infinitely more alive than the English writers. Are five years of a brutal Occupation less tiring than five of a grinding war? They had a raging hunger for books—'Haven't you brought anything with you? Didn't you bring even one?' I began to feel that I was denying a crust to the starving.

England has no Minister of Culture: it is in the highest degree unlikely that in a time of national breakdown its government would give a moment's thought to the lives of writers—even if half of them had been killed, and the survivors were penniless and homeless. I was astonished and humiliated to discover that a Polish writer who had written two books, or translated four, or whose work was vouched for by the Writers' Association (under its non-communist president), was being given enough to keep him alive and a roof over his head. A modest pleasant house in Cracow, the Writers' Club, housed some twenty writers, married and unmarried. After five minutes there, I knew what Captain Cook would have felt if instead of landing among savages he had found himself walking into a meeting of the French Academy, with nothing to offer it but a handful of beads.

Deprived, for six years, of even their own classics, these survivors were desperately eager to know what the scholars and writers of other countries had been about during the years when Poland was a vast concentration camp, and no voice from outside reached them—'except the wireless—not often worth what you risked on it,' Milosz said, smiling, 'your life.' Their curiosity might have been touching: in fact it was devilishly searching and informed—and a great deal wider than their questions about living writers implied. The small four-page journal they gave me—paper for printing was scarcer than gold—had translations not only from *The Waste Land* but from Crabbe and Cowper.

'Please tell me about T. S. Eliot,' Milosz said, and went on to talk himself, with cold impetuosity and vehemence, making one English word do the work of ten.

I had a fantastic sense not so much of unreality as of living in a different reality. A partly mediæval city, a wasted country, its capital in ruins, its people awaiting the winter with dread, and I was listening to a poet talking, with intelligence and keen enjoyment, about another. It might be any moment in the past, in an interval between two barbarian invasions.

He was saying that he respected Eliot as a great poet, and the one poet of our time who fused two realities, the sensuous and the metaphysical—which may be what a modern poet must do if he is to tell even part of the truth about an age which contains Picasso, Proust, and the Auschwitz gas chambers. Not that he had any impulse to imitate Eliot. On the contrary. He believed that there is something new to be said by Polish writers—not simply because they have an immediate knowledge of hell, but because when you must, out of a past which is almost purely tragic, create a future reached across a vast graveyard, you must find a new way of saying the new thing. Or give up.

Abruptly, he said, 'Tell me—is there the slightest hope that your country and America will go on taking an interest in us?'

'I don't know. Why not?'

He smiled with extreme delicacy and extreme bitterness. 'All this fuss you are making about the Germans we have turned out of the new provinces to make room for our own peasants who have been chased out by the Russians! They have been kicked and robbed in the trains, they are going to starve in Germany. I must tell you that what looks to you like an innocent farmer looks to us like the face and hands of a murderer. You have just been trying four of my fellow-countrymen; they have been slave-workers in Germany for more than five years, and they robbed and killed a German family. Terrible. They have become beasts. And now, after six years of the life that changed them from human beings into wild animals, you are going to execute them—because they killed one or two German civilians. I don't understand your people. You have hearts, yes, but do you think with them?'

Stammering, I said, 'If there is no such thing as justice, what happened here is irrelevant.'

He smiled with the same fine bitterness.

'Since the last years I ceased to be interested in abstract justice.

I can't accept as justice a verdict which kills Poles for killing Germans. That's all.'

The room was crowded, men and women, most of them young, talking with a serious gaiety—or gay seriousness. Since one cannot remember everybody I had decided to remember Milosz. But two other people forced themselves into my memory.

A young man, younger than Milosz, very lively, with the eyes of a mischievous girl. He was showing off, but it was impossible not to like him and want him to go on bounding and bouncing like a young hare.

'Why talk about what's over?' he said to me. 'All I want to know about the English is how soon they are going to stop the Russians from swallowing us. We're more than half way down their throats already.'

It was only when he flung his arms up that I saw he had no shirt under his jacket: like the others he was meticulously neat: since they were really poor, really on the edge of the abyss, they had no impulse to dress loutishly.

He laughed at my politic answer. 'You wait, Mrs Storm, we are going to fight them.'

'Don't expect us to help you,' I said.

Taken aback, he rallied at once. 'I knew you'd say that! But in the end you'll be forced to fight—you always are. When the tension between East and West splits right open . . .' He laughed again. 'The Russians are jealous of us and despise us—exactly what the Germans feel about the French. It's very interesting. Don't you think so? They're a dull people, any illiterate Polish peasant has more irony in his little finger than a thousand pages of Tolstoy. You wait! Nobody and nothing can regiment Poles . . .'

Eugenia K——, a young woman, a delicate creature, with clear fine features. She had spent five years in Ravensbruck. Like other survivors of the camps whom I met, she had curiously withdrawn eyes. How had anyone so frail been able to live? She said calmly, 'Oh, in Ravensbruck I became a Christian, because I saw that only God could help . . . You know, I don't like to hear people talk of punishment; what was done in Ravensbruck can't be punished, you can only forgive such cruelty.'

Thinking of Kowalski's half-mad secretary, I said, 'I know you are right, but I don't know that I could make myself feel as you do. After all, you were defenceless, you couldn't have done the Germans any harm, you weren't fighting them—any more than were the millions of helpless men, women, children, they killed as they might have killed vermin.'

'Don't ask me to defend what I feel,' she said, smiling. 'I can't, it is what I am.'

When we were leaving I looked over my shoulder at the still crowded room, seeing the lively shabby figures, movements startling in their energy, and everywhere, at the ends of eyelids, on young women's colourless lips, the print of smiles, as if from a distance. What when the Russians close in? What will happen to all this new energy? . . .

That evening we were taken to the ballet—the Ballet Parnella. Superb vitality, superb clowning. I was madly happy. I had not watched anything like it since Diaghilev's dancers. That was in a year when, the young dead of the first war having retreated to their place, it seemed that all of us who were left had only a future.

The first exhibition of paintings made during the war had just opened. There had been one earlier exhibition—the work of the thirty painters killed by the Germans. Among the living, one, Jonasz Stern, might have put his work in both shows. He was taken for one of the public executions, stripped, and lined up; still living, he fell under the bodies of the others, and after dark crept out, naked, and escaped. He had been dead and he lived—to paint these smiling landscapes. It seems that when you are living in hell you don't paint it: none of these paintings had a trace of the violence, the disintegration of all values, which surrounded the artists while they were working on them. Another curious thing: the experimental work was being done by the older painters, the young men and women had returned to an equilibrium, a passionate attention to sensuous forms, which might belong to a moment of ease and stability, not to the chaos they were living in.

Perhaps it was not strange. It is perhaps when you have too little other experience to set against the experience of cruelty and violence, that you keep the simplicity and humility to paint appearances. Or you paint them as a defence against one face of the reality behind them.

Looking at a plaster statue, about a foot in height, of a young woman, tears came into my eyes. The face had a purity and fineness I had begun to look for in the faces of Polish women, and, as well, a serenity the very reverse of resignation or passivity. The sculptor,

Pujet, looked like a village baker, in thin worn-out clothes covered with plaster from the mould he had been working on. I asked him if I could buy his statue and send the money from England. He asked twenty-five pounds for it, and I gave him the two I had in my pocket, all that was left of the little I had brought.

A young woman I took to be the original of my statue was standing near it. It turned out that she was a slightly older sister, and after I had talked to her for a few minutes Pujet told me a story about her. During the Occupation she had thirty children in her house, and clandestine papers passing through her hands. One evening, an unexpected raid by a German officer caught her with some of these in a bureau . . . 'Tell the rest yourself,' he said.

'They made a very thorough search, and when they reached my room I waited for the moment when they would find the papers, and either send me to Oswieçin or—more likely—shoot me there and then, to save themselves trouble. The walls in this room were covered by my husband's paintings, and the officer was interested by them. He examined them all carefully, one after another, then said: This place is all right, nothing here—and went out, without touching the bureau.'

'The first time your husband's paintings were worth something,' Pujet said.

The next morning, I expected Maria's sister-in-law. When I was waiting for her in the hall, an elderly woman, Julia Rylska—I can use her name, since she cannot still be alive—who had been a translator of plays, came to ask me to send her new ones from England, and burst into tears. Madame S. arrived, and I asked Rylska to forgive me. Drying her tears, she said decisively, 'I shall wait.'

I hurried Madame S. to my bedroom, less fetid than the Polonia but almost as unpleasant, and gave her Maria's messages and gifts, and a thousand of the eighteen hundred zlotys the Polish government had given each of us as pocket-money, telling her it came from Maria—as it would have done if I had been less cautious.

She was telling me, for Maria, about her life, she worked in some sort of kitchen, and about her son. Because he had been in the Home Army, he was still in some danger, but refused to leave Poland. 'He says it is everyone's duty to stay here now.'

'And Maria?' I said. 'Am I to tell her that it is her duty to return?'

'No,' she cried, 'no, no. There are too many arrests, tell her not to come now, tell her to wait——'

Someone knocked, and she looked at me in alarm, but it was only Rylska to say that she would wait in the corridor until I could see her. Vexed, I shut the door on her, but after a few minutes Madame S. had to hurry away to her kitchen, and the other woman came in, and stayed an hour, talking and crying noisily. She was the only woman I saw in tears the whole time I was in Poland, and the only one who complained. Heaven knows she had plenty to complain about and weep for, but she was a little unpleasant. She talked about the savagery of the Russians and the horror of being occupied by them—'We endured so long, we suffered so much, and now this.' And then, without a pause, she began, dry-eyed, to talk about Jews. 'We can't have them back here, you don't know them, you have never seen a child's, a Christian child's, arm covered with cuts where Jews had drawn off blood for their abominable rites . . .'

I can do nothing about it, I thought, it is a disease. To distract her, I made her write a list of English dramatists whose plays she wanted, and promised to send them. (I sent several but did not hear that she got them.)

When at last I was rid of her, and went downstairs, I found Milosz waiting, with a younger man, almost a boy, a journalist, shockingly thin, stick-like arms and legs, a face restless with intelligence and curiosity. I went with them to a café, where I drank three glasses of vodka quickly, to loosen my tongue. The two of them put me through a merciless examination in the English writers of the 'thirties, about whom they knew fully as much as I did.

'What happened in the last months before the war?' Milosz said. 'Did any of them become catastrophic? How did the younger writers wait for the war? Didn't they drop their emotional Leftism? I know Auden went away—was he afraid? Angry?'

Harried by questions, I disentangled for them the threads of the 'thirties, the thread of weak lamentation, the strong thread of Hopkins, the pseudo-Marxism, the surrealism. 'The Spanish war persuaded most writers that civilization can't any longer be defended in private—it cost the lives of three good English writers and spoiled tempers as well as closing the frontier between Left and Right.'

'Nothing like a war for killing off writers,' the boy said, with the sharpest of smiles. 'Now tell me the names of your new poets, all of them. I suppose they are absolutely different from pre-war.'

I could think of four names, and gave them to him. 'We, too, had a hard war,' I said, 'and two of the poets we expected most from were killed. Something is stirring in English writing, possibly a new humanism, possibly—I don't know—a rejection of all that my generation means by humanism. It's too soon to say much.'

Scowling, Milosz said, 'But surely there is already a revolt of critics and writers against all that childish Marxism? What are the *new* writers doing? Isn't there a revolution?'

'No revolution of any sort,' I said, 'yet.'

They were disappointed. Milosz said warmly, 'Well, we shall wait a little. I hope that you in England will try to understand us, and that you won't abandon us again, as you always did in the past.'

'I forgot to tell you,' I said, 'that two or three of our young novelists were very much influenced by Kafka.'

To my great surprise, they burst out laughing. 'You don't mean it! Any Polish writer who imitated Kafka now would be *sifflé* by the public and crushed by the critics.'

Thinking about this afterwards, I supposed that the reality of terror, violence, unmotivated cruelty, had blotted out Kafka's prevision of it, or made it seem childish to these survivors . . .

At the theatre that evening I was reminded that the future is not always a young poet; it is sometimes the smiling worn-out face of an old professor, the single survivor of more than a hundred and thirty teachers of Cracow University arrested and sent to a concentration camp. He spoke to me after the performance.

'I shall show you my dear possession,' he said gently.

Fumbling in his pocket, he took out a membership card of the International P.E.N.

Half way through the evening, the director made a short speech in which he said that a delegation from England was in the theatre: the audience rose, shouting and applauding, and we stood up and bowed, feeling ashamed, and forgiven for our shortcomings and our failure to send them the help they needed. This world of simply human warmth that exists, a minute kernel, inside the world of politicians, intriguers, the power-hungry, the indifferent, the cruel, is what justifies our existence on earth—if anything can.

I was fascinated by a Russian officer sitting in the row in front of ours—a Georgian, someone said. He was young, slender, not tall, with a dark face, very narrow and pointed, and black gleaming eyes, so black, so filled by a brilliant restless light that they seemed to be enjoying a life of their own in his face. He moved brusquely and gracefully; he was like a whip, no, like a young powerful animal. I noticed his hands; they were very small, white, and quick-moving and, like his eyes, seemed alive with their own impersonal energy.

On the way home, shots were fired in the road we were about to cross. The few people near us lay down, and we stood like idiots, not knowing what to do. A Polish officer came up and helped us over some barbed wire, out of the direct line of fire. Two Russian soldiers, he said, had robbed a woman of her money and coat, and to stop them the police were shooting over their heads. We walked on, keeping to the side.

Towards midnight, over a long drawn-out dinner, Antoni Slonimski talked to me with a frankness I was not expecting. I had been half asleep, but a sense that he was unhappy and disappointed roused me to listen closely. I felt for him the kind of love one can feel for music or a landscape, an emotion between gentle pleasure in looking at him, at his clear tranquil worn-down features, and affection, none the less deep for being sexless.

'You are seeing the heroic side of this country,' he said. 'I see it, of course, but I see other things which are not heroic . . . The survival of anti-semitism . . . an elderly Jewish baker . . . he had returned from Germany only the night before, and he was leaving again at once. No one expected him to come back, and a Pole had taken over his house and shop. It was dark when he arrived. He knocked, and stood knocking for a long time, an hour; at last the door opened a few inches, a hand came through it holding a knife, and was drawn back and the door bolted again. He understood what it meant . . . Few people's characters are improved by being forced to live for years in fear and slavery, and I'm not shocked by the demoralization —remnants of the partisan army hanging out in the woods and robbing peasants, decent men and women living by what they call speculation, young thugs going through the train-loads of Germans robbing and raping. One day killing, lying, stealing, is heroic, the next it is crime . . . the human tragedy of boys who have lived a hunted underground life as animals so long that they can't grow into men, not even into speculators . . . The new government is doing many good things. In spite of the censorship and the Russian secret police, and raping and looting by Russian soldiers—who will leave when they don't need to keep a line of communication with Germany . . . I am sorry, a little, for the old ladies living in one room full of the furniture they managed to save when they were turned out of their estates, but they have outstayed their welcome in history . . .'

He hesitated, looking at me with a smile of grief, and said, 'I should have known what to expect.'

'You won't stay here,' I said.

'No.' He added after a moment, 'Not yet.'

When he did come back to live, years later, it was at a time of less freedom and greater danger for writers than in the undisciplined Poland of 1945. He behaved then with a calm courage which, a young Polish writer told me in France in 1959, 'was to all of us young an immovable rock and a, what do you say? a trumpet-call.'

Anything less like a trumpet than my dear Antoni's voice . . .

Writing this reminds me that after less than four hours' sleep that night I woke up and heard, very faintly, the *hejnal*, the trumpet-call from the tower of the thirteenth century church in the market-place, broken off before the last note—it commemorates some heroic act, I forget what. For a few moments I did not realize where I was, and I was swept back across Europe and the North Sea, and half a life-time, to hear, as faintly, the distant bugle that ravished my soul every July morning in my ninth year, the year when a brigade of soldiers was encamped outside Whitby . . .

A handful of young men and women were trying to rebuild the film world from nothing, with almost no equipment. In a bare room they showed us an almost unendurable film of Auschwitz and Majdanek, composed from photographs: the monstrous piles of shoes, spectacles, false teeth, clothes, women's flimsy shoes, chil-dren's, even baby shoes, stripped from their wearers before they were suffocated, methodically sorted, and stacked: a dead baby lying on the edge of a pile of adult bodies, four children folded together still feebly alive and another tottering past without glancing at them. Least bearable of all, the twin children walking away, helped by a nurse: these were kept for a time when the others were gassed, because one of the pair can be used as a control in experiments carried out on the other.

At the end, as it might have been the moment when, turning his back on hell, Dante saw the stars, they showed an exquisite short picture of children's living hands.

Was it here or in Warsaw that I looked, forcing myself to look, at photographs the Germans themselves had taken? A street execution: the first line of naked dead lying against the wall, the second standing in front of it, a terrified boy, his face contorted with grief and fear, hands knotted together on his breast, an older man holding both hands queerly and stiffly away from him, as if to keep the bullets from entering his poor body, three younger men, expressionless. In another of these photographs a boy, his face beaten black, was surrounded by smiling young German soldiers, delighted with their false negro. A young woman being searched in the street, a soldier stretching the elastic of her knickers to look down them.

The passion of the Germans for recording their ugliest gestures is extraordinary: it foreshadows the impulse of a few writers of the 'sixties to write wilfully disgusting novels in which normal human acts are made filthy by language and tone. They appeal to readers who are amused by midgets and fœtuses in bottles.

It is a sort of blasphemy, a religious spitting on the human body and mind—and as deadly dull as any other monomania . . .

If all I saw of Poland at that time had been the musicians' house in Cracow, it would have been worth the voyage. The only guests, we sat in an upper room and heard a famous singer, Aniela Szleminska, old now, but an exquisitely clear true voice, too strong for the small room, and then a violinist, Uminska, of unforced charm and power. To see Uminska standing at the end of a bare room, in her thin shabby dress and poor shoes, playing without a score, behind her the frightful nothing, the crack in the ground which had swallowed up friends, possessions, the past of her own life, convinced me that short of a nuclear war Europe cannot die; or, if it dies, will have seeded into the future too richly to be lost.

They talked with the energy, simplicity, gaiety, we now expected of these survivors.

'When I got out of Warsaw I was quite naked under this suit. I lost all my music, all. I can practise now, but without music it is a little difficult . . .'

'Forgive me, this is my only dress. I lost everything in Warsaw . . .'

'You know that all but a little of our music was burned. We've begun printing again—so far, just six scores. But look, don't you think they're well done? Of course, the paper isn't good . . .'

'My husband and two of my sons were shot. The third—since 1940 I don't know . . .'

'They weren't all brutes. I have a friend who was living, with her children, in a village, there had been trouble with partisans, and the Germans began murdering everyone: an officer came into the house

and she opened the door of the living-room, pulling it on herself—
that, you know, was always the thing to do, in case they came in
firing. He was a middle-aged man, and seemed decent, and she
begged him to stop the murders. He asked: Who is doing it? S.S. or
Wehrmacht? She told him: Wehrmacht. He passed his hand over
his face, and said: We used to be civilized . . .'

'This week I had the most superb luck. I made an expedition to
look at a cottage my family had near Zakopane, it had been looted,
of course, but they'd overlooked one box, I opened it and it was full
of linen sheets. Five! Think of it! I spent yesterday selling them . . .'

Despair is not decent. Like the novel of disgust, it is the twitch of
a weak nerve.

A people which has the energy to turn from the agony of its past,
to accept that it has lost everything, and to look with interest at the
future, makes despair irrelevant . . .

We were leaving Cracow after an early breakfast, and at two in the
morning I was still packing, in a stupor of fatigue. There had been an
official dinner-party, I remember nothing about it except a fierce
argument afterwards with Milosz and a young officer.

'What the English don't understand is the anger we feel when you
talk about saving Germany for Europe. Why are you saving them?
So that they can start again? What use is it for us to build up our
houses and our writing if every ten or twenty years they are to be
destroyed?'

'I dislike Russians,' the soldier said quietly, 'but I don't hate them
as I hate Germans, with my bones and nerves.'

'Why should you think I don't understand it?' I said. 'And why
can't you understand that Europe must be pacified? It's the house
we all have to live in.'

'Yes,' he retorted, 'and you English have the most comfortable
room in it, while we live in an abominably draughty corridor.'

'The *va-et-vient* in our corridor is terrible,' Milosz said drily. 'You
English can afford to make the most terrible mistakes, Singapore,
Tobruk, Munich and the rest, and survive, but we have only to make
one, like the Rising, and we pay terribly, all.' He smiled. 'And for
your mistakes, too!'

'Was the Rising a mistake?' I asked.

'An abysmal idiocy,' the young officer said contemptuously, 'a
crime. To fight in an overcrowded city, with a large German army
concentrated on it. The Russians, who are not fools, let the Rising

destroy itself—and three hundred thousand civilians. To play politics with people's lives!'

What else are they played with—at any time? . . .

Pujet had promised to deliver his statue at the hotel; he turned up with it as we were leaving: it was not packed and I realized that I should have to nurse it from now on, until I got it to England.

Since then I have wondered with a little anxiety whether he ever got the rest of the money I sent from London, entrusting it to a Pole who was going back . . .

Half way between Cracow and Warsaw, our car broke down completely. After we had been sitting by the side of the road for two hours, a lorry stopped: it was carrying a few Russian soldiers in dirty shabby uniforms and two officers: Antoni, who spoke Russian, talked to them, and they roped the car to the lorry and towed us into Radom, and there piled us and our baggage into the lorry, the men outside in the open, and me in the closed cab, wedged between the Soviet captain, who was driving, and the major. They were both extremely hard-bodied and very broad, and smelled strongly of a stable: I might have been sharing a stall with two powerful good-tempered horses, jostled first by one, then by the other. Neither of them could keep still, and after a time I felt I was sitting too near a menacing current of energy, dangerous if it got loose, and not likely to respond to any rational appeal. A few miles out of Radom a wheel collapsed, and the soldiers and the captain jumped down to change it: the first spare wheel they tried gave them trouble, they threw it into the middle of the road, and the officer and two men stamped on it, shouting with laughter, until they had reduced it to scrap iron and shreds of rubber. It struck me that they would kill a man or woman with the same childish impatience; they might have been a separate species of human being with its own impulses and habits.

It was ten o'clock when we reached Warsaw, and midnight before a room was found for me. I spent the time writing down the heads of a broadcast for next day, and got up early to finish it.

In the newly-built transmitting station, Polish and Russian technicians were working together with noticeable ease, like friendly schoolboys. A world run by technicians, in love with their complicated machines, might be less human and more peaceful than the one statesmen cannot keep going without killing off every year, by war, hunger, political murders, an undue proportion of its inhabitants.

The Pole in charge of my broadcast was very young, with a calm handsome face, and completely bald. Caught after two years of underground work, and sent to Auschwitz, he came out barely alive —'and like this,' he said, smiling, touching his smooth crane. 'Curious, don't you think?'

He was friendly, very gay, and moved about the room as though sitting still were too boring an effort.

'You liked Cracow? Of course—it is full of nice people with nothing to do but write. The future is being put together here, by those of us who live with it. It's difficult, of course, the days are too short, but, believe me, we're not wasting our time . . . The worst of the Occupation wasn't the deaths or the arrests, it was the sense of time wasted—and the fear, the sitting drinking beer in a room and hearing that a round-up is going on in another street, and the waiting, the fear and the fear and the fear.'

He was touching one shoulder against the wall behind him: suddenly he leaned against it like a man on the point of fainting; the gaiety and energy of his face were wiped off it, he closed his eyes; for a second his face was as coldly empty as if he were dead. He came to life again at once, and looked at me with the same smiling vigour.

'We are all obsessed, imprisoned in the house of our memories. When you have blown out a man's brains, even an S.S., and when you have learned to lie, rob, kill, as a terrorist kills, how do you stop? Where is the frontier? Many of my friends have remained bandits even though they are living normally.'

He smiled again, politely. 'As a writer you must find us—what shall I say?—strange animals.'

At this moment it struck me that perhaps the only habit we need to acquire, and teach our children, is the habit of loss. Then, if civilization collapses, the survivors may be able to begin again without resentment or self-pity.

To my surprise, I was being paid a fee for my broadcast, I forget how much: I gave him the address in Cracow of Matia's sister-in-law, and he promised to send it to her. I ought to have sent it to Pujet, but pounds would mean more to him.

Driving back to the Polonia after dark, the lights of the car stroking the ruins, I had a moment of giddiness: starting here, the tangle of snapped threads stretched across Europe—women from murdered villages searching for the child last seen stumbling off in the screaming darkness, wives who had given up expecting a letter from the husband in a foreign army, or his return from a camp. In 1945, Europe was a hell of memory.

I had over forty letters in my bag, addressed to men who might be alive, but certainly were not living at the address on the envelope— care of a regiment which no longer existed. I was clumsy enough to tell our Ambassador I had them. His seemingly effortless friendliness and ease of the highly trained diplomat became very slightly mocking.

'Don't,' he said, smiling, 'tell me about them. If they get you into trouble we'll do anything we can, but it's on your head.'

At the airfield, no one took any interest in my suitcase, or in my statue.

It was an uncomfortable flight. I tried to clear my mind of its illusion that it could read the future. Unless I had seen and listened to them, I could not have conceived that men and women who had suffered atrociously could do better than exist. These people were not simply existing, hanging on blindly, they were living, on the other side of despair, with passion, some at least of them with joy. In totally ruined Warsaw, the sense of life and light was infinitely sharper than in London.

The joke about human beings is that they can survive anything except the thermo-nuclear death of the planet—that is, anything except their own intellect and curiosity. Their resilience is such that they can even endure what they do to each other.

For a few minutes I felt sure of it, as I am sure of nothing else . . .

It was too late when we left Warsaw to reach London the same day. When we landed at Berlin the airfield commandant groaned, and said, 'Oh, my God, I was praying there wouldn't be a woman on board.'

The sheets on the bed he found for me were very dirty, and the bed itself harder than the one in the Polonia, but I slept soundly.

Chapter 2

I had no wish to revisit a Prague last seen in June 1938, in its triumphant self-confidence before Munich, and I dreaded the meeting with Jiřina Tůmová and did not want to see the marks made on her by her husband's atrocious death. But I could not decently refuse to go.

Staring, from the embankment, at the massive self-assurance of Hradčany stretched out on its hill-top in the November sunlight, and at the river running full and very fast below undamaged bridges, I thought that the invader had left no marks on the city. Here, if nowhere else on this side of Europe, the roots were unharmed.

It did not seem possible.

P——, the amiable young Foreign Office clerk who met me at the airfield, said, 'Mrs Tůmová met all three planes last week. Today we didn't dare tell her you were expected.'

'I came in the first possible plane—last week's were full.'

'I know. We manage things badly.'

Not badly. With strict care for justice. In Czechoslovakia the privileged persons were a thin layer of Ministers and officials; everywhere outside and below it, an equality of discomfort and scarcity. My room at the Alcron was luxurious, and I ate atrociously, meagre unappetizing dinners, and at breakfast a cup of ersatz coffee, bitter and nauseating, without milk or sugar, and two slices of hard dry black bread. At the next table an American sergeant unwrapped package after package containing everything he needed to endure life: two eggs, slices of white bread, a tin of real coffee, butter, ham. The Czechs drinking a thin sour liquid and chewing their dry bread at the other tables eyed him without surprise, even with irony. To be eating only what they ate gave me a good conceit of myself.

At first glance I thought, scurvily thankful, that Jiřina had not altered: her profile had kept its strict purity, and her slight body, slighter than ever, its latent energy of a cord. After a few minutes, I saw the changes, a deep fold at the ends of her eyes, and a strangely fixed serenity drawn over them like a bandage. When she closed them her face had a deathly immobility and absence.

She had made a long list of people and things I ought to see—it did not include the one thing I knew I must look at, the internment camps into which German civilians had been pushed until they could be tried and deported—and left no time for the pleasure of being alone in the foreign streets. Also I felt that she might be making a duty of me, and this disturbed me.

It was not true.

'I'm not going to squander this miracle by talking about the past,' she said calmly. 'First because in Prague we are only thinking about the future. And my own past is entirely in a little dust, which I won't show you—not because I want to shut you out, my darling, but it is too narrow, too cold, without room for friendship and the perfect happiness I feel today. I have been praying for this since June. When I heard you had gone to Poland I was very angry.' She lifted small worn hands. 'You see these? I beat on the Minister's table with them. Poor man, I alarmed him, and it was not his fault.'

In the first four or five days I saw more than a score of her closest friends, older writers, actresses (she had been an actress), the young doctor who went into Terézin some hours before the German guards left, overworked professors at the university, women working for the government and in industry. I made, at once, a mortifying discovery. In seven years the shock of Munich had lost none of its bitterness. All these friendly serious men and women, only one of them a communist, admired England, read English books, spoke English, and trusted us as little as they trusted any other rotten plank. As most Poles did, they knew they had to be on terms with the Russians: unlike the Poles, they spoke of their 'Slav brothers'—who had not betrayed them and never would.

They could not help their mistrust of us; it broke through a warmth and politeness which were quite genuine—at arm's length.

It was the more mortifying that I felt deeply at ease with these energetic unsentimental warm-blooded Czech women, Jiřina's friends. They lacked the quickness and grace of Polish women, so that it was some time before I admitted to myself that they sprang from the same tough root thrust deeply into ground soaked in violence: they were hard in the same way, without a trace of aggressiveness; the lines under their eyes conveyed, with less lightness, the same intention to live without pitying themselves. The vivid intelligent creature designing fabrics for export, Josef Čapek's widow searching for her husband's paintings, singers rehearsing in icy rooms, young students making up for the lost years, old tired ill-fed writers, all talked continually about the future.

That, when it came, it was not the one they expected, bred stoicism, not indifference—and no kindness for stragglers.

When I think about the Resistance in the occupied countries, I wonder uneasily whether I should have had the courage to take part. Here as in France the temptation not to resist had been very strong— less, I think, out of fear or cupidity than from a Czech habit of accepting what is inevitable *for the time being*, and making shrewd use of it. They are an eminently reasonable people, and don't lightly throw away a happiness at hand. I was told, and believed, that women kept themselves more aloof from the occupiers, more intractable, than men, who were after all responsible for the day-to-day running of the country.

It is a question less of dialectics than of habit and very long usage.

If some catastrophe should overtake Russia, leaving it without the means to force other peoples to be happy according to rules laid down in Moscow, I would not give much for the myth of Slav brotherhood.

When I had been less than a week in Prague I was faced with one of those problems in which two and two do not make four. The government, then turning its benevolent face to intellectuals, had handed over a castle, Dobřiš, to the Writers' Syndicate. After I had accepted their invitation to lunch I was told, privately, that Dobřiš had belonged to one of the Czech-Austrian aristocratic families; its expropriated owner was in an internment camp, accused of collaborating. The accusation might not be true—remembering squalid stories of denunciations in France, I felt uncertain—and John Lehmann, staying in Prague with a friend, had refused, on principle, to go to Dobřiš.

He was certainly right, yet I could not convince myself that even the most honourable scruples made it right to deprive half-fed Czech writers of what a foreign guest meant to them: a tolerable meal and permission to buy wine and slivovitz for his entertainment. They called for me at the Alcron, eight young men and women, none of them known to me, huddled at one end of a large bus: it was a bitter day, with an air out of Siberia, the bus had no springs and as many icy draughts as the cave of the winds; we shivered and rattled out of the city, stopping at a wine store to present our licence and buy: they were all as shabby as their bus, and vigorously gracelessly gay. No one except a caretaker could inhabit Dobříš in winter, it could not be heated, but a decent lunch had been prepared, wine and slivovitz loosened all tongues, even mine to make the obligatory speech, and I reflected that the noblest sentiments, untempered by mercy, rarely add to the sum of human pleasure.

I still had to see an internment camp. When I spoke about it to my bear-leader he said easily, 'Of course. Why not? You will have to spend a night out of Prague to see one. I'll arrange it for you.'

That afternoon a Dr Bruegel—he and his wife are dead now—a close friend of one of our Austrian exiles, came to the Alcron and took me to an apartment across the river, in one of the old streets. He was a civil servant, with inward-looking eyes in a thin vigilant face. Over cups of the detestable coffee substitute, he gave me a corrosive analysis of the situation. I made no notes, and what I recall is chiefly his conviction—at the time I put much of it down to his scepticism and dry cold intellect—that in a year or two the country would be entirely and savagely communist.

'Czechs enjoy being bureaucrats, and they feel that nationalizing everything means that everyone will be a state servant, and perpetually safe.' Here he smiled sharply, a bitter smile with a trace of self-complacency in it. 'Very many high-ranking civil servants have served loyally Beneš, Hacha, Hitler, and now Beneš again. But the old fellow is going to find himself out of step and the music being played a great deal too fast for him. They'll push him aside ruthlessly.'

I felt no doubt he was honest—and unable not to use his mind to destroy. When I stood up to leave, I told him I was going out to the country to an internment camp.

He stared at me. 'Why go out of Prague to see an internment camp? There's one here.'

'In Prague?'

He was silent. A very curious expression, half reluctance, half an ironical complicity, twisted·his dark face. At last he said, 'Ask them to let you see Hagibor.'

'Is it in Prague?'

'Yes, yes. They won't be eager to show it, you'll have to insist—
that is, if you really want to know what goes on . . . if you're not too
polite—' he meant cowardly—'to insist.'

From the hotel I telephoned to the Foreign Office and told P——
that I wanted to see Hagibor.

'If you like,' he said, 'but it's practically empty now.'

'I'd still like to see it.'

'I've made arrangements to take you to a camp very near here,
twenty minutes by car.'

Only the memory of Bruegel's ironical guess at my timidity made
me say calmly, 'I'll see that, too, but I really should like to go to
Hagibor.'

'May I ring you up tomorrow? . . .'

At an Embassy dinner-party I had on my left a politician, named
Fierlinger, about whom I knew only what my host told me hurriedly
before we sat down, that he was the Vice-Premier, the leader of the
Social Democratic party, and had spent time in Moscow. Facing me
across the table, his back to a wide mirror, was Jan Masaryk. As the
dinner went on, with well-cooked food and excellent wines, he
became more and more wittily scurrilous and indiscreet, jeering at
Czech politics and politicians with all the mimic simplicity and
impudence of a satirical clown. Listening to him, I tried to guess, as
often before, what you would come on if you were able to peel off
the several bare-faced personae, the natural comedian (he played
only real parts), the gourmand, the ribald buffoon who enjoyed
using a coarse salty tongue in solemn company, the resolute patriot,
the hard liver, the son of his father, with all this implied of effort to
fill out the name Masaryk: his reckless tongue was one of the ambiguous signs he made that formidable shade.

But the melancholy, the quivering sensibility I had once or twice
caught sight of—where did they come from?

Neither were visible this evening. He amused himself by mocking
Fierlinger and the other Minister at the table, and said he was going
to form a fifth party which would have nothing to do with the
'rotten policies' of the others. Brilliant fooling and highly indecor-
ous and absurd.

Suddenly my eye was caught by the reflection of Fierlinger's face
in the glass behind Jan: he was smiling slightly, not an unfriendly
smile, neutral, and oddly feline.

This smile was the first thing I remembered when I heard that Jan had thrown himself from his room on the fourth floor of the Czernin Palace, less than three years after this evening. No death of a person I liked without knowing very well so shocked me as did his—a splash of blood across the false peace in Europe. It was surely the final moment of a pause which had lasted since the end of the war in 1945 and now was over, and I thought with dread of the future. Hard to believe that his lively dangerous mind and tongue had been so easily silenced. Staring at the rather haggard photograph in a newspaper, I saw him, on the evening of the 29th of June 1938, in the Czernin garden—the fountains, the exquisite seventeenth century colonnade, the half-darkness, wine, strawberries—and heard his mocking voice—'Wells says you're not going to fight, but who knows? There are decent Englishmen. There are even Englishmen as honest as Czechs. I am not by God particularly intolerant. You can see that!'

He didn't kill himself, I thought. The certainty that he had been murdered took complete possession of me. No one who so enjoyed eating, drinking, swearing, mocking, who had so much warmth and sensibility and unused energy, would kill himself.

And then the way he died: to get rid of inconvenient opponents by throwing them out of a window is a Czech habit . . .

The day after the Embassy dinner-party, Jiřina asked me if I would like to see the prison where she spent several months.

'I go there every week,' she said, with her fine smile, 'and take a little bread—only a little, because it is forbidden—to a prisoner, a woman. One of our guards, who was rather kind to us. Now she is as hungry as we were.' She smiled again, this time as if she were laughing at herself. 'I shall have no trouble in getting used to myself as a skeleton. When our men broke into Pankrác and freed us, I weighed thirty-two kilos.'

In the broad corridors of the prison, the young Czech guard had none of the habits of a warder, he laughed, swung his arms, talked. We waited at the foot of a staircase for the German woman; she padded down the stairs, blowsy, untidy, her hair in grey wisps over her cheeks. As soon as she saw Jiřina she began to cry, wringing her hands, groaning.

'What will they do to me? Tell me, please. What's going to happen to me?'

'Nothing,' Jiřina said soothingly. 'We are all speaking for you, all your prisoners. We shall get you off.'

She took the bread from her handbag, the guard turning away his eyes, and gave it into a hand that clutched and pushed it out of sight inside a gaping bodice. She was still crying and snuffling. Jiřina put an arm round her and kissed her lightly: the German woman clung to her slender shoulders, sobbing like a trombone, and smiling a little. Then shuffled back up the stairs, pressing the slice of bread to the body of a fat sluttish housewife.

'*We* did not cry,' Jiřina said quietly.

In a reflective voice she added, 'She was kind, she did little things for us, but you should have seen the chief woman guard, she was the mistress of the prison governor, they were in bed together. She was consumptive. She was a born killer, she strangled women herself— when you looked in her eyes you saw death. One day about five o'clock they went to Terézin and killed some people, and came back and were merry together. The Germans always showed this hygienic prison to the Red Cross, these tall innocent Swedish gentlemen praised it, all smiles, they couldn't know what went on in these hygienic cells, the poor blood spilt everywhere held its tongue.'

By now we were two floors underground, in another of the broad passages. The guard unlocked a door.

'This is the small bathroom,' Jiřina said.

A dingy little room, like the bathroom in a cheap hotel, cracked wash-basin, lavatory seat, and a single naked electric bulb. Pointing to the pipe of the cistern, Jiřina said calmly, 'They hanged prisoners from it with wire.'

The next room we went into was large, hung on all sides with heavy multifold midnight-blue curtains, the whole so like a set in some early German film of suspense that it was ludicrous, bestially ludicrous—the German imagination is club-footed. Apart from the curtains, the only furniture was a large desk, standing with its back to the farther wall.

I noticed that Jiřina's slender body had begun trembling, her fingers curved stiffly like small claws. For the first time she spoke in a voice harsh with contempt.

'They brought one of our men in here and pretended to judge him, but all they did was glance at him from behind the desk and say: You have not been granted mercy. There were four S.S. guards in the room, three of them took him through the curtains——'

Smiling, the Czech guard tugged at the black folds hiding the wall behind the desk. There was no wall. The other half of the room was in violent contrast with this: white-tiled walls like an operating theatre, concrete floor, and in the centre the guillotine. A thin hose for washing down afterwards was coiled beside it. To be used when the judges preferred it, there were steel girders grooved for the easy running of hooks like those in a butcher's store-room.

'—and drew them close again. But, of course, the judges and the next prisoner who is being told: You have not been reprieved, can hear all that goes on.'

I said nothing. I had brought down inside my skull the shutter cutting off an emotion. The young guard had been fiddling with the guillotine. Friendly, only anxious that I should not miss anything of interest, he said, 'You would like to see how it worked.'

The steel blade fell like a stone, with a loud dull sound.

Back in my room at the Alcron, I made notes of all I had seen, and only when I had written the last words did I realize that I was almost too weak, my joints turned to water, to stand up. Better than I did, my body knew what it was thinking . . .

For days now I had been groping my way through a fog of delays and excuses about Hagibor. For all his youthfully smooth face and pleasant smile P—— was turning into one of Kafka's ambiguous officials . . . The day after I had been to the prison, he came to take me to Hradčany: I had been asked to tea. I had the impression that he was surprised by a civility I had expected.

'I think,' he said, 'you have been invited alone—yes?'

'Why not?'

'It is not usual.'

Guessing that he felt uncertain about me for the moment, I reminded him that I was still waiting to see Hagibor.

'I shall have news for you tomorrow,' he answered.

In the failing light, Hradčany was even vaster, more impressive, more like an enormous crouching animal, than ever. Leaving P—— —'I wait for you,' he said kindly—and climbing the staircase, I felt a familiar anxiety. Should I find a word to say to them? I need not have been anxious. True, there were no other guests, but wherever Hana Beneš was, a silent warmth and safety spread from her, the overflow of her absorbed gentleness and passion to serve her husband, and he made it unnecessary for me to talk by talking, in the voice of a man speaking to himself, almost without a pause, for two hours.

At the time I was not in the least astonished that he took the trouble to give me, an unimportant English friend—I had, he knew, no power to harm, and could not be useful—a long lucid account of the situation in Czechoslovakia since he came home, and of his policy. Today, I cannot for my life understand it. Why the devil did he do it? Not, certainly, out of a wish to impress himself on an obscure person. That I did, this afternoon, see in him a human being —in many ways unlike the man I had admired across a distance—is irrelevant.

The answer may be that he was so wholly without a trace of the snob that he could talk as easily to me as to H. G. Wells, Churchill, Jules Romains. His politeness was a vocation.

In familiar talk, there is no faking the quality of simplicity: either the speaker has it, deeply, or the fraud is obvious. Edvard Beneš, the man of reason, the adroit diplomat, had it.

Even certain friends said of him: Beneš? Too clever by half, believes—when he has talked his way through a problem—that he has solved it . . . Listening to him, I became convinced that this was both true and stupid. And not the truth. The truth about this subtle clever reasonable man is simpler. Below every other quality, he had an intelligent peasant's belief in the virtues of hard bargaining, and in the wisdom of keeping a bargain, once made. What sort of a world would it be, if, after long cunning argument, after you have got the fellow down to his lowest price, and after striking hands, you went back deliberately on the whole thing?

There were other men in him. There was the self-cultivated intellectual, the sensible patient teacher who believed that reason and logic can be taught, the felicitous politician who enjoyed politics as a connoisseur. Obviously, he had enjoyed the difficulties of the first months, enjoyed balancing between extremes, enjoyed his own deftness in moving to the left without sacrificing his sober vision, laid up in the bosom of St Thomas Masaryk, of the ideal democracy (Czech water-mark).

Sipping his tea, he developed this part of his theme—to his class of one—for twenty minutes. His wife—who knew more about silence than anyone, and was aware of him to the ends of her fingers— moved towards me the single plate of small round cakes, but I was too self-conscious to eat in class. His voice changed suddenly, becoming oddly younger.

'I discussed everything with Stalin, freely and frankly. I told him what Czechs would and would not accept, I told him they would not adopt Russian methods. And he accepted completely.'

He looked at us with a slight smile. 'You know, I had far more trouble with our Czech communists than with Stalin. But I've brought them, too, to see reason: in speech after speech I've led them always a little further from the idea of an unparliamentary régime.' His smile spread to the lines round his eyes. 'You know, I can turn their own talk about democracy against them. Now I can say that a revolution has been carried out without a single shot. People were astonished at first that I talked so much about the need to go ahead in a *Czech* way, they were ready for anything, anything, if only they got rid of the Germans. But week by week they became a little stiffer, a little more stable and balanced.'

'You are clever,' I said diffidently.

He considered this for a moment, lifting a blunt thin finger.

'No. It is not cleverness. It is . . . to take everything into account, to take care not to be surprised . . . to speak to the back of the mind. So with the Slovaks—they came to me when I was in Moscow, and I said: My dear brothers, I will give you everything you want . . . They were startled, they suspected a trick. I said: It is not tactics, you can have everything you want, but you must pay for it yourself.'

I laughed. He looked at me with entire seriousness. 'And so their demands gradually dropped—and by the time I came back here the position was what it ought to have been before the war, they have their autonomy, and Slovakia is not one of my problems . . . You were in Poland in September?'

'Yes, I——'

He cut me gently short. 'Six months before Hitler attacked Russia, I asked Sikorski to come and see me—to put an end to the quarrels . . . I liked him, I could talk to him . . . And we were in complete accord, complete, until I said: We can do it only if both of us are allied to Russia. In any case, I said, I shall make a pact with Stalin . . . And Sikorski, even Sikorski, started back . . . I said: I know what you think, my friend, you think it will be like last time, Germany will defeat Russia and then be defeated by England and America. That would be a miracle, and miracles do not happen twice . . . He was not convinced, nor were the other Poles.'

He allowed himself a moment, no more, of ironic triumph. It pleased him that he had been so much more alert, far-seeing, sensible, than the Poles. They had not known—had they ever?—what was possible, they had not *le tact des choses possibles*, the one thing a statesman (and a peasant) must have.

'You see what happened, you see the state Poland is in now, no freedom, half the country wanting a rigid imitation of Russian methods, the other half impatient to fight both Russia and their own Left. What stability can there be in a country so torn and unbalanced? . . . *I* knew. I knew all along that we should have to come to terms with Stalin, quickly. I told Churchill so in 1941 and in 1942, I told Eden, and in the end I went alone to Moscow and had my friendly talks.'

The same flickering half-triumphant smile. 'You see the result. We keep our independent way of life. And there will be no second Munich. *Which could not be risked* . . . The fact that we are a small country, no prestige to consider, makes it easier for us. And we are Slavs. But—attention—we are also Western, our writers, painters, professors, look west. Always will. Believe me, the country will be kept open . . .'

Earlier that day I had watched the Russian troops marching out of Prague between lines of smiling hand-waving Czechs, radiant with a host's friendly pleasure in seeing the back of his guests. I said so.

Beneš laughed. 'I had to help them a little to go,' he said slyly, 'They said: We go when the Americans go. And the Americans said they would go when the Russians went. In the end I cabled to Truman, and it was arranged.'

Then—when I was not expecting it—I felt under my hand the roughness, the scar, of Munich. I had asked him awkwardly whether he thought Europe could be saved.

'Yes. Certainly. There will be years of trouble—Poland, Roumania, Hungary, Austria, Italy, will swing violently from side to side, but we shall go straight forward—' he held his hand out in front of him: he had a strong small hand—'like this, on our steady middle course. We shall be a *rock* in the confusion.' He paused. I could not read his expression—anger? grief? both? 'France . . . At the time of Munich I begged, yes, begged their statesmen not to do what would kill France. You are betraying France, I told them. And that is what Munich did, and what is wrong with France now. It will take them fifteen years to recover. Yet Europe cannot live without France.'

'Or England,' his wife said softly.

'Yes, or England. You are on the highest level of civilization of all peoples. Of all. And yet—' his voice picked up a thread of bitterness—'I don't understand, I shall never understand the folly, yes, folly of your ruling class, which could not see what it was doing in letting Hitler grow to his strength.'

'They were blinded by their fear of social revolution,' I said.

(We go on repeating this excuse, but is it the real one?)

'But they should have known there would be war—and that modern wars are followed by social revolution—and made their plans in advance to see that it was orderly.'

He did not say: As I have done. His eyelids lowered on lively guarded eyes said it for him.

'The English are not logical,' I said.

'Another thing . . . You knew perfectly well that since 1933 the Sudeten Germans were plotting to destroy us. You knew it even without Frank's cynical revelations. Yet you are shocked, you protest, when we insist on getting rid of these treacherous neighbours.' He went on coldly, 'Even after Munich—for six months—I tried to see in the future a Czech-German state. Then it became unthinkable. It is unthinkable for our people to settle down with them again now. They know themselves that they must go. I know, of course I know, what an ugly affair it is, hard, bitter . . . For us, too, the loss of three million people—a million workers—is serious. But—' he made so few gestures that the sound of his hand striking the edge of the tea-table shocked me—'for the sake of the future . . .'

When I was hesitating between two replies, both futile, Hana Beneš said in a low voice, 'We need all our friends. Tell me, please, about Mr H. G. Wells. We heard he is very ill.'

'He is dying,' I said. 'His last book was one of despair, black despair. Now he is dying.'

She murmured a sorrowful phrase.

Beneš moved his shoulders like a man shifting a weight. 'So—he has let his own death make him despair of the future.'

When I left, they stood side by side, closely, to shake hands with me, he short, stiff as a wooden post, collected in himself, she all outgoing goodness and smiling blonde serenity. I thanked her for inviting me.

'You are the friend of Czechoslovakia, and our friend,' she said.

'And you didn't want anything,' Beneš said, with a smile.

'Not everyone does,' I said.

'Of course not.'

Hana Beneš laid her hand on my wrist. 'Next time you come it will be still better . . .'

P—— was sunk in himself, half-asleep. It was seven o'clock. Looking at me inquisitively, he said,

'Two hours. And he received you alone. This does not happen.'

'I knew them in London,' I said shortly.

When we stepped into the forecourt, the cold drove a knife into my chest. Plunging downhill, from the Middle Ages to the seventeenth century, we were in Apollinaire's Prague, the oppressive and menacing city of his tormented passer-by. A feeling of grief—grief or fear?—seized me. As soon as we had crossed the bridge into the modern city, I made P—— stop the car, pretending I needed to walk.

Nothing could be more absurd. I had just left a man tranquilly sure of himself and the future, reasonable, obstinate, quick-witted and endlessly patient and resourceful, and a woman in whom devotion and courage were an instinct. Then why this grief? Why, in a commonplace well-lit street, the continuing weight on me of the darkness, the raw cold, the history-soaked night of Prague?

I had to leave the hotel again at once, to spend the evening at the National Theatre, with Jiřina, listening to *Libuše*. This opera goes on for ever, relentlessly melodic, high-minded, patriotic. Towards the end I slept with my eyes open. Afterwards I sat up in my bedroom until three o'clock, writing notes of all Beneš had said.

There is no point in recording here all the words, the life-sustaining illusions, of a statesman whom even his enemies have forgotten.

I am ashamed not to record what I believe. Politically I am naïve, and not much interested, but because I distrust people I know them.

About Edvard Beneš I know that, until it happened to him for the second time, he did not for a moment expect that men with whom he had talked 'frankly and freely' would, for reasons of their own, go back on their bargain. Under his adroitness, his casuistical intellect, his obsession with the idea he had formed of the future—expecting that what he had sowed prudently he would reap—he had this simplicity. In 1945 he was sure—oh, clever clearsighted wily Czech —that he had saved the country, by making terms willingly and in good time, from any second attempt on its freedom.

A press photograph of March 1948 showed him aged by twenty years, the short strong body stooped, his face creased and haggard.

What the agony of Munich could not do was done in a few weeks by his countrymen . . .

In the morning, telephoning to P——, I found that the reasons why it was no use my going to Hagibor had sunk without trace.

'I shall take you today to Modeřany camp and then, since you wish, to Hagibor—yes?'

I thanked him.

In my heart, I shrank from knowing how men and women lived in internment; I was forcing myself to feel curiosity. Getting out of the car at the entrance to Modeřany, I felt ashamed, almost degraded.

P—— showed our permit and we walked through the barbed wire into the compound. It was near the river, and there may once have been grass round the huts, now there was only a stretch of mud, and children running about in it, madly, as though just let out. Inside, rooms like sheds or large mangers opened on both sides of the central corridor: groups of women and very young children turned their heads to us with the avid fawning movement of a dog who thinks he has at last found his master again. An old woman pushed herself to the front. When she opened her mouth I saw that she was completely toothless. A twist of white hair hung over the dark wrinkled skin of her neck. She talked, quavering, in Czech, tears pouring down her cheeks, looking so closely into my face that I could not avoid her breath, which was foul.

P—— translated.

'She wants to go home, she's done nothing wrong, and they need her at home to cook for them—she doesn't know who can be doing it now.'

He spoke to her indulgently, patting her shoulder. Turning to me, 'Don't fuss yourself, I've told her, the neighbours come in every day and do the cooking for them—' he grinned—'whoever *they* are.'

'Why is she here?' I asked. 'What has she done?'

He spoke to her again. She lifted shaking hands and let loose another torrent of tears and gabbled sounds. He listened smiling.

'She doesn't know.' He shrugged. 'She must have done something—perhaps she gave someone away to the Germans, out of fear or spite. Or said something she shouldn't. Or one of her neighbours had a grudge against her and denounced her. It will come out when she's examined, and they'll probably send her home—at her age.'

'When will she be examined?'

'Oh, I daresay in a month—or six months. So many of our judges were killed by the Germans, and the rest have too much to do. Come, please.'

He tried to move forward, but the women came round us like shades pressing themselves against a living visitor. They held out babies to me. Two of these looked strong enough, the face of another was a minute wizened root, two inches long, the fourth—opening the rags covering it, its mother showed me a skeletal body covered from head to feet in sores like puddles. The smell was horrible.

'Has a doctor seen it?' I asked.

P—— spoke briefly to the Czech guard. The man went away and came back with the elderly interned German who was the camp doctor. Glancing at the child, he said with contempt, 'She's dirty, a peasant, she doesn't keep it clean.'

It might be true. But the woman was crying bitterly.

P—— forced a way through for us. I slunk after him—to inspect kitchens, a separate kitchen for the children's food, separate washing huts with basins.

'You see,' P—— said, smiling at me, 'it is not so bad, is it? It is very cold, yes, but many of us are cold.'

The doctor was following us, and P—— asked him to show me the hospital. He opened the door of a narrow little room, empty except for three beds and one patient. A very young girl, perhaps fifteen or sixteen, turned her head with an embarrassed smile: she was a beautiful creature, dark eyes under long arched eyebrows, straight nose, fine lightly curved mouth. Lifting the hair from her damp forehead, the doctor said gently, 'You're stronger again today, my child. In a few weeks, in no time at all, we'll have you up . . . She's been in here and other camps since May: she and her parents and two sisters ran away from the Russians, the others were killed, she's quite alone . . . But you're not afraid now, are you?' he said to her.

In a low voice, she said, 'No—but if only I knew what they are going to do with me.'

She was looking at me. I did not answer. Could I have told her that her likeliest future was the clearing-house near the Lehrter Station in Berlin, the stinking rags of her fellow-travellers and her own, the coldness, the distaste, of the German nurses when they had to touch her?

Outside the camp, P—— said, 'Perhaps now you do not care to see Hagibor?'

If he had spoken with less assurance, or looked—at that moment —less damnably like a Yorkshireman, I might have seized the excuse.

'No, I'll see it,' I said.

Dusk, the cold raw November dusk, thickened by fog, was coming down when we reached the place. It was much larger than Modeřany, half a dozen long huts set close together in the compound, and a shabby brick building. The guard, brisk, smiling, with enormous hands—he kept them cupped as if trying to catch trout in a pool—led us directly to the nearest large hut. We stepped into the narrow ante-room. A group of women holding tin mugs stood listlessly before the official who had brought them the last meal of the day: pieces of dark bread, one for each man, woman, child, the guard said, with his amiable smile, and pails full of the thin 'coffee'— I knew how bitter it tasted. A few heads turned towards us with less than curiosity.

'Speak to them,' the guard said in German, 'we're not jailers, they're free to speak.'

Awkwardly—it seemed as senseless and derisive to speak to these women as to caged animals—I glanced at the one nearest me, then at the bread she was clutching, and asked, 'Is this your supper?'

This brought down on me a loud shrill clatter of Czech and German, all of them speaking together; skinny arms thrust the hunks of bread and the tins in my face. A voice, piercingly harsh and jeering, belled above the others, speaking a precise pure English.

'Yes, and our breakfast, too. And at midday, we get watery soup and no bread. And that's all we have—nothing else, nothing, nothing. We're hungry!'

I looked at the speaker. A long dark face, with the large gauche eyes of an old horse; their gentleness and the violent contempt in her voice disconcerted me. At least they're not afraid to complain, I thought. I glanced at the guard, who shrugged his shoulders.

'They don't get much,' he muttered, 'and neither do we Czechs.'

He moved forward. Rank-smelling bodies flattened themselves against the wall to make room: as I passed her, the woman who had shouted at me leaned forward and stared into my face with an air of defiance and mockery: her lips were trembling.

Inside the long room, rows of triple-tiered bunks filled every foot of space except a narrow passage down the centre. In here it was nearly dark, and in the first moments I had the sense that I was pushing through a liquefying heap of bodies, here and there in it a livid face turned upwards, the eyes staring like open wounds. The stench was suffocating. Men, women, children, stood or squatted, alone or in small groups, pressed against each other and against the bunks. A few older children were amusing themselves by rolling in and out of the upper bunks, other children sat in them doing nothing, or crawled about between the adults' legs.

The warder took seriously his duties as guide. 'Whole families,' he said importantly, 'are living here, waiting to be deported. A good few of the women are Czechs who married Germans. Some of the Germans were born in the country.'

'Then why must they leave?'

I knew the answer.

'Why? They're Germans, aren't they? Do you suppose we want them here, with their murderer's hands?'

Incautiously I stood still. Instantly women pressed round me: a young woman unwrapped the strip of worn blanket round her baby and said quietly, 'Look—it's all he has. He's not warm enough. And what am I to do when he's older?'

'Mine—look at mine. He has nothing under what you see. He's two now, he's grown out of what he had when we came, and he has no shoes——'

The guard interrupted.

'We have shoes for some of them,' he said softly. 'But not the smallest sizes.'

I tried to turn back. The women stood in my way with their children, imploring me. I thought that each of these hoarse voices had been climbing through centuries to reach me, the cries uttered by any mother in any war, any sacked town.

'My children are hungry, I tell you. A few drops of milk for the little girl, for the boy, because he's six, no milk at all—only the soup and bread . . .'

'Feel his hands—he's always as cold . . .'

'Why are we here? How much longer? . . .'

'Please—help me . . .'

'Do something for us . . .'

Flailing with his arms, the guard forced a way through, and P—— and I followed him. A woman holding her child in one arm seized my hand, and kissed it. Another woman, younger, who was pregnant, caught hold of my arm, smiling and crying, stammering a phrase I did not understand.

'Do you want to go into the others?' the guard said, when we were outside the hut.

I shook my head.

'Well, see the hospital,' he urged. 'We have a hospital.'

This was the brick building, from the outside a rambling dilapidated house of two stories, dankly cold, with bare stained walls inside. The whole place, the guard said in an apologetic voice, had once been a Jewish stadium; the Germans had turned it into an internment camp for Jews and Russians, these had left it falling down and infested with lice: it was now just habitable.

He had sent for the doctors. There were two, a haggard young man and a woman in middle age, with a broad good face. She reminded me of Joan Malleson, the same smiling directness, the same warmth. Both were Germans interned in the camp. Hesitantly, uncertain that I was doing the right thing, I shook hands with them. The young man did not speak, the woman smiled warmly and took my hand in a strong clasp.

'You want to see the hospital?' she said, in English, in a quiet deep voice. 'A pity to visit hell without seeing every circle.' She glanced at her colleague. 'No need for you to come with us, Joachim.'

He did not answer, staring in front of him, blankly, as though he had ceased completely to attend to what went on round him. Clumsily, I offered him a packet of the cigarettes I carried to give away. He took them in silence, with the same indifference, and turned his back.

Touching my arm, the woman doctor led me up the stairs to the upper floor. P—— and the guard came with us.

This place—in comparison with the overcrowded stinking huts—was bearable, unspeakably depressing, dark, squalid, but bearable. On the landing she hesitated outside an open door, then said, 'You would give me great pleasure if you would speak to some colleagues of mine. Being men, they suffer more than I do from their . . . humiliation.'

In the small room, their beds touching each other and the wall at each end, were four men who might be any age from eighty to a hundred: too little flesh remained on their skulls to tell. The doctor introduced each of them formally, by name and profession. 'X., the distinguished brain surgeon . . . Y., the well-known heart specialist . . .' They lay rigidly still; each appeared to be intent on keeping alive a different part of himself, eyelids, an index finger, a tongue, a vein in the temple—concentrating in it a last charge of energy. The one whose tongue was still alive said with weak bitterness, 'A nice way for people like us to die—of hunger.'

'Nonsense,' the doctor said, smiling at him, 'you'll live to operate on a great many more brains.'

A faint contortion passed itself off as an answering smile on the old gentleman's face.

'Next time,' he murmured, 'I shall remove the whole brain, it's nothing but a nuisance.'

When we left the room, the doctor said calmly, 'They really were well-known, and they really are dying of hunger. They can't swallow the dry bread, and there's nothing else for them. And no drugs. It's the same with these.'

In a larger room eight or nine old women were lying in narrow beds, in strange attitudes of abandon—not as a child abandons itself in sleep, but like rags thrown down. None of them spoke, but one discovered in herself a flicker of coquetry and withdrew under the blanket a disagreeably fleshless arm.

A door at the end of the landing, wide open like the others, led to a passage. The doctor seemed to hesitate, turned to P—— and the guard, and said pleasantly, 'I shall shut the door to these rooms. And you will stay outside it. None of these women can run away.'

P—— stepped back. Looking at her with a curious expression of embarrassment and irony, the guard nodded.

This unlit passage was an image of the passage leading from one wing to the other in my first shabby old-fashioned school, and it should open into a room with a twisted old crab-apple below the window and a glimpse of the upper harbour: I felt a sudden stinging joy, cut off when I stepped into the room, windowless and no bigger than a cupboard—it may have been one. The young woman lying curled up in the camp bed—it was too short for her—had her few days' old baby in the fold of her left arm. She looked like a peasant. Turning her head, she stared at me with sudden eagerness, her grey eyes as clear, as without self-consciousness as a child's. The doctor bent over her.

'Yes, now is your chance,' she said.

With the swiftest of movements, the girl thrust her free hand under the pillow and drew out an envelope addressed, in pencil, in an unformed sprawling hand.

'It's a letter she has written her husband to tell him about the birth of their child. The address, the only one she has, is the village in Bavaria where he was stationed with his company when she last heard from him, eight months ago. He's a German, in the German army. Read the letter, and if you find it all right, post it when you leave the country. Will you?'

I put it in my handbag. The face of the young woman in the bed became radiant; a smile of ecstasy crossed her full colourless lips. Outside the room, the doctor murmured, 'Of course, he's not there, probably she'll never see him again, but you've made her happy. It is worth it.'

She walked past the next door. 'I won't take you into this room, the women in there had their babies only a few hours ago. For a week or two they'll be almost content. After that—well, you understand— their milk will dry up, they have the same food as everyone else, and their babies will begin crying from hunger, the few spoonfuls of milk I'm allowed to give them are nothing . . . You're cold.'

The whole place was glacial, but these rooms seemed degrees colder than anywhere else. Trying to control the helpless shivering of my whole body in its warm clothes, I felt in my handbag for the two bottles of haliverol capsules I had brought from England; they were for Jiřina, but I had forgotten to give them to her. I held them out.

'What are these?'

I told her. Smiling slightly, she said, 'Perhaps it isn't kind—but I'll make use of them.'

I saw, thankfully, that there were only two more rooms. The first of these held half a dozen beds, but their occupants were too far gone to notice a visitor. Lifting a young woman's arm to show me that it was only bone, the skin a grey membrane stuck to the wrists and the phalanges of the hand, she said again, 'No, it's not kind.'

The young woman sighed, opened her eyes, saw me for a moment. 'Help us, please,' she whispered, the animal speaking.

The last room—the last circle of this infernal place—was badly lit by a single weak electric bulb. Six cots, two of them empty. From the nearest rose a thin crying, only just audible, just not an absence of sound, and continuous. Two of the other babies were lying quiet, their tiny livid faces barely visible on the mattress.

'They're nearly gone, thank God,' the doctor said under her breath. 'There's nothing the matter—a teething-rash—babies born here have no resistance, they die of a scratch. This other one may live—I don't know yet.'

This other—the fourth—had been propped up in his cot against a folded blanket. He was older than the rest, perhaps a year old. He had four playing cards he was looking at without interest, one of them dropped from his hand and lay face down in the scrap of blanket across him: he let it lie.

'Couldn't someone sit with them?' I stammered.

The doctor looked at me, smiling a slow reflective smile, indulgent. 'Why? They don't know when they die.'

I bent over one of the cots: the tiny face dissolved and for less than a breath I saw through its soft skull the guillotine in Pankrác, the walls of the little bathroom, the terror of a boy in the instant before he is killed, the decent bodies of women heaped, naked as maggots, in Terézin and Auschwitz—the spume of agony flowing back and forth across Europe.

Then I saw only the dying baby.

After dinner in the Alcron that evening, the usual wretched meal, I told Jiřina about this one room. She listened, her glance absent, almost, I thought, with a gleam of irony in it. In a dry voice she said she would do what she could about it, speak to a Minister—Clementis.

Later, she broke off what she was telling me about the younger writers, to say abruptly, 'You are disappointed, my darling, not to find the young Prague of 1938, the Sokol children walking about the streets like dancers, and that confidence and gaiety and courage we felt then. I am sorry.'

'No,' I said, 'I didn't expect it.'

'We still, you know, have confidence in ourselves, we still think of the future.'

I hesitated. 'Suppose that Russia tried to take you over? How would you feel, what would you do about it?'

She lifted her thin small hands. 'What could we do? We couldn't fight them—what other friends have we? We could only say: Do not do us any harm, we are your brothers.'

And wait, I said to myself, with your habitual shrewdness and obedience, for the moment to shake off another servitude—and in

Guy in uniform again, in 1941

In Vaison-la-Romaine, in 1954

'Offered a pleasure . . .' At a party in the Macmillan office in 1957

The crew and the passenger

'She learned to steer a
compass course . . .'

the meantime build up a weight, a fearful weight, of resentment and anger which you could only work off on each other.

'Don't be afraid,' Jiřina exclaimed, 'it won't happen.'

'If I became afraid for this country, I should only have to think of you—you are courage, honesty, endurance, grace itself.'

'Oh, no, my dearest,' she said sadly, 'I am a fool. What to do with such a thing as a heart? Perhaps a clear mind would be some use, but after these seven years mine isn't even clear. Do you know that sometimes I am longing for Pankrác, where I had so much time to think? I used to have marvellous dreams. Once I dreamed about the destruction that was going on in Europe, and it seemed necessary, and still more destructions, if the new world was to be built. Each of us, I thought, will begin again, from the beginning, to reconstruct in himself the man, the human creature. I felt madly happy. Now ... My darling, fortunately we are not only our minds.'

I spent three feverish nights, neither sleeping nor fully awake. Images of Hagibor pressed against the inner walls of my skull, a frantic pressure that distended the blood in my veins until I felt that I was being squeezed out of myself, like paint out of a tube, a horrible sensation.

When I had time during the days, I wrote a long report on Hagibor, cold, factual, ending with the room of the dying babies, to be handed to Clementis ...

I was seeing too many people, and whenever I was in the house of a Czech friend allowed, for official reasons, to buy liqueur, drinking too much, to endure the cold and my growing impatience. At moments, Prague itself, with its superb palaces, its flights of baroque angels and monks, its secretive alleys and wide grey solid streets, started in me a fear of—what shall I say?—of something not so much evil as sly, and slyly cruel, like Fierlinger's smile.

Time you went home! I said to myself. That the happiness of living in a foreign city had failed me—for the first time in my life— was a little humiliating. I blamed myself for it, not Prague.

It was not easy to get away. The weather was atrocious, on some days the plane expected from London did not come, and after two or three such delays the returning plane was overfilled. I hid my impatience from Jiřina.

During these weeks I heard six operas—I adore opera, but Smetana folkishness, lively and often amusing, quickly bores me, and even Dvořak ... for an hour the long liquid translucent phrases of *Rusalka* enchanted me, then I caught myself stifling a yawn.

Nothing I heard, not even the music party His Magnificence the Rector of the University gave in a baroque palace, had the poignance of Uminska playing, without a score, in an almost empty room . . .

Jiřina's friends were of all ages and kinds. An evening I spent with her and two young men gave me a singular pleasure; both were intelligent, quick-witted, quick-tongued, and their affection for each other was open and curiously touching. One of them, F——, small, dark, lively, a Slovak, worked in the Foreign Office; the other was a dancer and choreographer who had worked in London with Ninette de Valois, and had served with the Czech brigade. Never were two gayer, more passionately hard-working, more sanguine young men, so confident that the country was on the verge of a renaissance in all the arts that for three hours I believed them.

In May 1952, I heard that F——, implicated vaguely in one of the 'conspiracies' of that time, had died in prison. Not allowed to go on working, his friend killed himself. What a waste of two minds and bodies made to give pleasure . . .

I got away at last, at the very end of November, after waiting on the airfield for three freezing hours, until the pilot decided to risk the trip: it was a day of driving snow and wind.

My last sight of Jiřina was of a dark thin almost transparent figure, a leaf blown against a snowy pane, dwindling.

The aeroplane, a converted Dakota, was, of course, unheated. Huddled in my seat, I made an effort to clear out of my mind its sense of a subterranean violence, in ambush below the friendliness, the hard confidence, the energy. The impression that undamaged Prague was actually worse, because invisibly, damaged than Warsaw, persisted. In Poland the destruction could be seen and touched, here only felt. Both countries were facing the same problems of reconstruction, infinitely less acute in Prague, both turned the same glance, trusting or fearful, on Russia. But, if both were forced to turn religiously towards the east, the Poles might, it was conceivable, ride lighter, with a margin of ironic reserve . . .

The cold crept from my limbs to my mind: I was becoming unconscious. Closing my eyes, I drifted into a nightmare, and after a time opened them to see the co-pilot standing looking down at me. He went away, and came back with a flying-jacket he laid across me. But for the slight warmth it started, I should have lost consciousness completely.

It was dark before we reached London, and I was stone deaf. I recovered my hearing, painfully, only when I was walking about my room in the King's Cross hotel in a trance of fatigue, preparing for bed.

I was catching the morning train to Yorkshire, and fell asleep thinking, with some primitive root of my brain: There you will begin a new life, sane, settled, not writing too much, not spending too much money, not knowing too many people: learn to say No! No! and No! to the people and occasions that are only an irreparable waste of time and strength. Already the total of wasted days in your life is appalling. How, when you are dying, you will regret it. Remember . . .

Chapter 3

In the morning, things looked different . . .

Is the excessive order in which I live, everything round me, on my writing-table, in my rooms, neat, dusted, or scrubbed, and in its right place, a cover-up for the profound spiritual disorder of my life itself?

Guy had been appointed to the Chair of Modern History in Leeds University; he was also head of the department. The small hotel in Ilkley, at the foot of the moor, was to be our temporary lodging until I found us a house. I succeeded—with twinges of guilt and a stubbornness of the devil—in living there for six years, in complete freedom, six of the pleasantest years of my writing life. Now and then, driven to it by my conscience, or by some kind meddling body, I looked at a house or flat, and found incontrovertible reasons for not taking it.

Guy had a working room and library of his own in the university or I could not have held out so long.

My days were monastically ordered and delicious: I wrote through the morning, then walked for an hour across the moor, not a North Riding Moor, not the moor above Sleights or Aislaby, but fine enough in its harsh way—ling, bracken, grey rocks, magnificent horizon, and a thin sharp northern air—and came home to write until dinner.

In May I went to Stockholm for the first P.E.N. Congress since the war. I remember little about the proceedings beyond the fact that the French and the Centres in other countries occupied by the Germans had drawn up a black-list of writers who had collaborated, even a little.

Only an eccentric like Paul Léautaud, or a wilfully obtuse 'liberal', could fail to understand their bitterness. None the less, Hermon Ould and I gave ourselves a great deal of trouble to stop any action being taken. It did not, and does not, seem to me decent for writers to proscribe each other. Leave that gesture to politicians. A writer has other, sharper, ways of expressing his detestation of his fellow-writers' wickedness than by black-listing them.

What I remember above all is the charm of a city into which the sea enters and gives the light its reverberating brightness and clarity. This light is the one I was born into on the north-east coast of England; it is the one, if there were another world, I would pray to find myself in after death. No other, not even the subtle light of the Loire valley, nor the hard smooth brilliance of Provence or Greece, would content me.

In Uppsala, seen at four in the morning, the lilacs were magnificent. It vexes me that I cannot describe them without looking round for metaphors. And what use is a phrase to eyes which did not see them in that light, at that hour, on that day, the 9th of June 1946?

My other distinct memories are, as always, of people. (I noticed, by the way, that the Swede you have listened to in the morning when he is stone cold sober and the same man after he has drunk enough are two different individuals: the first is more confident of his cleverness and wisdom than the second, who has doubts, and is capable of humility and poetry.) When I could do it without being seen, I stared at a middle-aged Swedish poet—I have no idea whether he was a good poet or only mediocre. He had the face of a mediæval devil or saint in a Gothic cathedral, or the stone effigy of a crusader: it was long and lean, with a very long, very narrow arched nose, pale eyes set so deeply in his skull that they disappeared easily, and down each cheek a groove like a wound. There was something infinitely attractive and absurd about a tortured mediæval head set on an elongated body in striped trousers and a dark jacket and carrying an umbrella.

I made notes of this face and used it for a character in *The Black Laurel*.

At one of the sessions an old Finnish professor, Yrgö Hirn, delivered in English a speech on humanism and its future: he had been preparing it since 1939, writing and rewriting it throughout the war. In a gentle voice he told his audience of writers from some twenty-five nations that we cannot rebuild the world we have destroyed without first restoring respect for the life and happiness of the individual. The true humanist cannot give up the detachment which is his way of life, but neither can he disregard his fellows, and must take the risks involved in social intervention. Today man is cruel and violent because he is bored and profoundly afraid of the technical monsters he himself has made. In the horrors of war he has forgotten the humanist philosophy, but the moral force in men, and in the power of sacrifice, will revive it . . .

His hands trembled violently, rattling the sheets of paper covered by the finest of fine writing. Immediately in front of him a female writer, English, took out lipstick, powder, an eyebrow brush and hand-glass, and touched up her face. Others of his hearers went out or sat yawning. He did not notice. For seven years he had seen and heard himself giving this speech, and the effort of giving it demanded the whole of his weak energy.

'. . . that past-master in revaluations, death. Now that the great buildings have collapsed, it is easier to notice the flowers among the ruins,' he said quietly and, gathering up his papers, stood a moment, waiting, then walked slowly off the platform to his seat in the audience.

There were no comments, and neither of his neighbours glanced at him.

At the end of the session, I congratulated him warmly on making the most important speech of the Congress, the one none of us would forget.

After this he came up to me whenever he caught sight of me, and talked and talked, until I took basely to avoiding him.

Among human beings I prefer the very old and the very young. I listen to the old with respect, even when they talk nonsense. They are so near death! Perhaps it has always been my own old age I see in them. And the very young? Ah, think of all they risk, the disappointments, the mistakes, the useless tears. No doubt it is still myself I see and hear.

This Congress had a strange flavour, sharp, delicate, a little bitter. There were no German writers, except the exiles—it was too soon to have sorted out the sheep from the goats, or to ask, say, a Dutch or Polish writer if he cared to risk shaking a hand which might have touched hands responsible in some degree for the extermination camps. There was this black-list, and there were joyous moments when someone caught sight of a friend from the other side of Europe whom he had supposed dead—'*Ah, cher ami, c'est vous! Enfin!*'

One of the two Polish delegates was a writer I had tried vainly to see in Poland—Jan Parandowski, president of the Polish Centre since its foundation. I was told he was alive, but in the incredible difficulties of moving between Warsaw and Cracow I missed him. Now here he was, with his wife and three children, and at first sight of him I understood the stupefaction of the French writer who exclaimed, 'Parandowski alive? Oh, impossible! A puff of wind would have killed him.'

He looked as fragile as a splinter of glass, stooped, sallow, with pale eyes under a magnificently arched forehead, and thin bones. Rather quickly I realized that his was the fragility of a steel watchspring. A scholar, learned in three languages, a writer of exquisite sensibility, incapable of a clumsy phrase, and so fixed on his one aim in life—to become more learned, to write with yet greater simplicity and elegance, to enjoy a more acute aesthetic pleasure in books, in sculpture, in music, in landscape—that he was invulnerable. The frightful hardship and dangers of the Occupation in Poland, worse than in any other country, fined him down to the bone, but did not kill him—I really think because his self-centredness made him transparent. A monument of delicacy, integrity, egotism.

A year or two after the worst of the Stalin decade, a young writer told me, 'Parandowski—yes, yes, a saint who shuts his eyes. But I respect the old boy—oh, not for anything he did, he did nothing, for being unchangeable. If it was a mask it was a good mask.'

He adored his three handsome children, and I suppose would not have hesitated to sacrifice his life for them—and possibly his work.

In Stockholm, I felt so fiercely that he and his family ought to have more than ten days' ease before going back to Poland that I persuaded the Swedish publisher of one of my novels to hand over to him a meagre sum of royalties owing to me. This accident began a friendship as formal as a minuet, friendship in the, so to speak, pure state, metaphysical and fragile, as might be the friendship between a human being and a bird. The distance between us is at least as wide as that between two species.

At one moment when he was thinking about writing his life, Stendhal reflected that, supposing there is another world, he would certainly go and see Montesquieu and ask him: Had I real talent as a writer?

Quite certainly he would do nothing of the sort, he knew perfectly well that he had a unique talent and what it was. I, on the other hand, who am not even remotely interested in placing myself, would dearly like to ask some female writer I respect what mental wear and tear, short of the death or illness of the human being nearest to her, was able to distract her except momently from the book she happened to be writing. The months after I came back from Stockholm were beyond words racked and torn by anxieties, but I got *The Black Laurel* finished—on the 12th of April 1947, a year and a half after starting to write it, many years after I caught sight of it for the first time.

The last chapter was written in North Wales, in the hotel where I had lived for a few months during the war. Towards the end I was working on it at night. I wrote the last sentence about one in the morning, slept for a few hours, and woke early, to a soft warm cloudy day. Lying in bed in a narrow room, its window facing the valley and, across a trout stream, the hill, I heard the first cuckoo. It is a sound that lays the heart open, disturbing in their sleep the remote past, youth, childhood, all that it is dangerous to remember.

The child moved in bed in the next room, and I went in. Wide awake, he looked at me with bright dark eyes, lively with intelligence and mischief. Far too intelligent and articulate for his age— five years—he was what the old women call a very noticing child; he noticed with his senses as well as his mind, everything set them instantly alight, a bus ride to Portmadoc, a line of nonsense verse, *Façade* played on the gramophone; he was ceaselessly active, impatient, but never bored. When he was younger, not three, his fits of rage had disturbed me until I realized that what started them was only a lack of words, he raged because he could not explain himself. I was more disturbed by a completely silent agony of grief over a broken toy. To be capable, at that age, of such despair . . .

At this time he reminded me a little of the central figure in Maurice Baring's finest novel, *C*, and since it was one of his initials, I thought of him as C.

I helped him to dress, and he came into my room and fingered the manuscript on the table.

'Is it finished?'

'Yes. I'm going to send it to the publisher.'

'Will he like it?'

'I hope so.'

'Never mind if he doesn't, we'll soon write another, I'll help you.' His eyes sparkled. 'I wrote a book once. Do you remember?'

'You began one,' I said.

'No, no, it was finished.'

I turned up in a notebook, and showed him, the half sheet of paper on which I had scribbled his 'book' at the time, a year earlier. (He had come into my room waving a scrap of paper covered closely with pencil strokes. 'Now just you stop working and listen to this. I've written a book and this is the first chapter.' A lively mime of reading the strokes. 'Once there was an aeroplane and it landed in a field, and there were wild bulls. The ambassador said——' I interrupted him. 'Who was this ambassador?'—'He was in the aeroplane. So they killed the bulls and they roasted them——'—'Who killed them?'—'The ambassador did and the other people. And what they couldn't eat themselves they gave to the farmer's wife.' He went off into a peal of laughter. 'Do you like it?')

I read it over to him. 'You see? It's only one chapter.'

'It's quite long enough.' He looked at me through his lashes. 'Probably yours is too long.'

'Very probably.'

'Never mind that, either,' he said gaily. 'We have plenty of time. How old will you be when I'm a hundred?'

'Dead a long time.'

'How I shall miss you,' he said under his breath, 'my *best* grandmother.' Smiling, he added, 'I forget about you when I'm at home, that makes me very melancholy.'

'What you've forgotten can't make you melancholy,' I said.

He laughed. 'Oh, yes, it can! Suppose you forgot where you lived. You would be melancholy in all the streets, until you came to the place.'

Delighted to have silenced me, he rolled under the bed, and came out on the other side, growling.

The Black Laurel is a very good novel, one of the few really good and sound books I have written. Its two central characters, David Renn and William Gary, came from *The Mirror in Darkness* series: when I dropped it in 1935, they refused stubbornly to leave my mind. I discarded a dozen narratives until, in one of the fragments I was tearing up, notes about the tragi-comic life of an imagined obscure German-Jewish refugee, I stumbled over the theme that bound together Renn, Gary, and a score of men and women, English, German, Czech, Polish—one of the oldest and darkest themes in the world, the problem of justice versus expedience. The action had to unfold where the problem itself had been opened to the quick, in Berlin and Eastern Europe, but it is neither gloomy nor political: there was room for the absurd and for gaiety and motiveless kindness as well as for cruelty, violence, ambition, failure, death. In spite of the circumstances in which, much of the time, it was written, I wrote it with the sort of confidence and humility which comes of writing about what you really know and care about intensely.

'If you think that what you have written is good, it is certainly very bad.'

This is a terribly silly axiom. No writer, unless he is very young, very green, or a hopeless amateur, fails to know the difference between a book which is competent, worth reading once, and another which has a germ of life. He knows it by the pricking of his writer's thumbs.

Published in 1948, *The Black Laurel* was all but done to death in England—the review in *The Times Literary Supplement* was a curiously cold assassination. With one exception, even the few kindly notices were stupid.

I do not know why I was not more dejected or anxious about the future. For a time I felt isolated—the isolation of being damned or praised for a novel which was not the one I had written. But, strangely, not much cast down, and not afraid. You had to write this book, I told myself; you enjoyed writing it, and it is just possible that in the year 2048 a reader will come on the one remaining copy and say: So this is what it was like to be living in Europe in 1945.

One of my least scrupulous critics, finding himself at my elbow in an over-crowded room, said, 'It would have given me so much pleasure to say nice things about your book.'

'I'm sure it would,' I said warmly.

'Yes.' He passed a handkerchief over his forehead. 'To be unkind hurts me. I'm unhappy for hours after I've written a bad notice.'

A gap opening in the crowd, he bolted through it before I could beg him, for his own sake, to take up a less self-mortifying profession.

Chapter 4

About this time I went into the black market for the first and only time in my life. Not many people in England knew that one existed. It happened because Paul Tabori was asking writers to send clothes to writers in Hungary. Since I knew no Hungarians except a man who was almost certainly dead, I asked him to give me a woman writer no one else wanted. The one he gave me was called Renée Erdos, I knew nothing about her except that Paul said she had been a good writer, a friend of the older Hungarian writers and artists, and was old, poor, sick. My troubles began when I got her measurements and a poor snapshot. She was not only very broad and heavy, but very tall: nothing I or any friend of mine had would come near fitting her, and I had no clothing coupons left. There was nothing for it but to buy coupons, and I did, from a Polish *emigré* who would have been astonished and derisive if he had known that my crime terrified me. When I handed them across the counter in exchange for out-size underclothes, it struck me suddenly that they might be forged. They were not.

Written in eccentric English, Renée Erdos's letters were a low voice out of the darkness and the past of Europe.

'. . . I am ill, my heart says to me: You were always a bad compagnon to me, now I have enough from you, I am tired and repose. The magnific shoes and clothes I received from you, and I reproached myself for making you so much trouble. But I did not think you would send me so splendid things. It is over my desire. I don't find words to thank you. Excuse me my writing, I can hardly move my hands. With the same post I send for you a small plaquette as remembrance of me when I must go away. Please behold it of my memory . . .'

The figure of an old woman living precariously in the misery of Budapest that winter was barely distinguishable in the shadowy multitude stretching back to the Trojan women and behind them into a darkness without a voice. She had been well-off . . . 'Oh, I am become a coward and a wheeping old woman, I can't wear my sort with dignity and resignation. I am full of rebellion and cannot find to join that new world round me. I have lost myself. When it was all in order and I lived at my house, when winter came I made always a journey vers Sud. In Italia or Sicily or to Grecia, to my beloved Dodekanesos and my adored Rhodos. I could not bear cold and I never wrote a book in winter. Is it not right that such an idle creature shall die of the cold and hunger in this epoch of existentialism? It is quite right, but not very easy. Not easy to be a *class-foreigner* (a new expression). My books are dead, and when my friends ask me why do you not write I am responding: I am not so full of vanity . . .'

She had two daughters, an invalid who lived with her, and another she called 'the talented little one', a doctor, for whom she was always afraid, since the young woman was a passionate communist—'and in those circles who is safe?' Her second husband, her junior by ten years, had left her to live with a peasant woman, and she was anxious to excuse him . . . 'he needs much a young woman who attends him, he has enough from the past of prince consort and now he is adored from her and that pleases him, I cannot be angry. He was here yesterday and told me he has married one day ago. He was sorrowful, I was obliged to console him and I did with tranquillity telling him: I hope she will be good for you and forget that you are old and she is young. But you must not forget it!'

Over the months her letters became more agitated and ambiguous.

I pored over them, straining to see through the muddy water. In my replies I tried to comfort her for what she had not complained of; I was groping in the dark to touch a hand I knew was there, needing to be taken and held, but I could not reach it. Then, in 1949, she stopped writing.

The silence lasted for thirteen months, and was ended by a letter posted on the 19th of April 1950, the handwriting almost illegible.

'My dear friend, I could not write to you for a long time—I am coming back from a pass where I walked between the abimes of death and madness. On the 8 February died my younger daughter Veronica in her 31th year with an unnatural death. I cannot tell you more about it. I am a little alive—I have yet another daughter, and my dearest friend Irene, and your mighty spirit is beside me. Renée.'

I never heard again. For some time I wrote short careful letters. In the end, partly out of fear for her, partly because this year was one of great personal trouble, I stopped, and let her slip back, poor woman-ghost, into the indifferent darkness.

Chapter 5

Zurich is as charming in its clean elegance as any city in the world. I would live there with pleasure. The old quarter, above the swiftly-running Limmat, is delicious, dignified and unassuming, like the last sober descendants of an aristocratic family, and the newer town is solidly discreet and makes no demands.

I saw it for the first time in June 1947 when I went to the second post-war Congress of P.E.N. This time there were Germans other than refugees. They had come to ask leave to refound the German

Centre, dissolved in 1934 at Dubrovnik, after the Burning of the Books, against which the Centre had not wanted or not dared to protest.

In the heat of an abnormally hot summer, the delegates of the once occupied countries lost their tempers, not so much with the Germans as with the lukewarm English, who felt that since sooner or later we should have to accept the German writers we might as well make a coldly polite gesture now, when they were still meek. It mattered very little to me whether or not they were treated generously at this moment. Rationally, I believed that they ought to be scrutinized and admitted. So far as my instincts were concerned they could wait on the doorstep for another year or two. I did not feel kindly towards them; their chief spokesman, Ernst Wiechert, who had spent a short time in a concentration camp before the war, annoyed me by his emotional speeches. Berthold Brecht, leaning against a wall, his thin lips tightly shut, was equally exasperated.

It cost me an effort to argue against the French. True, they were our friends in a strictly impersonal sense, and tolerated us only when they thought it discreet or useful. Their arrogant certainty (an illusion) that they alone possess what the Master called *la lo-gique*, and their distrust of the English, are an old habit. The ghost of 'perfide Albion' starts up behind our most innocent gestures. Nothing can be done about this. It is visceral. But I was unhappy. I recovered my equanimity when a Belgian writer, sweat pouring down his neck, attacked me with a virulence I listened to with the greatest pleasure, since he could not know that Hermon and I were holding our tongues about the letters we had been sent by two of his absent countrymen, denouncing him as a collaborator, with supporting evidence.

There was a second pleasant moment when Thomas Mann came to the microphone and made an impassioned speech on behalf of the handful of Germans who were being offered to us as pure in heart and soul. In a moved voice he said, 'I am ready to put my hand in the fire for these men.'

Immediately behind me, one of our German exiles muttered, 'If there is a fire, you can be sure that Thomas Mann's hand will be a thousand miles from it.'

From where I was sitting I had Mann and the French writer Vercors in profile, one appearing over the other's shoulder, the German heavy, square-shouldered, stiff, the other slender and nervously energetic. It is never going to be possible to reconcile them, I thought. And if they do come to terms, they will probably turn on us together . . .

A Swiss industrialist—he was also one of the directors of a bank with its own international intelligence service—invited me to lunch. Over a superb meal in a panelled room looking over the flying Limmat, he began by giving me a lecture on Russia.

'In London,' he said, 'it is not clearly understood that although Soviet industry and the army would be satisfied with a good strategic position, Stalin himself is set on world communism, and distrusts both the industrialists and the soldiers as the cadres of a new *haute bourgeoisie*. If he lives, expect terrible purges in both, as well as a cruelly intensified dictatorship in Poland and Czechoslovakia. The information we get here is fuller and sounder than anywhere in Europe. In New York, of course, they understand nothing, even their bankers are sentimentalists.'

'Sentimental?' I said.

'I mean that they can be swayed, in financial affairs, by emotion.'

'Surely the English, too——?'

'Oh, no, no. You are experienced and reasonable.' He went on in a very friendly voice, 'Such a pity that England is so far on its way to becoming a third-rate power. Even without the second war it would have been inevitable—in a much longer time. As it is . . .' He smiled gently. 'We shall take your place in world affairs, we shall export our brains to every country.'

I hoped he was premature, or a little drunk—I remembered the unintended pathos of the elderly Swiss lady, a warm-hearted very cultivated woman, who said to me about her countrymen, 'They become a little merry when drunk.' But, no, he was sober.

Moreover, there was nothing insolent or unpleasant about his self-confidence. It was purely a question of arithmetic, almost a moral question, in which neither sentiment nor effrontery had any place.

On our last evening, at the closing banquet, one of our exiles, an Austrian, came up to me. He was stammering with exasperation.

'There were only Swiss at my table. I *hate* the Swiss. I hate them because they're not real, they have no reality, no real sufferings, no real thoughts. They're *outside* history, they look on, they're sterile, they reproduce themselves in precision instruments and bank loans.

And they are so pleased with themselves, and tidy and comfortable—
if they'd been in a war they wouldn't be so filthily comfortable. And
they're not even ashamed of it!'

'Why should they be?'

'Even the Swedes are.'

'Only in the evening,' I said, 'only after a very good dinner . . . I
like the Swiss, and I find their freedom from guilt restful. And their
confidence and self-satisfaction and cleanness. I should hate anything to happen to this country to spoil it. For heaven's sake, let's
have one peaceful solid comfortable people in the middle of Europe,
if only as an example to the rest of us.'

He was disgusted with me, and went off. It had been a fine dinner,
and the Swiss had put gifts beside our plates, and were now going
round offering us more of their admirable light wine, not a headache
in a barrel.

I caught sight of Edwin Muir. Like the rest of us, he was pleasantly a little drunk, and looked extraordinarily young and sweet-
natured—a bemused young angel. And happy—as I was myself.

The day after I got home I began a novel on a double theme, the
struggles of an old writer to retrieve the memoirs he had sold unwisely, and the effects, whatever these might turn out to be, on a
younger man, of running away from danger. I worked on it for as
long as three months, and wrote several chapters, with a growing
sense that it was no good. It was on two levels of reality, and one of
them, the story of the old writer, was faked—that is, I was exploiting,
not re-living, the unhappy intrigues round Chateaubriand's memoirs
—and the other, the deeper theme, was too intangible to be told in
this way.

After a sleepless night, I made myself destroy the manuscript on
the 23rd of September.

That was the day I heard from the young Polish woman in Warsaw
who had translated *The Other Side* that it had earned fifty thousand
zlotys. Without having the faintest idea what the money was worth,
I asked her to give it to the fund opened in Warsaw for rebuilding
the city. A month later the President of the city sent me a handsome
certificate made out to Pani Margaret Storm Jameson.

'When the communists take us over,' a friend said, 'you will be
spared, when the rest of us are lined up and shot.'

I began again, a much less ambitious story about people who run away from their moment and place. I ought to have waited and meditated, but, as always, I needed money.

To avoid boredom, I wrote it in the form of a play.

This summer was like the summer of 1940, week after week of a hot sun, splendid cloudless skies, the trees heavy with fruit, no rain, and wide clear warm nights. And, as in 1940, we were in a poor way, an economic crisis, strikes, a dollar famine, and the threat that we might even run short of food. But, this time, there was no exhilaration, only a feeling of bewilderment and the demoralizing sense that no one knew what to do, least of all the government.

I had nearer, sharper griefs. Used to running madly between high and low water, I could pour out money and promises, but I could not come between a high-spirited child and the weight of violent unhappiness and resentments lived under his eyes. Nor take lightly the loss of his off-hand affection and trust.

I had moments of pure happiness. The first of these came when my son wrote about the small yacht I had helped him to buy. He was living in it, alone, between flights to South America or Singapore or Africa, very pleased with it, and contented. I felt all the gaiety, the absurd pride that used to fill me, a young woman, when I had given a child something he coveted and I could not afford.

After his second marriage, when I saw him recovering what he had almost lost, confidence, youth, gaiety, I felt happiness of another sort, a divine lightness of heart, the assurance that now nothing I did or failed to do for him mattered at all. He had everything he needed for a lifetime.

I should like to think that the rather gaunt nobility of the head Anna Mahler, daughter of Gustav Mahler and the formidable Alma, made of me in January 1948 is a likeness. But since she left out both the jeering northerner and the clown, I don't dare.

I finished *The Moment of Truth*, in its form as a three-act play, on the 24th of February 1948, and began to turn it into a nouvelle. This was finished on Easter Sunday, and in the evening we drank the last of six bottles of Tokayer Szamorodner 1901, bought in Vienna in 1930 from Franz Josef's cellars below the Hofburg. It was stronger than its taste of raisins suggested. On the wireless someone was reading from Gibbon a passage about the dilemma of early Christians in a pagan empire, unable, because of the reverence shown to false gods, to share in the ordinary ceremonies of everyday life, funerals, weddings, games. Through a light fog of Tokay I puzzled over the trouble human beings—*the only animal who knows he is to die*—give themselves to avoid simple pleasures. Old Captain James, methodically eating his Christmas cake during a typhoon, to save it from being wasted if his ship foundered, seems to me the model of a wise civilized self-respecting man.

This same Captain James was remembered in Whitby in my childhood for the moment when his modest elderly wife, standing on the wharf to watch him move his ship out of dock, tripped and fell. Leaning from the bridge, he shouted, 'H'Ann, H'Ann, if tha's hurt thi bottom, say so, and I'll put t'ship back.'

What a pity that when I am dead no one will remember him.

Chapter 6

Early that year, Guy was offered the chance to change places with a professor of Pittsburgh University for a year. At first pleased and excited, we began to be plagued by doubts. To abandon his pupils, set aside the book he was working on—a book, not a novel—was it worth it? The salary offered was miserable, and with the Treasury forbidding me to spend my dollars, we should be pinched, and—after all—why waste time on America with more than half France still to be visited?

With a book just finished, I was riding light, and seemed, even to myself, to be disinterested. On the one hand, I should see my middle sister, whom I had not seen since she emigrated to New York at the end of the war, and my young sister's two children, living with their father and his second wife, in Kansas City: on the other I had half-formed fears that I might be too slow-witted for America:

not fear of anything I could grasp, but of the amorphous monster that, when I said *America*, I saw.

'Very well,' Guy said at last, 'we'll refuse.'

Without warning, I was invaded by a storm of disappointment and grief. It rushed on me from some dark recess, nothing to do with my rational mind or my will. Until this instant, I had had no idea how savagely I wanted to go.

'We should be saved a great deal of trouble if you took a little more care to know your own mind.'

No doubt, no doubt.

I agreed readily to teach what the professor of English in Pittsburgh called Creative Writing. I took it to be an inflated term for English Literature, and felt sure I could rake together enough for a year's lectures. Had I known the goose chase I was in for, I should still have agreed, but less lightheartedly.

The evening before we left Ilkley I turned the wireless, casually, to a programme called: Women in Green: the informal story of the Women's Voluntary Service, told by W.V.S. members. It turned out to be W.V.S. women talking about their work during the war: one of them began a list of those killed in what had seemed safe jobs— three or four names, then, preceded by the split second of foreknowing, my young sister's: *Dorothy Pateman, killed while on duty at the People's Pantry in Reading.*

An absurd thought jumped into my mind: How pleased she would be if she had heard it . . . She had very little vanity. Hearing her name on the wireless, she would have laughed, pretending to mock herself, but with a secret warmth at her young heart.

On the day we sailed (the 27th of July), the papers were bristling with some crisis or other—Stalin, I suppose—and I reflected that we might soon be back. I have no wish to see a war through anywhere but in England.

Looking back at a year when every sensation, from happiness to moments of atrocious boredom, was sharpened to a pitch seldom reached in England, I find it difficult to say why this was so, why events, ordinary in themselves, carried a charge of excitement which was cut off, abruptly, when we left America. There is something exhilarating and reckless in American everyday life which, in England, rises to the surface only in time of danger, and only then if the danger is actual, as during the months of air-raids. The unmanageable size of America—a continent pretending to be a country—must have something to do with it, or the alarming violence of the climate.

This skulking violence seems to be reflected in the minds themselves of Americans: more than once, at innocent private gatherings, the sense of a repressed violence in the handful of people in the room became as clear as a knife opened in the hand.

An ignorant spectator, I caught myself wondering whether this pervasive violence, material and moral, was not part of an answer to the question: Why is it that, now, the big flawed novels—as well as the most crushingly bad, boring, hysterical—are being written in America while our own serious writers content themselves with an inbred spruceness? No American novelist is so urbane as Mr Anthony Powell, so careful as Mr Angus Wilson to weight his phrases with the precisely controlled charge of meaning, well this side of enthusiasm or vehemence, or so redolent of camphor.

There are exceptions in England—one every ten or twenty years.

Our Dutch boat (I have never been able to shake off a prejudice rooted in me by that old sea-captain, William Storm Jameson: he believed unshakably that only the English and the Scandinavians can be trusted at sea: none of the others can build a sound ship or navigate one safely if by some chance it turns out to be seaworthy) arrived too late to dock, and we spent the night off Staten Island, a night without a breath of air, without stars, on one side a shadowy hump of land, on the other an unbroken rippling chain of lights. It was some time before—coming from a country where shortage of petrol had cut the use of cars to a blessed minimum—I realized that it was made up of headlights.

In the early morning a sky of white-hot metal dwarfed the buildings sitting back on their haunches behind the water-line.

There is a very short time, to be measured in days or hours, after one sets foot in a country or a city never before visited, when, if not the truth about it, *a* truth, and important, is thrown between one's teeth. That first taste of America was sharper than any since. It was the salt taste of power—power, wealth, energy, restlessness.

This country, I told myself, shocked, doesn't want to conquer the world, but it will submerge us by sheer weight and impetus. Unless we repair our sea-walls quickly, the wave is bound to sweep in. And . . . *je regrette l'Europe aux anciens parapets* . . . What's more, I thought, it is an alien country.

Upon my word, I had not expected to feel more of an alien here than I would feel in any small Czech village.

I stress this feeling of strangeness, of alienation, because, after a few weeks, overlaid by the friendliness, the astonishing warmth, of ninety-nine out of a hundred Americans, it withdrew. But it had existed; it is what I felt in the first moment, before instinct began to be adulterated by reason, emotion, memories.

No one, no European, who has not lived in America can imagine it—the awful sense of power and size is unimaginable. So is a curious emptiness, rather, an absence of meaning, which comes across the scene at moments, perhaps in a train crossing the Middle West, where for hour after hour the same field, the same town— called Warsaw or Troy or Macon—is repeated and repeated, an endless stuttering of the same unintelligible phrase.

Have the Russian steppes this non-human quality, this really appalling monotony? It would not be the only likeness between two peoples in whom everything, their natural spontaneity, inventiveness, distaste for compromise, shrewdness in bargaining, all the way to a certain childish pleasure in destruction, seems designed to make them friends for life. Let us hope for it. And that they will be content to let the rest of us, harmless dwarfs, run about freely between their legs.

I spent ten days in New York, long enough to blur but not erase that first image. I came from a country still enduring, and with that surly pleasure the English take in being uncomfortable, almost cherishing scarcity of everything. But even before the war no London shop gave this impression of bottomless wealth, wealth poured out in a torrent, given off by Fifth Avenue. That and the waste—the first time I saw a waiter scooping butter off the edge of a plate to throw it away I exclaimed in horror—would have been unbearable but for the friendliness.

In any European town or city, the inconceivable happiness I feel when I dawdle through it for the first time is given me by the place itself. I scarcely notice the people. So far as I am concerned, they are supernumeraries, actors employed by the municipality to give an air of realism or gaiety to a scene before the appearance of the principal characters—for me, the streets themselves, the café I am sitting in, the dusty square lined with plane-trees, the river. In New York, for the first time in my life I was in a place where the streets and cafés were nothing much and the people everything. I don't mean that New York is not impressive, handsome, at moments even beautiful. Only that it is infinitely less interesting, less real, than its inhabitants.

In the blinding heat, I hung about street-corners and shabby side-streets, only to catch the tones, harsh or warm, but always vibrant with undertones, of the voices. A narrow shop off Sixth, as hot as an oven, crammed with cheap untrimmed hats. The elderly shapeless woman tried on her twentieth. 'You know what,' the exhausted assistant told her, 'that does something for you. Me, I'd push it back, but you do as you please.' What can it possibly matter to her whether this fat old woman gets a hat that suits her or not? In a London shop, no one would take the faintest trouble with her. The vivacity, the incredible energy, of ordinary New Yorkers, and their lack of even the most harmless forms of vanity, left me speechless with pleasure.

One morning I got into a cab driven by an unshaven bandit with a magnificent Greek name. A fag-end between his blackened lips, he told me,

'Listen. I been up with my wife till *four*. She's in *hospital*, with a baby, and her doctor told me: Bring her a few flowers. For a bouquet I need *money*, I've been driving round since four and I haven't made it yet.' The pantomime, both hands off the wheel, head turned over his shoulder, eyes rolling, paralysed me. 'She's English—like yourself, doesn't drink, doesn't smoke, and when I come home she brings me my slippers in the English way.'

I admired his invention, but I did not give him money for flowers. Not that I have serious objections to a liar, but he was too like the luckless loose-minded Elpenor.

New York is not as I had imagined it. I expected something harsh and a little intimidating, not to say exaggerated. It is exaggerated, yes, but I had not been told that it is gay, with an exciting delicacy in the outlines of buildings otherwise remarkable only for their height.

On second thoughts, exaggeration is not the right word for a touch of excess—in elegance and squalor. The saturated squalor of Harlem is excessive, the fantastic beauty of a line of lighted sky-scrapers at night is excessive, and not easy to describe, since the more overwhelming a sight the less there is to say about it. In the same way, the fashionable restaurants—all that a good Paris restaurant still is, discreet in their luxury, the food admirable—at some point exceed their model. The vice of perfection, perhaps? When everything has had to be created from scratch, and with that violent continent at your elbow, how can you be certain that enough is enough?

I believe that this subtle excess creates the feeling of unreality I had even at high noon, when the light picked out every crack, every stone, every angle in the great buildings. And had again and again— on the edge of a forest in Pennsylvania, flying between Chicago and Dallas, in Connecticut driving for hours under autumn trees, stunned by so many splendid monotonous miles.

And—no getting away from it—the country is oppressively large. In a war—that is, in the comparatively human wars we have lived through so far—an English or a French conscript is able to tell himself that he is fighting to keep inviolate something small enough to hold in a corner of his skull, the slope of an absurdly narrow field, an ugly village street, even, my God, the whole of England as a seagull might see it, crossing the country from the North Sea to the Channel. But how do you fit a continent into your skull?

On the credit side, a continent cannot be spoiled as atrociously as England is already spoiled, its high-hedged lanes flattened into motor roads, its trees and rich fields obliterated by mile on mile of faceless houses. Impossible to turn the coast line of America into a middle-class slum like the one that stretches from Kent to Dorset and beyond. There will always in America be untouched areas— anything but cosy or charming, but unmauled. With the worst will in the world you cannot—except with thermo-nuclear bombs— murder a continent.

Late one afternoon, I was in the Park Avenue apartment of my friends, Toni and Gustav Stolper. After they left Berlin in 1933, I had seen them once, in London, and I was prepared to find that America had changed them. I should have known better.

How easy to sit silent in this room, and allow a still living past to grow without shock into the present. The habit of reasoning without emotion, the instinctive tolerance, the politeness in debate, the lack of emphasis, the completely natural sophistication of a highly-cultivated and intellectually alert Austrian-Jewish household, closed round me. This room was Europe. I was no longer an outsider, an alien.

Another guest, a German, who had been back to his country, was talking about it. '. . . I knew before I went that it would be impossible to live there again, among people who allowed the gas chambers. But—I am forced to say this—I believe that a great many people did not know about them, at the time.'

'You believe that?'

He smiled. 'Let's put it that I believe that the one talent even stupid men and women have consummately is for avoiding unpleasant knowledge. They did not—all—know . . . I found—what shall I say?—no repentance. Sullenness, apathy. If souls can be indifferent, theirs are indifferent.'

Toni Stolper's voice, slow, clear. 'The only important thing is to remember how the murders came about, the mistakes, the fears, the dishonesty.'

When I came out into Park Avenue the daylight was going. This above any other is the moment and the place to look at New York. A violet haze fills the distance, buildings lose their substance and lighted windows their depths; the city becomes a living body, and the people for a few minutes unimportant.

I am told that Park Avenue has been rebuilt and vulgarized (like too much of London). A pity. But New York does not depend for its charm on its buildings, as Paris or Prague or Vienna depend. It exists by its rich physical life, its superb energy.

No doubt during my ten days I saw too much and formed too many rash opinions. Happiness makes me rash. But at the same time I could not understand why my sister preferred to live here—working hard at a dull ill-paid job—rather than come home. I understood it confusedly when I reflected that New York is the farthest she could get from Whitby. When I think of our birthplace, and the birthplace of our hard-minded sharp-tongued ancestors, it is with regret, with love for something irretrievably spoiled and lost. For her it is a memory of efforts to escape. She would go back there only as a last resort. That much I understand.

On the same basis, I understand our famous exiles—that they wanted to evade England or Europe. I cannot conceive any other reason why an English writer should choose to live in America.

I respect my sister's courage—and in a colder, the coldest possible sense, theirs. I myself would not have the courage to become an expatriate; I should have to be forced into exile. And America demands a singleness of purpose I lack. A writer, without money of my own, I should have to keep steadily in mind that the most important thing is to succeed and be seen succeeding, seen living with what my grandmother called an elegant sufficiency. I like elegance, I should enjoy living a polite much-travelled life, but that is not the only thing I want—and it is only by wanting nothing else so much that one becomes, by one's own efforts, rich.

In France, an ambitious writer devotes to becoming an academician as much energy and talent as would make him a saint if he were inclined that way. In America, after one very successful book, he lives in terror of failing. We English writers have both diseases, vanity and ambition, but in a milder, almost benign form.

The touch of excess in America, like the excesses of Elizabethan England, may at any moment throw up a great writer as well as giving lesser ones their energy.

The train journey from New York to Kansas City gave me my first taste of the dread this continent can start in a foreigner—and for all I know in Americans. It is the sensation one has in certain nightmares, that something, some pressure, both inside and outside the mind, is increasing at hideous speed, dangerous and all but unbearable. Hour after hour, the same cornfield running out of sight to the horizon, the same white clapboard houses and wide streets lined with trees. I suppose that at night, when you can hear the trees, these towns must be friendly, like a mountain hut when darkness hides the abyss on all sides of it.

In the early morning—it might have been eight o'clock, but the way time shifts about in America confused me—the train stopped at Elkhart, a small town of frame houses, like all the others. In large letters on a shop window I read: Mothers of World War 2. Unit No 9 —and made a note of it for the benefit of Giraudoux in the underworld.

(*Je ne veux pas mourir avant que les mères dont les fils ont étés tués soient toutes mortes: ce jour-là un grand pas sera fait vers le bonheur du monde*— Siegfried et le Limousin.)

We reached Kansas City at night. The family was there to meet us, my brother-in-law, his second wife, my sister's two children. The boy Nicholas was as I remembered him when they left England in 1940, the spit image of his father, but my first glance at Judy sent a shock of blood to my heart. At two, she had been any infant of my family: now she was at once my sister as a child and not her: her eyes, a greenish-grey in place of the cold pale blue of her young mother's, were shaped like wide short almonds, and her face, in every line my sister's, was curiously flattened over the cheekbones as if a hand had been pressed down on them: her neck and the line of her jaw were fuller than Dorothy's.

I took care not to show any feeling except pleasure. My brother-in-law had, I knew, been afraid that I should talk about Dorothy and perhaps start a flaw in the intimacy between both children and their kind warm loyal Texan stepmother. I was never tempted. They were American children, both of them, even the little girl.

The heat was brutal. In the streets the sunlight seared my eyelids as though they were being sand-papered. The walls, the pavements, sent out waves of heat from an open furnace. I imagined that now I knew the worst about the centre of America. This was an illusion. We had not yet seen the Ozarks.

In the kindness of his heart my brother-in-law had arranged for me to have the children to myself for two weeks, in a place in Missouri. It turned out to be a clutter of wooden houses beside a lake, miles of warm muddy lifeless water surrounded by trees and ugly hills. The hotel, thrown together out of some dark timber, consisted of a dining-room—the food fell between indifferent and terrible—a second vast room with pin-tables and a juke-box grinding out tunes of revolting sentimentality, and a great many separate cabins, each with its hard narrow bed and shower. The whole village stank of petrol, rancid fat, and a heat that clung like oil in the nostrils and round the eyelids. It was not a savage place, it was the quintessence of barbarism, graceless, tawdry, repellent, without a redeeming touch.

Yes, one. Wait.

We were no more aliens here than a New Yorker or a Bostonian would have been. The children rode the ponies I hired for them, and swam in the horrible dead lake. I kept the promise I had made, not to speak to them about their own mother, but I asked one or two not entirely innocent questions, trying deviously to find out whether one or other of them had kept an image of her, even indistinct.

'Where,' I asked Judy, 'did you get your doll's house and its pretty furniture?'

Looking down, she said absently, 'I don't know. For Christmas, I think.'

I saw my young sister's short deft fingers working on curtains for its windows and covers for the tiny chairs and beds she meant to surprise the child with when at the end of the war the children came home.

My poor girl, I thought, now you are really dead.

One day Guy complained of pain in his left ear. During the night, the pain became so severe that he did not sleep, and in the morning he was clearly very ill. In an agony of remorse—it was I who had dragged him to America to die of a mastoid in this uncouth hell—I began planning to fly him to New York. We asked if the village had a doctor. Yes—one. The door of his small comfortless shack, like every other, was ajar; we knocked, a voice said violently, 'Come in, folks,' and there he was in shirt-sleeves, standing in the middle of the room sewing a fly-button on his cotton trousers. While we stood waiting for him to finish, my heart sank and sank. I expected him to apply leeches to the ear, now insupportably painful.

Talking amiably, he peered at it and said, 'Well, I'll fill you up with penicillin.' He opened a small corner cupboard: the upper shelf held a few instruments and drugs, the lower only whiskey bottles. 'Ever had penicillin?'

'No.'

'Good. Virgin soil.'

'We'll give it until morning,' I said when we were walking away. 'If it's no better, we leave.'

In the morning, the ear was noticeably less inflamed. During the next few days Guy had heaven knows how much penicillin pumped into him with the same off-hand energy, and although he had to be doctored in Pittsburgh—with all the apparatus of sterilized tools and X-rays—this genial brigand had saved him.

There may be village doctors in England willing to act with as much lighthearted boldness, but I doubt it.

For hours during the interminable bus journey to Kansas we drove through a Judgement Day thunder-storm, the whole night sky in eruption: at one instant I saw at a great distance a hawk suspended against a hill the colour of steel, pinned there by the flash. We reached Kansas City about midnight and left again four hours later. Some time that day we spent several hours in St Louis, where in the merciless heat we could do nothing but sit in a hotel watching respectable middle-aged gentlemen playing the pin-tables as if their lives depended on it.

The next day we reached Pittsburgh. I was exhausted, and when I set eyes on the apartment the university had arranged for us to rent —on the eighth floor of a large block, two and a half rooms, shabby, airless, a grey film of dust on everything—I fell into one of the pits of rage and misery, bottomless and black as hell, scattered through my life. I can make shift to deal with a major misfortune; every now and then a minor one puts me out of my mind, blind and deaf to reason. The reporters arrived from the Pittsburgh Press, and I had to smooth my face to talk to them.

For days, locked inside my ridiculous despair, I was certain that the place was unendurable. The real root of my spleen was that I realized I had let myself in for something I was too stupid to manage. The thought of the fool I was going to make of myself, trying to teach anyone to write, I who begin each book in fear and trembling, sank me. Vanity?—yes. But rage, too, that—not for the first time— I had made a blunder. To spend nine months here, in these sordid rooms, doing badly what no person in his senses would even try to do—no, no, it was impossible.

Never make promises, my grandfather used to say drily. Implying: You may have to keep them.

My boredom and despair were atrocious and shameful. Pittsburgh is a splendid city. Built, like Rome, on hills, with two magnificent rivers, the Monongahela—five liquid syllables—and the Allegheny, meeting in the city to become the Ohio, it has a strange, awful, and at times overwhelming beauty. At night, looking down on the glittering bridges of the Monongahela from the heights at the back, it was Budapest, but the wide valley of the river, mile after mile after mile of steel mills, filling the dusk with bronze smoke, turning it brighter than noon in the minutes when a Bessemer converter flamed to heaven, was one of the faces, an inhuman one, of power.

The power hub of the world, I thought coldly: and they can keep it.

And it was another America. Another splendid fragment of a country which does not exist. Not as a country.

Even Americans had made derisive comments when I said I was going to Pittsburgh, and even in my first unreason I knew they were wrong; it is one of the finest cities in the world, the fable of the present as the Parthenon was the fable of Greece.

Also it is, or was in 1948, the city which has not yet completely resolved—dissolved—its European elements. It has more 'nations' than mediæval Paris. This—I once heard it called *this infection of Europe*—may be a source of its magnificent energy. Czechs, Poles, Hungarians, Syrians, Greeks, Jugoslavs, heaven knows what more, formed resistant knots in the pattern. By now this rich pattern may be fading, but in my day there were students in the university who, at home, never heard a word of English.

And there were Irish. The once or twice in America when I met hostility, it came from that quarter. One day as I left a street-car after listening to the account of England, pitched to be heard the length of the car, that an Irishman was giving his friend, I turned and said loudly, 'I hope none of you believes a word he says. It is all lies and nonsense.'

Trembling with anger, I hurried off before he could deal with me. I have a horror of scenes, and he had the face of a stoat and a complacent old woman.

There were a great many Catholics, but the city's ruling caste was Presbyterian, and very much in earnest. The atmosphere was Victorian, of the simplest and finest period, and so familiar—I was brought up in the shadow of that tradition living on·in a small northern English port—that I scarcely noticed it until the wife of a banker who had moved to Pittsburgh from New York spoke to me about it. She found the church-going habits of her new friends dowdy and ridiculous.

'How many better ways do you know of mitigating the inhuman size of this country?' I asked her.

'What do you mean?'

'If I were you I wouldn't pull down a single absurd out-of-date stockade. You may need them.'

'You're joking, of course.'

'No, I assure you. This country isn't humanized yet.'

One of Guy's graduate students, married, lived twenty or thirty miles out of Pittsburgh in a house he had built himself out of his own timber on the edge of a great forest above the valley of the Allegheny. We had spent two nights there, surrounded by huge lion-coloured trees. At night deer came out of the forest into the field round the house. It was superb country—I am working the adjective to death, but it would be affected not to use it—and its vast emptiness appalled me. A few human beings had made no mark on it at all. And what lay close to the surface was neither gentle nor, humanly speaking, manageable.

Or is it only eyes used to the tiny intimacies of English woods and pastures that find it alarming?

The university in Pittsburgh is like no other I have seen. Imagine the masons of a Gothic cathedral deciding to do without statues and, to make amends, elongating the tower to an enormous height. There are I forget how many floors—forty, forty-two? It ought to be absurd, as absurd as the monolithic limestone columns of the Mellon Institute near by, and is in fact very impressive, at night even charming. To look down into the great hall called the Commons Room when it is filled with students sitting about reading, arguing, drinking coffee, is to be reminded—distantly, but without any sense of incongruity—of a mediæval refectory or chapter-house.

I faced my own students for the first time in a lecture-room on one of the upper floors. They sat on tiered benches and looked at me with polite curiosity: four 'veterans'—the eldest twenty-seven, the youngest (he must have been drafted at the end of the war) about eighteen—two very young girls, and three women of my own age, friends of the Chancellor.

Even if I had had anything to say, I could not have handled them as a class. In an agony of dismay, scarcely able to fit one idea to another, I said that if no one had an objection I would give each of them a tutoring hour every week; they could choose their own times, and fetch me anything they were working on. In the meantime, had anyone a question to ask?

After a silence, one of the ladies, a warmly beautiful creature, asked me if I had read *The Naked and the Dead*. No, I said, but if she thought I ought to read it, I would, at once.

'What I think,' she retorted, 'is that the habit of using obscene words in these war novels is unnecessary and inexcusable, and I hope you agree with me.'

Disconcerted, I did not give myself time to reflect. 'Well, you know, war is rather a bloody business,' I said.

The veteran in the front row looked at me with a blank face. Weeks later, I heard that he had enlivened a number of social gatherings with his mimicry of my, as it struck him, genteel English voice saying: 'War, you know, is rather a bloody business.' By this time, he and I were close friends.

I am an intolerant disbeliever in the practice of teaching Creative Writing (save the mark) in universities—or anywhere else. It is infinitely worse than useless. What can adolescents be taught about imaginative writing beyond a few tricks, of no value?

And why, in God's name, encourage them to think of becoming writers at all? It is a profession which should be risked only by the few for whom not to write would be physical or mental torment. Or only with the backing of another profession, or a private income.

With horror I discovered that every year an emissary from one of the New York publishing houses visited the university in search of 'talent'. The individuals who make a living by encouraging young women to go on the streets do less harm.

I don't think I harmed my students, since I did nothing for them —except read through and argue about the short stories, essays, chapters of a novel, they were writing to please themselves or a genuine professor of writing. I never had time to find out how these last went about their grisly business. The most intelligent of my veterans made a mock of what he was being taught, but for one wary soul there must—it is an enormous industry—be thousands of young men and women wasting three or four years learning nothing of moment. The few who go on to write seriously can only have learned what they had better forget quickly—if they are writers and not hacks or charlatans.

For my so-called tutoring, I was given a room, on the third floor, which had been fitted up as an early American kitchen, with small leaded windows, low ceiling, beams, a vast open fireplace in which an iron pan swung from a hook over fake logs; at the touch of a switch smoke rose from them, and there were bellows, cooking ladles, bunches of Indian corn, real, a besom, a wooden scrubbing-board, a plastic candle stuck in the neck of a bottle and dripping plastic tallow, old lanterns round the electric light bulbs, a sampler, a rocking-chair, an old settle with genuine worm-holes, and a single short book-shelf. With my student of the hour I sat at a long table, he on a narrow backless bench, I on a chair so low I had to sit on the only two books in the room. There was also a narrow panel concealing stairs to the secret room used to hide from Indians: sometimes during a tutoring hour I was disturbed, not by Indians, by a conducted party of tourists.

I may have been lucky in my ex-soldiers, but I was never bored. Nor conscious of the gap between their age and mine, their attitude to life and mine. There were moments when, glancing up as the door of the colonial kitchen opened, I should not have been startled to see any one of the young men my friends in 1914. These young Americans had a natural self-possession, a lack of pretentions, a liveliness, that made it easy for them to be friendly: it did not occur to them to think of themselves as *the young*, that ghastly invention of twentieth century psychology (or pathology): even the youngest was a self-sited individual, and felt no need to put me in my (obsolete) place.

This escape from diffidence and boredom (the mortal boredom that seizes me when I try loyally to read the novels of the young English generation) is, of all the pleasures of my American year, the most exhilarating, the one I miss.

I had a second appointment, in a woman's college, to teach fourteen girls of seventeen and eighteen: I fell back on tutoring hours here, too. This place fascinated me. Perhaps it resembled the senior form in an expensive English finishing school—I am no judge— but I doubt it: it had nothing of the gynaeceum. My pupils ranged from the children of the very rich, preparing themselves to talk entertainingly about Sartre and O'Neill, to the anxious hard-working daughter of a senior clerk. This child explained to me that she must, since she was in her last year, think about making money; she must 'write for a market', now, at once.

'But why?'

'Unless I begin to sell now I've failed!'

'At eighteen?'

Her blue eyes shifted a point. 'I see you don't understand. What does my age matter if I'm not getting a foothold? I shall have to be a secretary in some factory or other.'

'Well?'

'My parents will be disappointed. Besides, I *want* to write.'

No, that's not what you want, I thought. But her anxiety was so real, so without vanity or the wish to impress, that it impressed me. This, I told myself easily, is the trouble with America—such good people, and all of them worshippers of the bitch goddess . . .

I had been in America seven weeks, I had seen New York, Kansas City, the Ozarks, Pittsburgh—an infinitesimal fraction of the continent—but I knew what was wrong! God forgive me, in time I learned a little better.

Twenty-two tutoring hours a week, scripts to read and annotate, a certain amount of housework, a great deal of society, forced me to work as hard as ever in my life. The horrible apartment was cleaned for me, in a fashion, in twenty minutes, by a yellow-haired brass-throated German, a ferocious creature—it was like harbouring a wild animal. But she chose to be friendly.

'Ha-a-ahn!'—a rasping yell—'For you I wash up. Not for other women. For you. You *work.*'

I worked, yes, but not for myself. I had brought to Pittsburgh the bloodless ghost of a novel, at its centre one of those aristocratic radicals our society throws up as naturally as an oak develops galls. I had no time to consider it. Figures which clearly belonged to it stalked at the back of my skull, and if one of them had the imprudence to step forward I pushed it roughly back.

This, though I did not know it then, was one certain way of nourishing the book, probably the only certain way. How many clever novels of our day begin with a company parade of lively characters, confidently brushed in, who after a chapter or two turn out to be hollow, a series of half-seen impressions or a screen play of naïve sensations, and cease to exist. Naïve because their authors are so engrossed by the functions of human beings that they have forgotten that the heart and the other organs are not interesting as organs: what is interesting is the double activity, seen and unseen, fed by these nerves and cells.

It is the fault of the incontinence, the myopia, the frivolity, which drives us to turn out our novel a year like articulate robots, to be praised or damned by critics as unfit as ourselves to talk about novels.

If only I could begin again!

Some time during the autumn I spent a weekend in Connecticut.

Here, and later in Vermont and Massachusetts, I had for long moments a tantalizing sense of *déjà vu*. Was it nothing more than the reflection, in this handsome glass, of books read and re-read in childhood, so sharply remembered that I caught myself looking for the spider-flowers, johnny-jumpers and buttonwood trees of *Ellen Montgomery's Bookshelf*? (I have it still, loose from its spine, the brittle foxed leaves crumbling at the edges. Absurd to care what happens to it when I die! But I hope it will not be simply thrown out.)

All that can be said about a New England autumn has been said already, by writers with an interest in scenery. The scene is, in any event, indescribable. Only in dreams do such trees exist, a broad river running out of sight to the horizon, its ripples gold, black-bronze, scarlet, lunar yellow. The exquisite small towns, half-village, half-park, their white houses, white wooden churches, lawns of coarse shorn grass open to the street, have the same dream-like un-reality—no, that is not strictly accurate, it is not reality they lack; in some indefinable way, they give back a hollow sound, like an empty vase or the wings of a theatre. The vase, the body, is beautiful, still apparently intact, but the soul has dwindled to a thread. During the dream, a change has taken place. Or, perhaps, the dreamer is losing his hold on it, on the unrepeatable dream that was New England, with its harsh undertones, its strength, its toughness, its narrow-ness, its fortitude, its innocence—if there is such a thing in the world —its candour, its spring-like delicacy.

Probably I am wrong, deaf, like all foreigners, to words I did not learn in childhood.

I came back to Pittsburgh with reluctance—and found that I was in love with it. Even Americans have mocked my infatuation with this place. What, they say, Pittsburgh? You must be mad . . . And like all love-affairs, this one had little to do with merit. Not that the city is less than very handsome, with an air of space, of elbow-room for large gestures, born, possibly, of the nearness of virgin forest and the immense skies of the West. But I recall with love streets which have nothing to commend them except a view across the Monongahela to the labyrinth of lights covering the flank of a hill, below an iron sky; I remember the Point, the tongue of land where the two rivers flow into the Ohio, in my day a place of derelict rail-way lines and stunted bushes, its one obvious charm the small dark block-house built in 1754 by the English, captured by the French, recaptured by General Forbes; I remember the rivers in winter sun-light, the many bridges, the tracery of tall buildings, spectral factory chimneys in snow, the fantastic colours of smoke from the steel mills, plumes and drifting clouds of rust-red, tawny, green, grey-blue, white. I even think with affection of the amiable store where I spent two-thirds of my salary on sending packages of food to England.

What else? The very young negress in the street-car, slowly walking its full length, her back as straight as a rod, swaying a little, with the nonchalance of a wild creature, and chewing. She was wearing a grey coat and a high-crowned fur hat on her black hair, smooth with oil. There was something insolent, almost dangerous, in her vitality and feral movements, but also something candid, free from the corruption of society.

This was my Pittsburgh, a city like no other. It has perhaps vanished. No city now knows enough to leave well alone—think of the mutilation of London since the last war.

Stranger than anything else—for the only time in my life since I left Whitby (where I had been living for at least five hundred years, so that whether I chose to be or not I was *of the family*), I was a member of a community. It was not homogeneous, except in so far as it kept traces of the New England theocracy carried south and west by earlier generations. The fierce Calvinism—Calvin rather than Luther—of the theocrats had crumbled, but something of their evangelical habit of mind remained. Apart from this, and a half-conscious pride in belonging to a province—when provincial stands for a certain freedom of spirit, a taste for experiment, a spontaneity —which marked even Pittsburghers who had come to the city from New York, it was a community of interlocking worlds: directors of steel companies and banks, professors, musicians, a well-known judge, an editor, business men, lawyers, politicians, a writer or two, all of them citizens in a sense we have almost lost, taking an active part in the day-to-day life of their city, from its splendid orchestra to its hospitals and universities and institutes.

Why am I not a member of a community in England? Oh, a dozen reasons—the exigencies of a writer's life, which demands the greatest concentration possible or endurable; laziness; my inborn fear of committing myself to live with other people. But here, thousands of miles from England, not only had I forgotten my first awful sense of being an alien, but I was at home as I have rarely been in any place for the past thirty years.

Credit where credit is due. Only a boor, a heartless idiot, would have rejected a warmth as natural as the generosity with which it was offered.

I was happy to be living with fifteen or twenty intimate friends I had known only for a month, intelligent men and women, alert, un-affected, without the vanities and jealousies of a closed society; happy to be overworked, not a moment to think of writing. Perhaps, ironically enough, this was a reason for my happiness. For the first time for years I could push aside the idea of a novel without the guilty sense of wasting time. Except in name, I was no longer a writer. I was playing a role, yes, but the role suited me.

No doubt I should not have been happy in a small town, or in a purely academic society. And no doubt I should have reached a point when the uneasiness of not writing stifled the pleasure of living a continuously active gay life. I did not stay long enough for that.

The evenings I spent in the houses and apartments of married professors might give out echoes, broken syllables, of Berlin or some other European capital—oftenest a German syllable: the United States is littered with the grandchildren of Germans—but the final word was American, Pittsburgh-American, mark 1948. Not only did our temporary colleagues take endless trouble to be friendly, but not once did I come across the vanity which uses friendship for its own gratification. Vanity is the only human habit, except cruelty, which wrecks me: I begin to be uneasy, to tell lies, to cajole it, and finally take to my heels, ashamed of myself. In this community I had not chosen, I was perfectly at ease, perfectly light-hearted.

One evening I had the illusion of seeing over my shoulder a Germany which no longer exists: it had had its throat cut soon after my first and last glimpse of it in 1932. A shabby comfortable room, dinner, cooked by the professor's wife, for eight guests: wearing her apron, she helped them to help themselves, then went into her bedroom to practise the sonata she was going to play with three of them.

It had been written by one of the guests, an old composer: it was in four difficult movements, to my refractory ear dry and discordant, inspired, he told me simply, by Dante.

When an American tells me that in his country materialism and a cancerous boredom have taken the place of the vision—what vision?—I only half believe him. The mere notion of adding snobbery, greed, vulgarity, to that room with its piano and the clumsy bunches of white lilac brought in as an afterthought is ridiculous.

Not that I did not come across snobbery, greed, vulgarity. Why not? Pittsburgh has everything.

The day before Truman won the Presidential election I was invited to lunch by six Republican ladies, all but one of them widows, immensely rich. The sum of wealth in the hands of ageing American women whose husbands died getting it must be enormous. In the kindest most friendly way in the world they told me what Dewey would do to the greedy American working-man and the Bolshevik-minded English.

'My dear Miss Jameson, tell me why, why, we should give you money to spend on socialistic experiments and social services—if that is really what you call them—for your lazy workers.'

The English worker has always been, not lazy, but taking his time—except when bullied, or in war-time, but I denied it. They smiled.

'My dear, every working-class is lazy—yours is not an exception. But why should *we* be taxed to support them?'

'I don't know,' I said. 'I was against Marshall Aid. It would have been infinitely better to be poor and independent. Better for you, too, since no one loves a benefactor.'

'You were against Marshall Aid!'

'Certainly.'

'Well—' she did not believe me—'with Dewey in the White House . . .'

'You are sure he will be elected?'

'Why, of course! No question.'

'The English,' I said, 'always vote Democratic in an American election. Did you know that?'

'Ah, yes—Roosevelt, that rascal, that lying twisting slimy monster, that socialist, that . . .'

All I could think of to say, at the end of the commination service, was, 'Forgive me, but no one in England, not his bitterest enemy, would abuse Churchill as you abuse Roosevelt. It always astonishes me.'

They were too kind and well-intentioned to do more than smile at my obtuseness. But I wondered whether the excessive rancour with which these dead hands are still raised against Roosevelt and all his works is due to fear—that they are defeated.

Not that I had any great inclination to defend him: his ignorance of Europe did us enormous harm.

'Pittsburgh,' a New York journalist told me, 'is full of Babbitts, you won't stay a month.'

He was wrong on both counts; the only two people I knew who might have deserved his contemptuous epithet were also amiable and energetic. They were a professor and his wife, both Republicans, which was unusual enough: all the others were Democrats to a man. They expected little good of an Englishman, but they had determined to be kind and Mrs B. took me with her to a woman's meeting in the Stephen Foster Memorial building on the campus. It was the week after Dewey's defeat. On the way in she said, 'I'm ashamed of America—the most terrible disaster! You, of course, being English, admired Roosevelt. People of our sort, the intelligentsia, hated him. He got his support from the mob.' She flung up plump arms, entangled in a fur. 'There now, I don't mean you're not intelligentsia, and my Johnny said I mustn't talk politics to you. Let's look at the shrine. See? These are bars of Foster's music. The only time music was ever carved in stone!'

The lecturer, a Valkyrie from the electricity company, talked about deep freezers with the cunning fervour of a revivalist. 'Oh, my stars is that good!' she cried, holding up a turkey frozen harder than Stephen Foster's semi-quavers. 'No, it's divine!' I sat in a trance of contempt as cakes, pies, loaves, were taken from the machine. Why freeze bread? Even the abominable American bread?

'Science,' Mrs B. said to me as we left, 'is what will save us—in spite of Truman. If it weren't for science, we should still all be Catholics. Oh, my, you're not one of them, are you? What would my Johnny say to me? Oh, fine. You must come to us on Good Friday, I always serve ham, our own—delicious!'

England is full of Babbitts, with less energy, less simplicity of heart, less kindness, and even more irrational. But they are rarely members of the professional caste, in which, with us, bigotry and unreason take drier forms.

One dark October afternoon, I answered the telephone in the apartment, and listened to a woman's voice, I thought a young woman, reading a cable from my son about the birth of his first daughter.

'Do you mind repeating it?' I said.

'I will.' She read it through again, adding, 'That's splendid news. I sure am pleased about it.'

'Thank you.'

'You're welcome,' she said, quickly, warmly.

Maxine Davis invited us to spend Thanksgiving in Washington. She had married since the last time I saw her in London, a Colonel of

Marines who knew China intimately in the way certain English soldiers, during the heyday of the British Empire, learned to know and cherish the remote country they served in. Courage, a biting intellect and expert knowledge, in one person, might have been intimidating. That I was not intimidated by Jimmy McHugh is due to a hospitality at once formal and highly personal, a *Mozartian* hospitality. Perhaps it was Chinese. As in Pittsburgh, I forgot to guard myself and was continually happy and amused.

Washington is one of the loveliest cities in the world, and civilized to a fault. The part of it in which we lived for three days, Georgetown, is so nearly perfect that I should have been delighted to come on a flaw: perfection has one drawback—nothing holds up the glance passed over it, so that one has trouble in recalling details. I have never been back to Washington, and do not know whether the light is always that of a fine September day in Paris, clear, faintly golden, faintly vibrant. Probably not. It was probably, during those three days, in a state of grace. As I was myself.

The McHughs had a great many friends, people like themselves, intelligent, uncommonly well-informed, liberal—writers, politicians, financiers, journalists. Having written that, I realize that the whole of society in Washington is to some degree political. It is like no other capital city known to me, in that political thinking, the whole business, technical and personal, of politics, is not diluted by an equal interest in art, industry, amusement, anything you like. I don't mean that these are non-existent in Washington—only that they are subdued to the ruling passion. English political society in its upper reaches is less concentrated.

This was the most sophisticated of the several Americas I touched. No doubt the charm and elegance of this house was a personal achievement, but it did not, as anywhere else it might have done, startle. Living in it, listening to the talk at the dinner-table, I reflected that if Europe dies of its political incompetence, of the different idiocies of ourselves and General de Gaulle, its culture might, for a Byzantine century, be preserved here.

But perhaps these people were a little too intelligent, too liberal, too disinterested. And they were not—though they knew everything about them—the people who make the decisions. An intimate knowledge of China was enough to ensure that its possessor was never in a position where he would embarrass the China lobby by his knowledge. (In any event, who does make the decisions in Washington?

The tug-of-war between a President and Congress never ceases to astonish and baffle an Englishman.)

On our second evening we dined in a club—very stately; it might have been the Athenaeum without its discreet discomforts and with the benefit of marvellous food. Among the six other guests were two people I had been hoping to see ever since we landed: Czeslaw Milosz and his wife. Since Cracow in 1945, I had seen them once, when they passed through London on their way to America: like other young Polish intellectuals at that time he had been drawn into government service, and from his letters since he became cultural attaché in Washington I had the impression that he was living uneasily in two worlds, Poland and an America he could not yet accept. To a survivor of occupied Poland the wealth of this country could seem an insult to so much death, cruelty, destruction, or a mockery of a Europe whose greatest thinkers have never given to happiness or success so high a value as to poverty, solitude and the tragic sense of life. The revulsion I had felt in the moment of landing in New York was instinctive—and I was not burdened by the ghosts of friends, parents, lovers, done to death in Auschwitz or in Warsaw itself. Nor am I a poet, with that heightened capacity for being flayed by my senses.

He looked much as when I saw him in Cracow, a little more solid. His young wife was unchanged, pale, blonde, quietly resolute; neither America nor the birth of a son had altered by a line the clear delicacy of her face.

One of the other guests was an international editor with the genial arrogance of his position, and after dinner, perhaps intending it, perhaps not, he provoked Milosz into an argument. When Czeslaw was in a rage he opened his eyes widely, and I had the sensation of looking through them into an endless cold empty plain. Without moving my head I could see four of the faces turned to him. That of the editor's plump good-humoured Russian wife was the most extraordinary; behind an air of simple curiosity there was a pitiless directness: her husband's face showed little but disbelief in so much passion and imprudence. Listening politely, Jimmy McHugh had all at once the look of a scholarly monk, impassive, possessed by a wryly ironical spirit. Maxine's face wore the expression of quizzical amusement she uses to hide a coolly critical mind; I was surprised to catch a trace, hidden normally by her warmth, her gaiety, of a certain ruthlessness, a masculine quality.

When I had the Miloszes alone for a moment, I asked Janka, 'Are you happy in Washington?'

She smiled very slightly. 'Yes.'

'Are you going to stay?'

Czeslaw answered for her. 'How do I know? How do I know anything which can happen to me? How do I know even what I wish to happen? . . .'

Blanche Knopf was staying in Washington, and next day I lunched with her. During the years, my affection for her had become a serene habit. She was now physically brittle, and so thin that I doubt she weighed five stone. Her elegance was of the bone, and her face had the purity of an abstract drawing.

'I'll tell you something that will amuse you,' she said, smiling. 'Mrs Eugene Meyer—you haven't met her yet but you will, she's immensely distinguished—I called her up this morning and asked her to dine with me. She said she couldn't because she'd been invited with the McHughs to meet a completely unknown English writer. She couldn't remember even this unknown writer's name, and asked her secretary. It was Storm Jameson . . . By now she will have had her secretary look you up and brief her. She's a very very fine person.'

Agnes Meyer was an elderly woman, immense rather than fat; her eyes, small and sagacious, were not unkind. When I was presented to her she smiled warmly and said, 'How wonderful. I've wanted to meet you ever since reading your *Cousin Honoré*. A remarkable book.'

I thanked her. The liking I felt for her was entirely genuine. Compliments which may possibly be sincere embarrass me terribly, but courteous kindly insincerity is the simplest thing in the world to accept.

In England at this time (November 1948) the butter ration was down to six ounces a fortnight, and eggs were almost non-existent. I discovered that I could send over by air boxes of twelve dozen eggs, and I sent one of them to F. R. Leavis's wife, Queenie Leavis, in Cambridge, a woman I respected infinitely for her own work and for an uncompromising devotion to her husband and his career, to which she subordinated her own without, so far as I ever heard, a sigh. By a stroke of luck for me, I sent them at the right moment.

'. . . we had a ghastly summer culminating in my going into the operation theatre on the 1st of September under suspicion of cancer and having a horrible operation which confirmed it . . . the whole business is working out very badly—the professionals do not conceal from me that they take a poor view of a woman who develops a cancer at the age of thirty-eight. This is of course very disturbing when one has a young family and no relatives. However, in view of the likelihood of an atomic war it seems ridiculous to worry about a little thing like this, and I try not to do so. My husband's, or I should say our book on the English novel [this was *The Great Tradition*] is at last out . . . It is being published in USA, too, but Frank is sending you a copy from this side in case the Am. publisher can't be trusted. I wrote a good deal of it myself, perhaps you can identify some. The children were quite overwhelmed at the sight of so many eggs and all boiling ones, and think the millennium must have come when they can have a boiled egg at breakfast, egg and cress sandwiches at tea, and apple sponge at dinner. I have already felt the benefit myself, because the op. and the radio-therapy treatment had reduced me to living on soda-water and oranges (when available) and there seemed nothing in our rationed state that I could take. One has been giving the children all the eggs, bacon, chocolate, milk, etc. for so long that when one gets ill and can't take starch there seems nothing else to eat. Egg custards and an egg for dinner have given me quite a lift. One feels ashamed when one thinks of Europe, though. Frank has had an awful time sustaining the house with one hand and the university English teaching with the other, and with the worry as well looks like a skeleton. It doesn't help that he is so sought-after that all his supervisions have had to be turned into large seminars and that his lecture-theatres are crowded to Black-hole conditions. I wish we could go visiting professorially to USA but he hasn't had a sabbatical year yet in an academic life of twenty-five years. I should like to go to California some day—we could put Kate in the swell girls' school where Auden teaches English, Ralph could study under Schönberg and Hindemith, and I should be able to enjoy little Robin before he gets too big to be nursed . . .'

I imagined I had only to tell the right people that F. R. Leavis might be willing to come to an American university for offers to rain on him, and I seized chances I was given at Kenyon and Columbia. In both places the answer I got was, in effect: Of course, we'd all like to have him, but my belief is he won't come; he'll never leave his position in Cambridge undefended for a year, long enough for enemies to do him a mischief . . .

I have no idea how just this was, or whether offers were made to him, but his wife did not get her Californian year, a misfortune which still vexes me.

I suppose there is no English university—I know nothing about other countries—where social tact (that is, a reasonable hypocrisy), smooth manners, discretion in every field, prudent scholarship, a habit of well-turned phrases, are not more useful to their possessor than all the originality and critical passion in the world.

Even before coming I had noticed that the American traveller, not rich and not a journalist, who knows Europe or a country of Europe as I know France—by heart—is rarely sentimental about it. His affection has a quality I came to recognize as peculiarly American, loyal, unpatronizing, but informed and very shrewd.

I had the luck to meet one of these uninfatuated lovers in my first week in Pittsburgh. Gay, tolerant by instinct, Ruth Crawford Mitchell knew Europe first at one of those moments when—for a moment—it seems possible that generosity, reason, and faith in the future, are stronger than injustice and old hatreds. In 1919, as a young relief worker in Czechoslovakia, she became director of the Social Survey of Prague sponsored by Alice Masaryk and an intimate friend of the family. Thus she knew about Europe not only its habit of suicidal wars, but its other habit of giving birth to great men in order to have something worth betraying.

I am an unreconstructed provincial, happy to have been born in a part of England which, in my childhood, still tasted only of itself. Paradoxically, this is what makes me an internationalist, in the sense that when I meet a man or woman of another race, it is with the greatest difficulty that I reflect: This is a foreigner, a Jew, a Frenchman, a Turk. So far as I am concerned, he is a man from another province, and if he has customs and habits very unlike mine, why, so had old Mrs Wear of Whitby, a Congregationalist, so prudish that she kept a doily at hand to throw over her husband's face when the servant came into their bedroom with morning tea.

Nationalism will keep its venom until we succeed in creating an image of the nations of the whole world as so many provinces.

This image exists in Pittsburgh, in the Nationality Rooms of the university, a series of twenty-seven rooms on the ground floor, each decorated and furnished by a National Committee in what it considered its country's finest and most characteristic manner. Thus

Chinese elegance completes and contrasts with French, Swedish clarity of form with Czech or Greek.

To this splendid stroke of sanity and imagination, Ruth Crawford Mitchell devoted an energy, an inventive passion, a loyalty, justified by the result, which is worth a thousand treatises on world government. Conceived between the wars, perhaps as a gesture towards the vision, already dimmed, of a new Europe, it grew quickly: one of the last rooms to be finished before the second war was the Czech, dedicated by Jan Masaryk a few months before Hitler occupied Prague.

In 1948 the room set aside for England was still bare. I have not seen the finished room, made up of wood and stone salvaged from the House of Commons after the air-raid, with carved stone bosses round linenfold panelling, and a bomb-splintered overmantel from the Aye lobby. There may be a grim rightness in the idea. Even an Englishman who did not feel that these fragments represent the finest period of English taste need not be displeased that they survive in Pittsburgh—together with the small dark blockhouse near the river. It will be a bad day when either country forgets that it shares a nerve with the other.

I was fortunate in my year. On the evening of the 11th of December, twenty years after the first ceremony, the National Committee, meeting in the great hall of the university, were handed copies of a book of water-colour paintings and an account of the rooms, to be sent, even the Russian copy, to the great university of each country. (In 1962 no way had yet been found of presenting copies to Jugoslavia, Poland, Hungary, Czechoslovakia, Roumania.)

As each chairman went up to accept his copy, his voice evoked a double image, of his past and of a country he thought of with grief, as for a dead child, or with the respect due to an ancestor, even, in the rather brash voices of the Irishman and the Scot, with a hint of defiance. Stumbling over the unfamiliar words, the Lithuanian explained that he had taught himself to read, but read English with difficulty.

'At home,' he said slowly, 'I wanted always to go to school. The priest would not let me, he said my brother was going to a school, and that was enough for one family, I must work in the fields. I thought: I will go to school in America. But I am here a baker, I could not even go to night school.'

Taking the large handsome book in his hands of a peasant turned baker of bread, he looked at it with surprise and smiling respect. In the long pauses between his words, a country of fields, forests, rivers, had its moment of freedom between invasions. But when he looked at us from his small pale eyes, full of a shrewd goodness, I supposed there were other images, less reassuring, at the back of his cropped skull.

After the speeches, people stood about in the great warm hall and —this was presbyterian Pittsburgh—drank an innocent fruit punch. There was an untidy fire of logs, a green tree, a choir singing old carols, a flag: the simplicity of a village harvest festival, and, distilled from it, and from sources as far apart as Athens under a blistering sun, Cracow, Delhi, a Balkan capital, the rue St Jacques, a spirit of extraordinary strength and purity.

'This,' I said, 'is your triumph, dear Ruth.'

Eyes and smile brilliant with fatigue, she shook her head. 'No, not mine. What you are seeing this evening is America.'

A charming myth and the truth. Every reproach laid against America, of materialism, idol-worship, can be true without destroying its real grandeur. Soberly I thought that I really had been given a glimpse of that grandeur, which may be distorted, lost, betrayed from within, but, if it survives, might do as much for the world as Greece did for Europe.

As so often happens to me when I have been excited and moved on a deep level of my mind, my dreams that night were of the past. I was with my young sister; she was helping me with something, as so often, and we were both laughing. Afterwards, neither asleep nor awake, I felt a terrible longing and grief. Ah, if she would come only for a minute, a single minute, so that I could tell her . . . what?

It occurs to me now that the impulse I had felt to indulge her, as a girl and a young married woman—inexplicable by anything in her character, gaily self-reliant and intractable—might be explained by the savage notion that her early violent death threw its shadow backwards over her, unseen but felt.

This speculation is idiotic—but not more insane than the custom of sending young men to murder people in small open towns from the air.

We spent Christmas in Rye, with the Henry Steele Commagers.

That house was a living spring of warmth, generosity, wit, gaiety, intelligence, all the active graces of living. At its still centre, Evan

Commager, a creature as purely good as salted country butter. Seeming to do little except talk in a slow warm voice, she was the point from which the wit and gaiety rose and to which it returned.

I doubt that Henry Commager slept more than four hours a night; the rest of the twenty-four was spent writing, reading, lecturing—at this time, when his children were young, he wrote through any disturbance, stopping only to take part in their violent games or to argue with friends.

I wrote a little in this house, an article ordered by Lester Markell of the *New York Times*. When I went to see him in New York he told me that the paper never paid higher than a hundred and fifty dollars for an article. This was four times more than I should be paid in London, by *The Times Literary Supplement*, for a comparable piece of work, but before I could stop him my grandfather had said, 'That's very poor pay.'

Mr Markell looked at me with extreme sharpness. 'Do you think so?'

'I do indeed,' I said warmly. Not only had I liked him at sight, but America, there is no doubt about it, had given me, an, alas, passing trace of its *je m'en foutisme*.

'We might go to two hundred.'

When I sent it to him from Rye he rang me up and told me that it was not what he had expected. I was dismayed, but I hate talking on the telephone, it stupefies me and I forget to be either prudent or tactful. Besides, it gives me more pleasure to throw away an article than to write one.

'What,' I asked, 'is wrong with it?'

'It doesn't fit the title.'

'Why not change the title?'

A silence. 'You may have something there.'

'It seems to me much less trouble than changing the article.'

'I'll think about it,' he said drily.

The thought of rewriting bored me, and I resigned myself to losing my two hundred dollars. I heard no more, and the article appeared as I had written it. I have not the faintest memory what it was about.

An off-Broadway theatre was playing Giraudoux's *La Folle de Chaillot*. I went to see it, not only because of my affection for his writing, not yet spent, but out of curiosity, to see whether in a city of hard outlines and parrot-shrill light anything could survive of a poet who saw the world in oblique images. That an astonishing number of these images are of treachery, despair, injustice, death, is overlooked by readers now, who find him affected, a maker of bric-à-brac. If a habit of turning reality slightly awry, to show its absurd, ironical, ambiguous sides is an affectation, they are right. But I would throw away the whole output of the last decade of novelists—except one—to discover an unpublished Giraudoux of his dexterous maturity.

La Folle de Chaillot, alas, belongs to a period when he was already tired, less able to keep cruelty and bad faith at a distance by mocking them. It was not the fault of New York, nor of translation into a hostile idiom, that the centre of the play was empty. A void. Jouvet could have filled it with his magnificent voice, deep, staccato, vibrant, and his controlled passion: brilliantly as she tried, Martita Hunt could not.

Each time I came back to Pittsburgh from New York or the half familiar charm of New England, I felt thankful that we had been sent there and not to Columbia, or to a place where the university dominates. True, my knowledge of Pittsburgh had narrow limits. I knew that Wylie Avenue existed and that if I walked up it at ten o'clock on any warm Saturday night I should hear real jive and see negroes jitterbug in the foetid air until their eyes rolled white and their pores spouted sweat, but I was not silly enough to go: it was no Nigger Heaven for curious visitors. And I was taken to look at a vast housing project for which the upper half of a hill had been sliced off as neatly as the top of a boiled egg: nothing in its vacant stare to tell me whether its tenants, moved here from the old quarter of foreign steel workers three hundred feet lower down in a pit black with its own smoke, had brought their brutal memories with them.

In the nature of things, I was not likely to get smell or hide of these, nor of the squally Pittsburgh of union organizers, coal miners, truckers, railroad flunkeys, bartenders, whores, derelicts of every tongue.

But even the bourgeois Pittsburgh I lived in was penetrated by currents of excitement which drew some of its virtue from these circles, and from being an inland continental city as well as an immense industrial nexus. There could be nothing precious, and not much that was ingrown, about a society boiling over with power

like a Bessemer converter, and with two great nerves of river joining it to the endless stretches of country arched by enormous skies
and licked by a searing light.

My memories of the months between February and June are confused—not because I have forgotten them, but because one memory
pushes aside all the others.

Towards the end of March I flew to Texas, to Dallas, to see the
two people who in 1940 took in my young sister's children and kept
them until after the end of the war. A lack of courage has kept me
from writing of this sooner—it should have been put first.

In the summer of 1940, when she came to Dallas, she was the guest
of a Miss Hockaday, the head of a girls' school, who had been her
guarantor when she applied for the visa to take her children to the
States. The school was more luxurious than an English school of its
kind, and she could have stayed there, teaching or helping in some
way, and kept her four-year-old son and two years younger daughter
with her. This was not her idea. She was determined to get back—
the thought of being out of England during a war, safe when her
husband and her friends were in danger, was intolerable. With that
generosity as natural to Americans as breathing, several foster-
parents offered themselves to her. She chose the Leakes, Sam and
Betty, because they were moderately well-off but not rich—reflecting
with good sense that it would not do to give two English children a
sort of life they would later miss—and (this was important) because
they were young, her own age: their kindness, their warmth of
heart, was a young kindness, a young gentleness, a young warmth.
She trusted her two to them with the confidence born of recognizing
goodness at its clearest and simplest.

I left a Pittsburgh scoured by an icy wind and flurries of snow. In
Dallas, less than seven hours away, the air was warmer than an
English June, the sky flawlessly blue and wide, wide, with magnificent sunsets, and streets and gardens were vivid with tulips,
wisteria, red-bud, azaleas.

At first sight of the Leakes on the airfield, or at first sound of
Betty's low voice, I knew they were what my sister had said they
were: the best people in the world. In a clear spirit one reads the first
lines first and quickly.

That evening when I came down the stairs from my bedroom,
calling some phrase over my shoulder, I found their black cook
leaning against the wall in the living-room, her hands pressed to her

throat. Staring at me wildly, pupils rolling from side to side, she said,

'Oh, Miz Daisy, you startled me near my death. I thought you were Miz Dorothy speaking.'

This was one of the few moments when I came across a trace of my young sister in this town where, for a few weeks, she was safe.

Dallas had more obvious graces and moved at a slower pace than any northern city. I met a great many people, and now and then I caught myself wondering what would happen to this friendly hospitable society when the last of the old negro servants died. I lunched in the splendid new building of the *Dallas News*, seated at one end of a long table, facing Miss Dorothy Parker, as terrible as an army with banners, in a Tyrolean hat, at the other. One evening in a restaurant I argued with a rich lawyer who *knew* that in England in 1949 we had a Communist government. I tried to convince him that all but one or two of our Labour leaders hold their noses when they pass a communist, but he knew better. Since he knew also that Roosevelt had been in the pay of the Russians, I had to abandon argument. He smiled kindly, stretching a thin-lipped mouth in the face of an elderly well-nourished baby.

'Don't try to mislead me. And as soon as they start shooting people, come back here. We'll look after you.'

I thanked him. You never know.

Another evening, as we sat listening to the wireless, Sam Leake suddenly jumped to his feet and switched it off.

'I can't stand that damn Yankee voice any longer,' he said.

No Englishman ever grasps the question of 'state rights' and their deep roots. He expects the United States to be a single-stemmed power, and is disconcerted when one of these buried roots begins to twitch in the ground.

I imagine that, even talking incontrovertible good sense—perhaps more easily then—a damn Yankee voice disturbs dust that the northerner has forgotten exists.

The whole time I was in Dallas I had one overwhelming idea, which I pursued, as reticently as possible, everywhere. I hoped, expected, that at some turn, in some word, some casual memory started up by my passing, I should catch up with my young sister. On earth as new to her as this, her light steps ought not to be confused and obliterated, as in England they were by the many times she had crossed and recrossed the same paths.

To Betty Leake I could talk freely. I told her—I had told no one else—that Dorothy's youngest child did not even know whose fingers had made the furniture for her doll's house.

'I think she does,' Betty said quietly. 'I think they both have memories they hide. As children do.'

I should have remembered this from my own secretive childhood. It might well be true.

Betty had a box filled with letters from my sister to the children, which she was keeping with the idea that she might give it to them when they grew up. I doubt she ever did this, or even whether it would be right. What could the pages of letters written by a young English woman, dead these many years, mean to two young Americans? Nothing.

Nothing.

When my sister left Dallas, she asked Miss Hockaday to let her leave a large suitcase at the school, telling her it held things that would be useless in England in wartime, she would take it when she came back for the children. Betty and I opened it together. There were clothes I had given her for America—*to mense herself*, as we say in Yorkshire—the blue taffeta evening dress, the black dinner-dress, the quilted dressing-gown (never worn), and some knitting wool, a pair of light shoes from Nieman-Marcus, and three steel pans.

Holding the shoes, I remembered that she had told me about them. 'They are beautiful shoes, too good to wear now; it will be nice to have them after the war.' She smiled, half at herself, at her habit, like my father's, of hoarding new clothes, half in pleasure at the thought of these fine shoes waiting in Dallas for her.

Oh, poor child.

'There's one person you've not seen yet, and you must,' Betty said. 'Dr Perkins is the best children's doctor we have, and he refused to charge for treating two English children.'

When I saw him, alone, I knew that any kindness he did would be the gesture of a naturally Christian soul—for all I know he was an atheist. He had a glance that raked your mind, but gently, and a singularly quiet voice. Afterwards I wrote down what he said.

'For me, your sister was England. Just before she left, she came to see me, bringing the little girl—who was, I think, just two years and five months. Since I was going to keep an eye on the two of them, she had come to tell me how she wanted them brought up—above all, to be self-reliant. At that time, you know, we all here feared and expected that England would go down. I and other people had done our utmost to persuade her to stay in Dallas, but she was absolutely insistent on going home. Looking at me, scowling at me, in fact, she said: "What I think is that Nick and Judy, and the other English children in America, will grow up and come back to England *and get it back*." I have never forgotten the tone in which she spoke the last three words, almost spitting them at the Germans—and at me if I had any doubts . . . The other thing I haven't forgotten is that when she dropped her handkerchief, instead of stooping for it herself, she told the child to pick it up . . . I have the greatest respect for your sister. As I said, for me she is England.'

No, I thought . . . She was a young English woman, the daughter of Hannah Margaret Jameson and grand-daughter of George Gallilee, that's all, that's all.

Several people spoke to me about her 'amazing composure'. I did not tell them—why should I?—that it was not, in their sense of the word, composure; it was the same impulse that makes me refuse to be seen suffering. Only to be told about this 'amazing composure' let me see the bitter scalding tears she wept when she was alone.

An older woman told me, 'I was with Betty and Sam the evening your sister left. She put the children to bed—I remember that it was Sunday—then came down and went off on the six o'clock train to Chicago on her way to Montreal, to the boat. All of us there cried, but not she. She smiled.'

The other memories of that time are less distinct. I worked harder than ever. I was inveigled into lecturing and making speeches, things I detest doing. I made the speech at the Thomas Masaryk Memorial meeting—for how much longer will that be a saint's day of the Czech colony in Pittsburgh?—preparing it with enormous care. An accident—I scribbled notes on it about the spare beauty of a Pittsburgh hillside under snow, white-roofed shacks, the spectres of steel mills—has saved the last page.

The sardonic gleam in Jan Masaryk's eye forces me to skip a lyrical passage. It ends:

'. . . Europe will survive, will emerge from the chaos it has fallen into, and begin again that effort towards freedom and unity it has made again and again through the centuries. In this effort Czecho-slovakia will be involved both by the character of its people and the need that any future, any imaginable future, will have of them. The two Masaryks, father and son, belong to the future, not to the past.

To say that Thomas Masaryk's work for his country must be done over again is a half-truth. The truth is that it was done once for all time. The country he created cannot die. The spirit cannot die, and Masaryk's Czechoslovakia is idea and spirit. In violent death once, in life always, the name Masaryk is simply another name for Europe, for the idea and everlasting life of Europe.'

If, but for an accident, I should have forgotten my words completely, I am not so likely to forget a conversation I had afterwards with an elderly Czech. He had a brown blunt face, long nose, deeply furrowed cheeks, thick coarse hair like colourless wool, a clown's mouth, from which came a voice of astonishing force. His English was uncertain.

'So, in 1945, you talked to Beneš?'

'Yes.'

'And he said that the future of Czechoslovakia was to be a rock between East and West. But his Czechoslovakia has no future!'

'How can you be sure?'

'Do you, you, believe that anything of Masaryk has a future?'

'Sometimes a man doesn't die at the time of his death. Do you think that Jan Masaryk died forever on March the tenth, 1948? I don't.'

'All that is literature!' he said, with a controlled violence.

Since I said nothing—I detest my habit of turning emotions into phrases—he smiled and went on, 'Talk of something else. Do you know that not one of my son's children speaks a word of our language? And you imagine that we here, in Pittsburgh, will keep the idea of Masaryk's Czechoslovakia alive? You are crazy. No, no, the fight is lost.' Stretching out splayed knotted fingers, he took a boy by the ear and said something to him in, I suppose, Czech. The boy grinned at him and escaped. 'You see?' he grumbled. 'My grandson, and he thinks I am an old buffoon and savage. He is an American, he knows less than my—' he slapped his lean buttocks— 'about Czechoslovakia, and cares nothing.'

Another occasion when I gave a lecture prolonged itself for more than forty hours. One of my friendly adult 'pupils' and her husband drove us some eighty miles north-east of Pittsburgh to a small town with a college where, after the canonical lunch of chicken salad and ice cream, I depressed two hundred women by talking about Sartre, Malraux, and the future of Europe. It was a very worthy lecture, and

could not have been less suited to its audience. Afterwards we drove
to the university town of Oberlin: it was dark when we reached it,
and I recall only tree-lined streets and a hotel where we could not
get a bottle of wine because it was a dry town.

The next day, we drove a great many more miles west and south
across Ohio to lunch with Louis Bromfield.

Not satisfied to be a successful novelist, this remarkable man was
running a large farm on a method he spent time, health, a religious
passion, to persuade other farmers to try. Had he any other religion?
From the astonishment with which Blanche and Alfred Knopf,
staying in the house, greeted us, I think we were not expected. It
mattered very little: no one, not even Mrs Bromfield, knew how
many guests to prepare for. In the end, after a formidable tour of the
estate in a jeep Alfred and I shared with four or five enormous dogs,
lunch was served to some fifteen people. Louis Bromfield questioned
me about the post-war English novelists: ashamed to say I had not
read them, I began improvising. He looked at me shrewdly and said,
'Don't bother, I was being polite.' He had a bottle of seaweed
tablets in front of his plate, and swallowed nine. 'To give me
energy,' he said.

Some time that evening we reached Kenyon. I have never seen
a more charming university, and I thanked God for Pittsburgh.
Cloistered in this park, what on earth should I have learned about
America except that it is vast and has magnificent trees and friendly
learned people?

The drive home went on for hour after hour, until two in the
morning. At night, even more overpoweringly than in the daytime,
the country has no beginning and no end, it stretches beyond belief,
a distance without imaginable limits. It will look no different, I
thought, the day after all human and animal life has been obliterated.

I have never had so strongly the sense that this can easily happen,
that we are on this planet on sufferance.

At long intervals we drove through or round the threadbare edge
of towns which might have been abandoned except by the couple
blotted against a tree or the groups of two or three young negroes
turning to the car faces made phosphorescent by the lighting. Lines
of street-lamps lit up trees, shadowy white houses, the ragged ends
of lawns, and stopped abruptly, on the edge of nothing. One of these
towns was called Warsaw. There are forbidding enough tracts in
Poland, but they are less irreducible by the mind, less inhuman, than

parts of America. The continent has not been gentled yet. With its brutal extremes of heat, cold, wind, light, its grass oceans, immense rivers, wild, untamed, and to eyes used to Thames and Tweed, monotonous, I doubt it can be.

At some point in the night journey, we crossed the same river five or six times. Impossible to imagine why, in this featureless plain, it should have turned on itself so often—unless for a joke.

We left Pittsburgh in June. The train journey to New York takes eight hours—by air we could have been there in one, but it is a horrible flight, over forests that suck the air into great precipices, and with too many chances of a thunderstorm: during storms I prefer to have sea or earth under me—and I had all the time in the world to think of what I was losing: friends I was obliged to for their incomparable *bonté*—I cannot find a more exact word—and the happiness of being part of a lively idiosyncratic society. I had gained —it has not, of course, lasted—a certain insouciance towards other people's opinions; I could talk to an acquaintance without the anxious sense that I must say what I know is in his own mind. No doubt this was because, for nearly a year, I had been liked, by a number of men and women who wanted from me only my company, and with whom I had no feeling of being surrounded, as in intellectual circles in London, by vanities it is only too easy, by a clumsy gesture, to offend.

None the less it was time I left.

During the last eleven months, as if part of my life had been amputated, I had written nothing except the odd article. All writers are more or less insane and lead an unnatural life. I had had a lucid interval.

Some time during the night, a yellow-haired woman in the seat behind spoke to me.

'You are English, yes?'

'I am.'

'I was in England, once. I am German. Not a refugee—a true German. England is a kind, beautiful country, and do you know why? Because for hundreds of years its people have loved it.'

'That could be one reason,' I said. 'Parts of it are no longer beautiful. I suppose that means——'

Offended by my manner, she interrupted me. 'I meant only to say what I feel.'

'Yes,' I said. 'Thank you.'

No one had asked her, true German that she was, to have an opinion on England.

And my own opinions on America? Were they any less uncalled-for, less ignorant? I realized that I had none, I had only a great many confused notions. Without trying, I had lost almost completely the sense of being in a country more alien than no matter what primitive corner of a Europe where the dust is half human. The nightmare of a submerged Europe that seized me on landing had been transformed into a conviction which seemed splendidly rational and was in fact no better than an emotion. Lying at the side of a lake in upper New York State, I made a note on the fly-leaf of a copy of the *Mémoires d'un touriste* that I had brought with me. Having made it, I thought myself dispensed from thinking of the question again. (This saved me a great deal of mental wear and tear during arguments about the Common Market in the months before General de Gaulle's egoism turned out to be more brutal than ours.)

3rd of July 1949, Lake Minnewaska

A nation can only grow by engaging in an enterprise which calls on all its energies, forces it to believe in itself, make demands on itself, discipline itself. The nations of Europe can go no farther as separate entities, they will become demoralized and run down, get used to living at a lower and lower intensity. The single enterprise which can summon all their energies, rouse, excite, is to construct a *European* nation. This alone can give us a new strong pulse of life. It only can match the discipline and force of Communism by holding up to be realized a gigantic human image. Oppose, to the new Russia, a new Europe, a new intellectual inspiration, a new plan of living—voilà tout ce qu'il faut . . .

How positive and clearsighted one becomes, on hot afternoons, with nothing to do but stare at an immense cloudless sky, listen to the croaking of frogs in a weedy lake, turn the pages of a book read many times already, and think over a problem at the greatest possible distance from its centre!

I could not live in America—I have Europe in my bones, and I should lose my memory if I left it for good—but I cannot think without envy of the benefits to a writer of being born into this exciting, dangerous, not yet fully humanized country. Its violence may crush him but, given that he is not morally impotent, is surely as likely to give him what the habit of the sea gave Joseph Conrad, infinite patience, infinite trust in fidelity to experience, a little arrogance, a sharp eye for the visible world, and the confidence of controlled power.

At the very least, it must save him from the literary inbreeding among English novelists, unavoidable in so overcrowded a *panier à crabes*.

Chapter 7

Landing in England was a rapid descent into a familiar valley; I was content to be living there again, but the air, no mistake about it, was noticeably less exhilarating.

As soon as we were settled again in the Ilkley hotel I let the characters of *The Green Man* take possession of me. They did so with ferocious energy. What had begun in my mind as the portrait of a scholarly Christian gentleman and radical eccentric, not unlike R. H. Tawney, became a society, the established society of the 'thirties and 'forties reflected in the lives of two brothers, their children and their friends and associates; more than a score of men and women of many conditions and ages; social and political intrigues and jealousies; young men at Oxford, in love, marrying, divorcing, climbing, failing to climb; the war; the shifting moral currents. A single character, the Jewish newspaper proprietor, Cohen, survived from the world of *The Mirror in Darkness*; the many others had pushed themselves forward during the year in America when I was not able to write.

'What are you working on?'

'A novel,' I said, biting back the answer: My finest novel.

In the end it brought me one of my sharpest disappointments . . .

I did not begin writing at once; for the first time in my life I was afraid of the first step. I spent weeks meditating and planning, and in September I went to Venice for a week, to the P.E.N. Congress.

Short of writing a book in which every narrow blackish-green canal, walled garden, vast empty square of shuttered houses and dilapidated church, every dark alley, museum, neglected palace, and artisan's workshop, is set faithfully in its place round the cathedral and the Riva degli Schiavoni—still, in the teeth of tourists, alive with Goldoni's characters, passing and repassing—what can anyone say about Venice except that it would be a marvellous place in which to learn to trust in Providence. Preferably in a room looking over one of the more luminous canals.

The Congress—unless I have forgotten too much—was peaceful except for the moment when an excited Italian rushed on to the platform and challenged Ignazio Silone to a duel on the ground that Signora Silone had, the day before, spoken of his friend, a woman of untarnished virtue, as having been Mussolini's mistress. 'And she was!' an Italian yelled in the audience, so enraging the virtuous woman's defender that the speakers' table collapsed under his fists. The delegate from Scotland, Douglas Young, immensely tall, wearing, I think, a kilt, led him gently from the platform. The duel did not take place, but the incident made everyone happy and interrupted the flood of Italian eloquence sounding, because of the merciless repetition of the name Croce, like a chorus in *The Frogs* . . .

I came back to some of the blackest days of my life—to one day in particular when a relationship I had built up over the months, at infinite cost, was pulled down on my head in a few hours of violent fury.

Much later, I thought that there had been one moment when, if I had been truly a loving person, I could have found words to stop the destruction. So that in effect it was another failure of warmth. This, which did not occur to me for several weeks, may be true and yet it may have been impossible *not* to fail . . .

I write that without believing it. A failure is always a failure. The respectable reasons for it, and the excuses, are irrelevant.

I sunk myself in work. One day, at the end of November, I told myself: Tomorrow you can start writing . . . That night I had a curiously lucid dream. Guy and I, dead, were going up to be judged. There was a curtain over a doorway. Pulling his arm, I said: Look, there is something inside. We went in, I had a paper in my hand and laid it in a shallow box. Someone indistinct, a woman, asked me: What have you to confess? Almost crying, I said: All the meannesses. We went farther into the room; there were papers to be filled up, some sort of examination, and a friend who had died lately was beside me . . . I woke thinking: But you have been much worse than mean. I thought of the things I wished I had not done. No use.

After breakfast, pleasantly a little cold with dread, I began writing. The discipline I had taught myself, and the innate egotism of the writer, his belief that what he has begun has a necessity of its own, kept me at work eight and ten hours a day, month after month, against the drag of acute anxiety.

I had not tried to discourage my son's plan to sail his 21-ton ketch to Australia, taking his wife and their baby; I had even, since he had set his heart and will on it, helped as well as I could, but during the months when he was getting the boat ready for the long dangerous voyage I lived with all the minute particulars of grief and panic.

I worked in this way at *The Green Man* through the first eight months of 1950, not letting a chapter or paragraph go until there was nothing more I could do to it. Half way through August, I put the manuscript in a drawer and we went down to a hotel on the south coast, a few miles from the yacht, for the last two or three weeks before they sailed. Longer would have been too long; I should have been in the way.

Bill had taken on a 'crew', a middle-aged ex-petty officer he had known for some time and trusted completely. He was a small man, weathered and agile, and in the instant of setting eyes on him I felt a pang of doubt, the briefest possible. It disappeared at once, and when my son asked, 'Well, what do you think of J——?' I said easily, 'Oh, he's splendid, just the man you need.'

Afterwards I thought that the old captain, my father, had jogged my elbow for a second; he had only to glance at a seaman to know whether the fellow were any good.

There was little I could do to help except look after Frances. Not two years old yet, she was an enchantingly gay sweet-tempered baby; she never cried and was never bored. (There was a moment during the first fortnight after they left when the sea came aboard: at the first moment she could leave the deck her mother ran below and found Frances sitting up in her bunk, laughing, drenched, salt water streaming off her. 'Yaining,' she said gaily.) She was ceaselessly active, and at the end of the day I was usually tired enough to be able to ignore a raging fear.

Her young mother, one of the bravest of women and very gay, had her own fears. For the first time, too late, I realized that she had been only half willing to risk the voyage. She was not afraid for herself.

One night of full moon I left the boat about eleven o'clock and stood for a minute to look at a pale sky plumed here and there with white clouds; a few barely visible stars withstood the deceptive light. The tide was out, and the mud flats had the fine seaweedy smell of the harbour at Whitby, the very same. It laid my life open—down to its earliest memory. A frightful cold lucidity seized me. Could I have stopped this mad scheme if—a thing I had never done —I had outfaced Bill's wish instead of helping it? Oughtn't I at least toh ave tried? And what else but my failure to bring him up carefully and wisely is responsible for his stubbornness, his reckless determination to prove himself at any cost?

I thought coldly: We do as we can . . . But I could not give myself absolution, and I did not know who could . . .

The evening before they left, we had Bill to dinner alone, and afterwards, standing on the jetty, talked for a moment about nothing.

'Off to Australia with you,' I said.

He smiled and went away.

During the thirty-nine days before I heard anything, I could not write . . . I sat holding my pen, to look as though I were working, and so avoid questions. A great deal of the time I was thinking about a lively well-tempered child. It was she I thought of first when the B.B.C. announcer began his account of the gale blowing in the Channel, with gusts of up to ninety miles an hour, and small boats forced to run for shelter. One day, in London for the week, I walked past Brompton Oratory, and turned back to go in and kneel awkwardly behind another woman who may have known better than I did how to pray to Our Lady. All I did was ask her that I, and not anyone else, not my son, not his brave high-spirited wife, not his child, might be punished for my failure.

During this time I had a letter from Maria Kuncewiczowa—I still have it—so purely warm and good, a luminous goodness, that if I could have taken it truly to heart I should be a humbler and better person. 'My dearest friend,' it began, 'I know you are frightened and

I know you are blaming yourself for anything bad that is or may be happening to Bill. I know it from my experience . . .'

The first word came from them early in October, a letter written in Brest.

'We must return, I am afraid. We were not beaten by the sea though it was moderately rough or by the weather which was mostly foul and half a gale. It was J—— who let us down, so badly I can't quite understand it. We spent a day or two down the Chichester Channel and finally sailed out against a fresh S.W. wind and beat against it all that night and next day, sailing 100 miles but only making 20 miles down Channel. So we ran into Yarmouth and waited nearly a week for a more favourable slant to the wind. It was here that J—— began to show his colours. He adopted a completely defeatist attitude and sat round glowering all day. Finally we got away and had a magnificent sail down to Falmouth in quite a hard wind, putting in there because it was freshening for the S.W. again. J—— did only his bare duty and spent all his standby periods lying on his back. Consequently Patchen and I had to do most of the work.

'We left Falmouth against a freshening wind from the west. It was hard going but not impossible. A certain amount of water came aboard, and everything got wet below. Frances behaved magnificently. J—— complained of the hard work and said of course we would be putting into Brest, wouldn't we. I, knowing the Ushant approach and the risks of being caught in the Bay of Biscay by a gale before we got into really deep water, drove the ship as hard as I dared to get over the 100 fathom line and into deep water. We managed to work her against a moderately westerly gale 90 miles south of Ushant 10-20 miles into deep water and with about 200 miles to the Spanish coast.

'It was here that J—— with a long face announced that he thought he had dislocated his back. It was obvious he wasn't going to be any more use and that Patchen and I couldn't carry on alone for another day, so we ran for Brest, at night. Most unpleasant. The mainsail began to give trouble and J—— started panicking about flares and rockets. He couldn't or wouldn't keep the ship on course, so I had to take him off the tiller, and Pat and I did it all.

'Just as we were entering Brest harbour a final squall blew out the mainsail, split it from leech to luff. That would not have been so bad out at sea or where it actually happened, but it would have been very

very awkward if it had gone off Ushant where we had no sea room.

'It was now that we were really shocked by J——. He grinned all over his face, said wasn't it a good thing we were in port again, hoisted Frances on his shoulders, swung himself up and down the rigging, and generally behaved like a two-year-old. I was speechless with rage. I had put my ship in hazard because I thought he was injured, and it was now obvious that he had decided he couldn't take it and would use any lie to get into port . . . We shall return when we get reasonable weather. Patchen is desperately keen to do the trip. We have proved to our satisfaction that we can stand it, that the ship can stand it, and most important of all that little Frances can stand it. Damn J——.

'Expect us when you see us. It depends on the weather, because I don't consider that messing round with Ushant in anything but moderate weather is a justifiable risk, not now.'

The wretched J—— jumped ship at Falmouth on the way home. A few days after the return, Bill began flying again, this time for one of the independent airlines. I suspected that the voyage, or one like it, was only put off to a better day, but I took care not to ask, and went back to my novel.

By now I knew most of the characters as I knew myself, and I took immense pains to mistrust each of them as thoroughly as I mistrust myself, disbelieving my first impressions of them, spying on them, doing all I could to penetrate their perfectly natural hypocrisy. In solitary walks across the moor, I pored over this and that act which I had accepted at its face value until I thought I had the truth.

About this time, too, in October, I was delighted, for a reason of my own, to hear that I had been sentenced by the Soviet 'peace fighters', with much more vehemence than in the Nazi Black Book of (I think) 1940. Harrison Salisbury, the correspondent in Moscow for the *New York Times*, sent me his article about the proposed 'Book of Death'—proposed by the Literary Gazette—containing 'the names of all those monsters and cannibals who openly preach destruction of millions of human lives and of the greatest values of world culture.' What delighted me was to find my name in a list which included one of the great novelists of our age, perhaps the greatest, André Malraux.

Chapter 8

That year winter began early and stayed late, weeks of freezing rain followed in the north by three months of thick snow. The surface froze and walking between the banked-up walls of snow was difficult, I fell every time I went out, but I have kept from my childhood a trick of falling light. Electricity was rationed, and between half-past eight in the morning until four there was no heat in the hotel; wrapping myself in a quilt off the bed, I sat writing in an icy room; my fingers stiffened, my brains luckily did not.

By April the last traces of the snow had gone, but the ground was water-logged and still frozen to a depth, so that the farmers could not start sowing and the lambs born earlier died. I saw the first leaf buds on the chestnut opposite my window when the trees and stunted bushes on the moor higher up were still bare and black, as though sculptured. Spring came in a headlong rush, at the very end of May, all the trees breaking into flower at once, heavy-tasselled lilacs, gross waxen chestnut candles, spume of hawthorn and wild cherry. The laburnums were magnificent, great fountains of yellow fire.

This month, June, the last visible thread holding me to Whitby was snipped by the death of my mother's sister, the last of George Gallilee's many daughters. As thin as a bone, lively, drolly kind to stray animals, detesting children as cruel noisy conscienceless little brutes, completely fearless—I am certain she never told a lie, not the whitest, in all her eighty-odd years—an unshakably firm and simple Christian, of Cromwell's sect, she had been living on in the house my grandfather bought for his children when he made his disastrous second marriage, alone except for a servant as old as herself, who had long given up expecting to be paid her wages. My aunt's income, shrinking in value all the time, was less than two hundred a year. The house, in a terrace of houses built without bathrooms, decayed, its one remaining grace a view across roofs and beyond the harbour to the ancient Parish Church and ruined Abbey on the opposite cliff. As the old servant grew older and frailer, my aunt's rooms on one of the upper floors were rarely cleaned, dust and cobwebs thickened in corners, leather-bound copies of the classics fell apart, and silk rotted: below, in the basement where old Catherine lived and slept, the walls mildewed, and larders and cupboards, alive with generations of mice, held little else except broken crockery, old yellowed papers, filthy rags.

I had never seen anyone so dead as my Aunt Jennie, so *gone*. The shrunken hawked face and thin tiny body made less mark in the bed than an infant.

When I was not struggling to clear up the disorder, I walked about the narrow streets on both sides of the harbour, talking to myself in silence. I climbed the one hundred and ninety-nine steps to look at my brother's memorial in the old church. I followed my mother's steps, at first impatient and light, then slow, in the streets, lanes, and moor roads where she wore her life away, beginning with old shabby streets she knew as a young married woman and ending in the fields behind her last house. For the last time, my very dear, I told her, for the last time.

I could not live in Whitby again, but in a sense I live nowhere else, since only there and nowhere else except on the lowest level of my being, do I touch and draw energy from a few key images, sea, distant lights, the pure line of a coast, first images and last, source of such strength as I have. Source, too, of my talent for happiness . . .

I wrote the last pages of *The Green Man* in June. It had occupied two years of intensely hard work, with several serious interruptions, the worst that of Bill's aborted voyage. None of them were of the kind that ruins me as a writer—no domestic drudgery, no responsibility for looking after a house. This was the last time I was able to write a whole book in freedom, at the full stretch of my—limited—powers. Since then I have contrived only weeks or a few months of that most acute of all mental pleasures. Uncovenanted mercies. Like February days when the wind is warm from the south-west and streams overrun their banks, days of false spring, no stir at the buried roots.

For what I have received may the Lord make me truly thankful. And more truly for what I have not received . . .

I had promised to write a long preface to the English edition of Anne Frank's diary, and began it at once.

A few days ago a friend spoke slightingly of this little book. 'Far too much fuss has been made about a thoroughly trivial book.'

'You are wrong.'

'Why? You know yourself it is trivial.'

I am not sure of that. I could argue, with Léautaud, that the finest because purest form of literature is written as easily and naturally as one writes a letter: anything else is pose, worked-up emotion, rhetoric. The fourteen-year-old child trying to hide from her butchers wrote as naturally as birds sing, as Léautaud himself. In the likeness which emerges from her diary there is nothing self-conscious, no trace, not the faintest, of showing-off, of acting a part, even before herself; she is even able to recognize the temptation to be a little sorry for herself and reject it, even comes to realize that to use a little hypocrisy would make her life in this over-crowded hiding-place easier, but does not come to using it; instead she breaks through to something like calm, to a half-tender, half-indifferent and unchildlike patience—almost to detachment; she has no vanity; she is candour, innocence, sanity, gaiety itself.

I don't rest on this miracle of simplicity my belief that her diary deserves to be remembered. Nor on the stupefying fact that to a number of her fellow human beings it seemed proper and necessary to send this charming intelligent good child to die, as people died in Belsen, of hunger, cold, weakness.

The mind cannot form any image of mass murder, and to say that the Nazis killed six million Jews evokes only an image of darkness, a shadowy river flowing sluggishly across Europe. But if, in that black stream, a face is suddenly turned to you, the face of a clear-eyed smiling child, you feel the horror in your veins, in the marrow of your mind.

Poor child. She did not ask to become a symbol. But, since she has become one, let us agree that a trivial story, a child's naïve observations and heart-searchings, are worth more to the world than all my industrious labours as a novelist.

'Possibly I would not ask you to do this,' Maria Kuncewiczowa wrote, 'if you were not yourself an exile in a cold tough world. I ought in honesty and love to add: One day, when you'll be in need of help, your insane generosity, on which we count, may not be reciprocated. This sounds bitter, and is only meant to be sober.'

She had founded a P.E.N. Centre for Exiled Writers. It included Poles, Czechs, Slovaks, Estonians, Catalans, Castilians, Hungarians, Russians, Jugoslavs, the definition of a writer-in-exile being: One who, were he to return to his country, would be in grave danger of denial of his human rights . . . Let it go as a definition.

'They are second and third rate writers,' Maria went on, 'or too young to be classed yet, but should they not be allowed their chance to write and to publish, since there is such a thing as a second and third rate public?'

Let that go, too. Any writer who is able to write against the crushing pressure of exile (cut off from his roots, his tongue removed) has something to say worth listening to. And any attempt an exile makes to break through his solitude, his alienation, implies a measure of courage, or defiance, I find moving and admirable, to be respected.

The new Centre needed money for its basic needs, paper, stamps, English lessons for those young enough to profit by them, cost of translating a few manuscripts worth the risk. Growling under my breath, I agreed to write begging letters to English writers. Since it would be no use sending out a circular letter, and I had to write them all separately myself, it took me into August to finish.

Years ago, in 1939, when I was begging for our desperately poor refugees, I had discovered that it is never the rich who give generously to causes or persons *of no importance*; it is the modestly well-off, the Olaf Stapledons, the E. M. Forsters, the Walter de la Mares. So it was now.

Next year I wrote to Walter de la Mare again, another begging letter. Jan Parandowski had taken it into his head to form a library of English books for the use of his students in Warsaw University. He wrote telling me I must ask English writers, at once, to send him —also at once—one or more of their books. 'You may ask any writer you please, with disregard of politics. Regard only his merits as a writer . . .' Notwithstanding this assurance that there was still, in Poland, a margin of freedom—or was Parandowski being treated as a cultural unicorn?—I chose my writers discreetly. Only one of them refused, and every book sent reached Parandowski in Warsaw.

In the letter Walter de la Mare wrote telling me which of his books he had sent, he went on, 'Do please be sure to let me know of any opportunity when you are in London to come to pay a visit to this old creature at Twickenham. He will show you a tree. When ever your name echoes in memory, for some reason it brings back to me an evening when I was escorting you to the Crystal Palace station; there was no room inside the tram, it was windy on top, you wore no hat—so I luxuriated in your hair!'

This was not the first or the second time he had reminded me about an evening when he went out of his way to persuade the youngest and certainly the most timid and least articulate of his visitors that she was no less important to him than the rest. For a moment, holding the page with its fine writing, I was filled with the secret confidence, the happiness, the insane hopes, of that time . . .

I went to Twickenham. It was a long time since I had seen him, and essentially he had not changed. The fragility of old age had effaced every uncertain line and colour, leaving a creature of such lightness, such transparent liveliness and gaiety, a human elemental, that he might have belonged to another kind of being, nearer the race of birds.

He had always been unlike any other person in the world—a difference hard to pin down without making him seem not altogether human. In a way—a way which did not preclude warmth, kindness, mischief, parental pride, and a quick direct heart—he was not. Not altogether.

Chapter 9

The rest of that year, after I had finished my begging letters, slipped through my fingers.

When Hermon Ould died, it was the quiet guttering out of a wick burned down to the last thread. During the thirty years he worked, for the wage of a clerk, as its International Secretary, P.E.N. had eaten first his talents as poet and dramatist, in which no one for years had believed, except, with less and less conviction, a few of his friends, and then his whole personal life. He became nothing but this detached overworked apparently serene figure who—with reserved irony—kept writers of forty-odd nations more or less at peace with each other, held his tongue about all he knew of their vanity, egoism, intrigues and jealousies, befriended exiles, talked to governments on their behalf. Now, having devoured everything else in him, his —call it what you like—his devotion, obsession, inner flame— started on his flesh.

I have never been certain whether or not he guessed that he was dying of an inoperable cancer. His loyal friend, David Carver, had made up his mind to tell him the truth if he asked. He never asked. But that might have been out of politeness of heart, or his habit of detachment from himself. Or it might have been a refusal to play the part of a dying man—he had no liking for playing a part, no talent for it, and no vanity . . . There is a lot to be said for dying in your own home, surrounded by the things you have taken the trouble to keep near you—a hospital is already an alienation. And even more to be said for having in your life one person, one is enough, to whom, without awkwardness, you can start a sentence with the words: You might, by the way, when I'm dead, write to . . . tear up the letters in . . . sacrifice a cock to . . . Everything his friends said to him during his weeks in hospital was falsified and emptied of meaning by what they knew and he did not.

Coming away from one of these unreal talks, I was struck by the newly youthful look of London. Buildings that had been drab and war-stained so long were being painted in light colours: one in particular, Hawkes of Savile Row, stood out with extreme clarity, and in another Mayfair street a small public-house had set two tables on the narrow pavement. The air was warm and soft. Again and again, in a walk that took me from Bond Street to Westminster Bridge and back by way of Pall Mall and St James's Street to the Green Park, I caught sight of the exquisite ghost of the old confident friendly London, stepping forward in a clear light in one of the last moments before the rebuilders laid their filthy paws on her.

Towards the end of the year, my six years of guilty delicious freedom came to an end when I agreed to rent an unfurnished flat in Leeds. It was an ugly flat in an ugly solid building and, as everywhere in Leeds, the building itself, and the unhappy trees and shrubs of the garden, were blackened by soot. In the days, or rather, the nights before we moved in I went through innumerable—I should be ashamed to try to number them—crises of infantile despair, anger, frustration, resentment, and again despair, alternating with resolves to honour the conviction bred in me by generations of iron-souled Yorkshirewomen, that it is a woman's bounden duty to provide a home for her family.

To be a little just to myself, I should add that these crises took place for the most part out of sight. The tip of the wild beast's tongue came round the door, but not the animal. Not even Guy, with whom I am least guarded, had any notion of the black suffocating wave of nausea, revulsion and all but ungovernable terror that submerged me, again and again, night after night, like a piece of driftwood tossing in the North Sea.

Time and again in my life since a girl went weeping and raging into her first house, I have broken loose, pushing roughly or cunningly past everyone in my way, and lived in precarious freedom for a few months, even, once, for a few years. Always in the end to be driven back inside, stifling insane panic. Like any other living organism which is being suffocated, I struggle and knock my head on the walls. I do it figuratively now, in secrecy and mental darkness; when I was young I did it in sober fact. *Let me out, there's no air here* . . .

The frightful tension of keeping the two halves of myself, the violent conscienceless rebel and the good child, from flying apart might have sent me mad if I were not—as I am—very solid, very strong, rather well-meaning.

I am a disciplined madman—the very sanest of madmen . . .

Without Guy my life would lack its salt and honey, but our two needs pull diametrically opposite ways. Yet surely I could have managed better, even for myself? . . .

I had been commissioned to write a play for the B.B.C., and I spent my last free fortnight writing it, a sad little comedy drawn, at a great distance, from Bataille's *Poliche*.

Our furniture and books had been stored in Ilkley; we moved them to Leeds on a cold overcast day in December. It was impossible to get help and—any Yorkshirewoman will bear me out— this corner of the West Riding is as black as the Styx. I polished chairs and silver, scrubbed, dusted. I cannot endure slovenly ways and rooms, cracked imperfect objects, ugly furniture. I am a fine self-taught cook, it rests with me to rise into the class of minor chefs, but I cannot understand why the soufflés and *boeuf en daube* I prepare for my guests do not poison them. I detest the heat of an oven, it makes me swear like a third mate, and I touch greasy pans as I would a viper, with loathing.

I darn beautifully—sometimes, when I watch it darning, my hand is my father's long-fingered hand (he darned his own socks, like any sailor): I have all his physical patience, and a metaphysical impatience of the devil.

At the day's end I was exhausted. This was the first time I noticed a real estrangement between my body and me. The beast was beginning to flag. But it was a good beast still, and needed little more than to be shown the whip—even although, under the pressure of rage and boredom, my immense energy can mimic total exhaustion to the life.

I began to understand what Dante intended by immersing sinners guilty of accidie—vulgarly called sloth—in the filthy Styx. Accidie is the wilful refusal of happiness, and a form of despair, which is the sin against the Holy Ghost. And against the spirit of a phrase I tried repeating to myself at moments: *In returning and rest shall ye be saved and in confidence shall be your strength* . . . But returning where?

In the end, that is, in four or five weeks, my resilience was too much for my ill-will—also, I was genuinely heartened whenever I caught sight of Guy's pleasure in working at his own desk in an incredible disorder of books, notes, unanswered letters, scraps of paper, odds and ends of every kind, the working tools of the scholar-bachelor he is at heart—and I began a novel on a political theme, laid in a South American state. Finished at the end of May, it dissatisfied me profoundly. It had a plot, an admirable one, but no theme, and my mind only exerts itself to its limit when it is given a bone to gnaw. I sent it to both my agents, A. D. Peters in London and Carl Brandt in New York, telling them I feared it was superficial.

Both agreed with me, and I told them to destroy the scripts.

'You are a good trooper,' Carl wrote, 'the only author without any vanity I have ever known.'

He was mistaken. What I lack is not vanity, but confidence. I cannot take myself as seriously, not to say solemnly, as do all, or almost all my nimble-witted contemporaries. This is a frightful drawback.

At the same time, I do know when I have written well, and then, if no animal understands me, I am vexed . . .

There was one marvellous break in this Stygian spring. In March, my fare paid by Unesco, I spent four days in Paris, at a meeting of the International Executive of P.E.N. I did little enough for the P.E.N. now, becoming active only at moments, like an amiable volcano. Like a torpid snake, my friend Robert Neumann said . . . It is possible. How do I know? One sees oneself in such a dim light.

We stayed, Veronica Wedgwood, David Carver, now in Hermon's chair, I in my ridiculous role of elder statesman, at a hotel on the Quai des Augustins, and in the morning I had the acute pleasure of watching the sun rise behind Péguy's Notre Dame, a ship moored in mid-stream, half hidden in the Seine mists.

The evening we arrived, Czeslaw Milosz came to the hotel and hurried me, in pouring rain, to a restaurant in the Place de l'Odéon. Looking at him as he talked, at a face smoothly youthful, younger than his thirty-odd years, it was hard to believe that the ironical despair and anger of what he was saying were more than a gesture. And indeed either word reflects only one facet of a mind as complicated as any poet's. Any genuine poet.

His uneasy situation at this time was even half accidental. Or rather, it had come about because he was not calculating, not adroit, not prudent, not in any sense of the word a politician. Eighteen months earlier, in October 1950, he had been posted to

Paris as cultural attaché. Leaving his young wife in Washington, expecting a child, he went to Paris, then to Warsaw, where he was told suavely that his duty as a Polish poet was to live and write in Poland; he would be given a comfortable apartment, and probably a professorship. Until now, if he had thought of breaking away, he had reminded himself that 'twenty-four million Poles cannot emigrate.' But faced with the necessity of becoming part of a highly efficient intellectual machine, he felt a violent repugnance. He left Warsaw and went back to Paris, where he had friends.

From now on, he was in trouble both as man and poet. A poet's whole reason for existence, like his only valid autobiography, is in his poetry, and he had cut himself off from his audience, a form of suicide. Moreover, he was far too intelligent to accept the myth of a world eternally divided between an enlightened West and a barbaric anti-intellectual East: he could neither throw himself into the arms of exiles clinging with blind rage to the ghost of a dead Poland, nor lop his imagination to work inside a dialectic which none the less he recognized to be a powerful intellectual structure, the scaffolding of a deformed reality. The illusion outraged his intelligence by its futility, the dialectic offended his emotional and intellectual need, as a poet, to be free.

And, final irony, the American authorities were hesitating over his visa. He was sometimes half mad with anger, doubts, anxiety about Janka and his children in America. Over and above all this, he was bitterly humiliated.

It is conceivable that the émigrés in London would have embraced a repentant sinner, but what had he to repent? That he had lived through the Occupation, the Rising, and served loyally a ruined Poland they knew nothing about, where one educated survivor counted for a hundred? He had survived and he was arrogant —the arrogance of a writer who reserves humility for his work.

I had already written heaven knows how many long careful letters to anyone who might be able to move the State Department out of its paralysis—the most famous American writers, the more aggressive liberals, Felix Frankfurter, Eleanor Roosevelt—'She cannot be so good woman as you say,' Milosz said, smiling, 'she talks too much about human rights.'

What stupefied me at the time—less today—was the reluctance of certain people, too powerful to be in any danger, to lift a finger, and the shamefaced advice of others.

'Tell him to be patient, to wait. Sooner or later the political atmosphere will change of itself.'

Nothing, in our day, can be more banal than this story. It starts a question in my mind: How long, or rather how short a time will it take, in certain circumstances, for the so-called civilized countries to start burning heretics and breaking traitors on the wheel? The story ended—after some years—reasonably happily. That evening in the modest friendly café Voltaire, I could only watch the play of irony, despair, humour, across his face, and wonder how much irreparable damage was being done to one of the subtlest minds I have known . . .

In the morning, under a gentle light, Paris with its cathedral and palaces had the silvered delicacy of an old engraving, every stroke clear and unbroken, and a little remote.

We had reckoned on a difficult committee; it was no better and no worse than we expected. There were moments of intense happiness. Supper in a restaurant called La Grenouille, an infernally hot narrow room, the loudest French voices I ever heard, rough wine and good rough food, and the sense that not a soul in the place, man or woman, cared about making an impression of any sort, they were going straight for the essentials of a sane life. And, the next evening, a concert of Italian music of the eighteenth century, so clear, so ravishingly fresh and lively, that I had tears in my eyes.

At the end, the Orchestra Alessandro Scarlatti, of Naples, played the overture to *Il matrimonio segreto*. I listened to it for Stendhal. He was seventeen, in Italy for the first time, when he heard it, sung by a third-rate company in Novara or Ivrea: it gave him *un bonheur divin*, and from now on he knew that what he wanted most in the world was to live in Italy and hear such music every night.

The secretary of the French Centre, Henri Membré, was one of a sort of Frenchman nearly unintelligible to the English, whom he distrusted with all the force of his shrewd logical half-peasant soul. When, immediately after the liberation of France, he came to England, Hermon and I had welcomed him with open arms, laying ourselves out and emptying our thin purses to entertain him. In vain. He was still nursing his anger and resentment that we had got rid of Jules Romains as International President in 1941, at a time, he said bitterly, when no French voice could be heard.

'You don't count Denis Saurat's voice as French?' I asked.

'No.'

No explanation we offered shook his conviction that there had been a vile English conspiracy against one of the noblest of Frenchmen.

He was a good man as well as a calculating Norman and a minor writer: in 1940, harassed by anxiety about his son, who was with the army in Belgium and either a prisoner or dead, he went on steadily with his efforts to save interned foreign writers, 'trying,' Arthur Koestler said, 'to pick needles out of a burning haystack.'

I thought myself still unforgiven. On our last day in Paris, after he had given us glasses of his own *marc*, he took us out of the city to the Château de Champs. The sun was miraculously warm, and the trees a light wash of green, transparent and exciting. This château—built in the first years of the eighteenth century by a former valet who enjoyed it for ten years until the Regent confiscated it—is charming in a way the great châteaux of the Loire miss; they overwhelm with their splendour, one or two are even boring, but the Château de Champs is not only enchantingly simple and graceful, it can be loved.

I was standing alone in a window. Membré, who was walking up and down with the air of a peasant proprietor, stopped beside me and said, 'Do you not like this?'

'If you had been able to take us anywhere in the world,' I said, 'you couldn't have chosen a finer place.'

He was pleased. 'If you really mean that . . .'

'Oh, I've reached an age when I needn't make excuses for liking the architecture of the past better than the present. It's strange that we were once capable, easily, of miracles like this, and now only of a monumental dullness.'

'Yes, it is a miracle,' he said seriously, 'a French miracle.'

'Well—I'm happier in France than anywhere else—with and without miracles.'

'You are always polite.'

'But I don't always tell the truth,' I said. 'I'm being truthful now.'

He barely smiled. 'I think so . . . Shall I also be frank? I always believed that it was you who overturned Jules Romains. Our friend Hermon would not have had the—' he hesitated—'the arrogance.'

I seized the chance I had not expected. 'If Jules Romains had come to London in 1940, he would be International President at this moment. The people who had a right to speak for Europe were in London—or in occupied France and Holland and Norway. Not in America.'

He did not answer, but I had the clearest possible sense that—in spite of his anxious devotion to the great man—I had my finger on one pulse of his mind. And I knew what to say next.

'Listen. When our two Centres act together, we control P.E.N.—which is not a bad thing. If, when you're annoyed with us, you'll write to me—to me, frankly—I'll do everything I can.'

'You're being very clever,' he said, eyeing me, 'but—I think—you are sincere.'

'I ask you very humbly to believe that I'm sincere. And that I have never wanted to make use of P.E.N. for some personal reason. Why should I? I don't want to go about making speeches, and I have my work to do.'

He looked, at this moment, so like a middle-aged second mate of my father's, who used to let me plague him with questions when I was five or six, that I could have embraced him.

'From now on, we act together,' he said.

I liked him very much, I was glad I had convinced him, and I felt a familiar jeering laughter, in the pit of my stomach, at the pair we made, shaking hands solemnly, in this splendid room.

As soon as I went back to England, he wrote me a long letter which began *Chère Amie*, setting out all the reasons why, after so many years, he felt he could trust me. Too late. He died six weeks later, suddenly—*il ne s'est pas vu mourir*, Jean Schlumberger told me—and my interest in Anglo-French co-operation in P.E.N. disappeared with him. After that day, I never lifted a finger to try to change what has always been the attitude towards the English of the French Centre—friendliness broken by outbreaks of suspicion and irritation, not to say enmity.

Chapter 10

The fingers of one hand would be too many to count the times when I have looked forward to the publication of a novel. I am too wary to let myself hope, and too sceptical, seeing too clearly the width of the gap between it and the great novels. Besides, by the time a novel is published, I am already—or in those years I was—in some fashion involved in the next. But—partly because it had taken me so long to write, and partly that a very severe critic, my friend and agent A. D. Peters, had praised it when he read the manuscript—I hoped much from *The Green Man*. Hence my mortal disappointment when, a few weeks, I think three, before it was due to appear, I discovered that its publisher had so little faith in its merits, or its prospects, that he had printed less than a third of the number of copies earlier novels had sold.

It was a bad moment.

Anger restored me. It seemed to me that I ought to have been told what the firm thought about it. I more than suspected that it was not one of their own readers—publishers' readers always make me think of the old honourable profession of *castrati*—who had damned the manuscript; I forgave the assassin, but not the deception.

With the greatest politeness—after all, praising one's own wares is an awkward business—I protested, A. D. Peters protested, and Mr Daniel Macmillan who, until this moment, had not looked at the book, listened kindly, read it, and doubled the printing order, but it was too late, the leeway couldn't be made up.

Worse than my disappointment was the fact that I had no money left, or only enough to last me, with the greatest care, for another month or so. It was three years since I had published a novel, and for the past twelve months I had been living on money borrowed, on the strength of *The Green Man*, from the publisher.

Obviously, I must begin another book at once. A familiar devil seized me by the elbow. What you need, he said, to give you fresh heart, is *to get away*.

To get away. Find money somewhere. Put off starting the book for a month, a fortnight. The world might come to an end in a month. Only let me escape from these walls built round me, before I knock my brains out on them . . .

Incautiously, I said, 'We'll go to France in July, the minute term ends.'

Guy frowned. 'You told me yesterday that you had no money left.'

'That's no reason,' I said gaily. 'I can always find money somewhere.'

This latest evidence of my impossible character drove him to exasperation and rage. 'I can't stand this—you overwork madly, you write book after book and throw the money away. When you're not giving it away—how many hundreds of pounds have you handed out this year?—you're spending it recklessly on things we could do without. I never knew anyone so totally indifferent to money, and so careless. Why? Why?'

Resentment—against everything that forced me to live in one place and prevented me from running about the world with a pen and a ream of paper—washed across my mind in a black flood. Surely he could see that I *must* go—that by keeping me back he was destroying me and everything in me that was still confident and alive?

'I don't know,' I said. 'I'm made like that.'

Deliberately I used the voice, hard, harsh, and contemptuous, which is less mine than a voice out of the ground, out of any one of a hundred obscure northern graves, long since overgrown. I am not surprised that Guy would like to strangle it. My improvidence was inexcusable, I knew it, but I did not give in. It was he who, in the end, said, 'I'm sorry.'

This was an overwhelming relief. I would never have said it. He is my closest friend, my marriage rests on a rock of confidence and gentleness, given and taken, but I need that hand held out to break my way out of a coldness not mine.

'We'll go to France next summer,' he said, to console me.

'Very well.'

Silently, I was determined to do this.

I had been disturbed too deeply to sleep; images from the past, from my first years, trivial things, swarmed in my mind, a wordless delirium. I could not control them; choking, I tried to tear them out and could not. Again and again I begged: Let me sleep. At last I did sleep, and, as so often when my mind has been turned inside out, I dreamed of my young sister, a long dream, still sharply clear in my mind when I woke. Much of it was fantastic, and had to do with the birth of a child, but towards the end she and I walked along a wide road, between shadowy walls, and here, abruptly, I remembered that she was dead, and said to her: You won't forget me, will you?.We'll meet in our next lives, and I'll try to do better, I've been so weak . . . Before this, it had been a very happy dream.

There was no uncertainty or fading; I woke suddenly, while it was all still vivid. The recollection that she was dead had been as it were the sign that the dream was coming to an end, but the end came in an instant, like a shutter falling.

I lay awake, thinking: I can never be reconciled to her death.

One of the ghosts at the back of my mind had been standing there patiently for several years. Each time I glanced at it the face changed slightly, acquired a line or a shadow round the eyes, but the thought behind them was always the same. Only—I did not know how to translate it into action. Briefly, it was the figure of a man trying to decide whether or not to take on himself *to do justice*, as Orestes did justice on his mother. The man or woman he might have to execute did not, in the beginning, interest me. All I wanted to know was: What goes on in the mind of a man who, with the strongest motives in the world, acts as executioner in his own family?

As soon as I began consciously to attend to the shadowy figure, a whole web of motive and intrigue rose to the surface and I had only to examine it. It was a question of treachery. In a country which has been invaded and occupied, treachery is inevitable, and involves, inevitably, actions we are in the habit of pretending do not now occur in civilized countries. Also, private vengeance or justice is likely to be more nakedly ruthless than in countries which have not been torn open to the roots of fear and hatred. (Or only a little!) Hence, I saw Orestes as a Frenchman, and with fearful anxiety laid the story in France, in a part I knew best at that time, the Loire valley. I saw it, too, as a play, not as a novel, and began to construct it as a play, with characters who seemed to take as sharp pleasure in giving themselves away as I in watching them at it. Either they had been long waiting behind my Orestes, or I know more about treachery than about any other human habit. But, in fact, the theme of treachery was subordinate to the other — to the question of what it costs a man to inflict justice on another who is wholly in his hands.

By the middle of July, I had blocked out acts and scenes, and even written down a few lines of dialogue . . .

We went to France then, for a fortnight. I forget where the money came from. From the B.B.C. play? I could look it up in the enormous account book in which, since 1928, I have kept a record, more or less complete, of my rake's progress. I pay my bills the moment I receive them, and add up the amounts. This gives an air of prudence and sanity to my worst extravagances.

On the way we stayed a night with the Liddell Harts. Like every place lived in by Kathleen and Basil Liddell Hart this large pleasant house was a cell of almost Chinese serenity, kindness, and intellectual excitement. I know only one other house where I am as happy, and for the same reason. I think myself supremely lucky to have been admitted as a friend into two houses where kindness, intelligence, good-humour and politeness rule. And there is only one other woman I admire as I admire Kathleen Liddell Hart, for the warmth and grace of the life she makes for her husband and their friends: she will die smiling, because her mouth curves up at the ends like a young child's, even in repose. (Look at the mouth of every woman you see during one day: over the age of fifteen, all have begun to turn down.) As for her husband, the more I admire his intelligence, his fastidious senses, calm irascibility, and uncompromising rationality, the more I love his kindness.

They had staying with them a French diplomat. He told a story which, since he is not a writer, he may never record. A pity. In a few words it concentrates a whole epoch. Two years before the war he was a young third secretary in the French embassy in Russia. The Front Populaire was at its height, every other week French socialists turned up *en pèlerinage*, and among them that autumn was the Minister of Education, Jean Zay, with his wife. The Russian in charge of the visitors was a man called Bubonov: in official circles it was known that he was already done for, but during these few days he and Madame Bubonova entertained the Zays and became very friendly with them. One day, the young Frenchman, in the Finland Station to see off a guest, noticed the Bubonovs seeing their fifteen-year-old daughter off to some safer place. 'They knew they would never see her again.' A few days later he was there to see off the Zays. The Bubonovs arrived, friendly and smiling. Leaning from the train, Zay cried, 'We'll see you in Paris very soon, you must come to the Exhibition and see us.'—'Yes, yes, we'll come very soon,' Bubonov said. Three days later he was arrested and executed: his wife, sent to some camp, was never heard of again. Shortly, a package arrived at the French embassy from the Zays, with a letter asking the young secretary to deliver it to Madame Bubonova. He opened it. It was a bottle of scent called *Moment Suprème* . . . A novelist would be ashamed to employ an irony so banal.

(Three years later Zay himself was dead, murdered by three of Darnand's men who took him out of one of the Vichy government's prisons on a faked order.) . . .

We spent our first night in France at Verneuil, in a small hotel facing the unpaved square of dusty iron-hard earth. To our great surprise—Verneuil is nothing, a dull little town of narrow streets and rather haggard buildings—the hotel was full, and we were given the last tiny attic bedroom. After dinner, sitting at one of the iron tables on the pavement, I picked up a local newspaper left lying, and read the account of a tribunal. It had just sentenced Mme veuve D—— to pay 900.000 francs to the mother of a young man who had been denounced to the Gestapo by Mme veuve D——'s daughter, Andrée, and died in a concentration camp. Andrée, a seventeen-year-old *drôlesse*, now in prison, had been the mistress (*concubine*) of a Gestapo agent, and her mother's guilt was that she had failed to bring her up to be incapable of such debauchery. 'She,' said the young man's mother, 'has paid penalty; it is up to you, Madame, who neglected your maternal duty, to pay in the civil court for the grief I have suffered.'

Let us be honest: there is nothing surprising or disgraceful in try-ing to poultice your grief with 900.000 francs. The dead boy himself would have been the first to approve his mother's eye to the main chance. What shocked me was the profoundly malicious satisfaction shown by the comments, printed in the newspaper, of Madame veuve D——'s friends or neighbours. It was even oddly impersonal, a so to say metaphysical satisfaction and cruelty. A little as though, looking into a clear river, one saw a thread of foully black slime flowing through it. But why expect anything else? Would it have been different in England if we had spent four years rubbing shoulders with an occupying army, even if only one in ten thousand of the occupiers were anything but a decent enough young fellow with no wish to be where he was? Shouldn't we, too, have felt less loathing for the enemy than for those of our own people who, for whatever reason, softened towards him? There is a certain satisfaction in tormenting an enemy, but it is nothing like the pleasure to be got out of cruelty to one's nearest. And when it can be enjoyed as a form of justice . . .

In the morning we were wakened at four o'clock by the noise outside. To see through the single pane of glass I had to kneel, almost lie, on the floor, and squint through it. The square was already half filled by stalls and booths and more were going up, men, women, and half-naked children running about in the first light with wooden planks, hammers, bolts of cloth, huge live rabbits, open boxes of fruit, hardware, bread. Never since I was a child and watched the last launching in a small shipyard have I seen people work with so reckless an energy and gaiety; it flew out of their bodies and voices like sparks from a bonfire. What the night before had been a place of shabby secretive houses was more candid and alive than a healthy child. Even Madame veuve D—— —supposing that yellow haggard face poked out between the shutters of the house opposite were hers—must feel a quickening in her veins. Later, in blistering sunlight, when I was pushing my way between the stalls of the market, buying bread, cheese, peaches, and a bottle of wine, for our lunch, I felt that there are only a few griefs I could not cure by sitting at one of the café tables in this graceless foreign street, listening to the foreign voices, smelling the foreign smells of new bread, ripe fruit and cheese, and, yes, drains. To be happy—as happy as I have been thousands of times in my life—I don't need handsome buildings, lawns, great art, sublime music. I enjoy these, they may give me the greatest pleasure, but so, and more easily because it reaches down to some secret and purely personal feeling, can an hour spent in a place as ordinary, even ugly, as the market square in Verneuil, where, at nine in the morning, the light, the noise, the voices, the toothless old hag wearing an air of sanctity to go with the religious medals she is selling, the colour of a young woman's dress, give me an exquisite happiness, the most poignant I know.

We drove south, towards the Loire. The road ran dead straight, mile after white-hot mile, between poplars, acacias, tall pines, walnuts, all old trees, and so well cared-for that they had an astonishing air of youth and gentleness, very reassuring.

The light of the Loire valley is like no other in the world, clear without a thread of stridency, inconceivably clear and suave. It changes continually, of course, but never loses this double virtue of freshness and strength, a young virtue. The river was at its lowest, narrow grey-green channels between blond sandbanks. Later in the evening, between nine and ten, the motionless water was doubled by a bronzed smoky reflection from the west, lying below the surface, and the arches of the bridge were completed, exactly, as if by an engraver's tool, by their pitch-black shadows. Standing at the end of the bridge, I watched a panel of clear bronze water, framed in the double arch, fading to grey. Bats flitted between the arches. There was a crescent moon, and two or three weak stars.

What disappointments can cancel such a moment?

Certainly not the one that caught up with me a week later, in Nancy, sharp as it was. *The Green Man*, published just before we left England, had been kindly treated by the *Spectator* and *The Times*, so, when I caught sight of a *Literary Supplement* of two days before in a *tabac*, I picked it up with confident excitement. A prudent instinct drove me to glance at the review of my novel before spending francs on it. It was brief and very contemptuous. Horribly taken aback, I did not buy the paper. I give you my word that, at four o'clock on the afternoon of the 3rd of August 1952, in my humiliated state of mind, the marvellous Stanislas square was the ugliest place in the world. The White Queen's advice to Alice floated across my mind. 'Consider what a great girl you are. Consider what a long way you have come. Consider what o'clock it is. Consider anything, only don't cry!'

No doubt that, for an instant, only for an instant, my face gave me away. Then I considered where I was, in the delicious town of Nancy, and what a long way I had come from my mother's house, and—not for the first time at such a moment—a wild gaiety filled me. This exhilaration, the peculiar exhilaration of disaster, is like being splendidly drunk, an incomparable lightness of head and heart. With luck, it will be my last sensation . . .

In Alsace, I was enchanted to discover that I had not distorted it when I was writing *Cousin Honoré*. But the town I had been longing to see, Ammerschwihr, and had promised myself an intense happiness from my first sight of the cobbled market square with its sculptured fountain and splendid sixteenth century houses and the charming double staircase leading up to and away from the front door of the old Hôtel du Commerce, was a heap of ruins, not a house standing. A woman in a shabby cotton dress, the only creature there, was standing staring at the rubble of what may have been her own house. I did not dare to speak to her, but she spoke to me. Looking at me with frank hatred, she said, 'D'you know who did this? The Americans!'

I have never heard in a human voice anything like the bitterness compressed into the last nasal trumpet-note of—*cains*. It curdled my blood.

Chapter 11

'Why,' T. S. Eliot asked, 'out of all that we have heard, seen, felt . . . do certain images recur, charged with emotion, rather than others? The song of one bird, the leap of one fish, at a particular place and time, the scent of one flower . . .'

Surely he knew? Any image so charged, overcharged, with emotion that there are no words fit to describe it, or to convey the emotion, is the moment's face of an image so old we have to grope for it in the darkness of infancy. It is the young glance, telling the onlooker nothing, which starts suddenly from the half-extinct eyes of an old woman. In Venice that autumn, twice I stumbled over one of these moments when past and present become one, in the body's memory rather than in the mind, moments worth a long lifetime.

Reaching the Lido after dark, I could see nothing from the window of my room except the darkness of a cloudy night. But when I woke, early, I saw wet empty sands, and sea, the steel-blue Adriatic, its horizon an edge of blindingly white light reflected from the risen sun, itself hidden behind heavy clouds. Looking back over my shoulder, I saw all my life to the mornings when, travelling to school along the twenty miles of coast from Whitby to Scarborough, I had seen the sea joined to the sky by this same gleaming half-hoop let down from the invisible sun, swallowed by a cloud-bank as it rose. And as the North Sea rose in my mind, overflowing the Adriatic, an excitement from the past filled me to an almost unbearable pitch.

And there was one evening, the evening of the 26th of September 1952, the time was between half-past eight and nine, on the Piazzetta in front of the Doge's Palace: the pinkish grey and white marble above was the colour of sea-corroded brick, and in the cloister below the gallery were a few benches against the wall, and worn stone paving: it was almost dark, and the crowd standing or walking about, between the old street-lamps, to hear the Banda C. Monteverdi play an air of Rossini, shivered a little in the wind from the lagoon. The musicians wore white uniforms. At the far side of the square, under rounded arches, the lit windows of small shops and cafés, and globes of white light at the end of the Piazza below the Clock Tower. In an interval of the music, the clock struck, with a deep note like that sent out by the Whitby bell-buoy. So there I was again in the Saloon (since miscalled the Spa), sharing with my mother a wooden bench against the wall, a seat chosen for the shelter it gave us from the sea-wind, and, in front of us, standing or sauntering in the gathering darkness round the band-stand with its uniformed musicians, a crowd of hardy ghosts, old and young: the air is, of course, Rossini's, and in the interval the tolling of sea and bell rises between the voices and the knocking of feet on old worn stone.

The passionate intensity of such moments is incommunicable. I am certain they will be the last part of me to give itself up . . .

As soon as I got back to England, we took C. to a hotel in the New Forest for a fortnight. I had not seen him for three years, since the troubles. As we neared the house—later than we had said we would come: we had driven a long way and lost ourselves in unfamiliar suburban streets—I saw this tall slender boy, as neat as a new pin, striding up and down outside it, with a curiously set face. Had he been afraid we would not come?

The fortnight was almost a success—that is, I succeeded partly in bridging the gap between the child and the handsome ten-year-old, half graceful intelligent boy, with an impenetrable glance, full of reserves, half young barbarian. An old German professor of history staying in the hotel got it into his Hegelian head that I did not appreciate the boy, and told me, in solemn rebuke, twice, 'But he is remarkable, he is even more than intelligent, I have never known a child so quickly to see into and through what I tell him and he is also smiling—you have here a miracle.'

At last I said coldly, 'Why should you think I don't know it?'

Miracle or not, I had one fear, that he was already hiding as many anxieties and mistrusts as I at that age, and one stubborn hope—to be allowed to give him, without expecting any return, all I could give, an education he would be able to use.

In November I took up the skeleton of *The Hidden River* again, and wrote the first scenes. Everything I had learned in France in July helped to quicken it. What can you learn in a fortnight? But it was a fortnight lived on the surface of a country where I lived the rest of the time like a mole, reading little except French, sifting my memories again and again, living in France by faith when I could not live there with all my senses. What mistakes I made were less the mistakes of ignorance than of an excessive fondness.

I spent two months writing it as a play, and another two to turn it into a short novel, in a version I like better, immeasurably better, than the one in which it was published. In this first version there was only the simplest and briefest love affair—not an affair at all, a mere hint of feelings given little chance to become articulate. I was at first pleased with it. But it had been written against the boredom, fatigue, and occasional despair I felt in the Leeds flat, and after a time, when I was copying my manuscript on the typewriter—at breakneck speed because I had promised to take Frances for a month when her mother had her second child—I began to think that very probably I had only made a hash of another theme.

By now, I and my body were entirely separate. It had become something I took about with me. When necessary, I kicked it into obedience—a Caliban—and it obeyed. For how much longer it would obey instantly I neither knew nor cared.

This was the third time I had had Frances staying with me. A much-loved child, who lived happily in the narrow spaces of a small ketch, familiar with sea-birds, tides, mud-flats, the clatter of waves against the wall of her bunk, she made herself at home anywhere. A child who by instinct noted the shape of moving objects, changes of sky, all the physical details of existence, and slept through the loudest thunderstorms. A child naturally gay, who chattered with rage when she fell on her face and I was so foolish as to offer to comfort her.

She stayed six weeks. After I had taken her home, I set to work—cursing my folly—on the manuscript sent me by one of the exiles. It had been written heroically in English, a fantastic English, and since it was intelligent I had not the heart to say to the author: Take your deformed infant away.

Long before I finished it my energy was out of sight; it came scurrying back when I wanted to fly to Dublin for the P.E.N. Congress.

I had discovered that Charles Morgan was prepared to succeed Benedetto Croce as International President.

I was comically astonished. When it had been laid on me to ask him, I felt certain he would reject it as an intolerable burden.

'I shouldn't care to stand unless I can be sure of election.'

'Of course not,' I said. 'But no one will oppose you.'

I was a great deal less confident than I sounded, and the thought of his being mortified irked me.

In Dublin I found that the French had their own candidate, André Chamson. And the Germans and Austrians were going to propose Thomas Mann. Mann was no danger—in 1953 it was still too early to put up a German, even one so eminent and politically impeccable. The Austrian president, a lovable spluttering old fellow, said to me,

'If we had known you had someone in mind . . . Of course we shall withdraw our candidate.'

It did not enter my head that there was anything absurd or unreasonable in pushing aside Thomas Mann to make room for an English writer, any English writer.

André Chamson was an animal of another species. I liked him extremely. His narrow head and lean prematurely haggard face, the bones scarcely covered, an almost lipless mouth that, in age, would close like a trap—it did now when he was meditating a stroke—were as attractively austere as his part of France, the Cévennes, a region of Protestants, probably, if one followed the roots underground, of Cathars; I would swear there are living roots of that severely logical faith, burned out by the Catholic church, in those hills . . . His early novels, laid in this region, were marvellously evocative and spontaneous, without pretensions. If he were English, I thought, he would go on writing them, to a chorus of respectful praise, and keep himself and his family alive by reviewing or writing art criticism: in France, far grander and more strenuous ways are open to him . . . Looking at the lines of his jaw, I felt sure he had read his maps.

He was standing beside me when the Austrian apologized for his tactlessness. His fine mouth was crossed by a brief smile of speculation and contempt. Too adroit not to know that if I were going to make the effort I could easily rally enough Centres to defeat him, he was sensitive enough to guess that the last thing I wanted was a contest, I wanted Charles to be chosen without one.

What he did not guess was that I had been seized by an overwhelming reluctance to go on with this farcical diplomacy. Never again, I said to myself.

I wrote a long memorandum about the unseemliness of a tug of war between French and English, offering, if the French would support Charles, to use any influence I might still have at the end of his term of office to secure André Chamson's election then, and arranged for this document to fall under his eye.

The next morning he came up to me outside the conference room with a friendly smile, as delicate as it was, perhaps, sincere.

'I have seen your letter to Denis Saurat.'

'Yes?'

'You know, he is not a good Frenchman, Saurat. He is—what shall I say?—denatured, he has been living out of France too long.'

Not wanting to annoy him, I did not say: What you mean is that he has lost that total ignorance of other countries which is a caste mark of so many French intellectuals.

'I am sure,' he said, 'that there are no serious differences between us.'

'None,' I said warmly.

He pricked me lightly with one of his rooted phrases. 'Il faut dire les choses *comme ils sont.*'

I forget which foreign delegate was given the duty of proposing to the Executive that Charles should be elected, but the proposal was supported, warmly, with faultless grace, by André Chamson.

The whole Congress spent a day—made violently uneasy by the

tension between the two Irish nations—in Belfast. We left at midnight, in a special train. Exhausted, clutching politely the anti-Republican leaflets handed them in the station by a dozen fierce young Ulstermen, most of the two or three hundred writers slept in their seats. Pushing my way through the crowded coaches, I came to one where a bottle of Irish whiskey was keeping a score of them noisily awake. Among them was the East German delegate, a personage waiting to be born into a novel by Günter Grass: sprawling back, he was singing in German and beating time with his shapeless arms, pitifully grotesque and happy. When he saw me he stopped singing and gave me a sheepish smile. I blew him a kiss. He tried to get to his feet, collapsed, and began to sing again weakly, tears trickling over the wastes of his face.

The violent quarrel between the two Germanies had become bitter, and his position was excessively uneasy. I felt a perverse affection for him, and went out of my way to be kind. He was grateful, and frothed over with explanations. 'Believe me, Miss Storm Jameson, I should say Madam Vice-President, it is my regard for truth that forces me to take this stand, only my regard for truth. Believe me, I don't want to annoy you, but I must speak the truth.'

With the greatest difficulty we patched together a compromise which no one expected to last. Nor did it. The moment he got back to Germany it was repudiated.

Years later I made good use of him in a novel.

With some twenty other writers, I lunched at Maynooth. By this time, almost the end of the Congress, I was so tired—I had chaired both business sessions and the not at all placid Executive, and sat up at night until all hours, talking—that the faces on either side of the table became a Masque of angels and devils like the chorus in a mediæval play: a mouth, thin and tightly shut, turned up in a sardonic V; the lame delicate Count de Morra was sporting a saintly smile, Ignazio Silone's dark heavy face scowled; Franz de Backer was as white as a sheet, a skull rather than a head; the lines running from Chamson's bony nose to his jaw had been cut into the wooden flesh with a knife; a bearded Peter Ustinov had by accident or design the air of an eminent ecclesiastic, affable and a little womanish, or, paradoxically, a little like an intelligent bull. The lunch had been a long one, with exquisite wines, which the President of the College and his priests poured out freely but did not drink. I drank a great deal, without any effect.

At the closing banquet that evening, a spectral face came towards me in a corridor, startling me until I realized that it was my own reflection.

Forty-eight hours after I got back to Leeds, I had recovered completely. Why? Because we were leaving Leeds, and this particular trap. Energy and an air as keen as salt poured into me from the door standing open at the end of the month. Guy was about to retire, and had compounded his tiny pension from the university for a sum he proposed to spend on six months in France, longer if by living moderately hard we could stretch it. We were allowed to take the money abroad only because he was writing a history of the Third Republic—scholarship still has its uses.

This is the place to remark that he has no clearer sense of reality than I have. I am recklessly improvident by nature—whose nature? what flaw in the line of sensible hard-mouthed Yorkshiremen? Guy is not reckless, not, as I am, wasteful, but he is equally devoid of any solid sense. He should have married what in Whitby they call 'a warm body, a good manager.'

I refused to look farther ahead than the coming months. Without a pang, I prepared to send our possessions and books into store again. Three weeks in Brittany with C. and then away, away. The sea-gull screech of Whitby fisher children, calling each other in the streets outside the first house I remember, echoed between the bones of my skull—*Ah-wa-a-ah*!

Every few years I am seized by a hatred of possessions. Since I cannot destroy all our books and furniture, I destroy letters and documents. The previous bonfire had been in 1940, when I burned every paper I thought might incriminate other people if we were invaded and occupied, and a great many I need not have destroyed. Now I set to emptying my files again. I came on a letter, dated the 26th of July 1946, from Leonora Eyles, David Murray's wife, enclosing the one R. D. Charques had written David saying that he (R.D.C.) had been given 'the rather grisly task of writing a stock obituary of Storm Jameson' for *The Times*, and asking David for details of my early life and career. What David, who was not only indolent, but knew very little about me, wanted—in effect—was that I should write my own obituary and send it to him to give to Charques. The mere thought of writing it filled me with the same vexed boredom I feel when I am asked, by some publisher or some editor preparing a book of reference, to answer questions about my-

self and my books. This has nothing whatever to do with reserve
or diffidence—it is purely sloth.

I sent Leonora a few dates and left it at that . . .

Re-reading her letter before tearing it up, I was hooked by the
phrase 'a stock obituary'. It struck me as mean and silly, and I began
to make notes for the obit I would have written myself.

'Storm Jameson, born at Whitby on the 8th of January 1891, died
yesterday, in obscure circumstances, at ——. From her father, a
master mariner, she inherited patience and physical strength, and
from her mother, who was the daughter of a shipowner, a restless
boredom which bedevilled her life. The ambition, a blind hunger
to become a figure, and to use her brain and exceptional energy,
which drove her to write and brought her a measure of success, was
undermined by certain weaknesses of character and by a paradoxical
lack of respect for money and honours, and her hatred of a settled
life. In her late middle years, the impulse to turn her back on the
world was strong enough to defeat her contrary effort to cut a figure
in it.

'From 1933 onwards her novels were increasingly concerned with
the state of the world, the mystery of cruelty, treachery etc. etc.,
but in daily life she showed an almost total lack of seriousness and a
frivolous indifference to her own interests. Where money was concerned she was incontinent. This and her ineptitude (due largely to
boredom) in practical matters, drove her to write too many books.
A few of these—notably *That Was Yesterday, A Day Off, Cousin
Honoré, Cloudless May, The Journal of Mary Hervey Russell, Before the
Crossing* and *The Black Laurel* (a single novel in two volumes), *The
Green Man*—were worth writing.

'When not harassed by responsibilities which bored her to death,
she was naturally gay. She adored amusements, and if able to please
herself would have gone to the theatre, or an opera, or the ballet, or
a foreign film, every evening.

'The great passion of her life, too little indulged, was for travel.
No other sensual or intellectual pleasure gave her a fraction of the
acute happiness it gave her to see a foreign city or country. No other
assuaged the restlessness which, more than any other of her failings,
laid her waste.

'During the early part of her life she was domineering and timid,
unfeeling and betrayed by her strong feelings, mistrustful and involuntarily reckless, malicious and soft-hearted, kind out of a

nervous inability to stand the sight of suffering. As she aged, she ceased to be domineering. Not because she was at last ready to admit that it is spiritually and emotionally unprofitable, but because she was bored by most people. The instinct for flattery of which some persons, even some friends, accused her sprang less from a wish to be liked and approved than from the wish to reassure. For example, sitting opposite a plain elderly woman dressed carefully and very unwisely in pale pink, she had to stifle her impulse to lean forward and say: How beautifully you are dressed today.

'The least gesture of kindness from a person who had injured her, even severely, wiped out the injury. One of the signs of a weak character.

'At one period of her life she had hundreds of friends, of several nations.

'Apart from her family, she loved deeply, to the end of her days, eight people: of these, two were friends made late in life and four were her first friends.'

Chapter 12

By one means and another, without too much austerity and with only a feather of illegality, we contrived to live in France for ten blessed months. When we left, without a franc, at the end of May 1954, the French official in Boulogne who reproached us for overstaying our *permis de séjour* did so with smiling indulgence: either he was in a good humour or he pitied us sincerely for having to leave his country.

The sentimental situation of France among the nations is curious. No country, not even Italy, not Greece, has had more foreign lovers. And no country with pretensions to being a great power rouses more exasperation and abuse. In the love there has always been a tinge of unreason, a nervous anxiety to find excuses for failings—which is a profound insult. The abuse, the mockery, conceal a sour grain of envy. And none of these sentiments has any but the most superficial relevance to the real France; they exist almost wholly in our minds.

Is it true that France today is not, as in 1953 it was, a country of extreme contradictions: stretched irritated nerves and peasant stoicism, intellectual seriousness and political frivolity and corruption, insolent wealth and downright misery: a country radically stable, resting on the habits of greed and thrift which the sons of peasants take with them when they move into trades and professions, and little moved by giddy changes of government? Is it true that in the space of a few years General de Gaulle has changed all that?

Though I scarcely believe it, it is possible. The country may only have been waiting for a more adroit showman and despot than Napoleon.

Or—at least as possible—it may be that all but a few Frenchmen care very little who gives the orders. The only emotion common to every soul I talked to during our ten months was an instinctive contempt for politics and politicians—apart from the respect felt for a few, a very few, individuals. No one tried to discount the extent of political corruption. Nor was it anything new. What seemed new was the indifference to it, the total lack of heat in talking about it. The very man who had just been spitting his fury that Wall Street had forced his country to prolong the war in Indo-China ('fighting Communism with *our* bodies') became calmly cynically amused when all he wanted to say was that such and such an editor or deputy who supported the war had been paid to do it by French colonial interests. A well-documented exposure of financial thuggery, involving deputies and ministers, excited no one except, professionally, the journalists. From the man in the street, the shops, the offices, a shrug of the shoulder, a fine smile, resignation.

I came to believe that, just as the French are immune to bad drains, so they are at least partly immunized against political corruption and inefficiency—except when this last leaves them, as in 1939, almost naked before an enemy.

'In France, when all seems lost, a miracle happens.'

The pleasant fellow who repeated this facile saying went on, 'And invariably it takes the form of a man, not of a government. Let me give you an instance—every winter in Paris, walking home after dark, you might have to step over the body of a homeless man or woman trying to find traces of warmth near a ventilator of the Metro or the wall of a kitchen, and every winter a number of poor devils or their babies froze to death in the horrible shacks on the edge of the city. It was considered a sad state of affairs, and nothing was done. Until, last winter, suddenly, a man said: No, it's too much. In a few days the Abbé Pierre achieved more than any government would have done in years. It's always the same with us.'

'But the miracle isn't always on time!'

He shrugged. 'Perhaps not. But I expect it.'

With millions of others, less intelligent, he still regards de Gaulle as the just and necessary dictator. Not because he is a fascist at heart. But because, provided he is not too heavily taxed, one form of State is as good as the next; the things he considers essential to his happiness are all outside politics. A few citizens of the Fifth Republic are annoyed by its disciplines as sharply as they were by the corruption and fidgets of the Third. There are not enough of them to carry through a revolution.

Anything might follow the latest Napoleon. Even a democracy on the old model . . .

Our journey did not begin, properly speaking, until I had taken C. back to England and returned in the next boat to Dieppe. Except that it still has graces lacking to England—the servants in small hotels who without a breath of servility or self-consciousness give the impression that they enjoy working like slaves for sixteen hours a day, mechanics eager to flatter a sick car into health—the edge of Brittany in summer is as little France as possible. There is always the sense that the English coast is craning its neck to see across. I understand the disillusion of one of General de Gaulle's Free Frenchmen who took himself to Dover for the weekend, to be able to stare towards his country, and came back to London filled with bitterness.

'Not only was there a thick mist, but every time I made some pathetic or friendly remark to the Channel, the brute replied in English.'

'What did you expect?' I said. 'It is English.'

Guy had brought the car to the boat. I stepped in, and off we went, under a sky as flawlessly clean and new as the rebuilt towns and villages of these parts. The rebuilding has been done with intelligence (even affection): I felt a little sorry for the women still living in dilapidated unbombed cottages on the edge of one of these handsome new villages—until I remembered the weight of memory, of old beds and chairs, lace curtains, hideous photographs of weddings, christening robes, casseroles, that vanished in dust and terror.

The next morning, in Senlis, I bought our first *ficelle* of French bread, our first bottle of cheap wine and half-pound of local cheese, to be eaten by the roadside. The first moment of perfect happiness. Ridiculous—but, when I am living the sort of life which suits me, the only sort, a thread is enough to lift me to the heights.

Moving south, we sifted the familiar places through our fingers. We were making for Bordeaux, but before that, for the pure joy of it, we circled east and south, staying a night, two nights, a week—Montbard, Bourg-en-Bresse, Grenoble, Gap, Digne, Riez, Salernes, Draguignan, Grasse, Cagnes, Aix, Arles, Albi, Cahors. Living is simple and delicious when the heaviest problem of the day is a choice between two bakers, or two small shops both selling cheese, pâtés, wine. Then away, slowly, trusting in heaven that the unpromising cobbled street ahead will in a few minutes become the road south. Day after day of the solid secure warmth of the French summer, villages which seem empty, a countryside at once wide and intimate, the straight narrow streets of small towns, squeezed between the leprous walls of a sixteenth century mansion and the stunted arcade with its two small cafés side by side, strong shabby houses, a dusty square with its half-ruined fountain, the medlars, yews, and box-hedges of a walled garden, a mile-long avenue of great plane-trees, hedges covered with white dust, vineyards, deep valleys, farms, dry river-beds, olives. And we can go where we like, take any unmade road in search of a little-known church or walled mediæval village. We are free.

The hotel in Bourg-en-Bresse, with its faded ease and dusty smell of polish and old wood, could only be French. If, when I have been buried for a century or two, I am resurrected there, I shall know at once where I am. In more than twenty years, nothing has changed: the dining-room, as bare as that in my first school, is still serving the same splendid food to the successors of the commercial travellers, the notary, the senior clerks of before the war, and the decrepit cages lining the seedy glassed-in landing we cross to reach our bedroom house the descendants, sulky and moulting, of the birds here then.

'Surely there used to be a small monkey?'

'Dead. He is dead.' A pause and a quick brilliant smile. 'We are all mortal.'

Grenoble. With the best will in the world to flatter him, I cannot see it through Stendhal's eyes as 'la personnification de genre bourgeois et de la *nausée* exactement parlant': it is an inoffensive city, not handsome but decent, and resonant of mountains.

What, to be able to love it, I look for in a landscape is a bare hard line—no doubt the line, scored across the brain at the back of my eyes, of a short stretch of the North Sea coast. This hill country of Provence fills me with a contentment which must be exactly that of an infant set to the breast, as vacantly sensual. I draw in mindlessly the naked sides of hills, grey and bone-white, covered by a cindery dust of brittle grass and shrubs, villages clinging like wasps' nests to their crests above a few roughly walled terraces of vines and olives, the livid bristling rocks, a few poplars and cypresses, the road turning on itself endlessly between eroded hillside and precipice, the hissing sound given off by scorched thistles and rosemary, the grey fields of lavender, sparse wind-stunted trees, spruce, oak, rowan, and ahead the Alp-fanged horizon. It is a landscape without a trace of sentiment.

Even before we reached Aix, the sun was beginning to press its thumb against the back of the skull. In Aix itself, it drew from the gutters and old handsome buildings a pervasive smell of decay, the August stench of a town in the Midi. Why, I wondered, have the French never managed to achieve either an efficient drainage system or an efficient system of government? The answer must be the same for both. They don't care. Charming dilapidated streets and small squares stank of a sour dust, like ancient ovens, and in the magnificent Cours Mirabeau the trees gave shade without freshness, their depths sucked dry and empty by the violent light. Giraudoux set the opening scenes of *Pour Lucrèce* in one of the unpretentious cafés facing them: the elegance, if it ever existed, has evaporated, but to sit there gave me a gentle pleasure, like fingering dried woodruff.

We stayed three days before going on to Arles. The heat now was all but unbearable, a molten torrent pouring from a sky of white-hot metal. Pulverized by the searing light, trees, the walls of houses, the road itself, flickered across the eyeballs as in a bad early film. I was rash enough to walk, in this murderous sun, the length of the Aliscamps. It was nakedly horrible. Nothing of the poetry Rilke found there clings round the double line of sarcophagi foundering in the thick dust, or in the small empty Romanesque church, its crypt filled with a sickening breath of decay and corruption. Down here, for the first and only time in my life, I felt death as an immediate reality, filling my nostrils, eyes, mouth. I could have spat it out, and I felt ill—no, not ill, I felt that I was disintegrating, the flesh parting from my bones, an extraordinary sense of uncertainty and dissolution. Either I am going mad or I have a fever, I thought. I managed to hide my vexing state, and carefully did not take my temperature; in the morning fever and uncertainty had gone, both of them, and I felt ready for anything. Except, ever again, the dust and tombs of that abominable avenue.

Bare as it is, the bones showing through the thin skin, there is nothing arid about the country near Albi, a landscape of smoothly sculptured hills, grey-green, white, ivory, yellow, dead-leaf brown, wide planes of extreme delicacy: the scattered farms of pink brick or sun-yellowed plaster, red-tiled, have an air of candour and almost of ease. Albi itself is not candid. How could it be, in the shadow of that superbly menacing cathedral, more fortress than church? Inside, an inconceivable turbulence of colour and statues, the work of sculptors whose heads were full of any but religious ideas: he was no pious fellow who modelled the fifteenth century Judith in the ambulatory, with heavy sensual lids falling over her slanting eyes, delicate nose, and fine greedy mouth and chin, long-fingered hands gathering up the folds of an opulent dress.

A slit window on the staircase of the Bishop's Palace, itself once a fortress, now a museum of Toulouse-Lautrec's profane art, looks over the old city. That day, under an unclouded September sky, the river Tarn was running clay-red under red bridges, between the faded red fleece of roofs and the massive dark red Cathedral; it was singularly disturbing, as though a vein had opened in Albi's bloody heretic-burning past.

In the bakery next morning, a middle-aged woman, tall, lean, beaked, in grey alpaca with an aggressive toque, spoke to me in a sudden harsh voice.

'Are you German?'

'No. English.'

'Ah—' an ill-humoured sound—'I was told there was a German woman here.'

Why should she have given it a second thought? France was full of Germans, in sturdy Volkswagens and immense self-confident Mercedes, more Germans than English, and with more money to spend.

Our last night before Bordeaux was spent outside Cahors, in the Château de Mercués. My room looked down a great way to the Lot, and across the valley of unhedged fields to the hills; in the clear light the reflections of trees in the water were sharp and unmoving, as sharp as their long shadows across the earth. I thought: I could stand here forever, looking.

I had twenty minutes of pure happiness—really without any reason. Charming as it is at this point, the Lot is no more beautiful than other French rivers I know. At another moment, in another light, I might have looked, and looked away.

There is no accounting for these invasions—the correct word—of an overwhelming force of happiness, irrational and piercing. Entirely unlike the pleasure one takes in a fine day, a meeting with a friend, warmth after cold, the taste of new bread, it is not dependent on anything I may be looking at or touching. No doubt it depends on what the scene itself stands for, the surfacing of a deep primitive image—in my life, the sea, distant points of light, the tolling of the Whitby bell-buoy, the burning purity of a field of dog-daisies, the line, hard, severe, living, of the Whitby coast seen from the cliffs.

To our astonishment, Bordeaux, on the 19th of September, was crowded, not a bed to be had. It was international football or a Congress—I forget. After a long search, we got a room, a very small dark room, airless and evil-smelling. At the time I did not know it, but it was the hotel in which our ambassador and members of his staff lived for a short time in June 1940—they were there when the Germans entered Paris. No doubt their rooms were more elegant than ours, but they felt the same need to console themselves by eating in the Chapon Fin, across the narrow road from the hotel.

My love for Bordeaux is a little more than the pleasure it gives me to be in any foreign city; it is twisted round my young mother's memories of its streets and harbour, and although I had given up looking for her, as on earlier visits I looked, trying to come up with her in this busy street, this narrow dark glove shop, this garden with its iron chairs and magnolia trees, something of that obsession remains, like the all but effaced outlines of an old photograph. It is a handsome city, not in the least gracious—*une ville de cadavres*, a young woman said bitterly, when I was speaking about it with affection.

I don't ask a foreign town to be sympathetic; all I ask of it is to be immovably itself, reserved, coldly oppressive, friendly, as it pleases, but itself.

After five nights in the hotel, we moved to rooms in a large solidly dignified house some twenty minutes walk from the centre. It belonged to the young-middle-aged widow of a civil servant, who ran it as a pension for American students. Since the university term did not begin for another four or five weeks we could have two rooms and a bathroom, at a cost less than the cheapest hotel possible. Obviously, the rooms would be cold—but we had to economize, and I liked Madame B. She had a quick dark-eyed vivacity and, for all that she had never expected to keep herself and her four children by turning her house into a boarding-house, no trace of resentment. She was a good manager, a little too good. The meals, except on rare days when *mon père* came from his estate near Agen for the night, bringing game, fruit, pâtés, and bottles of his own wine, were extremely meagre: a huge dish of beans, with a few slivers of stringy meat lost in it, appeared again and again during the week. At the end of a month I had lost a stone in weight. It was worth it to live in Bordeaux.

Mon père was intelligent and a sceptic. One day when he saw me reading a Paris newspaper he remarked drily that if he wanted news of what was going on up there he had only to read any pre-war journal lining a shelf in his loft. The same tricks, the same corruption, even the same names.

'D'you expect me to take an interest in these broken-winded old horses as they tumble round the ring? Some of them can't even tumble, they're stuffed with sawdust.'

I had brought with me to France the typescript of *The Hidden River*. Six months ago, when I posted it to New York, to Carl Brandt, I supposed I had done with it, but he persuaded an editor of the *Saturday Evening Post* that it only needed a few changes to be worth thirty thousand dollars, and—to make certain that I did not, out of impatience and boredom, throw away this (to me) unheard-of sum—he covered three folio sheets in his fine angular writing, telling me precisely what to do. None of the changes he suggested touched the theme of the book, it was the plot, only the plot, that needed more flesh on its classical bones, and if this could be done by involving the one English character in an emotional affair, why not? I regretted the blurring of a clear hard outline, but—more even than the money—I wanted Carl to approve of me. Most of all, I was ashamed—as I am always—to seem by refusing to put too high a value on my work.

As soon as we were settled in Madame B.'s house, I laid out Carl's pages on the table in my cold bedroom, and set to work.

Guy was working in the library of the university, and we met every day between half-past five and six in a dark worn little café on the Cours Clemenceau. I walked there, a long walk through grey sombre streets, becoming crowded and lively as they neared the centre. Very often it rained, and the cobblestones were unpleasantly greasy. I was always hungry, and our choice lay between the Café Cardinal and hot chocolate and brioches in a pâtisserie: once or twice I weakened, not many times. Not only was it cheaper to drink, but the waiter who served us was an amiable old fellow and treated us with great gentleness, as though we were friends recovering from an illness. One day when I arrived, wet and shivering with cold, he bent over me and said softly, 'Not an *amer picon* this evening. A grog!'

Heaven knows what, besides rum, was in his grog; it sent the blood swirling through my body to the ends of my fingers. After this I drank it on every cold rainy evening . . .

It was not always raining. Some days were fine and warm, with a light as smooth as honey, the light, exquisite, of the Dordogne in autumn. On one such day at the end of October, we drove the twenty miles to Saint-Emilion.

Anyone who wishes to see France in a day should ask to be set down in Saint-Emilion. It is a town of less than four thousand inhabitants, gripping the edge of a rocky slope above the valley of the Dordogne, in the heart of the great vineyards. The earliest houses were built by Gauls across the marks left by prehistoric man: Roman colonists added their splendid villas—did one of these belong to Ausonius?—and planted vineyards which produced a wine well thought of in Rome itself. The first barbarians to turn up sacked the villas, settled down, and let the place civilize them. Then came the

Saracens; then, at the end of the ninth century, Normans who did not entirely destroy the great church dug out of the rocky cliff itself. In the twelfth, Saint-Emilion—now a strong walled town of churches, monasteries, great houses—was confirmed in its civic rights by King John of England.

This was before the English were chased out of France, a disaster for both countries, which has not yet been righted.

In the following century, a French king seized the place. We retook it and, except for brief intervals, held on to it until 1453. Savaged with equal energy by both sides in the Wars of Religion, it became what it is now, a little town of steep narrow twisted streets, the fragments of great buildings woven into a living pattern: a vineyard stretches across a mediæval cemetery, wine is bottled and stored below the cloistered ruins of a thirteenth century monastery. The past is not dead here, it is in use.

It was too late in the year for tourists. We were alone in the great Collegiate Church. Its very small Chapel of the Dead had (I hope has) the most extraordinary of tombs. It was not beautiful—a mound of dry earth in the centre of the floor, the size and shape of a child's grave. Small fragments of stone had been stuck in the soil to mark out a cross, as children stick pebbles in a sand-castle. At the head of the narrow little mound, a small upright cross formed from two pieces of wood no thicker than a wrist, the bark still on them; a poilu's steel helmet rested on this cross, and a small card, pinned to the wood, read: *Les Enfants de St Emilion*. What this grave said was very severe and very simple. To hide my tears, I stared at the list of names on the wall, a long list for the war of 1914-18, a very much shorter one, fourteen names, for 1939-45, and a third list of *victimes civiles*, six men and four women. Two families, the Dubois and the Jardilliers, lost between them four men and two women.

The old chairwoman, a huddle of bones and black dusty garments, the skin of her face and neck riddled with cracks, was waiting to take us round the cloisters. I asked a timid question about the civilian dead. She made a curious gesture, as though brushing a hair from her face. 'Oh, not many, not many,' she said almost inaudibly, and began to talk about the Germans. 'Some of their soldiers came to the church. Why not? They were Catholics, after all. Everyone left them to sit alone.'

One day a German colonel came to look round the church, and asked her about a fourteenth century wooden statue against the wall.

'I told him it was English. He said it reminded him of the Baron de Rothschild. I asked him: Do you know the Baron? He said: Oh, yes, very well. Then he asked me what the English were doing here with their statue. I told him: They were occupying the place, like you.' She opened a black toothless mouth in a wavering smile. To excuse herself for her rashness, she added, 'After all, at my age—eighty-seven—can it matter what happens?'

She stood with us on the steps of the porch, the sunlight covering her wrinkled skin with a fine varnish. Her smile became ironical.

'I knew they would go in the end. Just as you went.'

Her certainty that France will always civilize or reject an invader was lightly reassuring.

Early in November we moved south to St Jean de Luz.

I am devoted to the Basque country, and I like and respect the Basques. Whatever part of Europe or Asia these people came from, they brought with them every virtue of the north except its jeering bitter humour; they are hard, direct, and seem to have no defensive vanity, either of the Southern French kind or any other. As for the coast, in certain lights it is like enough my own to bring a knot of grief and loss into my throat—and, at least once in the day, a few minutes of happiness without thought, the happiness of a child.

I wrote at a table set in the window of my bedroom. The days were warm, with only a little rain, and when I looked up from my manuscript I saw the wide bay under a sky of extraordinary gentleness and purity, even gentler after rain and when a wind from the southwest blew white flakes of cloud above the horizon as lightly as a girl lifts her long hair on the back of her hand. Towards dusk, the fishing boats, about forty of them, worked their way in. They carried one riding light, reflected in the wrinkled grey water. At the farther side of the bay, the hill was the colour of a pigeon's breast: a single red light flashed on the cliff, and another, white, sparked in and out at the end of the long jetty. There were the lights of houses, not many, along the side of the hill, above the harbour, sweeping me back every evening to my mother's childhood. Behind the low hill another, higher, darker, more blue than grey, rose brusquely at the other side of the Spanish frontier. The boats came in between the jetty and a long stone barrier, under a sky darkening to the colour of the hill, with a single very bright star.

We stayed here a full month and left reluctantly, to make our way east, very slowly, sleeping a night in Toulouse, Béziers, Aix, to Vence.

From Vence we walked about the naked stony country behind, pastures of thin turf, gnawed to the bone by the cold wind, rising, slowly at first, then steeply, towards the circle of hills, dry, flayed; a few leafless iron trees and stunted shrubs; a few villages, their outer walls so near in colour to the greyish-ochre soil that they seemed part of the rocky slope behind them, as ancient and unfriendly. A few terraces of vines and olives were scrawled with rough patience immediately below the crumbling walls. In the distance the amphitheatre of foothills hiding the real mountains, between each crest a sharp void, no softening mists.

Walking along the cobbled street of one of these villages, between squat shabby secretive houses, the only inhabitants we saw might be two or three old men with bodies like withered vine-roots, the flesh dried from the bones, sitting or standing immobile in their stained threadbare garments. They glanced at us, once, out of colourless eyes hidden instantly behind dark wrinkled lids. These men, Denis Saurat told us later, were all well-off; many of them owned property in Vence or in Nice itself. Their wealth was land, sheep, cattle. You could take away all their money, and not one of them would live any differently: they did not live on their money. The state in France has far less call on the real wealth of its members than it has in England. Hence the indifference of so many of them to its goings-on. Why should they care?

In December we moved down to the coast, to Nice, the Nice of the now unfashionable winter, belonging only to its citizens, very pleasant, and took rooms in a pension in the high Cimiez quarter. It was up here that Queen Victoria used to stay, in a vast hotel named for her, the Hôtel Regina, now a great haggard block of flats, with a superb view above the town to the sea. The pension, run by a Madame P., a shuffling active old body, the veins of her neck and legs in relief, was warm and shabby. My room had its own bathroom, which stank so foully that I had to be careful to keep the door tightly shut. When I complained, mildly, of the smell, Madame P. said anxiously that something, the root of a palm-tree in the neglected garden, was choking the drain. Nothing worse. One could not, surely I would agree, receive any harm from the root of a palm. I accepted the explanation, and indeed received no harm during the three months I worked and slept in the room.

Madame P. was so desperately anxious to please, and so friendly that I became fond of her, and could smile with a pretence of delight when for the fourth time in a week, '*pour changer les idées,*' she gave us fennel root, that most loathsome of vegetables. Another thing she served freely was *loup*, a fish with the texture of old flannel.

Everywhere in our zig-zag journey through France we had come on plaques and single stones carrying the names of men and women shot, hanged, or tortured to death during the Occupation. Entering the main square of Nice, we passed two of these memorials. If we had come this way on the 7th of July 1944, we should have had to pass the bodies of two young men, Ange Grassi and Seraphim Torrin, hanged and exposed in this place. The same phrase was repeated on both plaques: *Passant, incline-toi, souviens-toi.*

What, I wondered, did the French passer-by remember? True, the resisters were a handful of Frenchmen; true, the girding anxiety of most people in those years was to get hold of enough food to keep a child from becoming tuberculous; true, many men and women could say what a Parisian woman staying in the pension said to me: 'The Germans? Oh, they gave no one any trouble. Unless you were silly enough to get mixed up in something.' All true. But the discomfort, the hardships, the despair of a few, the deportations, the executions, must—surely?—have left a mark on the country. Only, perhaps, as an adult may be scarred, lightly, by an act of cruelty he heard tell of as a child. Perhaps not even that? My peacock-voiced Parisian? Madame P.'s youngest grandson, a handsome demon of four?

A village I saw later, five months later, Frayssinet-le-Gelat, on the road between Beynac and Cahors, has one of the most terrible of these monuments. Darkness was falling when we drove into the place, which seemed to be empty. I caught sight as we passed it of a large block of stone, and stopped the car to look at it. (It always seemed impolite not to stop.) There was the usual inscription— *Aux Martyrs de la barbarie Allemande*—and below the fifteen names the date, 21 Mai 1944, and the usual two words. *Souvenez-vous.*

A door opened in one of the grey houses, a woman profiled on the weak light looked at us for a moment, and closed the door again quietly. Even if she had stepped outside, I should not have dared question her. Something—the darkness, the heaviness of the stone, the dark church behind it, the silence, even the unprepossessing look of the village—started up a feeling of anguish so acute that later I wrote to the Archivist of the department (of the Lot) to ask him what had happened on the 21st of May 1944 in Frayssinet-le-Gelat. He told me. That day a German division on its way to Normandy was passing through, a shot was fired, coming, the Germans thought, from a cottage where three old women were living; the soldiers dragged the old creatures out and hanged them outside the little church, summoning the rest of the village to watch. Then they picked out ten villagers to be shot, among them a schoolboy from the philosophy class in Cahors whose parents had brought him here for safety. The father asked to be shot in his place, and the German officer added him to the rest.

That accounts for fourteen of the names. But there are fifteen, eleven men and four women. Who is the fourth woman? I feel something like remorse that I don't know how she offended or how she died, whether she was one of the two Lugan sisters, or Agathe Paille, or Yvonne Vidilles.

After a time I noticed that the apathy of many people to the political harlequinade broke, when it did break, precisely over the question of Germany. Possibly the break marked a still suppurating wound in the country's instinctive energy. No foreigner could have probed it without running the risk of an atrocious blunder. Suppose I had been unlucky enough to speak about Nazi brutality to the charming intelligent woman we met here whose husband and son had both been arrested and shot, as resisters, by the *French* police?

That happened before the Liberation. After the Liberation, thousands of innocent persons, no one knows how many, died, murdered by patriots acting on lying denunciations, or by communists getting rid at this convenient moment of political opponents, or—perhaps less often—by persons seizing their chance to lay hands on a coveted field, or to pay off old scores or to cancel a debt by abolishing the creditor. One evening at the end of September 1944, when Agen and the whole region had long been free of Germans, four officers of the local Resistance forces turned up at the farm of a family which had taken a serious and costly part in the Resistance; they walked in unhindered, and killed the twenty-year-old son of the house, his mother, and another young man, a friend. A girl, in the house by chance, was taken outside and machine-gunned, but survived. After nine years, the case came before the tribunal in Bordeaux: friends and relatives of the murdered family at last felt safe enough to tell the truth. That the *execution*—what is language for but to ennoble our actions?—had been a personal vengeance: the dead boy was believed to have in his possession a document compromising to his comrades in the Resistance.

A young man, the eldest son of a Catholic family, was denounced as a collaborator by his fellow-resisters, good Party members, and shot 'legally'. The denunciators were saving themselves the trouble of an *execution*.

The newspapers I read that December in Nice were filled with details, only now, nine years after the event, being dragged into the light, of the summary executions in the Limousin, Giraudoux's Limousin, in July 1944. During that month (two months after the Frayssinet affair), the greater number of the non-communist resisters of the region were shot and their bodies hurriedly pushed into the ground, in fields and woods, by their ex-comrades of the maquis, acting under the orders of their chief, the Liberation mayor of Limoges and a member of the Party.

'What d'you expect?' a Frenchman said—with an extraordinary air of reserve and contempt. 'That a few months or years in the Resistance would turn a loyal communist into a loyal human being?'

No person whose country has never been occupied has the right to comment. But if I were the leader of a partisan revolt or revolution, of any colour, I should be less afraid of my opponents than of the impatience of my followers. After three or four years of heroic killings what, I ask you, could be more natural than to see murder as a handy way of getting rid of an embarrassment? To think anything else about these—these exercises, is hypocrisy or moonshine.

I worked at *The Hidden River* all day. The new version was going very slowly because of my extreme boredom when I have to describe a love scene. This boredom had been growing in me for some years and had reached a point when I could write about the emotions of a pair of lovers—not to speak of their acts—only by a torturing and tortuous effort of memory. It began—my boredom—on the day when I became sensible and ceased to fall in love for a few hours with the head or profile of some total stranger.

Some time towards the end of the year I read, I think in *Figaro Littéraire*, that *Scrutiny* was going to stop, and wrote to ask F. R. Leavis if this bad news were true.

'... *Scrutiny* has stopped,' he answered, 'because I am beaten ...

The immediate cause of death is the impossibility of holding any-thing like an adequate collaborating team in the field. But the radical cause is my utter defeat at Cambridge. To run a review and a one-man "English School" (the two going essentially together) in ostracism—no, it couldn't be done forever. People flatter me about my "influence", but it has failed to get me a glimmer of recognition at the place where above all it matters. How could *Scrutiny* be made a permanency, except from a continuing centre of intellectual life at an ancient university? Actually, the result of running *Scrutiny* (the reward) is that I am more isolated than ever. The fact intimately associated with the death of *Scrutiny* is that my *Education and the University* has never been recognized to exist, even to disagree with, at Cambridge. What it did was to confirm my life-long exclusion from any say in the English School. When I am retired (on the pension of one who wrested a part-time lectureship from the Faculty at forty-two, and a full-time lectureship at fifty-two) all that I have worked for at Cambridge peters out.

'I *am* sad about it. Without a focus, a source of impulsion, at an ancient university, I don't believe that much can be done in the provincial universities, or the schools or anywhere (I mean, of course, what I—am I egotistic?—have fought for) . . . No one is without vanity, but I think I care as little about mere kudos as any-one. But the lack of recognition in any form that could compel corresponding recognition at Cambridge has been fatal. That's why the boycott mattered . . . What is so depressing is the evidence—of which I'm now getting so much—of a potentially formidable public opinion, and the complete absence of any bringing to bear . . . And what a loss!—how irreplaceable *Scrutiny* is!—that's the chorus now . . .'

In this letter, and in one he wrote a month later, he spoke of his wife's bitter sense that both their lives had been sacrificed 'for nothing'.

I understood that. I know the frightful recoil of the heart in the moment of defeat. I understood with the marrow of my bones that a lifetime of exhausting work, devotion, laying aside of personal ambition, slow loss of hope, must, at this moment, turn to a nearly inconceivable bitterness and anger. She had never compromised, never sacrificed a living soul to her own ambitions, needs, hungers. Her singlemindedness and honesty were as absolute as her hus-band's.

The contrast between their integrity and my bad faith in altering *The Hidden River* was bitter in my belly. For a short time I wrestled with the impulse to cable to New York that I could not finish the revision.

I lacked the courage. I could not face the loss of thirty—thirty!—thousand dollars, and Carl Brandt's anger. And, too, I lacked confidence, arrogance, call it what you like. Pushed to the wall, I could not believe that anything I had written, anything I could ever write, was so good, so important that I had a duty to turn away money I needed.

I wrote a careful letter to *Time and Tide* about the death of *Scrutiny*, and went back to my task . . .

We had friends living ten minutes walk from Madame P.'s, in a flat in the Hôtel Regina, below the flat where Matisse was living. Denis Saurat and his wife. They came here to live when he retired from his university chair in London, after his abrupt dismissal, on General de Gaulle's orders, from the French Institute. His crime: that he loved England a great deal better than he loved the General. Yet he began, in 1940, by a passion of devotion and gratitude to the man he came later to see as a potential dictator. In 1942, disillusioned, he asked me for an introduction to a visiting American journalist, Maxine Davis; he wanted her to warn her countrymen that whether they admired or distrusted the General it was for the wrong reasons. I arranged for him to see her.

'Can I believe him?' she asked me.

'Anything he tells you will be true,' I said. 'You have only to remember that it is the truth seen by a metaphysical poet, a descendant of Cathars, an intellectual, and a shrewd administrator.'

When I left her, I caught sight of him in the crowded entrance hall of Claridge's, waiting to be summoned to her room, a frail tiny figure of a would-be giant killer.

His punishment at the end of the war came swiftly—the General is not magnanimous. And his bad reputation as a lover of the English followed him to Nice. The official of Aix University—on which the University Centre of Nice depended—detested him as an 'English interloper', and saw to it that he was never made use of by the Centre. Theirs the loss—of a lucid inquisitive mind, a scholarly gadfly, a wit.

No saint, and not without self-esteem, he resented his exclusion. But he was not unhappy, perched, a brilliant bird, in a room high above the mists of the lower town. Bird or dancer? His mind had the disciplined lightness and precision of a highly-trained ballet dancer. He talked superbly. He was never able to resist a verbal pirouette, but he pirouetted on a base of knowledge and speculation in his fields.

Listening to him here, I thought that living on the edge of an old myth-soaked Europe, under a hot sun, had brought nearer the surface the fantastic side of his intelligence—*un peu sorcier, un peu thaumaturge de ses montagnes originelles*, André Chamson said in a brief obituary. (How the French love a Tombeau de . . ., and how well, how adroitly, they write it!) The scholar drew back a little behind the wide-awake dreamer of *La Mort et le Rêveur*, the mystical poet of *Le Soldat Romain*. He amused his leisure with myths, half-believer, half-sceptic. A root of his mind was Manichean, that logical ambiguous faith. And why not? He came from a part of France where it died hardest—if it is dead.

During this winter we saw him four or five times a week. Either he lunched with us in our pension, eating slice after slice of the pale tasteless veal Madame P. provided when she knew he was coming, or we went to his flat in the afternoon. He had a great many friends —among them a retired professor of history who was unable to believe that Germans and Americans were not one and the same barbarian on the frontier.

'They come here, your Americans, like a successful man coming back to his village and finding his old cousins still living their lives by a tradition he can't feel, which makes no sense to him. And no one can convince him that civilization and power are not the same thing. Let me tell you what I would tell Americans who are not bankers like Foster Dulles or amateur politicians like Eisenhower— if I could get at them. I would say: You are handing back to the Germans the arms millions of men and women died to take from them—you hope they will glut themselves by turning east. But why, to satisfy your bankers, should we loose these brutes on Poles, Czechs, Russians, whom we have no wish to injure, nor they us? Why for the love of God should we help you to set fire to Europe? Tell me that!'

'The Americans won't start a war——'

'Then why are they taking such pains to provoke Russia? Oh, I know as well as you that your American market gardener and the rest is as much a victim as if he were only a poor French market gardener. It makes no difference. Yes, there is a difference. More of them will survive another war. But they won't, for that, constitute a civilization. A French government with the moral courage of any poor devil of a second lieutenant would order America to withdraw its occupying troops and invite the rest of western Europe to join us in a neutrality pact that would satisfy the Russians they had nothing to fear in Europe. If Mr Dulles felt compelled to go on issuing his challenges it would be his funeral, not ours. No sort of obligation compels us French to join him in his bloody adventure. We should be rebuilding France, planting vines, breeding children. God send us an intelligent dictator!'

'It will serve you right if He does,' Denis said with a purely malicious smile. 'A people that can't run its affairs without one deserves nothing better.'

He had a weakness, dear Denis, for well-born women. One after-noon there were two drinking tea in his living-room: Madame de Broglie, and Madame de Clermont-Tonnerre, the first a short energetic old lady, the second holding together with difficulty a long ruined body and long yellow equine face across which an amiable smile came and went, never able to lodge itself in any of the folds of ill-fitting skin. They had brought with them a strong handsome Flemish mare of a young woman, a Comtesse de —— what? I have forgotten. A passionate argument broke out between the young woman and Madame de Broglie about loving God.

Speaking with the utmost respect, the young woman said, 'But, Madame la Duchesse, I must, I simply must believe that we can love God even though we haven't seen him. All the saints——'

Madame de Broglie had rolled a newspaper into a baton. Brandish-ing it, she cut the young woman short with arrogant familiarity, as though she were a tiresome child. 'My good girl, you are talking the most complete rubbish. Why bring in the saints? I behave as I was brought up to behave. How can I be asked to love any person, how-ever exalted, whom I have never met? It's ridiculous. And per-fectly unreasonable.'

Blushing a little, the young woman insisted. 'Excuse me, Madame la Duchesse, if I say that I myself——'

'No, no, no,' Madame de Broglie interrupted again, 'I could never do it. Respect, obedience, belief, anything you like, but not love. What do you want me to do about it? I'm made like that!' She turned to her old friend. 'And you, my dear? Do you love God? You know the difference between love and respect, I hope. Your husband should have taught you that.'

Her affable smile wavered across Madame de Clermont-Tonnerre's eyes, leaving them vacant and childlike.

'Yes, yes, you are right,' she said in a hoarse voice, 'between love and respect there is an impassable gulf.'

'I don't understand either of you,' exclaimed the young woman.

'Perhaps when you are older, my child, and have been married for longer than a year . . .'

How I regret that, a little over four years later, Denis Saurat died. We have a surfeit of visionaries without intelligence and scholars without gaiety. When he died, a little of its salt and honey vanished from this lower world. I could better spare a number of judicious intellectual heavyweights with both feet planted immovably and solemnly on the ground.

A village a few miles south of the road from Cagnes to Grasse, reached by an execrable road, is more familiar to me than the university city I am living in at this moment. There is no explaining these quirks of the mind: if I tried to say why, for several hours, I was perfectly happy and at home in a small lost Provençal village, without any obvious charm, I should write nonsense or literature.

We went there first in the middle of January, with Maria Kuncewiczowa and her husband; they knew it because they had lived in the village for several weeks, in one of the old houses of blackish stone which looked to be on the point of crumbling into rubble—if it had had a thousand francs worth of repairs done on it in three hundred years that was all, and it was good for another four or five centuries. A village of dark lanes climbing steeply, step by shallow uneven step of cobblestones and dry earth, smelling of garlic and urine, and two narrow streets of taller houses, a few of them empty, all strong and shabby, here and there doors framed in blocks of old sculptured stone. No lane or so-called street had been made; all were stony and deeply rutted, thick in dust in summer, in mud the rest of the year. Both streets cut across the side of the hill, so that houses with a single storey on one side of the upper street had three or even four on the parallel street lower down. The upper street dropped sharply, between dark shuttered houses, from the large uncouth square, a stretch of bare earth, on the edge of the village, and came to a stop in a narrow stony place and a shabby bistro: a few yards of low wall outside the bistro overhung the hillside scored across and across by neglected rows of olives, below them a rocky precipice fell steeply, flowing into the folds of less savage hills, coiling and uncoiling, and flattening at last into the thin glittering knife edge of the coast.

Outside the village, at its lower end, two women and a boy were gathering olives. One of the women was old, bent into a hoop of blackened skin and bone; the other, elderly, had the profile of a Roman matron, features perfectly regular under thick coils of black hair, pure black, shining with oil. I had seen others of these Roman heads in this once Greek and then Roman countryside, but never one so superbly carved and massive. Using a long thin stick, the boy whipped the branches, and as the ripe olives fell on to the sheet spread below the trees, the two women sorted them deftly into baskets.

The sun, the light wind, a sky of incomparable freshness, the movement of the Roman woman's arms, movements she had been making for a score of centuries, at least a score, ran together in my mind to evoke an image which may—how do I know?—have been formed there before I was born.

Maria had several friends in the place. No one, not even an inhabitant of these savage hills, could have refused to accept a friendliness as simple and graceful as the gestures of her fine Polish hands. She knew everything about the marital troubles of Madame Titine, who managed the bistro where we ate a magnificent salad and drank a great deal of strong red wine; she knew, about the families of a few peasants and the owners of one or two of these forbidding frostblackened houses, stories which form part of an Iliad of obscure hatreds, quarrels, adulteries, marriages. How, without asking a single question, did she discover so much? Simply by living here, by listening, smiling.

One of her friends, the gentle dark-haired boy who knitted and drew sketches of women's dresses, and confided in her that he wanted to become a fashion designer, turned, a few years later, into a girl.

But for Maria we should not have come here, and I should have missed a pleasure so exactly my size that I have been drawing on it ever since. Altered, merged with another of these villages which, seen from above or below, look like ossuaries, indistinguishable from the livid rocks of their hill, or identical with itself, it returned in three novels.

When, in March, to everyone's satisfaction except mine, I finished the new version of *The Hidden River*, we left Nice. Aix for two nights: Valence, where we ate the most superb dinner and were kept awake until dawn by cars and lorries clattering through the walls of the room and across the beds; Nevers. This unassuming old city climbing staidly above the Loire and the Nièvre is dear to me: I fell in love with it on my first visit, without knowing why. This time—as well as cheese and bread—I bought a copy of the *Mémoires d'un touriste*, to replace one left behind in Aix: it is the one of my travel books I carry as an act of piety.

From Nevers to Paris. We stayed four weeks, and I remember little except the cold: the leaves of plane trees and chestnuts remained folded and the river as grey as though, higher up, it were full of snow: which was impossible. We saw *Pour Lucrèce*, so finely acted and presented—except that Madeline Renaud was too old for the part; she looked middle-aged, almost haggard—that it was easy to overlook the weariness, like the turns and twists of an old acrobat, still clever but tired to death, of the writer.

My other clear memory is of a visit to the remnants, outside Paris, of Port-Royal. The guide who took us round the commemorative chapel could exist only in France. Hands in the pockets of his workman's blue overalls, he discussed, with enthusiasm and knowledge, the events of the period, the characters of Louis XIV, Pascal, Arnauld, points of doctrine. No intellectual, adept in the history of Jansenism, would have shown himself subtler and more acute. A guide in a shrine little visited and, except for the death-mask of Mère Angélique, little notable—it seems nothing much. It was everything. Outlined on the clear cold March sunlight of the Ile-de-France, a whole irreplaceable civilization . . .

Longing for warmth, we went south again, to Provence. Still the spring did not come.

An ice-cold knife of wind moved through St Paul de Vence, and among the monstrous remnants of Les Baux and in the steep dark street of mediæval Vaison-la-Romaine. Snow began falling in May. We crossed the Rhône and drove through snow-storms and an icy wind as far east as Roquefort: the only guests in a hotel filled with scaffolding, we were served a dinner Petronius would have found a

little exaggerated. In the morning the cold drove us away from caves
filled with cheeses.

During the four days we spent in the Château de Mercués, a
slight warmth began to come into the air: at midday the sun was
almost strong.

Although I had seen the cave drawings at Lascaux before this, and
looked at them, as I thought, carefully, I had forgotten the one
radical thing about them, their purely sensuous energy. The men
crouching in these dark passages in the rocky cliff had behind their
eyes an image of the animal they were drawing so shockingly clear,
so detailed, that it inhibited every energetic impulse except the
primitive impulse of the artist, the maker, to set it free, without
distortion or interference. I don't for a moment believe that they
made these drawings only because they thought that in some magical
way the effort helped them to hunt down the beast they drew. But
no matter. The directness of these paintings and sketches, the life
captured in them, places them at the farthest possible distance from
abstract art—which is a sort of rhetoric in paint. A rhetoric in flight
from the naked statement. Where these first artists wanted to stalk
and free the force of life behind the image, the compelling wish of an
abstract painter or sculptor is to free *himself* from the coils of nature.
To create a style which has no frame of reference outside himself.
The price of his freedom is the isolation of his work on a mandarin
level of existence.

Looking closely at a modern *construction*, in iron or glass or wire, I
have the sense that its maker has tried to grasp and project some
hallucinating image proffered him by the nerves behind his eyes.
Even successful, the attempt excludes me. Excludes any spectator
unwilling to dupe himself. I could, as writers on art do, turn his
constructions into literature. That is, into a construction of my own,
which, if I am honest, I know has nothing in common with his.
Most criticism of abstract art is, in this sense, dishonest. Reading
that such and such an abstract painting of a naked man 'reveals an
imaginative energy at once abstract and sensuous,' I feel that the
writer, if not consciously dishonest, does not know what certain
words mean. The energy in the painting he is describing is intellectual, not imaginative, and what has been ignored (by the artist) is
precisely the infinite possibilities, the magnificently subtle sensuous
organization of the body.

Moreover, the finest constructions of this sort are extraordinarily clumsy and childish compared with the complicated and very beautiful machines and machine tools designed and perfected in a modern engineering works. In September 1940 I visited a number of armaments factories—to write a short book for the Ministry of Supply, which in the end I did not write. The machines and machine tools I saw in various heavy arms works were in a real sense the modern successors of the figures of Michelangelo. Beside them, the work of any constructivist is puerile, inept, empty, derived from the brain and nerves. These machines are made with the entrails as well as with the brain.

Oddly enough, there is one art which is able to be supremely sensuous and in the highest degree abstract—music. The phrase about an imaginative energy at once abstract and sensuous applies truthfully to Schönberg. Why? I am too ignorant to know why. Possibly the ear is the channel for a subtler, more complicated sense than the eye?

Crossing the empty country north of the Pyrenees, we passed continually from sunlight to rain, brilliant colours in the fields and hedges, then a long grey rippling curtain—a chameleon would have gone off his head. At last, in Bordeaux, spring rushed in, barely ahead of summer, bringing in everything at once, acacias, lime blossom, incandescent skies at noon, long warm unblemished evenings.

We stayed in the Chapon Fin itself. It was a delicious hotel, not many bedrooms, discreet, old-fashioned, with majestic mahogany furniture, like the bedrooms in my grandfather's house, breakfasts of strong coffee and magnificent croissants worthy of the creators of the most lovable, most finely civilized, least assuming, of great restaurants. Alas, a casualty of our insensitive heartless sinister age, it has vanished. Serve us right for surviving into a time which prefers computers and the Hilton hotels to peace of mind and body and the Chapon Fin.

Nothing, surely nothing, can mar the Dordogne valley. A short way beyond Libourne there was—I have never dared to go back to see that it is still there—an avenue of limes. In the hot sun they were alive with bees. All the summers of my childhood spilled from the continuous deep note, warmth and light turned to sound, the scent of green ling and peat on the moors, the choking smell of meadowsweet in narrow sunken lanes, even the tiny clatter of small waves running against the pebbles. Like an old dog, my mind turns in narrowing circles round the same point—a few yards of earth and coarse salt-bitten grass, a few undistinguished streets, the rotting timbers of a wharf, a laburnum.

Time was running out. From Bordeaux to La Rochelle, from La Rochelle to Angers. And then, for the last time, the Loire.

When we came into Saumur at six in the evening, the light was a thin, clear, amazingly clear and watery gold. Two hours later all the clarity had been drawn into trees and the walls of houses, in sharp relief against an overcast sky: a strong wind from the west was blowing the river under the arches of the bridge in a flurry of steel ripples: later still, about nine, a long sorrowful crimson gash opened suddenly in the livid clouds, and poured out a torrent of light the colour of tarnished bronze. Much later, glancing from my window at the trees on the other side of the Loire, I saw a tree-trunk, in an amphitheatre of leaves, turn to a figure of light, curiously menacing and archaic—Apollo in a mood to punish.

One more fortnight, and it was the last day of our ten months. Walking about Amiens, in search of a street no longer there, I comforted myself with the certainty of being dead before this country ceases entirely to keep alive a civilization, a way of living, of which man is the measure. A ceaseless patient and cunning effort has humanized the earth itself of France. Nowhere, but nowhere in the world, is the precarious truce between men and nature, between us and our own nature, so nearly friendly, informed by so tough and resilient a spirit. In no country is the past, the memory of human toil and genius, so part of the living present. Blois and Amboise, Chartres and Albi, Saint-Emilion . . .

It could be destroyed. Saint-Emilion could be wiped out, brutally irremediably ruined. The long story of the centuries still unfolding there could be cut short.

Something would survive. In a Provençal village the strong shabby crumbling houses would, as now, merge imperceptibly into the naked bones of the hill. Its peasants would work from dawn to dusk. Old women would die, smiling toothlessly, filled by a lifetime of labour. Women with the faces of Roman matrons would kneel in the weak January sun sorting the olives whipped from the grey trees. The rough unmade streets would keep their secrets, some of them bitter, behind closely shuttered windows. As now.

But peasant France is not the whole. The roots might be saved, yes. But how long, how many decades, before the flower?

Fine rain, a low curdled sky, flying splinters of gold. Turning a corner, I saw the long narrow spire of the cathedral, bone white and dark steel-grey, pencilled on the misty sunlight. I stood and looked at it, with an entire happiness, for two or three minutes, until the rain quickened and it was time to turn back.

Chapter 13

Next year, in April 1955, I came near enough death to imagine that I recognized her in the person of an elderly matron of a hospital. I meant to go to Vienna, and since, as happened now and then, I had worked myself to a standstill, I agreed with my doctor that this was a good moment to spend a few days in bed. (I agreed reluctantly—I have every intention of dying like Emily Brontë, in my chair.) 'We'll get rid of that,' she said, touching a fine knot of vein, 'and you'll have a week's rest and go to Vienna refreshed.'

I did not go to Vienna, and I stayed in that London hospital for eight mortal weeks.

So much for doctors and their powers of prediction.

I took it that the pain after the operation—which became agony when I put foot to the ground—was a perfectly normal thing. After a day or two, I asked for a walking-stick, and was refused it—on the ground that there were none on this floor. So much for hospitals.

I had begun to find it difficult to breathe.

Late in the afternoon of Easter Sunday I stopped breathing. Luckily for me, a very young nurse was in the room at the time. I had an instant left in which to say to her, 'Goodness, I'm going to faint,' and hear her cry, 'Oh, *no*!' A weight of darkness dragging me backwards, then nothing, then a sort of tent over my face, a voice telling me to breathe, and I breathed.

'How long,' I asked later, 'did it take you to get that thing into my room?'

It looked like the work of a surrealist sculptor, I thought it sinister, and wanted it taken away.

'Exactly one minute.'

It was a few minutes after this that I saw the elderly black-clad woman. The door was to the right of my bed: she came in silently, and, still in silence, walked, eyeing me the whole way, along the wall facing the bed, turned at the corner, and went out again. Well, that's Death, I said to myself: who could have known she would look so expressionless and respectable.

I remembered that I had seen her before—during the night after my son was born. But that was in a half-dream.

'Who on earth was that old woman?'

The nurse almost crossed herself in surprise at my blasphemy. 'That? That was Matron herself!'

Later still, much later, my surgeon came into the room. I was surprised to see him, but even now it did not cross my mind to wonder why they had thought fit to bring him up from the country on Easter Sunday. He leaned against the wall near the door, listening to my duologue with the house doctor. I liked him: the nurses gave him a reputation for foul language when he was operating, and he was certainly something of a brute, as some surgeons are, but I prefer a controlled brutality to what used to be called a good bedside manner. My sense of smell is as acute as my hearing: the smell of very good brandy reached me across the room, and I thought: I interrupted his dinner. I intended to use his dark hooked Welsh face some time, in a novel, and I kept one eye on it when I was answering the house doctor's questions.

'Describe the pain in the chest.'

I did so.

'How long had you had it?'

'Oh, about three days.'

'Why didn't you speak about it?'

Useless to tell this severely patient man that I had been brought up not to bore people with my ailments. 'It wasn't a bad pain.' I lacked the insolence to add: Not like the other, for which I was refused a walking-stick.

'And then this afternoon it suddenly got worse,' he said.

I detest having words put in my mouth. I was delighted to be able to contradict him. 'No. No worse at all. Exactly the same.'

The lightest possible twitch of amusement—noted for use—crossed my surgeon's face, but he said nothing until the examination was over, then all he said was, 'This afternoon I had to pick up a child who fell out of an apple tree, and——'

For some reason I now felt pleasantly excited, as if I had been drinking. I interrupted him. 'And tonight you had to pick up an ageing witch who fell off her broomstick.'

He laughed.

That night turned out the most extraordinary I can remember. In the first and longer part of it I did not dream. I was asleep, but in a state of heightened consciousness, a contradiction, a paradox that I grasped clearly enough to think: So, after all, the darkness is not dark. In this marvellous lucidity I passed through sensations as if I were moving from stage to stage of consciousness. My brain was full of light, like a plain flooded by the moon. In the morning I wrote down as much as I could recall, but the words distort even that little.

I was an impulse, a sort of energy, reflected in an image of myself. This circle was broken by an image stepping out of the image. I felt I had lost something, some harmony, and I began to multiply the images in the hope of recovering it. But it was useless, I only fell farther and farther down, an immeasurable distance, until I was looking at what seemed the final image. Now I began reasoning. This creature, I reflected, is entirely irrational and on the point of dissolution: I need not wake her up unless I decide to, I can let her die here and put an end to the whole coil of waking and sleeping, changing, making, and not-changing. It means depriving her of her acute senses, but why not?

At this point I began to be afraid of the distance I still had to fall, and made an effort to wake up. I woke in the first light, with a feeling of pleasure and sadness, some hint of the ravishing lucidity still there, but only for an instant.

I fell asleep again. This time I dreamed. One of the worst dreams I ever had in my life—I think the worst I remember. My son, a baby, burrowed under, or rather into, something like a vast mattress. I called, he answered, but I was certain he must be suffocating, and I began to tear my way into the thing, tearing up cork carpet and the boards of the floor, searching frenziedly and calling, calling. He was nowhere. I found odd things, including a little clay group of three figures together, which I vaguely knew to be a votive object: one of the figures was a minute elf-like boy. By now I was in agony of mind. Do, my sister, a young Do, about fifteen, was there, and my mother, also younger, about fifty, and they helped me a little. I went on with my anguished search. My sister came to me, exclaiming that they had found a clue; she had the tiny figurine in her hand, and said smiling, 'You see, Dear Dog, it wasn't a boy at all.' With despair, I realized that I had lost him, there was nothing to be felt in the mattress, no little body. There were other rooms I went into, and other incidents, which I forgot.

I woke in the same heavy despair and grief. It was lighter in my room, but still very early. I lay thinking—for the ten thousandth time—that leaving my child and going to London at the end of 1919 was the first fatal error of my many errors, the one for which there is no forgiveness, no redemption.

Thirty-seven years. A long time. Perhaps it is because I have never suffered any of the physical or metaphysical anguish which is said to afflict ageing men and women at a certain period in their lives that these other regrets are still alive and young . . .

During that interminable morning, the consultant of the hospital was called in, an amiable simpering comforter. My own doctor was on holiday abroad, and no one thought fit to tell me what had happened. I waited day after day, expecting some kind of explanation— and too determined to show no concern for myself to ask for it. But apart from telling me, almost in an aside, that the deep thrombosis which in a few days followed the lung embolism had been expected, they explained nothing. The simperer overflowed with sweet oil, and evaded me when I asked, 'How long am I going to be here?'

As the weeks passed, I not only became used to my weakness, I began wearing it like an old comfortable coat. I was not bored. If a prison cell were airy, with a good bed and a window, it would suit my unsociability, my distrust of people, very well. I had as many books as I chose, and as few visitors.

The visitors I enjoyed were those who came with a story burning the ends of their tongues. They sat down, asked one or two ritual questions I could evade, then laid in front of me some tale I listened to with the delight of a child brought a new toy.

There is something strange, and a little disconcerting, about the readiness with which people confess themselves to a friend they imagine to be very ill, perhaps dying . . .

The food in that hospital was no more horrible than in any other. Why in the name of Aesculapius must patients in English hospitals choose between a fast to the death and an insult to their helpless bodies? My friend Doreen Marston twice brought smoked salmon and brown bread, and my friend A. D. Peters brought eggs from the country. In the two months I was there these were the only tolerable meals I ate. They eat a great deal worse in concentration camps. True, true, but do hospitals fall into that category?

During these lost weeks I made efforts to balance my moral account, in advance of another death. But I fell into endless reveries in which I was not thinking but drifting from scene to scene, some recalled, some, the most charming, invented. In the end, to keep my mind at heel for an hour or two, I took to writing and folded the pages into a volume of Kafka I had been yawning over—in a cell the hermetic is a bore.

Here is part of it:

I am ashamed of my growing indifference. It couldn't be said that I live as I please, but what has become of that burning political passion of the 'thirties when I wrote and signed manifestos against fascism, attended meetings called to condemn the coming war, and toiled at every sort of flimsy barricade against it? Dust in corners . . .

I began calling myself a socialist when I was sixteen. Mine was the simplest and most emotional of creeds, a violent anger when I thought of children growing up in cancerously mean streets. All the economic arguments in the world are irrelevant to this single injustice. That there are people not shocked by this separation of children into two categories never ceases to astonish and offend me. Moreover I detect a line running underground from this relatively innocent inhumanity to the sickening inconceivable inhumanity of the gas chambers.

I am exaggerating? Oh, if you think so. What you think is not my business . . .

This has nothing to do with liberty, equality, fraternity and the rest of it. Equality is an illusion—attempts to enforce it involve the death of liberty. But brotherhood—ah, that is God, the Son, and the Holy Ghost of my creed . . .

I have no energy left to do anything about it. Spurts of flame from the ash, impotent rage. Nothing more. I was never a revolutionary

—an instinctive rebel, but not a believer in revolution. Too much cruelty, too many deaths, merely to replace one autocracy by another. The Labour Party, which began in the fraternity of poor men and is now another power machine, is necessary: two, three, ten power machines are more tolerable than one. But why should I feel any devotion to the politics of a machine? . . .

Of all my passionate concerns—in the Quaker sense—two remain.

I can give very respectable reasons for the concern I still have for those of my friends and fellow-writers who are exiles. They add a sharp taste to our dull island soup. So much new energy, so much courage, so many new minds, added to the spiritual life of this country, are pure gain. They form a new *ordo vagorum*, carrying ideas and opinions across the barbed wire that disfigures and brutalizes Europe, and remind us that our fellow-countrymen bear names like Čapek, Unamuno, Freud, Einstein, Pasternak.

But they are my fellow-countrymen in a deeper, colder sense. The country they return to in sleep, filled with voices from the other side of a closed frontier, voices of estranged friends, of a dead mother, a lost child, is as much mine as theirs. And if they delude themselves that they can return in reality, that Ithaca is not lost to them forever, that, too, is one of my own delusions, not the least indestructible.

And the other concern? One I share with millions of equally helpless men and women. Between 1914 and 1918, though I subscribed with my tongue to the protests of out-and-out pacifists, in my heart I thought less well of them than of my friends who were fighting, even the conscripts, either for an idea they had of England or out of a simple wish not to be safer than the others, or with no reason at all except that they had been conscripted. In that war, the vileness of what one of its soldiers, Major-General Fuller, called its 'ritual of slaughter' could be set against the patience, courage, and decency of the young men. Even in the second war it was possible to feel that Belsen was a worse evil than bombed cities. But nothing, not even the Belsens still existing in Europe, is as evil as what is politely called megadeath. Or overkill.

My young brother, killed in 1917, was not alone in believing, with the greatest simplicity, that the war he was fighting in would be the last. Poor child. What he died for was Hiroshima. And that affair was only a rehearsal, almost gentle.

What is so hard to believe is that any creature with only as much human warmth as serves to pick up a fallen child can think of the act of using thermo-nuclear weapons as possible, let alone as one of the things he might be obliged to do. Or can dupe himself with the argument that the existence of these obscene objects makes another world war less likely because we shall fear to use them.

We no longer believe that greater knowledge will benefit us. Traditional knowledge, the experience of our ancestors, ceased to be a help to us as soon as by our inventiveness we had destroyed the kind of society they knew how to live in. It has become fashionable to mock or snub humanists who distrust 'science'. But science is as disgraced by some of its fruits as the Christian church was by the Inquisition.

Reading a cold analysis of the condition of a world which has been only partly reduced to radio-active rubble, one exclaims: No, it's not possible!

On the contrary. It is possible that man is the only creature with the ill-will to make an end of himself.

Then you would rather not be defended by thermo-nuclear weapons?

Much rather.

And the children? You would leave them defenceless?

If their temporary safety can only be bought by the agonized death, the flesh seared from their bones, of other children, yes.

I was not always without equivocation in this bloody business of war. Just as I was not always without political principles—without principles *tout court*, some of my friends would say. (Our friends are not our friends for nothing!) The last war was the turning point: up to the day it broke out I was frothing over like a mustard-pot with political commitment. At the end, nothing was left of it, nothing—except my involuntary neighbourly love for our exiles and my hatred of war . . .

I was writing the last words of this apologia when my friend Adela (not her name) came into the room. I was delighted to see her, because she felt no need to treat me gently, as an invalid. We argued, I forget about what, but it ended in her saying sharply, 'You are always so calm and decided. A monster of confidence! You know exactly what you want to do and how to do it. You don't know what it's like to be an ordinary woman, full of misgivings and indecision, as I am—perfectly ordinary and normal.'

When she had gone, drawing on her elegant gloves and smoothing her hair under a new hat, I wondered whether or not to congratulate myself on the air of confidence and strength of mind behind which I hide unplumbable weakness, indecision, nagging anxiety, hesitancy, uncertainty, moodiness—inherited, or made to measure.

Perhaps I had once been what she called me—a monster of confidence? Yes, of course—young, very young, I had the greatest confidence in my talents, and the energy of the devil. My dreams were all of love, glory, excitement. And then, gradually, it all ebbed. Now, I thought, I have almost none, I'm no longer able to take decisions, for myself or others—as if my will had snapped. I'm indifferent—an indifference at the roots.

Who, what, is to blame? No one, nothing. Myself. With both hands I destroyed myself, denaturing my senses, tearing out energies, desires, greeds, the innocent with the corrupt. I *tamed* myself. Why?

Even the desperate need to be right, my mother's need repeated in me—I have overcome even that . . . It took a long time. Not until I was at least fifty did it become even barely possible for me to admit that I am not invariably right and moved by the most irrefutable motives.

I began to laugh, and laughed quietly but uncontrollably until the pain in my body checked me . . .

Later, a nurse came in and switched on a lamp. When she had gone, I lay looking at the white globe, and wondering why only to hold it in my mind gave me this feeling of happiness, as fine as a fine blade, exquisite. Suddenly I knew. It had the same shape and slightly oily gleam of the huge hard ostrich eggs my father brought from Africa, on which I painted, in oils, exotic birds, copying them, feather by minute feather, from a large book.

We had a round dozen of these. Where are they now? Smashed? Given away by my mother in one of her clearing-out moods? One of them may still be lying in some room in Whitby or in a junk-shop. I should know it if I saw it.

I have a puritan horror of drugs, but always at nine o'clock I accepted thankfully the mild pain-killer they brought me. I could have had it at any time during the day, but I made a foolish point of enduring. I fell asleep at once. My mind in these weeks sent me a succession of landscape dreams, the happiest I ever have. Happiness as sharp as a knife. Nothing exists in them except a landscape— sometimes remembered from an earlier dream—of intense beauty or grandeur. Very often it is a coast, one of my five primordial images. In others I recognize the east cliff at Whitby, the harbour and the Esk valley, but only as a basis, an outline overlaid by the colours and details of the finished painting. Others may be memories of foreign cities seen in my earliest years, rising in all their freshness, as without blemish as the eye that saw them.

In these dreams I don't act. I *look*—with an ineffable happiness which, in the moment of waking, becomes a longing heavy with the loss of the heart of life, the worth, the meaning.

The pain woke me soon after midnight. Then I called round me images from my happy life, to deceive it and protect me.

The last notes of the 'Nachtmusik' in Vienna, played in the small courtyard in the Hofburg, dark except for the musicians' lights and a few windows in the Pallavicini Palace, rose, died away, swelled and became Monteverdi's *L'Incoronazione di Poppaea* heard on the 13th of September 1949, in the Palladian theatre in Vicenza: I moved my hands over the stone seat, feeling the smooth cold in my fingers, staring into the deceptive distances of the stage, drunk with the Italian voices, in which the vocal cords seem part of the whole sensual system of the singer. The double sounds moved inside my skull, coiling and uncoiling like snakes warmed by the sun.

The forms and colours of water. The sea off the island of Tjømo in the Oslo fjord in June, completely naked, a blue without flaw, the air carrying lightly its splinters of salt and the hot scent of pines: the narrow water-lanes in the centre of Amsterdam, flanked by houses too self-possessed, too charming, for their weight of secrets, some of which have been cruel: the estuary at Portmeirion, a faint bloom of mist over the hills, softening and blurring their already soft green and black-green colours, the water a glass reflecting sharply grey clouds and an acre of blue sky, the sun, withdrawn behind massed clouds above the hills nearest the open sea, its unseen rays turning their peaks to a mountain range of blinding incandescent whiteness. And very thin, and piercing the brain, the screech of gulls.

I was near the oldest images now, the seething whiteness of marguerites, the sea-bird voices of Whitby children.

On many of these nights, because it was closest to me in time, less than half a year away, I went back to Cyprus. My son was stationed there, living with his wife and two children, the younger less than a year old, in a bare white house: the street, filled with stones and deep ruts, was called Irene Street. This was before the madness began in earnest. We could climb safely in the ruins of mediæval castles holding crazily to the steep flanks of rocky hills, and walk about these hills, between the stunted cork trees, the scented herbs crumbling to dust in the fingers, the Greek columns on a headland above a sea passing from blue to dense violet-green, the colour of a ripe fig . . .

Since I had a room to myself I was able sometimes to quiet the pain by a familiar thread of sound:

> There was an old woman went up in a basket
> ninety times as high as the moon . . .

What chaff for a grown woman to cling to! But this woman's mother had taught her tune and words; she in turn taught them to her son, who very likely did not remember them. Why should he? These memories have to end somewhere, or the world would be choked by them like a gutter by dead leaves. The almost tuneless old tunes, the lichened stones of old walls, the innocent curve of lanes, have to be effaced to make room. And if the future is less harmless? So much the worse for it . . .

The days became weeks, and I could get no satisfaction out of the simperer. I had better hopes of my surgeon, and when he came to take the stitches out of my wounds, which he did with sadistic speed and efficiency, watching to see me flinch—the only coquetry I have left is to do nothing of the sort—I asked him what had happened.

'The operation was a disaster,' he said coolly, 'you'll go out worse than you came in.'

I hardly believed him—but he was right. At the time his frankness stiffened me against the smiling deceit of the consultant, whom I despised for his good intentions.

At the end of eight and a half weeks I limped out of that place, to begin the long task of restoring myself to life.

Chapter 14

Since a degree of bodily pain, several degrees, is infinitely less demoralizing and destructive of my wits than domestic life, I lived happily in a country hotel in Surrey and wrote a novel, *The Intruder*. It was laid in the hard Provence of the hills behind Vence, in a village resembling the one I knew—to which I moved the remnants of a Celto-Ligurian city. These ancient cities sunk in the earth are the subconscious mind of Europe, its obsessions and its layer on layer of memories and races. The book was a study of obsessions, among them an old archæologist's obsession with the springs of cruelty. I explored my own through his.

The village we lived in had no railway station, and was simple and empty, a green thought in a green place, not much more than the houses and cottages scattered round a large rough common, and the friendly hotel itself. The garden ran away gently into corn-fields and meadows, and I looked at them—watching the colours change slowly through a dry summer and autumn—as I wrote, the sweat of pain trickling over my forehead in drops that fell on the paper.

I have never been more content.

My only distinct memory of these months is of a crisis not in my life, but in C.'s. In September, now a tall good-looking boy of thirteen, he started as a weekly boarder at Westminster. Something —perhaps the strain of living in a large exacting community after years of easy triumphs as a clever day-boy in a small school—touched off in him an uprush of anxiety so violent that if he had not had a basic strength of character—such as none of us had the right to expect in him (but I took it for granted)—he might have come to grief. And if he had not by the grace of God had a housemaster of the greatest wisdom, kindness and patience. I can well believe that in earlier generations he might have been handled in a way that would have ruined him for life. With his mother he raged like a mad creature. At school, during the week, he was dangerously controlled.

'He looks at me when I talk to him,' his housemaster told me, 'with polite cold hatred, it is like talking to a caged wild animal or a block of ice. I can't reach him.'

Had I been less sunk in my work and my racked body, I should have been more anxious. And more conscious of the risks we were running. The letter he wrote at the end of September, to tell me that I was wasting my money on sending him 'to a school full of reactionary traditionalism', was so acute in its feeling for the words that would be the most likely to shake me, so calmly intelligent, that I felt more admiration than pity for the young creature writing it, coldly, out of his irrational anguish.

By the end of the first term he was, if not yet entirely reconciled, on an even keel.

At the end of the year, *The Intruder* finished and revised, I began another novel.

It was one I ought to have tackled years before, when the doctrinal split of our time—between a militant communism and a liberalism gone in the tooth—seemed as deep and incurable as that between an uncompromising early Christian and an educated Roman outraged by a faith which seemed to involve the death of society and demand of its adherents that they hand over their conscience to a narrow merciless creed. I might have done better to obey my first impulse and lay the novel in Roman Gaul. In 1956, the split was already beginning to lose every quality of a religious war except its bad temper, and the excuses it offers for cruelty, intimate betrayals, devotion.

My mind still houses the ghosts of an abandoned task, and two of these seized on me, the children, now grown up, of Frank and Sally Rigden, humble characters in *Company Parade* and its sequels. *Pour changer les idées* (Madame P. would have said, handing the abominable fennel root), I wrote this book in the first person—the person of the Senior Tutor of an imaginary Oxford college—intending to turn it into the third when I came to write the second draft. Its title, *A Cup of Tea for Mr Thorgill*, annoyed reviewers who read enough of it to discover that Mr Thorgill was a minor character, but not enough —or they lacked the wit—to notice that he was a measuring rod for the *mauvais foi* of the others. The book was perhaps written only to bring him in.

I wrote the first version quickly, and finished it in April. It was six months before I had time and peace of mind to take it up again and rewrite it in the third person.

During the next two or three months I had a recurring sense that I was living backwards. Many things I touched split open like husks to let fall a sharp kernel of the past. In May, when the Society of Authors was giving Osbert Sitwell a piece of glass engraved by Laurence Whistler, I was asked to make the presentation—and the speech—at a luncheon. The thought that I might not do it well enough chilled me, but I was ashamed to refuse.

It was not a large luncheon, perhaps twelve people, held in a private room at the Ritz. As if he were accustomed to doing it, the head waiter cut up his meat for Osbert, who could no longer grasp a knife. Sitting beside him, in anguish about the speech I was going to make, I was uneasily two persons. I was the schoolgirl, Daisy Jameson, listening with passionate attention to adults talking about the legendary Sitwells. Ten years and a war later, I was in Whitby with my three-year-old son, penniless, a little desperate about our future, mine and his: a General Election, the mean-souled Khaki Election, was going on, with Captain Osbert Sitwell standing as Liberal candidate for the Scarborough and Whitby division (I usually write this the other way round, incorrectly but involuntarily). Who can have asked me, an unknown young woman, to sit on one of his platforms, and what, except vanity and the wish to outrage my Tory father—my mother, a Tory from habit, was indifferent, and secretly pleased by the sly glances of her friends ('Ha, I see y'daughter's got herself into politics')—made me do it?

I did not remind him of an episode he must long have forgotten. We talked a little of his novel about Scarborough, and he asked me how often I went back to those parts.

'Very seldom,' I said. 'Whitby and Scarborough have both been vilely fingermarked—the marks show worse in Whitby because it is a small town. I don't want to efface a living memory by the dead graceless reality.'

'No, no, you're right, don't go back. No point in tormenting oneself. A writer has all too many reasons to be irritated and angered, he must defend himself—all the more if he refuses to join a herd.'

'How does one defend oneself?'

He moved a shaking hand in a curiously light gesture. 'One way is by arrogance. A writer must be arrogant.'

'That,' I said, 'may be natural and easy for a Sitwell. My father was a sea-captain.'

'I always supposed that sea-captains were very arbitrary individuals,' he said, smiling—a warmly gentle smile.

I thought that, unlike his formidable sister, whom I admired and had never feared, he made little use of a mask: his arrogance, his aristocratic feeling for equality, his innate kindness, did not entirely hide a certain insecurity. I did not know enough about him to be able to guess where this thread of insecurity came from, but I could not be mistaken. I knew the trait in myself. I liked him the better for it, and for his polite heart.

What did I say in my speech? I have forgotten that completely.

In the letter he wrote to thank me for it, a phrase struck me: 'Even elderly writers like myself need encouragement, and you have always been one of the people who have given it . . .'

A polite gesture, yes, but also, without his intending it, an admission.

Once the past has opened a breach into the present, there is no damming the icy trickle. During the splendid London Congress of P.E.N. in July, I met ghosts at every turn, once in the shape of an old Jewish refugee who said very softly, 'I think all these days of the Congress in 1941, yours and Hermon's, simple and friendly, where I am someone. Here, what am I? Nobody.'

'Ah,' I said, taking his hand, 'the past is a fine place, and you and I are together in it, two nobodies.'

This comforted him, but there was no comforting the elderly lady, a Pole or an Italian, I am not sure which, who seized my arm during the reception in the Mansion House, and spoke in a deep voice, hoarse with despair.

'*Pour moi, madame, un buffet froid, c'est une catastrophe.*'

Czeslaw Milosz had come over from Paris. When I was talking to him in the crowded hall of Bedford College, I caught sight at the other end of Antoni Slonimski. It was the first time I had seen him since he went back to Warsaw for good, and I felt a sudden warmth and lightness of heart. It struck me then that these two Polish poets had not spoken to each other for a great many years, and without giving myself time to doubt I said, 'Antoni Slonimski is over there. Will you talk to him?'

'Why not?' Czeslaw said slowly.

'Don't move from here.'

I pushed my way through the chattering groups. For a moment, in the pleasure of seeing him, I forgot my purpose: then I said, 'Czeslaw Milosz is here. Will you meet him?'

'If he wants it,' Antoni said quietly.

I hurried him the length of the hall. Czeslaw's face wore the look of simplicity with which he covered up anger or excitement. The two stood some way apart, eyeing one another.

'Who the first?' Antoni said.

Czeslaw stretched his arm out and they shook hands. It was pure Conrad. Since they were both too polite to speak Polish so long as I was with them, I went away. Glancing back once, I saw that, still a yard apart, they had begun to talk with a certain unsmiling liveliness.

On the last day, unable to face another reception, I went down to the Embankment and stood a long time looking with pleasure at the ripples curling over behind a string of barges. The evening sun poured a yellow oil over the water, it ran away in veins twisting and sliding below the surface. Every now and then a smell like the smell of an old wharf, rotting wood, seaweed, tar, wet rope, overwhelmed the stench of petrol from the road. I had a delicious sense of freedom and lightness.

If instead of standing here, I reflected, you were in that ship moving down river, you would be perfectly content.

Chapter 15

Immediately after this, all panic stations manned, I moved into what my sick fear of being trapped saw as a black stifling tunnel.

It turned out to be less like a trap than any place of my own I ever had. In the first place, a window in the living-room, the length of the wall, looked clean over Hyde Park to south London and, on a clear day, to the edge of the Surrey hills. We had been able to rent a flat on an upper floor in the terrace of tall white houses facing the Marble Arch end of the park, so well-bred and puritanically elegant that it is surprising they have not yet been torn down; and from the day we moved in this view made the joy of my life: at any hour of the day, in any light, I had only to stand and gaze at it for my body to free itself: the paths crossing stretches of grass still, at the end of July, a vivid green, drew my glance, as smoothly as a ship is moved by its tugs, to the broad chimneys of the power station on the north bank of the Thames and beyond them into a distance I could stretch as far as I liked: the human figures sauntering across the park were dwarfed by the great trees and the spaces. This same scene in winter under an overcast sky, the black leafless trees, their trunks smeared by yellowish lichen, the dark iron-hard paths, with perhaps two figures turning away at the end of an avenue of naked branches became almost unbearably full of regret and smiling bitterness, like the lines it evoked ... *Dans le vieux parc solitaire et glacé, Deux spectres ont évoqué le passé ... Ton coeur bat-il toujours à mon seul nom? Toujours vois-tu mon âme en rêve?—Non* ... Silhouetted on the mist, the tall buildings south of the park slowly became formless; at four o'clock, street lights came on, blue, white, orange, circling the park; an hour later the pent-houses of Grosvenor House hotel floated to the surface and hung there above a street visible only as two double lines of cars and buses, inside and outside the park, their movements too smooth to be those of wild animals, yet oddly menacing in the icy dark.

Lights sunk in the night have always, since I saw them first as a child in Whitby, given me one of my rare moments of ecstasy, immense joy rising through my veins to my throat, until I can scarcely breathe.

One day in the week before we moved in I had gone to bed in the grip of the insane panic, unmanageable and instinctive, that seizes me when I am being forced into a house. I fell asleep after a time, and seemed to be wakened by a voice, not like the voices in dreams, which are felt, not heard, a cold slow northern voice, speaking aloud, which said: My girl, you need a lesson . . . I knew at once that this voice came from the horse's head nailed above the doorway in the fairy-tale of the goose-girl, and, at the same time, it was my father's.

With this voice in my ears, I woke.

The lesson was not long in coming. Guy had been coughing a great deal, and now the X-rays discovered a shadow on one lung. He was to go into hospital for an operation, on a day three weeks ahead of us, at the end of August. We were preparing to go to Sweden for a month, taking C., and I decided that it would be better to go for two weeks rather than hang about in London, waiting.

We went. In that clear air, as clear as the finest glass, in the white light, among black pine-trees breathing salt and resin, spectres are easily kept at arm's length.

Two days after we got back I went with him to St Thomas's Hospital, splendid worn battered ugly pile, and left him in a room looking across the Thames to the House of Commons. At that hour the river was running fast and dark.

That night, getting ready for bed, I thought suddenly: I am an old woman walking about an empty house . . . The staircase in the first house I remember climbed unknown depths to reach me, and I saw myself standing with a lit candle in the doorway of my bedroom, an attic, listening to the beating of my heart and the sound, far out at sea, of a ship's whistle. I had an instant of overwhelming excitement, as though I had only to move a finger to touch the cold rim of the candlestick. Something—what?—moved in me to begin again . . .

'Don't,' the surgeon had said to me, 'ring up the hospital. I'll ring you.'

In the protective apathy I can—often—sink into, I waited all day, walking between the window of the living-room and the telephone, which was on a shelf in the entrance hall. The brilliant green of the grass rasped my eyelids. White smoke from the power station stood in relief on a sky of rusted steel, fading to a tarnished yellow in the west above the dying sun. There was a wind. For the first time I noticed the stone drinking-trough opposite the window, at the other side of the wide road; I watched the reflections of branches in the water: it was a long double trough, the lower part almost on a level with the pavement, within reach of any creature, however weak and small . . .

'Everything went off very well. You can go to bed and sleep. Everything is all right.'

'Are you sure?'

'Of course.'

I went back to the window. In my brief absence the view had changed radically; the distances had become lightly foggy, and the chimneys and domes south of the park a delicate pencil sketch in mauve behind the dark mass of the trees. I stood for an hour, two hours, watching the black gleaming road, the sheaves of light thrown down on it by moving cars, the lower branches of trees an acid green, the dark sky, the dark cliff of Park Lane, the livid fish-belly white of faces, the livid white columns of the park gates, the single point of light on the crane, a gigantic antenna, on the roof of Grosvenor House, the sombre fermenting crowds at Speakers' Corner. Torn rags of sound, the cries of hawkers, a woman's shrill voice, and, below everything, the ceaseless rumour of traffic, thunder and clatter of the North Sea breaking on the rocks below an old pier.

At this moment I knew that the basic need of any human life worth the name is need and pity, the need to accept the death of the senses, the sinking to a little ash of sensual and primitive love, the pity born from the knowledge, taken into the mouth and chewed like a bitter root, of death. We have a minute in which to be kind, I thought. And in the end, nothing I do, nothing I could do, minor writer that I am, nothing I want, is anywhere nearly so important as this. This truth, and my knowledge of it, lie as deep in me as my hunger for freedom. But I touch it only in a moment of crisis, like this one.

I was asleep when the telephone rang in the early morning. Shaking, cold with the certainty that I was being called to the hospital, I ran to answer it, and heard Guy's voice, clear, weak. His instinctive

movement when he woke had been to stretch a hand to the telephone on his bed-table, to talk to me.

The supreme warmth of my life.

Late in October, I took up *A Cup of Tea for Mr Thorgill* and rewrote
it in the third person. On its level it is a good book, at times a little
too violent—it should have been laid in France or some Central
European country where doctrinal passions are still apt to be
murderous—but worth writing.

I finished it on the 23rd of December. One of my rare, very rare,
sleepless nights followed (like the old sea-captain, I can go without
sleep for two nights running, and fall asleep by closing my eyes).
Feeling feverish but not restless or unhappy, I lay awake and got up
before daylight. The first sign of light came at seven o'clock, a
sharpening of the delicate outline of the crane and the tops of
buildings. The sky changed almost imperceptibly. Then came a
tinge of colour in the east. Slowly, very slowly, the sky roused, with
the sluggish motion of a treacherous sea. The street-lamps were still
burning. The finest conceivable web of naked branches moved, with
infinite gentleness, against the grey void of the park.

I shall only deform or destroy the happiness of these moments by
trying to describe it.

Chapter 16

Guy made a good recovery, but the London winter, fog and an
acid grime in the air, was hard on his lung, and in the New Year we
rented one of the Portmeirion houses for two months. The air in
that corner of North Wales is soft and clear, and since the hotel was
closed there were only a few people living on or near the estate;

farmers and landowners: the handful of young and middle-aged intellectuals who had had the good sense or the supreme confidence in themselves to settle down here and attend to their minds and bodily needs, as in the Middle Ages they might have looked for a not too austere monastery.

The greatest of these was Bertrand Russell, a great mind and, in the proper sense of the word, a personage. His head would have made the fortune of a mediæval stonemason at work on a Gothic cathedral: the arched forehead, powerful nose, fine sensual mouth, narrow jaw, lean sunken cheeks, and, above all, the eyes—half closed under heavy lids, with a smile of sly amused malice. How many times have I seen that smile on statues in the porches and ambulatories of the great French cathedrals? In conversation— when he was not involved in a hot argument—he was amusing, affable, friendly. I felt a cold respect for him and small liking, and this was not out of fear of a great man: for another great man, R. H. Tawney, I felt as much love as respect. His high screeching laugh rasped my ear-drums. Yet many women were drawn to him, he had had four wives: three of his marriages had broken down, the fourth was completely successful and happy. He was not a libertine; whatever his lustful or ecstatic reasons for falling in and out of love, a polite and puritanical regard for the conventions drove him into marriage.

Listening to his voice rather than to what he said, and watching with pleasure the flicker of irony across his gargoyle of a face, I thought that he might be capable, at moments when another human being ceased to be anything more than an object in his mind, of intellectual cruelty—not of physical violence, he was infinitely too fastidious—of a shocking anger, of cold metaphysical unkindness.

After a time, I realized that he was a late heir of the Enlightenment in a sense which goes some way to account not only for the impact of his powerful intelligence on two or three young generations, but for the particular affection—or hatred—in which he is held. To put it shortly, too shortly, he invests in Reason so great an imaginative passion, so furiously religious a belief, that he makes it a question of conscience. And nothing, but nothing, so claws at the innermost spirit of an irreligious age as respect for conscience: it is in the name of conscience that a radical supports the ruthlessly nationalist ambitions of an African politician, in the name of con-

science that he pulls down the old shaky dykes against nihilistic drift
before erecting others.

What forced my own respect, cool but boundless, for him, was
much less things I had been told about him—his aristocratic sense of
family duty, his generosity—than the fact that he, an old man, who
could have said: What does the future matter to me? was as passionate as an adolescent. An act of injustice, the thought of nuclear war,
provoked him not only to rage but to do something about it. What
he did might be useless, but he had given in neither to old age nor
human folly. He fought.

So much holy anger in an old man is to be respected.

> Do not go gentle into that good night
> Old age should rave and burn at close of day . . .

In so far as they are intellectuals, Elizabeth and Rupert Crawshay-
Williams were living here on the same terms as the others. But they
had made their own terms with the place—to give it more than they
took. Their house was, is, a cell of friendly warmth and sanity in a
shaken world, a perpetual reproach to my restlessness, as Elizabeth
is an involuntary reproach to my spiritual clumsiness. She is what
Rilke required the poet to be, a praiser of life. The strict truth is that
she is a genius in living by virtue of the same hard work and devotion that makes another woman a great dancer: the muscles she
exercises are kindness, spontaneity, scepticism, gaiety, tolerance, a
mocking indifference to pretensions, and a saving salt of wit, even
malice. I could say to her what the Earl of Salisbury wrote to Henry,
Prince of Wales, in December 1608—'Such is the disproportion
between you and me (you the son of Jupiter and I his poor beagle)
. . .'

The estuary at Portmeirion is more beautiful in winter than at any
other time. As I wrote I saw it from the windows of the room I slept
and worked in. At low tide, there were only thin channels of water
between the stretches of sand. The tide came in swiftly, a grey flowing light, merging the channels into a flood the colour of the sky.
Black hills overtopped the lower grey-green slopes shutting in the
valley. Except the cries of cormorants and gulls, there were no
sounds.

At my age no image is single, just as time is not a succession of
minutes but a labyrinth where the threads of past and present cross
and recross, fusing, separating, turning on themselves, without rest.
The estuary at five in the afternoon, a winter sun gone, the sky

above the open bay beyond the mouth grey and primrose yellow, the very colour of the half moon, the tide far out, the water in the channels yellow and slate-grey, the sand a dun grey, the hills dark heliotrope, without any substance, was also the lagoon between Torcello and Venice seen eight years earlier, a stretch of grey silk, saturated with light, and, flowing in me at a great depth, below every other image of water, the estuary of the Esk emerging between low hills into the harbour and the North Sea . . .

We had brought C. with us for a week. He was now, within a month of fifteen, six feet tall, handsome, with a clear narrow face, half composed young man and half intractable schoolboy. He was very impressionable, and yet controlled, for his age remarkably controlled, so that in spite of the liveliness of his mind and quick humour I had a sense of his watchfulness. It worried me a little, but he was gay, he thought clearly, and had his own ideas and views.

The day he left I started to write a novel I had been carrying about in my mind, like all my better novels, for a long time. The theme, too large for me, was exile.

Only a great writer, the poet of the *Inferno* or the creator of *War and Peace*, could find words direct enough, hard, burning to the touch, palpably real, to contain the vision of our age of exile: the unnumbered thousands of men and women trying to escape the bestialities of the totalitarian states, lucky when they were not turned back at frontiers or crowded into the rotten holds of ships without a sure harbour. I had the wit or the heart to know that an exile is a man, or a child, who suffers the human condition directly, without benefit of a cloth over his eyes, turned violently round to face the void from which the rest of us, as long as possible, look away, but not the imaginative energy to do more than say it.

The actual plot of the novel had to do with the bitter depth of the abyss dividing a man, a Pole, who had lived in Poland after the war, from his fellow-countrymen who left it in 1939 and were frozen into their memories of that now vanished country. When he talks to them they don't hear him.

'The truth is, you haven't a future. You've committed suicide. Like me, you're a Ulysses too many. Even if, in Ithaca, a few persons remember you, or only your name, the place itself rejects you. You will never reach it, never live there again. The people at home have forgotten you, they're living in another age—their own. You can't go back. The country you dream about returning to isn't there. If the young men you know nothing about are ever able to free the country, you'll have to wait on the doorstep. And, if you're let in, keep your mouth shut—like any other *revenant*, any anachronistic ghost. The very best you can hope for—if a revolt starts—is to get over the frontier and be allowed to fight in it as an obscure nameless person. Not a leader—you have no right to that, and no qualifications.'

You, too, I thought, as I wrote, you, too, and the Ithaca you think you are seeking. When in fact you expect nothing from it, and don't want to arrive. All your happiness comes from the harbours you touch at, the foreign places you see for the first time. Ithaca is for the old.

My own age—I could not remember it off-hand and had to do a sum in my head—seemed to me irrelevant. Or less important than, let's say, my long sight, acute hearing, and indifference, in the last instance, to failure.

As soon as we were back in London, in March, I had the two children, Frances and Troy, to stay in the flat. They were astonishingly unlike. Frances, self-contained and smiling, used her quick wits to get her way with as little trouble as possible. Capable of sudden brief rages, she was physically placid, and fell asleep as she stepped into bed. Troy, fine, small, stubborn, was more difficult in every sense. She slept lightly and woke at a touch.

One night she was still restlessly awake at near midnight. I lifted her out of bed and held her, rolled in the quilt, in the window of her room, to look at the fantastic view. I thought: These are the things a child remembers. I thought I might be passing on to her my own childish ecstasy of pleasure in lights seen at night. But perhaps she noticed quite other things, the three ghostly beds of daffodils (now buried under concrete) on the edge of the park opposite the house, or the gleaming piebald trunks of trees, or the young, very young, very black prostitute in a yellow coat, walking up and down, up and down, a few paces each way, twirling a small yellow umbrella.

When I felt her little body relax in my arms, I put her back into bed. 'Now go to sleep.' Closing her eyes, she said, 'No, I'm still wide awake.' A moment and she was asleep.

The only change I noticed between myself now and myself twenty years ago was that the exhaustion of looking after two young lively children was not cured by a night's rest. And yet I was tireless. I galloped to the shops and back, carrying heavy parcels, took pains to cook well, wrote, when I could, for long hours. Offered a pleasure, or a visitor, or a task there was no getting out of, I rose gaily from the dead. ('Tha's unabateable,' a servant said to me when I was four, 'but time 'ull cow thee.'—'That it won't,' I said.)

After the children left, I had to take the chair at the meeting of the International Executive Committee of P.E.N. Nothing on the agenda interested me except the suggestion to do away with the Centre for German-speaking Writers Abroad, founded in 1933. Why, merely because they preferred to live in London, should any Germans be allowed in 1957 to pose as exiles? Why indeed? I was determined— a question of sentiment—to keep the illogical indefensible Centre. During the long rather surly debate its president made two speeches, the first sensible and moving, the second clumsy. Germans always say a few words too many. But I got my way.

A Roumanian writer, president before the war of a Centre in Bucharest, had written to ask us to admit a new Roumanian Centre.

'Is it really his signature?'

'Yes, yes.'

'But is it certain,' Paul Tabori asked calmly, 'that he hasn't already been sent back to prison?'

A little irritated by this purism, André Chamson said, 'We are in a situation where arrests are too usual . . .'

At the other side of the table, the Belgian delegate stroked his heavy sensual jowl, a proconsul in a good temper.

'*Ils* sont dans cette situation,' he said, grinning . . .

What moved intelligent men, and one or two women, hard-working respectable writers, to spend their time and energy on these committee meetings? The pleasure of saying Yes or No to Roumanians or Germans? The weak impulse to escape from the isolation of a writer's life? I watched the face of the elderly delegate from Tokyo, a wrinkled simian mask stretched over a tiny skull, surely the most menacing mask ever used to hide an anxious friendliness and a child's pleasure in being accepted. The sight of his skeleton at the resurrection won't surprise him, I thought; he sees it every time he passes a looking-glass . . . Our exiles had at least one good reason for coming: the longing to be in touch for a moment with the young man imprisoned in an ageing thickening body and still living in a country which no longer existed except during these two or three days when they were able to talk about it . . . The dignified ex-ambassador who was not displeased to be addressed as Your Excellency, the Catalan professor who wanted us to protest against Franco's restrictions on his language, the once blond now greying Latvian poet who enjoyed sitting in my flat and drinking glass after glass of sherry while he read out to me the clandestine messages he had received from 'my friend who did not come with me in 1939 . . .'

And you, why do you waste your time?

Perhaps merely in order to read a letter like the one the German-speaking Writers Abroad sent me after this meeting. 'May I in the name of Dr Hans Fleisch, our members and me too, thank you for your kind, I must even say, touching words on our behalf at the Committee meeting. I will forget these as little as I have forgotten what you have done for our comrades in 1938 . . .'

A month later I finished the first draft of *A Ulysses Too Many*. It was reasonably complete. There would not be much new writing to do.

The first minutes after finishing a book are extraordinary. At one moment I was living with every sense but one in the sordid little bedroom above the bar of a seedy café in Nice, plagued by memories of an enemy, a friend, a mistress, and making energetic plans for my future. Future of a character who is existing in the last sentence of a novel. I dropped the pen, moved my stiffened fingers, and went over to the window. Below drifting slate-grey clouds in the east, the sky reflected the colours of the setting sun, celandine yellow, bronze, pale peacock green. The stink of anchovies, tobacco, acid urine, equally acid coffee, dust, cheap strong alcohol, from Bouttau's café, was still in my throat, and I saw a stained wall, a skylight, and a strip of worn dirty carpet, and through them the deep pink brown of houses in Park Lane, forced into relief by the level rays. Then the last images of the attic bedroom, and the images of past and future *in Nadzin's mind*, faded completely, and I saw only the first quick pointed lights at the far side of the park, and the young green, each furled leaf a thread of bright colour, of the trees immediately below the window.

I felt something very like remorse. What was to become of Nadzin and the others, men, women, children, even the two people who existed only on the last page but one, Bouttau's new baby, a scrap of yellow flesh, and its mother, smiling, showing the gaps in her teeth and a cross wedged in the fold between baggy discoloured breasts? To create and then to destroy—or create in order to destroy—what do you call such an impulse?

Creation and cruelty may, may they not?, be two sides of the same coin. And if that is true, it explains a great deal that puzzles me. The deaths of children in gas chambers . . .

Chapter 17

During the thirty and more years it had been there, my young brother's memorial in the Parish Church of Whitby had been eaten away by the sea air. Another few years and it would be as illegible as so many of the ancient wrinkled stones outside, leaning, sunk, in the coarse salt-bitten grass between the church and the edge of the cliff. Even if no one looked at it now, I could not let that happen. I sought and after a long time found a firm of engravers who could copy the original brass in a hard metal that salt would not corrode. The new tablet had been in place now for a year and I had not been to see it. In May, I went up to Whitby.

On a brilliantly clear morning, the sea glassy smooth, sky and gulls immaculate in sunlight, I climbed the one hundred and ninety-nine worn-down steps from the old street by the harbour. The ghost walking with me, her remote glance fixed, unseeing, on the ancient houses sunk, one above the other, in the side of the cliff, could only climb them slowly. At the top I turned aside from the stone-flagged path to find the Church Maid's house, and get a key to let us in to the gallery of the church. A small cottage, two rooms, very old, very solid, it looked down to the harbour and across it to the other, the west cliff, and the line of the coast running north. Not what you would call a civilized landscape, or even a friendly one, but *my* coast line, my place. My only place.

A friendly lively old woman, the Church Maid. The entrance to the gallery is by an outside staircase. At the top a narrow door opens on a passage that leads to the gallery, wide enough for one person to walk between the wall and the high timbered walls of the pews. A little light comes through low windows. The boards creak.

His tablet had been fixed to the wall at the height of the eyes of passers-by ... To the memory of 2nd Lt. Harold Jameson, Médaille Militaire, D.C.M., M.C., Royal Flying Corps ...

'It looks well,' I said.

'Eeh, you did right to change it,' the Church Maid said, smiling. 'What's the good of these things if you can't read'n?'

'Does anyone read it?'

'Oh, ay. Sometimes. Last year there was an American came and asked me to let'n see it. He said he'd read about it. Fancy! I showed it to'n, and he asked how old is this church? Eight hundred years, I told'n, and he said—nay, I forget what he said, they say owt, and half the time I don't listen.'

I walked round the gallery to my grandfather's pew, to look down from it into the body of the church, at pews like square roofless rooms set round the three-decker pulpit—lower deck, main deck, bridge.

'You won't remember my grandfather, George Gallilee, or Hannah Margaret Jameson, my mother?'

'No,' the old woman said. She smiled again, ironically. 'You can't remember everyone.'

I did not stay in Whitby overnight, for fear that the squalid changes in it since the first war became fixed in my mind. As things are, I forget them, and when, in unguarded moments or in sleep, I go back, it is to the old simple town I lived in as a child, the town my mother lived in in her childhood, and her mother, and the ancient dead. I was staying in Goathland, a moor village a few miles inland.

It is a small scattered village, naked to the sky, almost treeless, the air as thin and pure as anywhere in the island. You have only to cross the rough turf of the common and you are on the moor. I had been happy here often enough as a child, I was happy now.

The place judged me, of course, judged coldly my restlessness, my egoism, my foolish ambitions, my greeds, but in some curious way I felt, oh, not acquitted, but—for a few moments—free. As though I had been mercifully forgotten.

If you had the courage, I thought, you would stay here.

After three days I went back to London, to the second version of *A Ulysses Too Many*. I finished it, and put it away to be looked at again later, and the next day I began to think hard and patiently over another novel, and make notes. It, too, had been lying in germ a long time. Or its characters had. A man called Mott, born in Whitby in the same street of small houses where I was born, had made his way up to a position of respect and influence as a writer and Director of an Institute of Fine Arts in London, remodelling himself, with instinctive sureness and pleasure, as he went. At fifty, he was a complicated and impressive *construction*, a Christian of the Anglican persuasion, living a carefully civilized life, even to his choice of wife and friends, a sensitive kindly man, without crude vanity. Suppose that at this point he made an error, one clumsy error, social or moral—and made the further error of lying about it? What would take place in him as the truth began to eat its way into his life? (My first name for this book had been *The Man Sought by God*. Later, when I thought I knew too little to call it that, it became *The Road from the Monument*.) I found that already I knew him intimately, and a number of other men and women. Never since *The Green Man* had I had this sense of overwhelming energy, of being assailed by characters who forced themselves on me, demanding their chance to live through my nerves and blood.

In spite of this feeling of power, I could not start the book. Heaven alone knows how many times I wrote and tore up a first chapter—ten, fifteen. I lost count. After a time, driven almost out of my mind by this perversity of—of what? characters I knew as well as I knew myself? my mind?—I began to suspect that there was a piece missing. Now and then I caught sight of a figure, a man, a shadow losing itself in shadows, but never saw him distinctly. For a time I thought he might be the old sea-captain, Mott's dead father, but I was forced to drop this idea: that gaunt stooped old fellow had his part in the story of his son's discovery of himself, but it was not at the beginning.

That year June was abnormally hot, day after day of blistering oily sunlight; the nights were close and airless, dulled by an acid breath of dust, petrol, dry leaves, sweat-soaked bodies, shoe leather. I wrote and tore up, wrote and tore up, day after day, evening after evening.

The nights were hallucinatory. I heard voices, and watched scenes play themselves through, but I could not write them, because I could not flush the missing creature out of its earth.

I spent hours standing in my window. In June it was still daylight at nine, but the light was filtered through a thin veil, it glowed dully, like over-heated metal. Lines and colours had an extreme sharpness and precision, as though bitten in by an acid, or as in the background of a mediæval painting: the massive green of trees, the contours of buildings south of the park, heavy grey-white plumes above the power station, the white stems of flag-staffs, the white pillars of the park gates, a woman's red dress splashed on an asphalt path, the violent scarlet of buses. The coffee-stall at the other side of the road, near the drinking-trough, was open all night. People stood round it in groups, and sat, a long row of bodies leaning slackly against each other like cheap puppets, on the low stone coping at this side of the park fence: in the sodium light of the street-lamps their faces and bare arms looked to be in the first moments of putrescence. Only the young black prostitute, yellow handbag swinging as she walked, was impervious to its virulence—she, and a negro in overcoat and bowler hat inviting a woman to dance with him, posturing in front of her, gesticulating, smiling.

Even I could not sleep in the exhausted air. At two o'clock one morning the moon glared into my eyes, and I got up to look out.

The coffee-stall was still serving a score of people, youths in white shirts, a young negro with fluttering hands and a curious out-of-date elegance, really exquisite, four stork-legged street-walkers in their summer uniform of full skirts, thin almost transparent blouses, and long wide scarves: one of them was laughing her head off, her mouth a black hole in the face of a corpse. Three boys with skiffle instruments started to play, jerking like marionettes, faces wooden, and a girl in the tightest of black trousers cut short at the ugly bulge of her calf swung her buttocks from side to side like captive balloons. A tramp, a heap of bones and rags the colour of dark clay, slept, arms dangling, head between his knees, on the low wall.

It was light enough in the room to write. I made notes, I knew I was not making them for myself, and I went on scribbling and staring until half-past four, by which time it was beginning to be day, the coffee-stall man was rinsing cups and plates in the trough, the last customers were drifting away, dragging their toes, and the tramp, sunk deeper into himself, still slept.

I slept a little then, until I was wakened by the thin spattering cries of birds, piercing the roar of traffic.

The summer was a hell of visitors from abroad (these included a stray professor from Zagreb, sent by the P.E.N.). I have never known how to keep what Montherlant calls *biophages* at a distance.

'But surely, as a writer, you need to meet a great many sorts of people?'

'No. No, no, no. As a writer what I need is strange countries, solitude, books, music, the theatre. Nothing else at all.'

'Then as a human being.'

'Not even as a human being. There are a few people, not all of them English, to be counted on the fingers of both hands, whom never to see would be an amputation. To be forced to meet others costs me as much moral effort as writing a book.'

'What intolerable egoism!'

One of these torrid afternoons I had a visitor who started in me a conflict of admiration, respect, and mild discomfort. A face and body burned down to the wick, black and as it were fused eyes, the look of a slightly mad mendicant friar. Except for this dissolution of his flesh in the flame of a single vision, he had changed little since my first sight of him—one day either just before the second war, or shortly after it started. I arrived at the office to find Hermon Ould involved with this curious figure.

'This is Miron Grindea. He wants to start an international literary review, and he wants us to support him, morally and with money. I've already told him that you'll give him your approval, but that what little money we have we're spending on our exiles.'

'Surely,' I said, 'this is the wrong time to start such a review?'

The glance Grindea turned on me was that of a Savonarola at the stake: anguish, a blind resolution, serenity. I thought him mad, and certain to fail. Worse, as I always am I was repelled by an implacable obsession. But at least his mania was innocent—in a decade fouled by every sort of cruelty and guilt. What I could do to help him, very little, I did.

Nothing defeated him, he started *Adam*, and kept it going, year after year, without money, with fanatical devotion. At one time or another every celebrated writer in Europe gave him a piece of writing, shamed into it by the spectacle of a total dedication. His life since the idea seized him had been that of a *monstre sacré*, prepared to

sacrifice everything—and everybody—to his hunger. If the only way
to bring out another issue of *Adam* had been to throw every stick of
furniture, every object in the house, his wife's clothes, his child's
toys, into the furnace, and himself after them, he would have done it
without a tremor.

I looked at him now, three-quarters consumed, a thin flame. He
had come to ask me to help him raise a ludicrously small sum of
money to keep the review going. Surely I must know rich people
who would give it to him?

Not only do I know very few rich people, but I felt certain he
would not get even the little money he needed. He had no alloy of
self-interest in him; his lack of it, and his obsessive idealism, made a
great many right-minded people uneasy. He was, they felt, unmanageable. *Perfecti* of his sort can count on praise, respect, flattery
even, dislike, but money—no.

After he had left, a little comforted by my promise to write to one
or two people, I sent him twenty pounds I could not afford. Not out
of generosity. In the same spirit as a sinner gives away alms on his
deathbed, in the hope of earning divine grace.

Chapter 18

Guy had been invited to go to Princeton in September, to the
Institute for Advanced Studies. I looked forward to it with an indescribable joy—as an escape from a state of affairs that made it
impossible for me to work. I was profoundly disgusted with my life
at this time, and with myself for not managing it better.

Before then, to give him the semblance of a holiday, we took C. to
Switzerland for three weeks.

A Swiss writer had talked to me about the marvels of Einsiedeln, and on the way back from Lake Constance we stayed a night there. It is a place of pilgrimage, with a Benedictine monastery and a Gothic Black Virgin. Whatever the village may have been in the past, it exists now for pilgrims; the shops on both sides of the narrow street are crammed with holy images, in plaster, in sandstone, in papier-mâché, in glazed pastry. The street climbs towards an immense square, the splendidly simple façade of the monastery stretching the length of one side: in the centre, dwarfed by the space, a fountain, a squat semi-circular arcade of booths like loose-boxes for the sale of images, and a flight of wide steps becoming a stone ramp rising steeply to a narrower flight: beyond this, another clean ordered waste of cobblestones before you arrive at the portico of the monastery, flanked by towers.

Our rooms in the hotel looked out across the square to the steps, the ramp, and the great sandstone monastery. At this height you saw the hill behind it, black with firs, and a vaporous sky which gave the impression of being a superb back-drop using real trees, real clouds.

A suave authoritative manager—no doubt an actor rehearsing the part—said, 'You will want to hear the *Salve Regina*—sung at four o'clock. You have fifteen minutes.'

C. refused to go with us—his amiability drew the line at a religious service.

I was stunned by the inconceivable extravagance of the interior: a jungle of painted walls and ceilings, a swarm of saints in the likeness of fauns and over-ripe nymphs and—breaking out on all sides, springing from ledges, from brackets, from the arched vault, hanging by a wing-tip, a single foot, a finger—angels with trumpets, with out-spread wings, with scrolls, with wreaths, smiling, gesticulating, half-naked in flying garments, gilded, painted in all the colours of a shoal of tropical fish. Like the village, it stank of the profits of piety. And, as I sat listening to the singing—a choir of monks out of sight behind the high altar—an extraordinary feeling of peace took possession of me, a strange deep joy. I felt that I was dissolving into a silence created by the voices—a sense of absolute security, absolute quiet.

It was unexpected—and undeserved.

Late in the evening I was looking from my bedroom at the square —empty and, except for a circle of coldly unreal light near the steps, dark. As I watched, the first ripple of a thick black stream of men and women appeared at the far edge; it flowed sluggishly up the steps, and up the ramp, endless. Priests carrying large candles came towards it from the church and waited at the upper flight of steps. Between them and the monastery was black night. After what seemed a long time, a shadowy mob—here and there a face picked out by a candle hung in the darkness like a fish in the artificial current of a tank—had seeped up at the foot of the monastery.

When the last figure, the last candle, disappeared into the church, I went to bed.

Ever since we landed in France, I had been living again in the world of my unwritten novel. Everything I looked at was attached to it at some point by an unseen thread: walking about the enchantingly dignified and friendly library of St Gallen I caught glimpses of its characters, and overheard remarks, even whole dialogues. This novelist's trick, which is involuntary—I never heard of anyone who can induce it—has a drawback: the actual world loses substance, or, rather, since one has withdrawn part of one's attention from it, the kind of things happen that might happen to a shortsighted man who refused to wear glasses, blunders, errors, stupidity. And something else which can be humiliating or shameful. A real incident which relates itself, suddenly, to something the writer is in process of inventing (or discovering) may cease entirely to be real in itself, and become real, charged with emotion, only in the imaginary world of the novel.

This happened to me in Einsiedeln. The clatter of bells woke me before daylight. I lay still for some minutes, listening to the sound of feet striking the cobblestones. At last, driven by curiosity, I got up and went to the window. It was a little after four o'clock: a grey sky closed in the monastery, the black fleece of trees on the hill, the vast square, and the slow-moving file of pilgrims. Had they been coming up the street and across the square all night? At this hour no one met them; they went straight into the blackness of the church. I watched the last in, and was going back to bed when I caught sight of something—a large dog?—moving in the empty square.

After a moment I saw that it was a man in a dark macintosh, shuffling forward on his knees. Infinitely slowly, he moved up the first flight of steps, the ramp, the second flight, and on towards the monastery. For less than an instant, I had an impression of atrocious despair and anguish. Then I thought coldly: You must remember this for Mott, and use it.

When I was making a note on the back of an envelope in my hand-bag, I thought that there is something positively evil in the way a writer makes use of other people's emotions, even of agony. It was not the first time I had thought it.

It may not be only evil. Nothing is pure or single; there might be compassion in the impulse as well as coldness and inhumanity.

I finished my note and put it away carefully. The dog-man had reached the church and vanished.

We spent our last night in France, in Rheims, a sordid hotel and a sordid city, an ill setting for the smile of Rheims.

Chapter 19

The relief and joy of getting away lapsed into the familiar excitement of landing. New York at six in the morning: in an overcast sky a magnificent arc of sunrise, fading quickly into a dull glow more like a sunset. Then a subdued daybreak, the lights on shore becoming fewer and dimmer, and the dark outlines of a tower, houses, taller buildings, cranes, leaping forward like animals—even on a grey day, the energy of America has this quality of brightness and menace.

In Princeton we lived in the Nassau Tavern, in two narrow over-heated rooms looking over a garden. I was continually happy, as always when the burdens and irritations of a domestic life are lifted from me. There was an admirable small shop across the street, kept by an unlikable German, where I bought sandwiches of rye bread and bottles of thin Californian wine, very drinkable, and five evenings out of seven we dined on these in my room, in great contentment of mind and body. Guy spent his days at the Institute, and I sat in my room from breakfast until five or six, writing.

I had scarcely arranged my papers on a table set in the narrow window, the first morning, when the figure I had been groping towards for so many weeks moved into the light. He was no one I had ever known, and I knew him at once. An underpaid old schoolmaster, widely and curiously learned, a mathematician who could not pass examinations, at seventy almost penniless, wearing a threadbare, repellently stained and creased suit—a small shrivelled old-womanish old man, in no way attractive, with harsh ungracious manners and a maliciously sharp eye. I saw him with astonishing clarity, even to the well of tenderness in his ruined body.

To see Mott first through old Paul Gate's eyes was in a sense to judge him before he had spoken for himself, yet it was right, because the old man loved Mott. And he himself was better worth recording than any of the obviously important persons in the book.

The short first part of *The Road from the Monument*, thirty-seven pages, is better than anything else in a long novel. Would the book have continued on this level if I had been able to live in the Nassau Tavern until I had finished it?

I don't know. It is not important.

This was the first time since *The Green Man* that I had the acute happiness of writing in freedom. It was also the last.

In Princeton, too, we had the uncovenanted good luck to make two friends. One of the scholars working at the Institute was George Steiner, a young man overflowing with intelligence, kindness, malicious irony, incomparable energy of mind and body, erudition, gaiety. I lacked the courage to talk, but I listened to him, and watched Zara Steiner moving about the room with the tranquil dignity of a good child. She was carrying her first child at the time. I should have liked to know where this extremely intelligent young woman, an historian by training, had learned to cook like a Frenchwoman.

If I had not, in the first moment, noticed the reckless generosity and warmth behind George Steiner's subtly aggressive genius, I should have been intimidated by it . . .

I was in Princeton when *A Cup of Tea for Mr Thorgill* was published in England.

Can I write about the reception given to this novel without seeming to be resentful, or worse, low-spirited? What, in sober truth, I felt was stupefaction. I had written a novel round the forms a para-religious doctrine can take in the heart and mind, and among its characters were two—or is it three?—communists, and one smeller-out of heresy who boasts that she is able to detect treachery by its 'vibrations'. Several critics (they included a comically outraged woman in that most respectable of liberal papers, the *Manchester Guardian*, who thought it 'unworthy and dishonest') persuaded themselves that I had set out to expose Oxford as a 'nest of communists', or 'riddled with communism.'

I was absurdly baffled. Indiscreetly so when a journalist well-known to me by name, wrote me an angry letter about my slander on Oxford. I could not believe that an intelligent man could be so obtuse, and I took the trouble to answer truthfully that if I had not wanted to write a little about the marring of Oxford I might equally well have laid the novel in Leeds or Cambridge or anywhere. From the abusive reply I got I realized that I might as well save my breath, he was in a completely irrational state of mind.

Is it possible for educated people to be, in good faith, so fatuous? I take enormous, but enormous pains to write clearly, and with as much or as little elegance as is suitable. What happens? Through naïveté or dullness, or, perhaps, ill-will, only a few people read what is under their eyes. (In the case of professional reviewers, this may be due only to laziness or lack of time.)

It is absurd, and I should despair if I were not, in the final resort, indifferent . . .

In December this blest interlude came to an end. Leaving Guy to follow me in the New Year, I left in one of the small Cunarders, to prepare a family Christmas in the flat. It was a fairly rough crossing, on the second day the life-lines were run out along the decks, and on the third we spent hours hove-to in what seemed the tail of a hurricane. For most of the voyage I was alone at my table, which pleased me. I am vain of my steadiness at sea.

One evening the only other person in the small bar was an American, a staff officer serving in Europe, a charming man with a passion for German baroque churches and German poetry. One of the recurrent crises in our relations with Soviet Russia was under way, and he talked very sensibly about the suicidal results of the thermo-nuclear war.

'Not,' he said, with a reassuring smile, 'that it need—I say: need—be a totally destructive multi-megadeath affair.'

'Do you mind translating that?' I said diffidently.

'Oh, there might be as many as a hundred and eleven million

killed in my country—that is, a hundred and eleven megadeaths. In a nuclear exchange between missile sites and airfields. I'm not talking about anything more than that.'

'It should be enough.'

'What one hopes, of course, is that between us—assuming that the Russians are not determined to reduce strategy to national suicide— we shall keep conventional forces large enough to provide a rational alternative to nuclear war.' His thin face of a mediæval monk was serene; there was even a faint gaiety at the back of his deep-lidded eyes. 'We must pray it won't come to that, but—in a war against evil itself . . . if our choice lay between that risk and the abandonment of all spiritual values . . .'

When I hear military men talking about spiritual values I am outraged and contemptuous. They chose a profession which in its principles, its methods, is the negation of the spirit. I feel more respect for Napoleon's generals; most of them were uncultivated brutes, but they did not discuss spiritual values. Any such value supposes in its holder the refusal of cruelty, an absolute respect for human freedom and dignity, without exception or reservation. If, by an awful paradox, we must kill to preserve a measure of these, let us do it without cant.

These are obviously the reflections of an obtuse irrationalist. And unjust to a man who will probably die quoting Rilke.

But I shudder at the state of mind which sentences children to death, and the unborn generations who might, even under what is misnamed communism, a religion I detest, *aller à la chasse au bonheur*. If it echoes the mental state of the American ruling classes, what hope is there that anyone will survive on this planet longer than a few more years? Paradoxically, the impulse to write is sharpened by danger. 'Depend upon it, sir, when a man is going to be hanged in a fortnight, it concentrates his mind wonderfully . . .'

In London I laid in vast stores of Christmas food, and a tree on which to hang the self-same glass bird, the very stars our mother had bought in Whitby market. In a few days I had dissipated the energy brought from America.

Recovered, I took out the manuscript of *A Ulysses Too Many*, revised it, polished it a little, and sent it to the publisher.

I had the weakness at this time to ask its English publisher how many copies he had sold of Mr Thorgill's book. Only a few over eight thousand. This was no worse than, from the notices, I had expected; it dejected me only because so much depended on what my novels earned now.

One mid-January night, about eleven, I was looking at the power station south of the park, flood-lit—two great columns, with a column of white smoke blown horizontally from west to east so that it lay across them, the image of a ruined acropolis, lifted up against a restless sky, such as I love. Lights flashed along the edge of the park between an amorphous mass of buildings and the black spectral web of trees.

I thought: I no longer believe in myself. I am ready to agree wholeheartedly with any ass who thinks or writes against me. I expect nothing for the future.

In this instant I realized the exact difference between expecting and hoping. To expect nothing, or very little, does not mean to be without hope. Hope is a talent like any other. I have as stubborn a talent for hope as for going on living.

In the shock of hearing that Charles Morgan was dead, I remembered that his last letter—not his last, the last I had kept—had saddened me, for no good reason, and I looked for it and read it again.

It was not unhappy. Yet I had been right, the shadow was there. A light shadow, very light, distant.

'. . . I have been wandering in France becoming an Academician, wearing a beautiful frock by Lanvin, and eating and drinking and talking too much . . . France was very happy and triumphant. As no other English novelist except Kipling has ever had that particular honour, your young man of *My Name is Legion* is happy. But the older man is tired . . . And for heaven's sake let us meet when we can.'

If I had thought about it, I should not, let me be honest, have expected the sudden end of more than thirty years of cool enduring friendship to grieve me as it did. For all his singular kindness, he had not the gift of intimacy. But, once given, his friendliness was given for good, with a modesty and loyalty not to be shaken by circumstance, divergence of views, age. It was given with reserve: there was always a distance, a space of—the word coolness will not do, it carries an overtone of indifference which would be entirely unjust—of, let us say, quietness, as though his affection, its warmth, its simplicity, had to cross a space set between him and the world. It was not set by self-regard. Perhaps by his perpetual attentiveness to an inner world. Certainly by a diffidence, an instinctive delicacy, which forbade him to do more than lay the lightest possible pressure on the mind and spirit of a friend.

I had heard him accused of arrogance. And defended as seeming to be arrogant only because he was very shy. Neither word is exact. Arrogance begins in a greed for personal power—of which he was wholly free. And in a grown man shyness—I know this about myself—is usually the fear of not being taken at one's own value by the world. Charles's values were centred outside himself, in the world he entered when he sat down to write.

The same man who accused him in my hearing of arrogance went on, 'He reminds me of that detestable fellow, Chateaubriand—the same hard vanity, the same superciliousness, coldness, stiffness.'

I could only say angrily, 'You are entirely wrong,' without being able to offer proofs. One cannot *prove* that a certain image is just, a certain landscape or a certain concerto beautiful. And he had to die before I needed to think about him with an attempt at detachment.

He was not cold. He could—a few persons know this—be burned to the bone by a passion, driven to the edge of madness. And could oppose to it—nothing self-interested, nothing timid—a living idea of order.

Although he did, during the years I knew him, construct from the author of *My Name is Legion* a self already there in the seed and, touch by touch, work on it until he died, what drove him was not vanity. It was an imperative impulse towards elegance and control in word and gesture. When he had to make a speech he worked on it with the care of a great actor preparing himself to play a part. I have heard a number of eloquent speakers, usually French. None of them, not Jules Romains, nor André Chamson, is able to send a shock through the nerves of his hearers like that started by the opening phrase of Charles's speech, in 1954 in Amsterdam: *A June night and no war* . . . Because, as in so many of Charles's contrived strokes, his heart was involved.

Tormented by his passion for elegance, for perfection, he quite deliberately wrote at a remove from life. He was not a great novelist —these monsters devour life whole. But he was a conscious artist, and dear knows the animal is rare, all but extinct.

Dead, a new trait showed in his face, a something feminine in its strength, that is, a vein of steel. The other traits, masculine delicacy, withdrawal, reserve, were even more marked than in life, since they had to do without the flicker of gaiety, the twisted smile, the kindness. Above all, the kindness.

Thinking of his reserve, his half deliberate distance, I might have expected his death to be no more than the widening of an existing gap. Not true. I felt and still feel a new loss. It is a little more than the loss of a friend who made no demands. In a world growing daily colder and more menacing, his calm greeting, the good manners directed by a polite heart, are a continuing lack. He would not have identified good manners with morality, but he knew instinctively that to mind one's manners, in daily intercourse, in friendship, in writing, is a better road than many to a society fit to live in. So much so that, with him gone, the moral climate of our writing world has worsened a little.

Nonsense, he would say, with his curious smile, nonsense; the climate changes with every young man writing his first book, suffering his first fever of hope, disappointment, renewed hope.

Perhaps. But something strictly irreplaceable had disappeared from my life and from a world increasingly indifferent to perfection, reticence, politeness, measure.

Chapter 20

I have never known—how should I ?—why my son, whose life as an airline pilot is anything but monotonous, had this stubborn wish to cross the Atlantic in his small yacht. Perhaps the familiar reason— because the Atlantic is there; perhaps because the pilot of a jet plane sees only the wrinkled surface of the sea (if he sees that): perhaps only a habit of mind common to so many obscure men whose graves, foundering in the harsh grass of a disused churchyard, carry the words: '. . . master mariner of this parish, drowned at sea, March 18, 1771 . . . died of fever in Vera Cruz, June 3, 1735 . . . lost with his ship off Archangel in the winter of 1783 . . .' Or perhaps an echo of my own restlessness—but then where did that come from, if not from these others?

His defeat in 1950 when he was forced to turn back from Brest in his first ship, the ketch *Nina*, had exacerbated his obstinacy.

He and his high-hearted young wife had lived in yachts since they married. The one they owned now, *Tally Ho*, was their third. Built in 1910 by Stow, she won one of the early Fastnet races, a fine ship, with a good length of straight keel, deep bulwarks, and full-bodied hull. They had worked on her, modifying the sail plan and replacing the heavy tiller by wheel steering, and late in 1957 they began to make her ready for the voyage, working patiently through the endless list of things to be done, spares and equipment to be bought, stores, charts, radio, a trawler's emergency four-man rubber dinghy and survival pack, a pump able to shift some ten tons of salt water an hour, down-wind sails to make her self-steering in the Trade Winds: the abortive voyage of 1950 had had its life-saving lessons. The preparations went on through the winter and spring, and in April I put aside *The Road from the Monument* and went down to stay near the Hamble river. They meant to set out at the end of May or early June—this time without a crew. On this point I was corrected by Frances.

'Nana, you forget. Troy is a passenger, I am a member of the crew.'

'This time,' my son said, 'we haven't made the mistake of wasting time smartening the ship to Cowes standard, she's fairly smart, and she's completely seaworthy. She looks well, don't you think?'

'Yes.'

I thought she looked even smaller than her overall length of forty-seven feet, forty-four on the water-line: between two Atlantic rollers she would be invisible.

'You don't have to worry. I know what I'm doing.'

His likeness at this time to photographs of my father in his handsome youth and young middle-age startled me, as if the lean shambling body of the old sea-captain had split open under my eyes to set free a younger self. But at no age would my father have dreamed of crossing the Atlantic in a twenty-nine ton ship with his wife and two little lively girls.

Of the five weeks I hung about, helping where I could, I remember clearly only the last day. I knew that they did not want to be seen off, and I arranged to leave before they did. That morning I woke early, a few minutes before half-past four—half-past three by sun time. After a minute there was the first weak bird note, alone for a few seconds, then another, and a third, and in less than two minutes the chorus belling out, filling the whole air with a web of differing cries and single notes, the strong whistling of one bird piercing the rest. Now and then the prolonged cry of an owl. Then, behind the bird chorus, a distant noise of hounds, like a peal of bells flawed by a shriller cracked note, something of a pigeon's throaty groaning cry and something of a wild duck, a curtain of sound rising and falling in the grey light. And then, some long way away, the cuckoo.

Without warning I was invaded by a sadness inexplicable even by my fears, an awful swollen tide of grief in my throat. Then, very distinctly, as if I had only to reach an arm out to touch him, I saw my son as a young child, perhaps two: he was smiling, his hair a yellow cloud round his head, his eyes widely-open and brilliant.

If you cry it will be for yourself, I thought. I said, 'Forgive me.'

He had already gone. With despair, such despair, I thought: Who will forgive me?

During the week before they left, the wind blew stubbornly from the west, sometimes gale force, the worst quarter for them. It was still coming from the west when Bill rang me up to say that they must start. 'We can't wait forever.'

'When do you go off?'

'Tomorrow morning at eleven.'

'Well, the best of luck.'

'Thanks for all you've done. We're very happy.'

'That's fine.'

'Very happy. We'll write.'

'Ah, do.'

Beginning young, I have had a great deal of practice not only in hiding my feelings but in hiding from them. It embarrasses me to be pitied. A membrane in my mind closes at once over any strong emotion—anxiety, dread, hope. A membrane is not a shutter: what is behind it can be felt moving. I went on with my novel, and took care not to say that I was afraid. The truth is I was afraid the whole time, whatever I was doing. And at night.

I am not a stoic. No doubt even my fear of pity and ridicule come down to me from long-dead women who were not encouraged to make a song about what went on inside the hard bones of their skulls.

After they left Falmouth in early June, the first news came from Corcubion, a tiny dilapidated village round the corner of Finisterre. They were trapped in the little Spanish harbour, with the tunny fleet, by southerly gales. When they went ashore the first time, the village had waiting for them its one English-speaking inhabitant; they were led to the store and the children given bunches of larkspur and carnations: the difference between the two of them leaps to the eye in what they did; Frances carried hers politely and patiently all morning, young Troy, disliking the messy stems, handed hers to her mother to carry.

On the 21st of July I had a telegram to say they had reached Lisbon. The same day I finished the second draft of my novel and put it in a cupboard, to revise later.

They had a rough passage, eight days, from Lisbon to Gibraltar, and wired asking us to fly there to see them. My heart leaped crazily. It was impossible to go, I was in Portmeirion with C.—his only holiday—and I drove the thought from my mind. Suddenly, when they reached Las Palmas, it surfaced, and I dragged a reluctant Guy round the shipping quarter of east London in search of a ship with room for us. There was one sailing from Southampton in less than a week, a Spanish boat. She turned out to be an emigrant ship for Venezuela, shabby, the passage-ways and bare cabins filthy, every water-closet blocked most of the time and stinking to heaven. And speaking of heaven—after I had watched the Spanish crew knocking out the rotten wood in the lifeboats and patching the gaps with white deal, I decided that she was as unseaworthy as she was squalid. The captain and officers were invisible, rigorously in-communicado, but the crew were gay and friendly. Indeed, apart from the stench and discomfort, she was a sympathetic ship. The bread, baked in what no doubt were appalling conditions, was delicious.

At Corunna we took in our first emigrants—two hundred of them. Something like a fiesta raged on the wharf, a laughing yelling chant-ing weeping mob of friends and relatives. Women carrying children, and younger women, newly married, with gawky boyish husbands in stiff new clothes, came aboard with faces swollen to twice their size by three hours of hard crying. They settled down quickly, and took over the ship. The eight or nine so-called first-class passengers were not merely in no way privileged, they were discriminated against in a score of ways. Since I was not going to spend longer than ten days with hundreds of restless parakeet-voiced Spaniards, I liked this. I liked it still better when I thought about the clean unnatural luxury and horrible diversions of the English liner we might have been in. At the same time I decided that, should we run into weather that was too much for the ship, I would not compete for a place in one of the four lifeboats. Simpler to drown at once.

Of the two weeks of heat and smooth massive light we spent in Las Palmas, a single scene stands out with the sharpness of an illuminated initial in a half-obliterated manuscript. The afternoon when I was alone on the sands with Troy and, suddenly, she ran into the sea, which that day a hot wind had blown into great clawing breakers; the under-current sucked her little body out like a twig, in mortal fear I rushed after her and dragged her back. I scolded her furiously. Sobered by the shock of feeling herself pulled into the sea, she sat curled up in my lap in silence. I held her, and to calm myself stared at the very strange hills behind the port, bare, sculptured, changing in the light from the livid grey of dry earth to lion colour, with that velvety blackness *under* the tawny glowing skin. Gradually an extraordinary peace came from—from where? The child and I were enclosed in a bubble formed of the hard bright light and the foreign voices. I had the brief sense that I had been born only for this one action, these silent sheltering minutes.

We were returning in a Union Castle boat. When we left the hotel for the last time I gave the servant some pesetas, not many, I was saving what I had left, to give to Bill. A flame of surprise and joy ran across her sallow face, she poured out a long smiling sentence, of which I understood only the last words—*Vaya con Dios*.

The family came on board with us. Looking round the ship with a fine smile, Frances said, 'I like *Tally* millions better than this great thing—don't you, Troy?'

Troy did not answer.

I sent them away an hour before we sailed. The sister ship to ours moved out ahead of us, and ours blew long ritual farewell blasts. The deep note echoed back and back through my childhood, tears forced themselves under my eyelids: I got rid of them before they were noticed.

Later I stood staring at the long waves, leaping, slavering foam, green above black-veined troughs. Let them be safe, let them be safe. *Vaya con Dios. Vaya con Dios.*

In London I took the *Monument* from its shelf and revised it very carefully. In the end, since, for once in my life, I had a year's income in hand, I decided not to publish it for another two or three years, to give myself a respite from reviewers.

(To be entirely honest, I was naïvely a little confident that they must and would praise this book.

This was an illusion.)

Another novel—its theme as old as humanity: how much evil, how much violence to the rooted decencies of the human spirit, can you bring yourself to do for a good end?—knocked on my skull. I kept it at arm's length, to give it a little room to grow.

During the whole of this time I lived and worked in front of a vast screen stretched behind my eyes: everything I did, between waking and lying down, took place in front of it. Behind every gesture I made, every image, every event, there lay the waste of water, under a dull sky grey and menacing, in sunlight a web of glittering points running out to infinity. Nothing, not even hearing of a friend's death, blotted it out.

It invaded the Memorial Service for Rose Macaulay, blunting the strange pang I felt, less for her than for the changed figures I watched come in, changes which seemed to have been hurried into overnight—the church was full of people who had not yet learned their roles of ageing men and women—the yellow sagging jowls of a celebrated woman writer, Harold Nicolson's heavy movements, another well-known face so creased and misshapen that for a full minute I did not recognize it. The images of Rose herself were less desolate. I could look full at the slender young woman with the head of a Greek statue, and at the older woman turning on the stairs of the Portland Place flat to look back at me and say: Margaret, you don't know what it's like to watch the person you love dying. And at the skeletal Rose of the last ten years . . .

They had left Las Palmas on the 7th of November. There was silence for thirty-three days, then the telegram from Barbados: ABILITY 33 DAYS ALL FLOURISHING LOVE.

Ability is the old merchant sailor's code word, standing for:

Arrived all well. My father always used it, and I had taught it to Bill.

One thing in their first laconic letter—apart from the incident of the cockpit drain broken at the skin of the boat eighteen inches below the waterline and plugged, in mid-Atlantic, with a cork—that struck me was that in thirty-three days they sighted only one ship, the *Jessie Gulva*, a small Danish cargo boat, which changed course to come and look at them and wave, but did not speak to them. Another was that Frances really had the right to call herself a member of the crew; she learned to steer a compass course, and in good weather took the wheel for an hour, alone. I tried and failed to overhear the thoughts of a ten-year-old child confronting that steep immensity of sea from an eye-level not much above that of a gull's resting on the crest of a wave. Thought is a clumsy word: probably she only *saw*— light, space, glitter of water, clouds.

What was I at ten? Already anxious, ambitious, eager to please, something of a hypocrite and a mule.

I was assailed at this time by a novel I had no intention of writing. It began one night in sleep. A woman was playing hide and seek with her young child, in a large garden, like a Welsh one I knew. She was a little bored, but she went on alternately hiding and seeking, calling dutifully, 'Hello, hello,' as she sought. For a time the child answered in an excited voice. Abruptly, he stopped answering. Becoming afraid, she ran wildly from shrub to tall dark shrub, calling, looking, not finding him.

When I woke the whole novel moved in my brain. It was about a woman whose life was shaped by a conviction of sin, an unreasoned agony of guilt. Driven by her savage energy, she went out into the world, coming back at intervals to see an only child. One day she came back to be told that he had disappeared. The rest of her life became a frantic search for him, like K's search for the Castle, or his baffled efforts to find out from his accusers what crime he had done. There were moments when she caught or imagined she caught a glimpse of him, and others when it seemed that he was in some other room of the house. Her life went by. Now and then she saw a young man who resembled him, and now and then spoke to one of these, who jeered at her. When she was dying he came into her room for a few seconds, an indistinct figure, glanced at her in silence and went out.

If I were a poet I could perhaps have fused these innumerable images and sensations into a poem, without deforming them—a novel cannot do this, it operates at too slow a heat. A talented choreographer might make them into a ballet. Or a childless writer, able to keep her cool distance, pick them up without burning her hand to the bone.

She can have them.

Chapter 21

I am always being reminded that English writers exist at several removes from reality.

Last year (June, 1964) I was reminded of it again at a P.E.N. Congress in Oslo, where the subject under discussion was semantics. On the first day it became clear that semantics is not only a mode of life, one of the most deeply-rooted, but one of the most dangerous. Words an Englishman can hold in his hand safely, play with, use for a rhetorical exercise, may kill the writer of another country who handles them. The delegates from countries where honesty or rashness or want of adroitness in touching certain words mean torture, imprisonment, death, were speaking on another wave length, and their English colleagues heard them, if at all, very indistinctly. (On this occasion, their French colleagues heard nothing except their own eloquence, and did not try to hear anything else.)

'Listen to our tears, our grief of small nations at the mercy of great ones,' the Vietnamese delegate said—explaining quietly and patiently that, in his country, the meaning of the word *freedom* was *freedom to go to prison*. 'Help us to endure, to reach a level where life will have a meaning . . .'

In 1959, a meeting in London of the International Executive stumbled over the same word. Several of the delegates had come determined to get rid of the Hungarian Centre, for the sound reason that Hungarian writers were being jailed as political prisoners and the Centre had made no effort to help them. I looked down the long table. There was an almost visible mark on the foreheads of delegates from the Iron Curtain countries: the East German's small lined worn-out face carried it: not in any English sense of the word free, sitting there quietly repeating his instructions, Bode Use was none the less in some way more real than most of us, the dangers he was facing were real dangers.

Speaking for the Writers in Exile, Paul Tabori made an unanswerable speech, answered at once by the delegate from Prague, a charming and intelligent young woman.

'Don't forget,' she said, smiling, 'that the four Hungarian writers you are speaking about were not put in prison as writers, but because they had broken the law.'

'They were not put in prison because they had stolen or murdered,' Tabori said quietly, 'but because they had written something.'

One of the East European Centres had tabled a resolution which allowed the offending Hungarians another length of rope. The committee of the English Centre had instructed me to vote against what it considered, rightly, an indefensible compromise. Listening to the debate, I thought briefly that more than a continent separated the warm room we sat in from Tibor Déry's uncomfortable (if no worse) cell. The Chinese delegate from Taipei had just said, with a diminutive gesture of quite astonishing beauty: We shall be making history . . . What is coldly termed *little history*, I thought, the history of unimportant persons, that is, of ninety-nine and nine-tenths per cent of the whole. Even though the effect of any protest we make here is probably, certainly, zero, we need not think too lowly of ourselves . . . I reflected that, if we expelled the Hungarians, then the Czechs, the Poles, the East Germans (about these I cared little), might be forced by their masters to expel themselves, and my poor friend Parandowski would lose one of his chances of talking about Mallarmé to a French scholar. A number of weak threads—but stretching across frontiers—would be slit . . . The resolution was being voted on by naming Centres. Against: the exiles, the Chinese Centre at Taipei, the American, the Latvian, the Estonian, the Australian . . . I can be something of a Calvinist and something of a hypocrite in a good cause, but could I carry it to the extent of asking writers in Budapest to risk their own lives to save Tibor Déry's?

Who am I to ask them to be heroes? . . . On the other hand again, I could not support the motion.

Four Centres had abstained from voting. It was my turn. My friend Tabori looked at me confidently.

'I abstain.'

I avoided Paul Tabori's eye. Not that he would reproach me. Too humanely cynical, he expected too little good faith or singleness of purpose from human nature, or from my nature.

What is more, my dear Paul, we are both right, you to be uncompromising in a matter of political and human decency, I to compromise, English fashion, to the limit of tolerance. The damage either of us, acting alone, is able to do, is halved by our co-existence . . .

Again and again, staring across the abyss dividing the provincial-minded English from the continentals, I realized that the last are in a situation from which there is no issue—except through the death of society. Two years later, the Hungarians were up for judgement again, with the difference that the Centre had rid itself of the police dog and elected a scholarly critic as secretary and a new president who was a professor. They came to London as delegates—or defendants—and David and I seized our chance to see them alone, before they faced the Executive. The argument ran, lap after lap, round the same track. The secretary coldly, the other with warm anxiety, reminded us that Budapest is not London . . . 'Déry is in prison for urging writers in the factories to come out on strike. You don't understand what that means. Here you can have strikes and nothing happens, all are calm, friendly, like lambs. In Hungary there are no political lambs, agitation is less than one step from civil war. We *can't* go through that bloody business again. Try, please, to understand us . . . If this new resolution of the English Centre, suspending us, is passed tomorrow, it will make a terrible impression on Hungarian writers. We are full of hope now, we have a new active Centre, we are prepared to do all we can to work with you. Don't make it impossible for us.'

For a moment, I saw what the speaker was seeing, our abysmal distance from the naked realities of power, our self-righteousness, our easy chatter about democracy, lambs frisking in the absence of wolves. If I were to say to him that pretence has its uses, that we English are right to behave *as if* freedom (the freedom to advocate what you will) is an absolute good, he would look at me with polite contempt and curiosity.

When they were leaving I told the secretary, 'I'll do what I can for you.'

He thanked me drily.

I liked him. He was as hard as nails, and without vanity; it had been burned out of him by an acid stronger than that used to cure warts. My friendliness appears to him as nothing more than liberal-minded weakness, I thought, but just possibly he suspects that I know what he thinks of me.

From Brussels a year later I brought away a single document from a session at which I took the Chair. Scribbled on the back of a page of 'Resolutions proposed by the French Centre,' it runs:

3 inconnus
1 libéré
1 libéré
1 amnestié
1 libéré
1 libéré
1 libéré
1 libéré
1 libéré
1 condamné pour des meutres: ancien S.S.
1 agent
1 } action criminelle—trahison
1 }

Voilà fifteen out of twenty-four, the others not traced yet.

As a comment on Europe in 1962 it could not be more concise.

One of our self-imposed duties is to make lists of gaoled writers in countries where imprisonment is an occupational disease of writers, and to plague authority with questions about them.

Imagine for yourself the state of mind of the secretary of, say, the Hungarian Centre, confronted by his virtuous English confrères with a dozen or so names of imprisoned writers and the demand to press his government to release them. I have my share of obtuseness, but that—I confess—goes against my grain.

That year the longest list was the East German one, and the commonest answer to letters about the East German prisoners was silence, or invective in the correct Cold War language. I was the more surprised when the East German delegate rose and began his reading of a long statement, name by name. He read it slowly and calmly, in French.

A pale slender handsome creature—thirty-five? forty?—with a fine arched predatory nose, hard very well-shaped mouth, small fine ears, rather pale eyes, bright and deeply-set, thick hair—a face at once delicate and powerful: good teeth and good strong hands. I watched him while I pencilled my notes. He was guarded, adroit, intelligent, and, I thought, a really first-class tactician.

He was heard in silence.

When I spoke to him afterwards, he smiled with the greatest sweetness and frankness—across an impassable no-man's-land. It is possible to talk as a friend with a Pole and, a little less easily, with Czechs and Hungarians, but not with an East German. I was the ambiguous liberal, to be politely or contemptuously discounted as not fit to grasp either his situation or his mental reservations.

In fact I understand our East Europeans a great deal better than they do me. And I can never shake off my sense that they—unlike us, with our lists and scandalized questions—are playing their heads. Reality in England, even in the 'sixties, is not edged.

My less reputable reason for being in Brussels this week was that—in the conditions of civilized society—no group of human beings offers so many *monstres sacrés*, displays so many naked emotions so shamelessly as a body of writers. The president of the Centre was a brilliant lawyer, a poet (praised by Cocteau), a brave citizen, a force of nature, and an orator of vehement eloquence with the voice of a cathedral organ. At the closing banquet, he recited a long roll of dead writers.

'. . . je pense à Piérard—mort, à H. G. Wells—mort, à Charles Morgan—mort . . .'

At each reverberating cry of *mort*, the chandeliers and the wine glasses rang, and an icy shiver moved down the spines of his listeners. He used his authority to persuade a Minister at the table to sign a document allowing the East Germans to stay two more days in Belgium. Turning to me, he said amiably, 'Not another country in Europe would do that.'

'Perhaps not another president of P.E.N. has so much influence with Ministers.'

He smiled. 'That also is true.'

At this moment, a card was handed to him along the table. He read it, frowning, and threw it down in front of me.

'Inconceivable! Abominable! What do you think, eh, Madame Storm Jameson.'

It was the place card of the elderly Iranian delegate, on the back of which he had scrawled: 'Cher ami, je sais qu'on dira quelque mot de moi. J'aimerais que vous disiez un mot sur mon livre *Le Prophète*. Merci.'

'Not in the least inconceivable,' I said.

He reflected for a moment. An expression of profound simplicity and guile crossed his face. 'If he asks me about it, I shall tell him that van Vriesland promised me to say some words about it in his speech . . .'

Forgive this long parenthesis. I am trying to soften the image of myself as a female Tartuffe.

At the dinner-party given to the 1959 Executive Committee by the English, the guest of honour was the German Ambassador— because the forthcoming Congress was being held in Frankfurt.

I found myself sitting on his right. Before we went in to dinner, an official of the Foreign Office talked to me about him: he was fifty-five—he looked twenty years younger—and had been posted to London as 'a goodwill envoy.'

'What kind of a diplomatic animal is that?' I asked.

My friend smiled slightly. 'You'll see.'

Calculating rapidly as I took my seat, I made him thirty-five in the year the war started. He was charming. He took every opening, the smallest and least promising, to convey his distaste for Hitler and the Nazi régime. It was done with fine tact, without affectation, without the use of a single clumsily assertive word. He knew what he was about. *What he did not know is that he was being listened to intently by an equally accomplished soft-speaker.* On his other side he had the president of the Dutch Centre, our dear turbulent highly culti-vated Viktor van Vriesland, who had learned during the Occupation to detest Germans with such bitterness that he would not be able to bring himself to go to Frankfurt. Turning to me after he had been talking to Viktor, His Excellency said seriously, 'I have been thank-ing him for speaking to me, he a Dutchman, in German . . . I hope you are going to enjoy your week in Frankfurt.'

I did not tell him that I had no intention of going. I said I was sorry that Goethe's birthplace there had been destroyed during the war.

He smiled finely. 'Well—we started it, after all.'

He went on to tell me that Anne Frank's father had called on him. 'He thanked me for receiving him. I said, "It is for me to thank you for coming." I was having a gathering of English boys and young Germans, one of them a young von Moltke, in the afternoon, and I invited him to come to it. He came, and it was a great success, it turned out that all the German boys had read the Diary.'

The ghost of that lively intelligent child must have smiled a little.

In his speech he made the same subtly unstressed confession of regret.

Afterwards, invited by Viktor, he came to Brown's Hotel to drink coffee and brandy, and was so charming, friendly, simple, neighbourly, that I saw myself and dear Viktor as two Neanderthal ghosts. I remembered suddenly the Radziwill I met in Warsaw in 1945. Unlike this German aristocrat he was unhappy.

Chapter 22

Throughout the first months of 1959 I was at peace about the yacht. They were moving gently about the Windward and Leeward Islands, Bequia, St Lucia, Martinique, Antigua. On the 25th of April, they left Antigua and sailed north—twenty windless days to Bermuda. From there they wrote that to attempt the North Atlantic crossing before the middle of June would be suicidal folly. Good, I thought, I have four, five, even six weeks: we can safely lose ourselves in France.

I have given up trying to explain to myself why I have only to cross the Channel to reach a state close to perfect contentment. The run of the grain—my grain? Or the existence of wide, but not too wide spaces—say the Landes, all that immense area of pines, dunes, fields, charmingly plain villages and single houses, many of these very old and very dilapidated, yet keeping a touch of dignity, a little the fold of self-satisfaction in an old woman's ruined face? Or the sense of eternity in a shabby changeless town of two or three thousand inhabitants—let's say in the Dordogne?

This recurring sense of eternity, of the unimportance of time and change, may have everything to do with a happiness I can no more account for than a young man can give an account of the emotion one face among many rouses in him. He can enumerate features, a smile, a turn of the head, and I could run off a catalogue of images drawn from this six weeks alone, the green quiet of the upper Garonne, the exultant dead calm of certain ancient buildings, St Savin, St Bertrand de Comminges, St Michel de Cuxa, Conques, fields of wild flowers in the Ariège, the friendliness of a bare clean hotel in Espalion, the sun of Perpignan and Banyuls lapping bones stiffened by the northern winter. But none of it explains my love of France, my deepest sensual and mental pleasure, even to myself. Why not simply say: A love affair? And leave it at that.

In six weeks we drove slowly 3,500 miles, turning aside again and again to follow thin veins of road to some neglected church, fortified village, river valley enclosing silence. We slept in twenty-eight towns, villages, isolated small hotels, without a trace of harassment. The sense of eternity again? Or the taste of the bread.

Between Perpignan and Foix we turned off the road to look for the ruins of Montségur. In the thirteenth century, some four hundred persons, men, women, children, believing Cathars, held out in this remote fortress for ten months, from May to March, against the Crusading force. Defeated in the end by hunger, thirst, sickness, they surrendered to the besiegers—that is, to the Inquisition—on terms which issued in an immense pyre, large enough to burn two hundred persons at once, erected on the south-east face of the mountain below the castle. Sick and wounded were thrown on to the faggots, and in a few hours two hundred living bodies were a mass of raw blackened bleeding flesh, slowly burning to cinder under a thick cloud of smoke, and filling the valley with the stench of burned meat. A triumph for the true faith, and the visible end of the heresy of Catharism.

It was a hot brilliant day, a jewel of a day, the air so clear you could see a mote at the farther end of a room. The narrow road to

Montségur climbs in a series of hairpin bends, steeply. Suddenly, between one breath and the next, the castle leaped into sight ahead, at a great height. More climbing, more narrow turns, and there, on the left, the high green hill, thinly wooded on its lowest slope, then short rough grass with a thin spatter of broom and yellow rattle, then naked rock, the whole tapering to the blunt point into which the castle digs its claws. Other hills, with the light mark of all but obliterated terracing, stood round, pressing closer on two sides, and mountains craning their necks behind the hills. To catch sight of the village sunk in the deep valley between Montségur and the bare nearer hills, you must walk on farther, until you can look down, over the crumbling edge of the road, on to the fleece of tiled roofs, none of them less than centuries old, in every colour of faded reds and yellows, pressed into the ground by the hills, by Montségur, by an immense sky.

That day there were no other visitors, not a soul anywhere, and no sound except the crickets. The sudden noise of blasting in a quarry sent a current of fear through me, thunder clattering from hill to hill and curling like a lash round Montségur itself. Then the silence closed in again, empty of everything except fear and the burden of the grasshopper.

Ruin that Montségur is, all other castles seem no more than its shadow. It draws up into itself the whole hill. It sends strong tap-roots down into the Manichean underworld of the human intellect and spirit. Catharism is surely the most logical of faiths. That may be why it laid no stress on the duty to burn your neighbour.

We stayed five days in the mountain village of Le Vernet—a village which has a charm and dignity not wholly due to its magnificent position at the heart of savagely wooded hills. It is a village with the soul of a civilized city. And it contains one thing I have seen nowhere else, a monument to the dead of 1914-18 which recognizes that France had allies in that war. Standing at the highest point of the village, in a small square, the Place Entente Cordiale, with ruthlessly cut-back acacias, it has no aesthetic worth of any sort. But at the back of the pedestal it has this plaque which recites the name of every ally, in Europe and outside, beginning with Bolivia and ending with Uruguay. Lower panels on the four sides list the battles, the fourth ending with the triumphant words: *La France sur le Rhin*. Above the wide main panel bearing the names of the dead of 1914-18, a smaller panel records those of 1939-45. A family name which appears three times in the earlier lists appears again on this. The monument itself is of two expressionless female figures seated side by side, England identified by her trident, France by a sword. Both have plump cheeks and buns of hair, good middle-class housewives transmogrified.

One afternoon when I was sitting in this minute airy Place, a very plain-faced young woman, holding the hand of her very plain dark-haired child, a little girl, walked past singing, in a low tuneless voice, to words I did not catch, a tune my young sister sang to her first child as she bathed him . . . Nick nack paddy whack, give a dog a bone . . . The thread of sound led back and back to my sister in her dark underworld: weak as it was, inconceivably weak and thin, it was strong enough to carry across almost twenty years the voice and smile of a young woman bent over the child in her hands. Everything else, the room she sat in, other faces and voices, have sunk without trace. Since I have forgotten so much, why have I kept this and a few other fragments as senseless? The word is unkind, and just.

I have remembered what I can. But she is dying, I know it, from the earth, the traces on it of her light feet, in streets and lanes, becoming fainter every day, more nearly effaced. And nothing, since I can't live forever, to be done about it.

The yacht left Bermuda on its return voyage on the 11th of June. There was no word until the 18th of July. Then I had a letter from the Azores.

At the time I read it I did not know how dangerous a passage it had been—gales, four of them of Force Eight or better, three following each other with scarcely an hour's interval. In one of these the top-mast snapped off level with the mainmast head. It took three hours to clear up the mess, with Frances steering. Cracks, which could be seen working, appeared in the rudder head, and Bill spent some hours hanging over the stern in big seas, head downwards, fixing into place a strip of brass taken from the locker and fashioned to fit the stock. It was to repair the rudder that they had to make for the Azores.

London in July was stifling. I had no help in the flat—the genteel young woman who had been coming two or three times a week had given it up. Oppressed by the hideous traffic noise and fumes, and the flow of *biophages*, Guy was raging to leave London for good. The half of my mind holding a mirage of country solitude and quiet agreed with him. The other half was in the blackest rebellion against the effort of finding a house and moving to it, and tormented by the reflection that since I finished revising *The Monument* I had written nothing. Between doubts and frustration, I drifted.

I knew indistinctly what I wanted, and that it was out of my reach. My fever, inherited, transmitted through my blood, was incurable.

Writing is only my second nature. I would infinitely rather write than cook, but I would rather run about the world, looking at it, than write. The person I have spent my life defeating, the silly sinner (the old sea-captain's word for a fool) who panics at the thought of being shut up in a house of her own, is not the writer.

After they left the Azores on the last leg of the voyage, I waited without patience, in growing fear. On the 13th of August, I wrote in the front of a book: The 21st day has come and gone.

The telephone rang less than an hour later, and my daughter-in-law's light gay voice said, 'Hello, darling, we're at Falmouth.'

It is impossible to be happier in this world.

Next day I started work on *Last Score*. I finished the first draft in September and began rewriting at once. I finished this second version late on the 26th of November, and put it away.

In the morning I woke a few minutes before seven, and saw a singularly clear last quarter of the moon on her back in a smooth darkish grey-blue sky, with one brilliant star above. Far below her, a bank of dark clouds behind the lighted buildings of Park Lane, and, south of the park, a building lit over its height and length, like a liner. I stood admiring it, and thinking—no doubt I had been thinking it as I slept—that I had wasted too much time in the past year to leave my manuscript lying in a cupboard.

I took it out again, and finished the third and final version in January.

Its theme was the one that has obsessed me all my life: Why are human beings so cruel? Life so short, and the world so beautiful, why do they give so much time and ingenuity to torturing each other? Why does cruelty give pleasure to a creature of flesh and blood and spirit? So acute a pleasure that it supports a vast intricate web of argument, sophistry, poetry, reasoned justification of a sensual act. *Last Score* was an enquiry into two aspects of the mystery. Is torture ever justified? (The other day I listened to an intelligent warm-hearted woman arguing that it is clearly right to torture one man to save the lives of, say, a hundred. I take this to be heresy, an infinitely viler heresy than that held by the thousands of Cathars burned by a Church which had no doubt that torture can be justified.) What is the effect on a deeply civilized man if he decides that, in some instance, it is right to use torture?

Not one of its English critics noticed what the book was about. The anonymous reviewer of *The Times* decided easily that it was 'an enquiry into the problem of responsibility and power', adding that C. P. Snow would have done it much better. While being very sure that anyone could do better what I had not tried to do, I was irritated by his dullness, as I am when I cannot explain myself to some wretch who is perhaps less ill-willed than vacant or pressed for time.

The failure was partly my fault. My passion for economy in writing, which had become an obsession, is hard on careless or stupid readers—but this is not a valid excuse. Had I thought over the book for another year or years, or worked it out at greater length . . .

Chapter 23

The young Greek engineer in Rhodes said, 'No one is too old to come to Greece for the first time.' Perhaps not. But to wait so long was a mistake.

17th of April 1961
We left London at night. At the air terminus an official glanced up

from Guy's passport and said drily, 'I suppose you know this is out of date?'

Our luggage was already on its way to the airfield. After dismayed minutes, another official advised us to go on, and risk being sent back from Athens. 'If you had been going to France or Germany, or Spain, I'd have said no, it's no use. But Greece—well, you stand a good chance of being allowed in.'

We landed in Athens in the first calm light. I took Guy's passport and laid it, with mine, in front of the first of the three men waiting to look at them. Not knowing whether he had any English, I pointed to the date and said we would take it to the consulate and get it put right. He glanced at it with indifference and waved us on. The other two did the same.

Later in the morning we bought a street map and walked a long way, in searing heat, to the consulate. Exhausted, I thought I had been a fool to come, I should have gone to France, to the Dordogne, and slept for two days. Each step on the way back was a fresh effort.

Our hotel was on the edge of the old quarter below the Acropolis; by leaning dangerously far out over the narrow balcony I could see four or five white columns, and a thread of excitement wound itself round my throat: the window on the other side of the room looked down into the attics of a house I thought derelict until I caught sight between crumbling boards of a heap of rags which moved and became two skeletal children and an old woman with a dark wrinkled neck, her body hanging from it like a dead branch.

Watching her hands as she touched one child's face lightly and drew its rags round the other, I thought: One says, How could they find a single human being willing to push children into the gas-chambers? But is there no single thread joining that indifference to the passive discomfort with which I peer into this attic?

I lay down, and fell asleep like dropping through a black sea, and woke able to go out. In the darkness we stumbled along streets not a great deal wider than gutters, until we found a small very plain restaurant at the far side of a dusty courtyard smelling of tarred rope, where we ate a decent enough meal.

What unless it is the light sets Greece apart from all the foreign places where I have been happy, serenely happy? Not only the light, nakedly clear, but the hardness. Greece has the hardness—not of stone, which can soften—of marble. The sunlight glances off it, piercing the eyelids. Thus the Acropolis is not simply a remarkably handsome ruin—which no Englishman can look at without a feeling of shame: when are we going to have the decency to send back what we as good as stole?—it is alone, isolated in time and space by the burning whiteness of the light recoiling from it.

And then, the firmness of the lines—the cape at Sounion has no distance to go to join in my mind the line, dark, living, severe, of the coast curving north in my first memory of lines and curves. A line as pure as these gives me the same pleasure music must give anyone for whom sound is all. But only in Greece is there this double intensity, the clearest light, a light from the first day of creation, joined to the clearest line. I saw it over and over again.

I saw it at Mykonos at five in the afternoon on the 2nd of May: a pale hot sky, the sun two hours from setting, one wide segment of the sea a moving fleece of light, blinding, the water nearer the island an unwrinkled stretch of grey silk, without brilliance, but alive. The single fishing-boat leaving the harbour drew after it a tail of separate explosions of light. The nearest island a black rock: behind it a violet shadow that was Rhenea, the island to which the dying and women about to give birth were sent from ancient Delos, too sacred for these first and last convulsions. At my back the flat-topped houses of Mykonos were white against the bare hill, dark, blackish brown tinged faintly with green, verdigris on a bronze shield.

In Delos itself, apart from the small admirable museum and a shabby building or two, there are only sun-warmed ruins, and the bounding whiteness of the lions. And the quiet, like an old smile, older, far older, than the smile of Rheims, less evasive, less subtle, with a divine indifference.

And again, in the bare calcined hills of Arcadia, the lines, not only of the corroded hills themselves, but of the villages clinging under their ribbed acre of bleached tiles to the sides of cliffs, are drawn not in colour but in a light out of my past.

And at Delphi, where—all those olive-trees—we might have been in Provence, except that the cliffs at the back of the shrine were made immeasurably older than anything Provençal by the way the light, not softened even by the fine rain, worked on them, stripping them to the bone. Large eagles flew off the rim of the cliff and dived upwards into a thinner and more dazzling light. When I stooped over the spring to drink from it, the water in the palm of my hand was cold, as cold as any northern beck.

Rhodes is completely different, a different grandeur, suaver, a little corrupt. I have no idea where the suavity comes from—not from the Templars who left the city of Rhodes their street of superb houses and a few tombs in the museum, not from the reticent houses of the Turks, and certainly not from the tactless Italians. All these successive invaders made marks on the island—which is green, full of trees and flowering plants—without erasing the older marks. In some inexplicable way the acropolis at Lindos seems closer in time to the village at the foot of its headland than any of the later fragments, but this might have been because our meal of fish and white resinated wine cannot have been very different from meals eaten in the tenth century B.C. by the builders of the acropolis. Or by St Paul when he landed in the little harbour.

When we came back to Rhodes from Lindos I was rash enough to buy *The Times* of the day before, and found in it the contemptuous notice of *Last Score*. It should have warned me against buying the Sunday newspapers when they came. All three of them damned it heartily. This I thought an excess of zeal.

Somewhere—I think in *Racine et Shakespeare*—Stendhal remarks that the writer and the soldier need exactly the same kind of courage: the first must take care not to think about the journalists, and the second to forget the field hospital.

He is right, of course he is right. But there is always the first moment of disappointment, and the image of oneself as the circus clown who gets slapped. And the fear that no one will buy a novel which has been damned in four important—commercially important —newspapers.

But—according to these same papers—it was raining in England, and I was in Rhodes, in brilliant sun, eating macaroons and drinking Turkish coffee at a table facing the harbour. It would need a more serious misfortune, some personal loss—a danger threatening my family or a close friend—to get past my happiness in being in a foreign country.

If I could spend my life travelling I should escape entirely these moments of diabolical self-doubt and boredom.

Kamiros, where we went next day, made the disrespect of—the names have gone—seem only a bad habit, like nail-biting. The road turns and twists, steeply, between pines. Suddenly, at the top of the hill, there is the dead city, with the temple on the lip of the cliff; below it, far below, the splendid valley and the hills folding it in; on the right the peacock-blue sea and the three green headlands. The silence is not a dead silence; not only do the Greek inscriptions on the stones keep it alive, but there is all that soft fine hair of grass springing between them, and the small flowers, and in the clear heat a scent of herbs and pines.

And the light, passing its sharp edge over columns, stones, pines, sea, all.

I suppose that one reason for the stubborn persistence in us of Greece, a seed, a face waiting to be recognized, is that, in this light-scoured country, one is able, no, forced to impose a myth on the reality. At Mycenae the myth becomes more than the reality, even more insistent and harder than these hard fragments at the top of the dusty hill, or the great bee-hive tomb. Standing in this tomb, I did not at first know what the sound was, a ceaseless deep murmur, until when my eyes were used to the half-darkness I saw the bees moving outside the crevices in the wall. Agamemnon a black bee.

There were other people at the top of the hill, in the ruins of the palace, but the guide took them to look at some fragment or other, I forget what, down the other slope of the hill. I pretended to be too tired to go with them, and was left, alone, sitting on the dusty earth, my back against a broken wall. Where the country is concerned—I am not talking about cities—I have little liking for any but a bare landscape. This one was bare, an anatomy, and at the same time violently alive. The sky was immense and immensely blue, white wisps of cloud scrawled across and across it; the hills were dark and bony, like Provence, but the bones here are even harder; in the empty plain a few cypresses, a few olive-trees, a few narrow strips of green. The silence over it was as naked and enduring as these cyclopean walls, what is left of them. The light wind raised the dust in tiny spirals. Some flower I didn't know the name of, a deep lilac blue, like a small periwinkle, grew close to the ground under my hand. Two swallows darted from wall to wall, so near me that I felt the air from their wings, and I watched a large black ant, Clytemnestra, suddenly attack a black bee crawling on the ground as if it were wounded, kill it and carry it off, pushing it in front of her: again and again a puff of wind blew her back, and again she set off with her prey, and disappeared behind a wall.

I recognized the desert of dryness inside my skull. Unlike this empty plain below Mycenae, it was a sort of nothing, a meaningless abyss, not even memory. It struck me that I had been running away all my life, and that I was very near the end of this flight into words.

There was nothing more I wanted to say, and no more words to escape into—and I couldn't now, even if that had ever been possible, escape into some sort of action.

There was still, if I could have afforded it, one way of escape open —into the distraction of travel, into the pleasure which has never yet failed me, of looking at a fresh country. Impossible.

What I must do, I thought, is to find some other way of enduring the silence, the regret, and wait in it, as I am sitting here, in the light, perfectly content. Perhaps the escape into death is like escaping into words, a substitute life?

For the first time since I was left alone here, I heard sounds, men's voices a long way off, in the Argive plain, and a single sheep bell, also a long way off—as far as the Whitby bell-buoy ringing at sea when I was a child. However far you go, I thought, even here, under this incomparably brighter sun, the original images, the original sounds, follow you.

Now the others came back, toiling up the hill in the great heat. The charming Frenchwoman with the small black darting eyes asked me, 'What have you been doing all the time?'

'What did you expect me to do?' I said. 'I slept.'

Chapter 24

There is something truly comic in the way I run head on into the same mistake, the same trap, again and again. In December 1914 I went into my first house. Today (21st of November 1960) I began living in a place I like no better—the same flat country, the same absence of a view, against which my glance hurls and hurled itself like a demented bluebottle. And the same revulsion and panic, entirely involuntary, of my whole being. The two moments con-

front each other inside my skull. The difference between them is not
that the first house was small, mean, shoddy, where this one is
spacious and uncommonly well-built, it is that in the first I was
young, seething with an angelic (or devilish) energy. Today I am
forced to notice, with rage and exasperation, that my once unabat-
able energy is flagging, I can no longer live two or three lives at
once.

I might have begun the story of my life here and worked backwards to the moment almost half a century ago of despair, tears,
rage. Time, for any organism, is circular, a continuous present filled
with ghosts and chimeras. In the darkness of the underworld I
cross and recross my tracks. I change, but only into myself, until the
minute of the last irreversible change.

Nothing is harder than to collect the fragments of oneself. Even I,
a comparatively immature person, have as many walking-on parts as
there are leaves in a bundle of grass. Which one you are talking to
depends on what you asked. In all but a very few actions of my life
I have been acted—by my fears and diffidence, by greed, by a
sensual obsession, by politeness, by a wish to give pleasure, by a
well-meaning child still making gestures of love towards an alien
adult world, by my nervous dislike of the sight of unhappiness, my
skill in playing a part, my dread of boredom, and by my ancestors,
silent powerful ghosts.

Time to settle the account. To arrange to make a friend of the
knowledge that wherever you go in the short time left you will find
yourself in the same street, the same place, landing in the same
harbour.

When I was young, when my magnificent strength, given me, was
at its height, I wrote book after book, always against time, when I
was well, happy, tired, ill, confident, afraid. What an ape! What a
fool! What an ignorant clumsy provincial fool.

Any writer who says that this—this respectable breeding and
raising for market of a novel a year—is what he intended is either
half-dead or a liar. Unless he was always only a clever swindler, he
must once have believed that he was going to write what would
change the men and women who read it. Nothing else is worth
writing, and no novelist worth glancing at but knows it, even
when he is busiest combing and clipping another of his marketable
books.

'Il n'y a pas de pire carrière que celle d'un écrivain qui veut vivre de sa plume. Vous voilà donc astreint à produire avec les yeux sur un patron, le public, et à lui donner non pas ce que vous aimez mais ce qu'il aime, lui, et Dieu sait s'il a le goût élevé et délicat . . . J'ai toujours dans le mémoire les figures tragiques d'un Villiers de l'Isle Adam, d'un Verlaine, avec les restes de talent sur eux comme les derniers poils d'une vieille fourrure mangé. Il n'est pas honorable d'essayer de vivre de son âme et de le vendre au peuple.'

Claudel had taken the precaution to get himself into the French Consulate in Prague before writing this to his friend Jacques Rivière in 1910. Would to God he had written it to me a few years later. But should I have believed him? Probably not.

For one thing, although I wrote too much—I spend recklessly and needed money—I did not write to make money. The spectacle of humanity on the edge of the pit, the darkness closing round us, excited me like a fever. Any European writer, I told myself, who concerns himself with anything less than the life and probable death of Europe is a cheap-jack, even if what he peddles is amusing, charming, comforting—especially if it is comforting. I became André Malraux's humblest disciple; I admired even his faults. When he wrote that by virtue of our passionate curiosity, our rage for discovery, Europe would not only survive but 'mould a new man from the clay', I thought I had found the subtle Hermes I was seeking.

(Had he lost faith in the saving virtue of curiosity when, for whatever good reasons, he lodged himself in a wing of the French cultural establishment, and seems to be without further interest in *la mise en question de l'univers*?)

The raw nerve-ends of our time are all outside England. Problems which with us have remained embryonic, come monstrously to life in countries where a moment of disloyalty or fear could condemn a score of men and women to torture and death, and where the most commonplace, the least heroic might suddenly have to take a decision involving the life and death of wife, child, friend. With bitter dread and anger I returned again and again to ideas, events, that I had neither force of intellect nor strength of imagination to turn fully into words. They needed a Tolstoy—at the very least a Malraux. In my fascinated search for answers I laid novels in France, Poland, Norway, Czechoslovakia, risking the mistakes due to ignorance, to the impossibility of knowing what a Pole means when he says *bread* or *forest*. Some few of these novels are admirable,

Cousin Honoré, Cloudless May, Black Laurel with its prologue *Before the Crossing, The Green Man,* one or at most two others. The absence of my name from critical summaries is not wholly deserved.

Indelicate? 'Damn your delicacy. It is a low commercial value.' (Byron).

The irony, the side-splitting joke, is that I cared far more passionately about what goes on in the human heart. Not the soul. The heart, a less exalted organ. The world and the frightening things I knew about it distracted me and kept my eyes opened outwards when they might have been sorting the entrails. Yet what writer, having seen the room of the dying babies in an internment camp in Prague could do less or more than spell it out?

'You would have done better to write humbly what would have been, if not the truth—that chimera—your truth.'

No doubt, no doubt.

I have an inexcusable fault—what Valéry called *le mal aigu de la précision.* I hold that the writer has a duty, sink or swim, to be lucid. To be, when it is fitting, profound, subtle, allusive, sincere, startling, difficult, but to struggle with all his energy to be clear. Not concise, not correct, not simple, not single-stranded—but lucid, as lucid as possible. A lucid sentence may not convey the truth, there may, at a given point, be no expressible truth. But incoherence, confusion, obscurity, which do not yield to hard effort to grasp what is being said, are always the work of a charlatan, a self-deceiving humbug, or a clumsy idiot. Writing—since about 1933, when I first realized my clumsiness and dishonesty—with a fanatical attention to clarity, I have deserved the epitaph on my tombstone: Here lies an accomplished writer.

I am genuinely puzzled by the indifference, even hostility, so many writers (critics and others) feel for clear writing. I am prepared to work hard and loyally to find my way in the deeper, less readily intelligible levels in a work, but only if I can believe in the writer's good faith. Only if I can believe that he at least tried to be accessible.

What makes a wilful or careless obscurity—that of a great deal of experimental writing—seem a guarantee of intellectual virtue, and the obese messy incoherence of a William Burroughs excusable or exciting? A legacy from that distrust of the rational meaning which issued in surrealism and its fragmentation of the image? The

Sartrean anti-humanism reflected in a cheap cracked glass which distorts Sartre's creaking metaphysics, his agile word-spinning, into raw contempt for a culture taken to be morally bankrupt?

I recorded this dialogue at the time.

'What you call the classics—in writing or music—make me vomit.'

'Can you explain to me why?'

'Easily. They're part of the dead cat's meat forced down my throat at school. Read the right books, pick up the right accent, eat the right toads—toads, turds—and you'll rise out of your uneducated family and class as from a dung-hill. You'll get the right values and with the right values you can go anywhere. Oh, can you? Try it— that's all. Try to break through the unconscious condescension, the oh so unaffected friendliness, of the pair of upper-class socialists who ask you to dinner and play you Webern on their hand-made record-player.'

'I was a scholarship brat, and so were my friends. It never occurred to us that we were inferior to anyone except a genius——'

'I never said I felt inferior! I said that Trollope and Pope and Mozart and Dante—and Eliot on Dante—nauseate me.'

Without kindness, I supposed he was afraid that if he once let in Pope and Mozart he would be asked to revere all the other idols of respectable well-heeled *salauds*. These exist to be mocked by the young, but not, my God, with this sourness.

Financiers assure us that all our troubles can be summed up in the single word: Inflation. This same mortal illness has infected language. I am prejudiced in advance against a novel I might enjoy, sensible, perceptive, a decent very drinkable little *vin du pays*, when I am told that its author is 'the English Proust'.

Reading over what I have just written, I see that I shall be thought ill-tempered. I am not, I was never gayer. I am in a passion, yes. And why not? *Avec les passions*, said Stendhal, *on ne s'ennuie jamais: sans elles, on est stupide*.

If I live much longer I shall be reduced to re-reading the nineteenth century Russians, Proust, Stendhal, and an occasional new novel by a talented eccentric. And my rather friendly young anti-classicist will tell me I am an arid snob . . .

Is it possible that I became a novelist from the least pure motives —to enjoy a sense of power: the child other children called a freak avenging herself? An abysmally ignorant young creature who supposed she was writing when she was simply trying to draw attention to herself and her cleverness? It is possible.

Writing was a chimney for my blazing ambitions.

Yet, yet, my passion for words was genuine. They delighted me. Like a character in my absurd first novel, I turned everything I noticed into phrases, repeating them to myself with voluptuous excitement. At the time I did not suspect the penalty for practising this trick. The very act of writing, of turning pain, grief, joy, into words, creates the Doubles of these feelings, so that innocently the writer places between himself and reality a charming or dreadful mask. Unless he fights with these masks they end by replacing him. That is not all. In a final sense, the truth is exactly that which can't be got into words. We are forced to lie, a little or, if we are inferior, much. The writer's mind is a country of words sundered from his being, alien to it, almost hostile. A cruel paradox forces him to realize his living self only in silence, when he is not making phrases —that is, when as a writer he doesn't exist.

For a time I used words without precautions. I wanted to disappear into them, I fled into the bovaryism of the writer trying to create an effect.

I feel some sympathy with young Daisy Jameson's craving to be not-there; it is even joined, somewhere in the darkness, to the child hiding in the water-closet at the end of the long passage in No. 5 Park Terrace, putting off for a few minutes the beating she is about to receive. Oh, and to the wish to be not the freak but the someone gay and free I think I was born . . .

I don't understand the foxy glances of my English reviewers. The strict justice I receive baffles me, since I seem to myself to be gentle and well-meaning. Nothing to be done about it. A little late in life, I realize that sympathy and aversion rarely have a logical base. Yet there are moments even now when I should be enchanted if—like F. Sarcey on some occasion—I could say to one of my young judges, 'Bah! Après moi, c'est vous qui serez la vieille bête!'

For a long time I was madly ambitious. I dreamed about worldly success. But, alas! I also despised it.

This is too clumsy a definition of a natural process. Suppose that in 1930 someone I admired had said to me, 'My dear girl, the mistake you and people like you, who have fought their way out of nowhere, are prone to make is to believe that to be respected, reasonably well-off, etc. etc., it is enough to have a mind and teach it to write as well as possible. You imagine that because this was true *at first*—clever little Daisy Jameson could and did climb right out of the world of her childhood—you had only to go on working hard and loyally. This is an illusion two other sorts of clever persons do not fall into. First: those who realize at an early enough age that respect and success depend only half on merit; the other and equally important half demands a certain impudence, the patience to force or coax other people to notice and applaud that merit, which not enough of them will do without being persuaded. And second: people born into an already influential circle who assume as their right advantages their birth gives them, use them naturally, and are as naturally admired for their grace and self-confidence. This is not cynicism, it is the recognition of a rule so seldom broken that it is childish to overlook it.'

The advice would have been wasted. I am lazy, and solitude comes easier to me than *camaraderie*. I have never tried to attract *useful people*, never taken the trouble to secure my lines into the future. In the first moment of receiving an invitation to a party my impulse is to refuse—since it will be impossible to go disguised as the English Proust.

I am forced to agree that this lack of sense is not due either to virtue or pride. It is partly vanity—there is no merit in rejecting the world out of a fear of being unable to shine in it—but much more a deep, an unseizably deep sloth. In the last resort I can't be bothered.

Because of this ineradicable indifference and imprudence, I can blame no one for my lack of reputation except myself.

'*Méfiez-vous d'un écrivain qui a fait sa carrière sans rien demander à personne, et qui, à cinquante ans passé, n'est pas décoré. Ce ne peut être qu'un mauvais esprit, et dangereux.*'

Oh, my dear Léautaud, to whom is he dangerous—except, a little, to himself?

There was, after all, something I wanted more, infinitely more, than I wanted reputation. That was to look at the world. My God, to look.

I cheated the energy and restlessness of my born nature by writing books. If I could put in one scale the displeasures they have brought me and in the other the pleasure, gaiety, the thousands of moments of perfect happiness that I have had through my eyes, the second would far, far, far outweigh the first.

And now? I am very cool (it is time!) and I see distinctly what is left. Three things. Precisely this fury and cruelly fierce pleasure of looking. The fear and sharpness of love, sharper because of the fear. The sense of being almost pure memory, the coming nearer of the dead who, for a few years or many, have been content to stay quietly in their place.

Who moved, turning the head in a known gesture, at the back of this room? Oh, nearer to me than my hand.

I am thankful that I was alive during the short exquisite flowering of life in the last year or two before the first Great War. You who were not there cannot imagine what it was like for the very young. Never to have known anything about war, and so never to have been afraid. To fear nothing except that, with so many roads at our feet, we might not be able to walk on all of them. Walk? Run.

Children born during the second war seem like us—far more so than any generation in between—lively, sceptical, inquisitive. They are, I think, very fine. So were my friends.

16th of March 1965

This morning Gerald Bullett's last letter fell out of a volume of his poems. No, not the last. The last of the few I kept. '. . . your letter has raised me from the dead. You describe just the kind of poems I want to write—and imply that I have written them. That what you say is too good to be true doesn't in the least diminish my happiness in hearing it said . . . I won't pretend to you that I think ill of them: I allow myself to believe that the best of them are good in their way: but God forbid that I should indulge in visions of posthumous glory. That kind of daydreaming is the last refuge of frustrated vanity . . . What annoys me when I look back on my "career" is the thought that if only I had had more character, staying-power, perseverance and what not, I could have made at least a respectable living and have enough money now to support me (quietly) in my declining years—instead of being always nagged by anxiety about the future . . .'

Dear Gerald, it was not character you lacked, nor courage, nor loyal perseverance. Now that you are dead, I will tell you. Your novels were those of a poet forcing himself to use his genius and lucid senses to do well a task they were only half fitted for: you had irony, sly humour, a shrewd and thinking heart, a fastidious mind—and little or none of the born novelist's gross appetite for life. Your instinct as a writer was the poet's to fuse memory, emotion and experience in a single resonant image. And you had even less instinct for making yourself secure than I have. It was not simply that you had no gift for putting yourself in a favourable light, you did not put yourself in any light at all. You never lifted a finger to call attention to yourself by the half deliberate, half natural man-œuvres of novelists no more intelligent than you were but more adroit and more personally ambitious. Critics in a hurry, used to writers who take themselves and their talents with devastating solemnity, were able to ignore you. They knew, they knew by instinct, as a hog smells out truffles, that you neither could nor would repay them in kind for any good they did you, or any ill . . .

I knew him when we were both young and poor. A year or two before he died in 1958, I turned in a brightly-lit and overcrowded room and saw in the doorway the young man I used sometimes to see coming into my room in Sloane Street in the 'twenties. Even when he was standing in front of me, the change in him was slight—a look of fatigue, a certain heaviness of movement, a few, remarkably few lines. His youth had not been obliterated by time, it had stepped back a little—that was all. It may be that we are ravaged not by time, but by our lies and the compromises we make. Something recklessly truthful and uncompromising remained alive in Gerald, some reality of innocence.

I think I have had better friends than I deserve.

With any luck, I shall be outlived by the three I made first, Oswald of the flaming hair, now white, his brother Sydney, still the most unsubdued and inquisitive of scientists, Archie, whom I respect more than anyone.

One of the uncovenanted benefits of living for a long time is that, having so many more dead than living friends, death can appear as a step backwards into the joyous past, to the edge of a morning sea, for instance, or into a warm shabby room in a vanished London, with the broken-down sofa and the large creaking wicker chair.

Chapter 25

24th of March 1965
How many times have I drawn back from an underworld darkness I
fear, closing my long-sighted eyes, blocking my keen ears? Possibly
the journey backwards, against the current, through the tangled
roots of withdrawals, evasions, lies, was from the start no good. I
may have pursued a phantom: the person I made bit by bit out of
my fears and greeds—that fake, that *construction*—may have strangled
whatever infant reality once existed.

When I was a child I had already cut my stick to be famous. I was
born as stubborn as the hardest wood and unwilling to learn what
bored me. I read for pleasure and, now and then, to astonish my
teachers by seeming to know more than I did. (One day, during a
visit home, I was turning the pages of an old encyclopædia my
mother bought when we were children. I found words—*Good*—
Yes, I see—*To be looked into*—pencilled in a large perfectly round hand
beside the articles on Plato, Hegel, Kant, Leibnitz and some others,
and remembered the afternoon when I decided to read the philo-
sophers, all of them: filled with excitement I began by reading about
them, and chased them through the eleven large volumes with
baffled patience.) As I look over my shoulder, the years divide:
beginning in eternity, I came early into the suburbs of time. The
years from my twelfth are marked off by public examinations that
fell in December and June; I went at these like a man cutting steps
in a rock face—they were my road to the world. I had no guide but
my devouring ambition—not a guide, a thorn in my flesh, a fever.

More than anyone I knew then, I wanted to live. My hunger was a
wild animal in my senses and brain. Perhaps its violence defeated it.
The savage beast was probably blind.

I am deeply convinced—so deeply that it will be no use citing
against me married women who are famous scientists or architects
or financiers—that a woman who wishes to be a creator of anything

except children should be content to be a nun or a wanderer on the face of the earth. She cannot be writer and woman in the way a male writer can be also husband and father. The demands made on her as a woman are destructive in a peculiarly disintegrating way— if she consents to them. And if she does not consent, if she cheats . . . a sharp grain of guilt lodges itself in her, guilt, self-condemnation, regret, which may get smaller, but never dissolves.

Yet I could have managed my double life better than I did. A choice—in spite of the error of an early disastrous marriage—was possible. I could have chosen the monk and let the restless greedy mountebank starve. Even to refuse to choose is a choice. Say I *chose* to drift, to let the mountebank make a hare of the monk and debauch the writer, and the monk trip up the poor restless mountebank, in a perpetual bedlam. But why? Why construct round myself something more intricate than any abstract sculpture, and again and again, sitting silent and unmoving, hammer on it in impotent rage, shout unheard, weep inwardly tears as bitter as gall? Why?

'It is a strange madness,' Petrarch told his travel-worn secretary, 'to be forever sleeping in a strange bed.' The secretary, a good one, could not bear not to go away, he left and came back more than once. Petrarch himself never stayed long in one place.

Alive in me forever, ports not touched at, voyages not made.

Years ago I said Yes when I should have said No. That Yes took me out of my way. But it was I who said it. And I who, long before that moment, encouraged the birth of the smiling fake other people, beginning with my mother, drew out of me to take my place. I *am* my choice. I am what I made of my original condition.

Ah, say it, say it. You had not the courage to choose the creature you were born, avid *to get away*, to be perpetually footloose, without responsibilities, material or human. This famished *vagus*, as in-disciplined, graceless, arrogant, as his mediæval kind, clown, spend-thrift, gay, eager to be amused, has made antic hay of my life with-out doing himself any good. I clipped his nails. If he drove me to a series of departures, I hamstrung him by clumsy attempts to live what my forbears called a decent life, tearing pieces out of myself to make the remnant match, compromising, dancing like a bear, speak-ing softly. I could pretend I did it because I was ashamed to dis-appoint human beings who depended on me—including the one who is the salt and armature of my life. It would be only half true. The habit is only a few years younger than I am.

Robert Graves is of the poetic opinion that only the baser sort among the dead rush to drink from Lethe. Perhaps—but there may be no other way of reconciling me with myself. As the old women say: What you can't forgive, forget. The grain of guilt is still there. Look for it in my dust.

The early sun of my setting-out was a cold northern sun—sun and salt, a great deal of salt, in the air, on the lips. My confidence was limitless and absurd. It took a long time, years, to vanish out of sight, its place taken by a blind patience—promised in the persistence of a six-months-old child climbing stairs she was beaten for climbing, six attempts, six beatings, before her baffled young mother threw her into her cot to sleep it off. Today I feel my knees failing me before those stairs, but there is no escaping them. How many times, how many more times, before, unforgiven, I find my way back? I have the gross strength of my original hunger. Punished—sometimes justly—I get up and start again, always with less ease. I know whom I have to thank for my power of resistance, for the habit of enduring, the habit and pleasure of hiding behind lies, dissimulation, tricks.

I am writing this at a table of plain wood. Just now, when I ran my hand along the edge, a tiny splinter caught the edge of my palm. Pulling it out, I felt a wave of happiness, even gaiety. It had not come from one of those exultant moments when, dropping with sleep, alone in some cold room, I stumbled on words that I believed came from a centre of my body rather than my brain, but it belonged to that family. Another instant and I had it . . . I am in the kitchen of my mother's house, facing an iron range, the curtains drawn across the window on my right, one weak lamp throwing its yellow hoop on the square of cardboard under my hand. The calendar I am making for my mother in the hope of pleasing her and being praised has the months, days, figures, copied in red and green ink, and the wide margins filled in with an intricate pattern of small blue flowers, each petal painted separately with the point of the finest brush, scores of flowers, hundreds of petals. Slowly adding flower to flower, stopping only for a second to pull out the splinter my left hand has picked up from the rough edge of the table, I am happy, my God how happy.

Surely, somewhere, it is still alive, the gaiety, the simple patience? Of course. How else could you live?

Chapter 26

Voices out of darkness, out of sleep, enclosed in memory as in a black bubble. Briefly, as I listen, it is myself I hear speaking in a young barely recognizable voice.

Are these phantoms who live in me lighter than the few, very few objects towards which I feel piety and shall carry about as long as I can—to be sold or destroyed by my heirs?

Phantoms. In half-sleep it can seem that my mother only yesterday stepped out of reach, and the feeling of desolation is acute. At other times I see myself turning from her at a dip in this path between bracken and foxgloves or at that end of a narrow steep street.

Showing a friend round Westminster Abbey, I took her into a side chapel, the St Nicholas Chapel, and there—I did not know it existed —found the W.V.S. book of volunteers killed in the last war. I turned the pages to the county of Berkshire. There was only one name, my young sister's. It seemed to belong to her less than did two words I saw afterwards cut in a wall in the cloisters—Dear Child. No name—only Dear Child.

No one can tell the story of his life. I have tried not to lie, and doubt I have told more lies than truth.

I could have written it in several ways, all half true, half a lie.

As the story of a young woman raising herself from obscurity to a shadowy success.

As a chain of failures. Always, under different forms, the same failure—to love enough. Only to write this makes me tremble with cold.

Why don't I forgive that restless young woman? Only a fool measures himself for a hair shirt. Very well, I am a fool.

In a world like ours, brutal, violent, menaced, is anything more important than faithfulness, than the loyalty one human being offers

another? Anything? Your life, the lost years, foreign cities and
harbours, the fever in a young body . . .

I may have been hoping that if I looked my trespasses in the face
they would disappear. Idiot. Failures to love are irremediable and
irredeemable. The best I can do is live with them, and make no
appeal against the judgement my heart passes on them.

The hunger of the spirit for eternity—as fierce as a starving man's
for bread—is much less a craving to go on living than a craving for
redemption. Oh, and a protest against absurdity. Atheism is ultim-
ately a question of will, not of intellect. Left to itself, the intellect is
bound to reject the notion that human life is a scurf lying in patches
on the surface of the universe, the immensity that frightened Pascal.
A thinking scurf? What nonsense.

What fascinates me about life itself, what is most astonishing and
unassimilable, baffling, absorbing, is its steady movement towards
death. You enjoy, suffer, ask questions, work, and all the time this is
what is coming. Surprise will be my last emotion, not fear. When I
think of the young dead of two wars, of my young brother, my
young sister, of the boys I knew in 1914, who have preceded me
with their light quick bodies, how could I be afraid of the last
minutes?

Yes, surprise and a light regret that I cannot go on looking.

I hope that the very last moment will be without emotion, a pure
act of memory. That the images I carry in my skull, clinging to them
with a passion I should be put to it to it to account for in rational terms—
a shabbily-furnished room for four poor scholars, the vanished
London of the sixpenny gallery and the Vienna Café, fields of nar-
cissus between Espalion and Le Puy, the Loire in sunlight, a dark
bookshop in Nevers, a Vienna without neon lights, the bare savage
country between Vence and Manosque, broken columns asleep in
the Greek light, the great curved eyelids of the gold mask in the
Museum in Athens, a street in Bordeaux—will detach themselves,
one after another, hesitate for less than a moment, vanish, leaving
room for the few I had in my hand at the beginning, the North Sea
flowing over the foreign rivers, the grand violins silenced by a boy
whistling the first line of *Sir Eglamour the valiant knight* in a street of
small houses.

Surely I can hope to end where I began, in a Whitby which no
longer exists, small, stubbornly old, not yet spoiled? In an un-
changing present, in an intense clarity, among my few indestructible

images: the distant points of light, the dazzling whiteness of a field of marguerites, the pure curve of the coast, the sea-gull screech of children—*ah-wa-a-ah*!

Away!

This is sure. However sudden, the last of my departures will start from the half-darkness of the kitchen in Park Terrace, along that narrow passage with the stairs going up on the right, down that flight of stone steps into the garden with the laburnum and the lilac, down more steps to that tall iron gate, cold passing from it into my fingers, into the empty morning street and the hired cab, down the steeply-falling North Bank to the harbour—the tide out, ebbing back from the mooring-posts and the broken timbers of the shipyard—past the plain-faced houses of Windsor Terrace to the low grey squat station, through its dark entrance, and away. Away.

An old woman dies. Elsewhere the sea rolls to the foot of the cliff, the coast runs north, the fields dazzle with flowers, quiver with long grass, stir with tiny creeping insects: light breaks. 'Friends, we do not know where the darkness is, or where the dawn; where the sun that shines for mortals rises, or where it sets . . .'